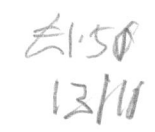

Israel and Judah:
How Two Peoples Became One

IGOR P. LIPOVSKY

Cambridge Publishing Inc.

Copyright © 2014 Igor P. Lipovsky
All rights reserved.

ISBN: 0692343687
ISBN 13: 9780692343685
Library of Congress Control Number: 2014958727
Cambridge Publishing Inc.

In loving memory of my uncle
Alexander I. Lipovsky
1918-1998

Acknowledgments

First, I want to express my gratitude to Mr. John Nicolson who translated my book from Russian. I am grateful to him for making my work available in English and for his painstaking labors on my behalf. I also want to thank my sons, Daniel and Ilya, for their help in preparing the manuscript for publishing. Daniel's contribution was so significant that I do not even have the words to describe it, but I do thank him, and most warmly.

My book would not have been possible without the love and support of my mother, Nina N. Lipovskaya. Finally, I owe thanks to my spouse Helen, who showed her patience and understanding through time of research and writing.

Contents

Introduction – The Greatest Secret of the Bible 1

Chapter 1 – The Biblical Family 5
   1. The True Nature of the Patriarchs 5
   2. How Two Forefathers Became One 9

Chapter 2 – In Egypt 17
   1. The Hyksos 18
   2. The Hebrews and the 'King-Shepherds' 26
   3. The Departure of the 'House of Joseph' from the Nile Delta
      in the 15th Century BCE 28

**Chapter 3 – The Exodus of Hebrew Tribes at the
Beginning of the 12th Century BCE** 33
   1. When Did the Biblical Exodus Happen? 34
   2. The Mission of Moses 36
   3. The Strengthening of Egypt and the Split of the Tribes of Moses 43

Chapter 4 – The Peoples of pre-Israelite Palestine 49
   1. Western Semites 49
   2. Indigenous pre-Semitic Population 52
   3. Indo-Europeans 53
   4. Hurrians 56

**Chapter 5 – The Conquest of Canaan in the Light of
Biblical and Archaeological Data** 59
   1. The Limits of Biblical Archaeology 59
   2. Three Stages of Real Conquest 60
   3. Peaceful Coexistence Instead of Expulsion 63
   4. Separate Wars of Joshua and Caleb 66
   5. The Fate of the Tribe of Reuben 67
   6. The Settlement on the Land 69

Chapter 6 – The Age of the Judges 71
1. The Judges and their Gods 71
2. The Israelite Tribal Confederation 74
3. The Mystery of the Tribe of Dan 77
4. The Philistine Threat 81

Chapter 7 – The United Monarchy 83
1. The Rise of Saul and the Hegemony of the Israelites......................... 83
2. Saul and David: Allies and Rivals 89
3. David's Accession and the Transition of Power to the Judahites........... 95
4. The Struggle for the Ark of the Covenant between the
   Northern Levites and Southern Aaronites 99
5. The Extent of David's Rule and the Discontent of the
   Hebrew Tribes: The Revolts of Absalom and Sheba 102
6. Solomon's Palace Coup and the Change in Political Course............ 111
7. Contradictory Accounts about the Epoch of David and Solomon...... 117

Chapter 8 – The Divided Monarchy...123
1. The Secession of Northern Tribes... 123
2. The Religious Break-up.. 134

Chapter 9 – Israel: Successor to the 'House of Joseph'..................................137
1. The Historical and Ethnic Roots of the Northern Kingdom............ 137
2. The First Israelite Kings and their Policies 139
3. Under the Rule of the 'House of Omri' 142
4. The Reign of Jehu's Dynasty 153
5. The Assyrian Expansion and the Fall of Samaria 166
6. The Myth of the Disappearance of the Northern Tribes 175

Chapter 10 – Judah: Heir to the 'House of Jacob'...185
1. Confrontation with Northern Kingdom. Incursions by
   Egyptian Armies... 185
2. Alliance with Israel 190
3. The Growth in the Influence of the Aaronites and their
   Interference in Judahite Policymaking.. 198

Chapter 11 – Judah as the Only Hebrew Kingdom..215
1. King Hezekiah: Religious Reforms and Uprising against Assyria........ 215
2. King Manasseh: Liberalization of Worship and Time of Peace........... 227
3. The Monotheistic Revolution of King Josiah................................... 234

Contents

    4. Between Egypt and Babylonia 242
    5. The Siege of Jerusalem and the Downfall of Judah 252
    6. The Babylonian Exile: its True Scope and Significance 256
    7. The Governorship of Gedaliah: an Attempt at National Revival 260
    8. The Escape to Egypt. A New Invasion by the Chaldeans and the Destruction of Ammon, Moab and Edom 263
    9. The Transformation of Judah during the First Temple Period 267

Chapter 12 – The Levites and Aaronites – Keepers of Tradition and Memory 277
    1. The Origins and Destinies of Two Priestly Groups 277
    2. Yahwism and Canaanite Cults 289

Epilogue – The Emergence of Judean People 305

Selected Bibliography 307

Index 313

Introduction

The Greatest Secret of the Bible

This book gives its readers the opportunity to penetrate the mysteries of the Old Testament – mysteries which have been concealed from us for millennia. The book does not substitute for the history found in the Bible, but it does add to it and explain it to a significant extent. The need for this book arises from the weakness of the many 20th century academic theories proposing interpretations of the darkest periods in Old Testament history based on facts unearthed by modern archaeology. Instead of relying on the contradictory results of archaeological discoveries, the author has focused on 'archaeological excavation' of the Bible itself and on analyzing biblical texts and comparing them with sources from the ancient Near East. This approach has made it possible to solve many of the Old Testament's mysteries, for, as it turns out, the keys to these mysteries are contained in the Bible itself.

But can the Bible be considered a reliable source on the history of the ancient Near East? Biblical scholars have tended to give this question the most contradictory answers – from an unconditional 'yes' to a categorical 'no'. The world of biblical scholarship continues to demonstrate two opposite extremes of opinion on this subject. At one extreme are the 'maximalists', who insist on the absolute reliability of all books of sacred scripture; at the other are the 'minimalists', who deny the historicity of the Bible, believing that it was composed by Judean authors during the Hellenistic period. Most scholars, however, occupy intermediate positions between these two extremes, with some inclining towards one and others towards the other. What, though, of modern archaeology: which side does it take? Unfortunately, even in the 21st century, in spite of the fact that literally every inch of the biblical lands has been dug up, archaeology is unable either to confirm the truth of the Bible or to refute it. Here we should note the acknowledgement made by the well-known Israeli archaeologist Amihai Mazar, author of one of the best monographs on the archaeology of Palestine: "Can archaeology throw light on the question of the origin of Israel? The answer is not affirmative, as the interpretation of the archaeological evidence is not clear-cut."

We may admit it or not, but we have no alternative to the Bible. All the discoveries made by archaeologists in the 19th-21st centuries, including the writings known to us from the ancient Near East, cannot even remotely compare in importance with the books of the Bible, the most fundamental work of religion, history, and literature ever created by man. However, the Bible is not a history textbook. Its authors were interested not in history, but in theosophy and the relations between human beings and God. They used their people's past for purely edificatory goals, as material with which to educate future generations. For this reason the books of the Bible are not so much historical as didactic. When evaluating the extent to which the Bible is historical, we should not forget the enormous interval between the time when the events themselves occurred and the time when they were written down. For instance, before the narratives about the patriarchs Abraham, Isaac, and Jacob were recorded, they were transmitted orally from generation to generation over the course of 800-1000 years. Furthermore, the books of the Bible were set down in writing and then copied over the course of many centuries by ordinary human beings who were prone to making mistakes. So both the Bible in general and the earliest part of the Old Testament in particular inevitably contain historical distortions and errors.

The main problem of the biblical books, however, is not that they are insufficiently historical, but that they are too fragmentary. Analysis of the biblical texts tell us that the initial part of the Old Testament, including Moses' Pentateuch, was subjected to heavy editing from deepest antiquity forwards, and a considerable part of the story, without which the Old Testament account is not always consistent or comprehensible, was removed. But how did such lacunae arise? Who removed part of the initial story, and when and why?

The chief protagonist depicted in the Old Testament is the Hebrews. The latter – and this is the greatest of the Bible's mysteries – initially comprised not one, but two peoples, or, to be more exact, two West Semitic tribal groups. Each of these groups had its own past, its own family tree, and, furthermore, its own religion. The two groups arrived in Canaan and then left for the Nile Delta at different times. Their stays in Egypt were by no means identical in duration (the northern tribes were there for 250 years and the southern for 430), and, even more significantly, the two groups occupied entirely different positions when they were there. Finally, they made their Exodus from Egypt at different centuries and reconquered their places in Palestine independently. So when modern archaeologists try to find traces of the events set out in the Bible, they very naturally come up against irresoluble contradictions which cast doubt on the authenticity of the Old Testament account. For where they look for the history of one people, there in fact lie the submerged pasts of two distinct, even if related, peoples who were for a long time utterly distinct from one another. For an entire century (the 11th to 10th centuries BCE) the northern and southern tribal groups were compelled to join forces in a united kingdom in order to beat back the onset of their common enemies. Yet their different origins, histories, and political interests could not but come to the fore and the two groups of tribes, which subsequently came to be known as the 'Israelites' and the 'Judahites', parted forever, creating their own, separate states. However, it was their short alliance that gave rise to the lacunae in the first books of the Old Testament. In the 10th century BCE, during the rule of kings David and Solomon, the compilers of the earliest books of the Bible – Genesis, Exodus, Leviticus, and Numbers – were faced with a task of great difficulty: to put together, without changing anything in the narratives of the two tribal groups, a shared ancestry and history for them. This objective was dictated by both the political interests of the united Israelite-Judahite kingdom and the Yahwist priests' aspiration to establish the cult of the one God among both tribal groups. The idea that the northern and southern Hebrew tribes had a shared origin was something in which the then ruling southern Davidic dynasty had a very strong interest. It was thus that the initial version of the Pentateuch, which mixed the narratives and family trees of the Israelites and Judahites, came into existence. It also contained the manuscripts written by Moses himself, the first man to start recording the history of his own people (the southern Hebrew tribes). Recognizing the special role played by Moses, the editors of the Bible gave his name to the entire collection of manuscripts. Of course, the first books could not have been written without extensive lacunae in the overall story, since to join the narratives of the northern and southern tribes turned out to be a by no means simple task. These difficulties are most clearly visible in the book of Exodus, where several centuries of the Hebrews' stay in Egypt are almost completely passed over.

In spite of the falling apart of the United Monarchy, work on the initial version of the Pentateuch continued during the following centuries in both Israel, the kingdom of the northern tribes, and Judah, the state of the southern tribes. This unparalleled work was carried out by the Levites and the Aaronites, the priests of the first monotheistic religion in the world, a religion which in both Hebrew kingdoms established itself only with great difficulty. The result was that two versions of the Pentateuch emerged. One of these, the so-called 'Yahwist', was created in the south, in Judah, while the other, the 'Elohist', was written in the north, in Israel. Regardless of the differences between them, the two versions were relatively similar since they were based on what had initially been a single version, that which had been set down in the United Monarchy. Furthermore, the two versions' authors – the priests of both Hebrew kingdoms – had originally come exclusively from the southern group of tribes and were interested in spreading their monotheistic religion and shared history and ancestries not just in Judah, but in Israel too. This same principle – the common origin of the Israelites and Judahites – shaped the composition of the biblical books that followed, the books of Joshua, Judges, Kings, and, in the 7th century BCE, Deuteronomy. The last redaction of most books of the Old Testament took place after the Judahites had returned from the Babylonian exile. This work was probably managed by the lawgiver Ezra, who returned from Babylonia in the 5th century BCE to help in the spiritual revival of his people. He was not bold enough to change anything in the ancient manuscripts that had come down to him; he merely combined them at his own discretion. Thus both versions of the Pentateuch – the Yahwist and the Elohist – were joined together and the codex of priests' laws and the Deuteronomy were added. The result was the creation of the Pentateuch (Torah) in its present form, which subsequently became the book most respected by both Jews and Christians. When editing of the Old Testament was complete, this put a final seal on the secret of the biblical story – namely that the Israelites and Judahites had different provenances. Thus the earliest history of the northern tribes, the Israelites, right up until their joining forces (in the 12th century BCE) with the southern tribes, the Judahites, was for the most part hidden from view. Instead of this true account, we find set out in the Bible the story of the southern tribes, the Judahites; and this history is presented as the shared past of both tribal groups. There is something else we should remember: both the Israelites and the Judahites were not so much direct descendants of the Hebrews as an ethnic mix of all the native peoples who had lived in Palestine from prehistoric times. The Hebrews did not drive out these peoples, as is commonly thought, but united them around themselves and gave them their own name, history, and religion before eventually completely dissolving in their midst.

Chapter 1

The Biblical Family

The True Nature of the Patriarchs
Who was patriarch Abraham and to which people did he and his family belong? The names of the biblical family members, and in particular, the time at which they appeared in Mesopotamia, Canaan, and later in Egypt too are signs not only of their West Semitic origin, but also of the fact that they belonged to the Amorites or a related people. We have no information on the ethnic origins of Abraham's family up until his arrival in Canaan. It is only in the episode involving the captivity of Lot, his nephew, that the Bible identifies the patriarch himself for the first time: "One who had escaped came and reported this to Abram the Hebrew [Ivri]" (Genesis 14:13). Today the word 'Hebrew' (Ivri) is translated from the biblical Hebrew as 'Jew'. 4000 years ago, however, this word had a different meaning and was pronounced differently – 'Habiru' or 'Apiru'. This was the name for semi-nomadic Western Semites who did not have their own permanent tribal territory. Even if we assume that the Habiru were not actually Amorites, they were certainly their close relatives. From an ethnic and linguistic point of view, the Habiru hardly differed from the settled West Semitic peoples of Syria and Canaan who surrounded them. They all had common roots and the same provenance; in terms of life style, however, there were important differences. The Habiru remained nomads and did not settle on the land until the 12th century BCE. In Abraham's time the Habiru were a large group of tribes scattered throughout Syria, Canaan, and Mesopotamia. They were to be found in all corners of the Semitic world of that time, but especially in Canaan and southern Syria, where they were a serious military and political power.

From the beginning of the 2nd millennium BCE southern and central Canaan was already considered to be the land of the West Semitic nomads. It is significant that, when he found himself in Egypt, Joseph said of himself: "For I was forcibly carried off from the land of the Hebrews" (Genesis 40:15). Today this phrase means 'from the land of the Jews'. But at the time it sounded and was understood differently, namely as 'from the land of the Semitic nomads'. The Hebrews constituted merely a part of the Habiru who were in Canaan and southern Syria.

The Bible speaks only of Abraham's family; however, the episode describing the liberation of Abraham's nephew Lot makes clear that the patriarch was leading, at the very least, his entire tribe. "When Abram heard that his relative had been taken captive, he called out the 318 trained men born in his household and went in pursuit as far as Dan. During the night Abram divided his men to attack them and he routed them, pursuing them as far as Hobah, north of Damascus. He recovered all the goods and brought back his relative Lot and his possessions, together with the women and the other people" (Genesis 14:14-16). In order to assemble a force of 318 warriors, Abraham's family must have numbered at least 6000 - 7000, which made them not even a clan but what at the time must have been a large tribe. Given that, according to estimates by archeologists, the entire population of Palestine at the time amounted to no more than 150,000 people, Abraham's tribe was a force of no small strength – and that is in spite of the fact that on the eve of these events some of their number left to follow Lot to the east. In order to pursue the enemy from today's Dead Sea to Damascus, you would have needed not just a large number of people, but also well-trained and experienced warriors. From the biblical narrative it follows that the local Amorites – Aner, Eshkol, and Mamre – entered into an alliance with Abraham. As a rule, families did not conclude alliances among themselves, so what we have here, evidently, is an alliance between the local Amorite rulers and Abraham as the head of one of the Habiru tribes. One should, of course, treat the numbers given in the Bible, especially in its earliest texts, with the utmost caution. And yet, even if the number 318 is for some reason unreliable, it still remains an eloquent fact that Abraham and his allies were able to put to rout the whole coalition of southern Syrian rulers who had invaded Canaan. This testifies that the biblical 'family' was an entire nomadic tribe or tribes – an alliance with whom would have been a desirable objective for many rulers in southern Palestine.

At the very beginning of the biblical narrative concerning Abraham's stay in the land of Canaan, we encounter a new fact confirming the supposition that the biblical 'family' was not only a tribe, but a group of tribes:

> Now Lot, who was moving about with Abram, also had flocks and herds and tents. But the land could not support them while they stayed together, for their possessions were so great that they were not able to stay together. And quarrelling arose between Abram's herdsmen and the herdsmen of Lot... So Abram said to Lot, 'Let's not have any quarrelling between you and me, or between your herdsmen and mine, for we are brothers. Is not the whole land before you? Let's part company. If you go to the left, I'll go to the right; if you go to the right, I'll go to the left'...So Lot chose for himself the whole plain of

the Jordan and set out toward the east. The two men parted company: Abram lived in the land of Canaan, while Lot lived among the cities of the plain and pitched his tents near Sodom (Genesis 13:5-9, 11-12).

The very description of the places where Lot settled – a region extending for more than 70 miles – is evidence that what we have here is not families, but tribes. Lot's separation from Abraham was only the first division among the numerous tribes of nomadic Amorites who had come to southern Canaan. Those who went east with Lot came to be known as the 'Sutu'. It is possible that 'Habiru' was established as the name for the Hebrews later, when they were already in Canaan, and that, when they lived in Mesopotamia and up until their arrival in Canaan, they had been known as Sutu. The Egyptians were very familiar with the nomadic Sutu and had their own name for them – 'Shasu'.

Of all the tribes led by Abraham from the upper courses of the Euphrates River, it was the 'house of Jacob' which received the best land, suitable not only for cattle breeding but also for arable farming. Jacob's fellow brothers from this large tribal union – the Edomites, Moabites, Ammonites, Ishmaelites, and Midianites – had to content themselves with land that was of significantly inferior quality. With a few exceptions, they occupied the extensive but semi-desert lands of southern and eastern Canaan, north-west Arabia, Sinai, and the regions bordering the Syrian Desert – a place where nomadic cattle-breeding was the only real possibility. The patriarch Abraham led these tribes into Canaan too late; all the more fertile and well-irrigated lands located in the northern and central parts of the country were already occupied either by local settled peoples or by other nomadic Western Semites – for example, the ancestors of the northern Hebrew tribes who had arrived earlier. It is true, though, that the houses of Jacob and Edom also had luck on their side: their founders derived from Isaac, the son of Abraham's principal wife, Sarah and, in accordance with the laws of the time, their father therefore had the right to the best part of the inheritance. But of the two twin sons born to Isaac, Esau (Edom) was considered the elder and therefore his tribal group was supposed to inherit the land that subsequently came to be called Judah. The rivalry between Jacob and Esau mirrored the real battle between the closely-related tribes for southern Palestine, a territory that was becoming increasingly cramped. Esau's line, later to be called the Edomites, won the first stage in this battle. They ousted some of the Hebrew tribes from their habitual places in southern Canaan. The episode recounting Jacob's escape to his mother's relatives in Haran may be indirect evidence of the temporary departure of part of the Hebrews for their old native-land in Haran. These were the ancestors of the southern tribes of Judah, Reuben, Simeon, and Levi. But there, in northwestern Mesopotamia, there occurred precisely that of which Abraham had been afraid when he had been unwilling to send his son Isaac back to his native Haran – namely a conflict of interests between returning and local Habiru tribes. The land belonging to those who had left for Canaan had already been long since occupied by their kinsmen. Although the latter took the fugitives in, they evidently placed them in a position of dependence. Jacob's fourteen-year service to his uncle Laban testifies to the difficult life of the Hebrews upon their return. Inevitably, there were conflicts and disagreements and these were reflected in the dispute between Jacob and Laban. In the end, the southern tribes decided to leave for Canaan once again. This choice was informed by the news that the West Semitic nomads from northern and central Canaan had gone to the Nile Delta in Egypt; their land, which had formerly been inaccessible to the southern tribes, was now available for occupation. So Jacob led his tribes back into Canaan. The warm meeting with his brother Esau in the north of Palestine was by no means unexpected. The departure of the northern tribes for Egypt had made continued hostility over land absolutely pointless since there was now land in abundance. Moreover, the departure of a large number of nomadic Western Semites weakened Esau's position in Canaan and made the return of his kinsmen from northwestern Mesopotamia extremely desirable. This explains why the chiefs of the two southern tribal groups now met amicably. Admittedly, in distinction to the canonical biblical text, the apocryphal book of Jubilees asserts that peace between the two brothers did not last for long and that after the death of their father, Isaac, their dispute over the inheritance led to a war between them. This war was won by the 'house of Jacob'.

The Bible tells us that Jacob decided not to hurry to the south but to delay for a considerable time in the central part of Canaan. He lived nomadically for a long period in the Shechem region and his sons pastured livestock in the Dothan Valley – something that had never occurred earlier in the time of Abraham and Isaac. This is incontrovertible confirmation of the fact that in central and northern Palestine pastureland which had previously been occupied when Jacob left for Haran had now become available for the nomads (the area nomadically farmed by the 'family' of Abraham-Isaac-Jacob did not, as a rule, extend beyond the borders of Judah's tribe). Here we encounter yet further evidence that Jacob's tribes were inferior in strength to the ancestors of the Edomites. Jacob was frightened by the fact that Esau had so many warriors (Genesis 32:6-7). Indeed, in order to field 400 warriors, Esau's tribes must have contained at least 8000 to 9000 people, which once again makes a poor fit with the idea that Abraham-Isaac-Jacob was a 'family' of patriarchs.

Thus the patriarchs were, in reality, leaders of entire tribal unions and the biblical family was nothing less than a group of closely-related peoples. Abraham was not merely the head of his family, but the leader of a large group of tribes which divided up over time into separate and independent peoples. The biblical family's move from Ur to Haran and from Haran to Canaan, as well as its temporary departure for Egypt, were, in fact, migrations of the West Semitic nomads. Behind the complex personal lives of Abraham, Lot, Isaac, Ishmael, Jacob, and Esau lies the history of their peoples – peoples who variously entered into conflict with one another and united with one another against their common enemies. The separations from one another of Abraham and Lot, then of Isaac and Ishmael, and finally of Jacob and Esau were not the 'splitting up of relatives', but rather the divisions of related tribes which had gradually become sufficiently large and numerous to function as independent peoples. Nomadic cattle breeding, the principal occupation of these tribes, did not allow a large group of fellow tribesmen to come together on any one piece of territory, but instead forced them to constantly search for new land with sufficient pasture and sources of water for their cattle. This was the economic background to the biblical family's divisions. Abraham's departure to the south of Palestine was not a result of the high density of population in the central part of the country, but of the lack of available pasture. There, in southern Canaan, Jacob and Esau, his descendants through Isaac, found a new homeland for themselves and their tribes.

How Two Forefathers Became One

Two particularly important moments in biblical history are connected with Jacob's return from Haran to Canaan. Both episodes deal with the giving of his second name, Israel. The first took place during the night prior to his meeting with Esau and his warriors near a tributary of the River Jordan, the Jabbok. This is how the Bible narrates the incident:

> So Jacob was left alone, and a man wrestled with him till daybreak. When the man saw that he could not overpower him, he touched the socket of Jacob's hip so that his hip was wrenched as he wrestled with the man. Then the man said, 'Let me go, for it is daybreak.' But Jacob replied, 'I will not let you go unless you bless me.' The man asked him, 'What is your name?' 'Jacob,' he answered. Then the man said, 'Your name will no longer be Jacob, but Israel, because you have struggled with God and with men and have overcome.' Jacob said, 'Please tell me your name.' But he replied, 'Why do you ask my name?' Then he blessed him there. So Jacob called the place Peniel, saying, 'It is because I saw God face to face, and yet my life was spared' (Genesis 32:24-30).

The second episode happened later, when Jacob and his people arrived in Bethel, where the sanctuary of the Hebrew tribes was located. When on his way to Haran from his brother Esau's, Jacob had prayed at the sanctuary. This time,

"God said to him, 'Your name is Jacob, but you will no longer be called Jacob; your name will be Israel.' So he named him Israel" (Genesis 35:10).

God likewise repeated his promise to Abraham and Isaac – that he would give the land of Canaan to him and his descendants. In this way God twice presented Jacob with a new name: 'Israel'. This giving of the new name and the promise that Jacob would father a great people and that his descendants would be granted the land of Canaan are very much reminiscent of the covenant entered into with Abraham at Elonei Mamre. It is possible that initially the point of the episode was a renewal of the vow made between Jacob and the God of his fathers, which was a traditional ritual that was common in Canaan at the time. However, the first compilers of the Bible gave the episode an entirely different character. They did not simply change Jacob's personal name, as was the case with Abraham; they endowed him with a completely different second name as well. Moreover, this did not happen at his birth or at his acceptance of a new faith, and not even during a period of dramatic military events, but during peace. The Hebrew name 'Israel' literally means 'fighter against god'; of course, at the time the gods that were meant were the pagan gods with whom human heroes had to fight. But what we know of Jacob's life from the Bible has nothing at all to do with warfare or religious reform. The Bible tells us of no events which could have justified the taking of a new name or a title. The entirely unexpected incident of the fight with an unknown person (a god or divine messenger) does not clarify anything. Rather, it creates the impression that an episode from a different story about a different person was inserted in the oral narrative about Jacob at a later date in accordance with considerations that were relevant at this later time.

From the moment when Abram received his new name (Abraham) from the Lord, it completely ousted the previous version and everywhere in the biblical texts only this later modification was used. Something very different, however, happens with Jacob's second name. In spite of God's word, "Your name will no longer be Jacob, but Israel..." (Genesis 32:28), the biblical texts make equal use of both names. Moreover, the compilers of Genesis emphasize with suspicious frequency the identity of Jacob and Israel, as if wishing to prove that this was a single, common ancestor instead of the forefathers of two different tribal groups.

The situation with the patriarchs' wives is similarly interesting. The forefather Abraham had had only one principal wife, Sarah; Isaac likewise had had only Rebekah. But Jacob had two wives simultaneously and both held the same status, something which had never been the case for any of his predecessors. Was not this the device by which the family trees of two groups of Hebrew tribes – the northern and southern – were artificially united into a single genealogy? Jacob was first given the wife and sons of Israel, the forefather of the northern tribes – and then he was given the latter's name as well. Undoubtedly, it was

The Biblical Family

by no means every branch of the family descended from Abraham that was included in the official biblical canon. Mention is made only of those which do not call into question the primacy of the Abraham-Isaac-Jacob line. It is likely that the oral tradition of the nomadic Western Semites included many legends associated with the history of the northern Hebrew tribes that were later known as Israel. However, only a few of these narratives were woven into the genealogy of the southern group, that of Jacob. Jacob's struggle with God's messenger during the night before his meeting with Esau was undoubtedly taken from the oral tradition concerning Israel, the forefather of the northern tribes. Jacob's second wife, Rachel, and their sons, Joseph and Benjamin, also belong to the genealogy of the northern tribes. It is most probable that the northern Hebrew tribes came to Canaan from northwestern Mesopotamia before Abraham's time, around the 23rd century BCE, and occupied land that was vacant in northern and central Palestine. Only later, in approximately the 20th century BCE, did Abraham arrive in Canaan with his group of tribes. Unlike their kinsmen from the northern group, Abraham's tribes, or at least a part of them, had already lived in southern Mesopotamia. So, since they arrived in Canaan later, they were forced to be content with the more arid regions of southern and eastern Palestine.

The southern Hebrews (Jacob) consisted of only four tribes: Judah, Reuben, Simeon, and Levi. The largest of these was the tribe of Judah, while the smallest was Levi. It would therefore hardly be incorrect to identify this southern Hebrew group as Jacob-Judah, all the more so since the Southern Kingdom took its name from this largest tribe. Unfortunately, until the 12th century BCE we know nothing about the northern Hebrew tribes since all the biblical history known to us from before that time was, in fact, only the history of the southern Hebrew group of Jacob-Judah to which the genealogy of the northern tribes was subsequently added. The combined history of these two groups began only in the 12th century BCE, when the southern group returned from Egypt and a part of it joined the already existing tribal union of Israel in central Canaan. The basis of the biblical canon that we have today concerning the family of Abraham-Isaac-Jacob and the twelve sons of Jacob-Israel was most likely written during the United Monarchy, in the reigns of David and Solomon. It was then, following the political interests of the United Monarchy, that the keepers of the tradition – namely the Levites and the Aaronites – unified the genealogy and history of the two different Hebrew groups. The northern tribes were written retrospectively into the biblical history of the southern group, Jacob-Judah, even though they evidently had an even more interesting and dramatic history than the southern tribes.

The basis of the northern Hebrew tribes consisted of the tribes of Ephraim, Manasseh, and Benjamin. The first two of these tribes were the larger and stronger, tracing their genealogy directly to the legendary Joseph, which is why they were known as the 'house of Joseph'. The third tribe was significantly smaller and had special relations of kinship with the first two. Given that Joseph himself was considered the favorite son of Israel, the father of the northern tribes, this entire group may be identified as 'Israel-Joseph'. The 'house of Joseph' not only occupied a privileged position within the group of northern tribes, but was also the founder of the Israelite tribal alliance, established in central Canaan in the 13th century BCE. Other tribes such as Dan, Naphtali, Gad, and Asher played a secondary and subordinate role – something which is reflected in the biblical canon: these tribes' founding fathers were also considered the sons of the patriarch, but by women of a lower social status. The tribes of Zebulon and Issachar were on an intermediate level between the first and the second groups. At the same time, all these tribes, including both the 'house of Joseph' and the secondary tribes, traced their origins to a common patriarch, Israel.

Sometime at the end of the 18th century BCE the Israel-Joseph group abandoned northern and central Palestine and left for the Nile Delta in Egypt. This is most likely to have happened in the time of the biblical patriarch Isaac and during a period of drought and famine in Canaan. The Bible says as follows:

> Now there was a famine in the land – besides the earlier famine of Abraham's time – and Isaac went to Abimelech king of the Philistines in Gerar. The Lord appeared to Isaac and said, 'Do not go down to Egypt; live in the land where I tell you to live. Stay in this land for a while, and I will be with you and will bless you. For to you and your descendants I will give all these lands and will confirm the oath I swore to your father Abraham (Genesis 26:1-3).

Thus Isaac and his southern tribes did not leave for Egypt. The fact that the compilers of the Bible emphasize this, however, is indirect evidence that the other part of the nomadic Western Semites did leave Canaan for the Nile Delta.

It was usually the southern part of Palestine that suffered most from drought, and it was here that the two related southern groups of Jacob and Edom lived nomadically. But if they did not leave, then why did the northern tribes? After all, there was more water in central Canaan than in the south. Evidently, the reason for the departure of the northern tribes, or some of them, was not so much drought as civil strife. The legend about Joseph and his brothers can shed some light on this problem. The compilers of Genesis took this narrative from the oral history of the northern tribes, but they considered it necessary to add to it the founding fathers from their own southern group in order that the new version of the legend should confirm the single genealogy they had created for the two groups. Above all, our attention is drawn by a geographical misunderstanding: the forefather Jacob is situated in the valley of Hebron, i.e. on the ancestral land of the southern tribes, but sends his sons to pasture cattle right in the middle of the territory of the northern tribes – in the region of Shechem and the Dothan Valley. Anyone familiar with the geography and natural environment of Palestine would find it difficult to understand why it was necessary to drive the cattle such a distance, even onto land that belonged to other people, if pasture of the same quality existed near Hebron. Secondly, it is striking that only the forefathers of the southern tribes, Reuben and Judah, act as Joseph's saviors. It is possible that this legend is founded on a real historical fact – an internal conflict within the northern group of Israel-Joseph. Such a conflict could have broken out between the 'house of Joseph' and the other northern tribes. It may also be that the Jacob-Judah southern group adopted a neutral position at a key moment and allowed the 'house of Joseph' safe passage through their territory into Egypt. It would then be clear that the ancestors of the tribes of Ephraim and Manasseh arrived in Egypt first and that the reproaches they directed against their fellow tribesmen might have been well-founded. It may also have been possible that it was not drought or famine but the privileged position of the 'house of Joseph' in Egypt in the time of the Hyksos that subsequently led the other northern tribes to come there. By contrast, the southern group of Jacob came to the Nile Delta much later, only in the second half of the 17th century BCE, and its life in Egypt took a different course than that of its northern brothers.

The biblical narrative about the family of Abraham-Isaac-Jacob is the oral narrative of the two nomadic West Semitic peoples – the southern tribal group of Jacob and the northern group of Israel. The compilers of the earliest part of the Pentateuch did not simply set down oral legends transmitted over many centuries; they went much further: they wove these legends together to create a single genealogy. They succeeded so well in intertwining the various pieces of narrative about Jacob and Israel, the forefathers of the southern and northern tribes, that all subsequent generations of the Jewish people considered Jacob and Israel to be a single forefather with a double name, Jacob-Israel.

Genesis, the first book of the Pentateuch, ends with the death of Jacob in Egypt, where the southern tribes had come to escape the drought and famine in Canaan. In accordance with the patriarch's last wish, his body was brought from Egypt to Canaan and buried there in the famous Cave of Machpelah near Hebron, where the remains of Abraham and Isaac had already been laid to rest. Thus all three patriarchs, the forefathers of the southern tribes, found their final resting place in the area where they had primarily lived, the Hebron region. Their wives were also buried there: Sarah, Rebekah, and Leah, but not Rachel. Rachel was buried in Bethlehem, which was called Ephrat at the time. But why? After all, Bethlehem was literally located only several miles from Hebron and the Cave of Machpelah. If it was considered possible to bring

Jacob's body even from Egypt, then why did not his wife Rachel (who died giving birth to their son Benjamin) receive the same treatment? How did Leah, although not Jacob's favorite wife, as the Bible itself admits, come to lie next to her husband upon her death, while his dearly beloved Rachel, who was also his legal spouse and, moreover, the mother of his beloved sons, end up outside the family burial-vault? There is another aspect that is also of interest. Joseph, the beloved son of Jacob-Israel, was the only person who, according to the Bible, received the honor of having his bones brought from Egypt when the Exodus took place. But, like Rachel, he too was not buried in the Cave of Machpelah near Hebron; his tomb is in central Palestine, near Shechem – the principal place of residence of the northern tribes. The answer to this enigma is self-evident: it is probable that both Rachel and Joseph were historical characters from the narrative of the northern tribes. Perhaps Rachel was the principal wife of the legendary forefather of the northern tribes, Israel, while Joseph would have been considered his eldest son. From the biblical episode about Rachel's death, we know that it took place on the road southward from Bethel, and that her death took everyone by surprise during some kind of mass move; thus it was necessary to bury her quickly in the spot where she had died. In their effort to compose a single family tree for the two peoples, the authors of Genesis found an interesting compromise with regard to the wives of Jacob and Israel. Leah, Jacob's principal wife, was given senior status, but is presented as unloved while Rachel, principal spouse of Israel, became the second, but only beloved wife of the common patriarch.

In this way the authors of the Pentateuch managed to preserve the primacy of the southern tribes as legal heirs while giving the northern tribes love and acknowledgment of their own special merits. The compilers of Genesis felt the need to merge not only the patriarchs of the two tribal groups, but also their sons – the forefathers of the specific Hebrew tribes. In this respect, we should note the words of the forefather Jacob to Joseph: "Now then, your two sons born to you in Egypt before I came to you here will be reckoned as mine; Ephraim and Manasseh will be mine, just as Reuben and Simeon are mine. Any children born to you after them will be yours" (Genesis 48:5-6). It is significant that Jacob 'appropriated' only Joseph's eldest children, but did not lay claim to any of the children of his other sons. Such echoes of the original existence of two separate tribal groups with different family trees have survived in many biblical sources. For example, one of the psalms of gratitude to God clearly states, "With your mighty arm you redeemed your people, the descendants of Jacob and Joseph" (Psalm 77:15). In spite of the fact, that according to the biblical version, the 'house of Joseph' was only part of the 'house of Jacob' – or, to be more exact, one of Jacob's sons, – the ancient tradition puts him on an independent and equal footing with the entire 'house of Jacob'.

Thus the life stories of the biblical patriarchs indicate that the ancestors of the Hebrews were semi-nomadic Western Semites who came to Canaan from their native land near the upper courses of the River Euphrates. From the very beginning, they were two different tribal groups who appeared in Canaan at different times. The first to come were the ancestors of the northern Hebrew tribes, who led semi-nomadic lives in central and northern Palestine. Later, a new and large tribal alliance which was headed by the biblical patriarch Abraham came to Canaan. His alliance included the ancestors of closely-related peoples who subsequently became known as the southern Hebrew tribes, the Edomites, Moabites, Ammonites, Ishmaelites, Midianites, Kenites, and Amalekites. The sons, grandsons, and great-grandsons of Abraham enumerated in the Bible were the forefathers of the tribes and clans. The Abraham-Isaac-Jacob family tree was only a small part of the genealogy of the rulers of the nomadic and semi-nomadic Western Semites (the Sutu and Habiru). Many centuries later, when the southern Hebrew tribes had already returned from Egypt, a new branch was woven into their family tree – the 'family chronicle' of the northern tribes with whom they united in a single kingdom. Thus Jacob became simultaneously Israel; the number of his sons (tribes) increased to 12; and the remarkable legend about Joseph and his brothers became the shared property of the northern and southern tribes. What could have united two different groups of semi-nomadic Amorite tribes? It was Egypt – or rather that which happened to them there.

Chapter 2

In Egypt

The narrative of the Hebrews' stay in Egypt is the most mysterious and obscure part of the Old Testament. In fact, by comparison, even the more ancient narrative about the Hebrew patriarchs is a much richer source of information. Amazingly, the Bible tells us hardly anything about the four centuries which the Hebrew tribes spent in Egypt. While the book that comes before it, the book of Genesis, is full of names of individuals, peoples, cities, and countries, the book of Exodus, which deals with the Hebrews' stay in Egypt, is enigmatically reticent on the 400 years when the Hebrews lived in this country. Yet the Egyptian period lasted longer than the time which Abraham, Isaac, and Jacob had spent in Canaan. Moreover, the theme of slavery in Egypt is so important that it subsequently becomes a leitmotif of all the biblical books, being mentioned more than 100 times. This complete silence ends only with the birth of Moses, after which all the information we have about the Hebrews in Egypt relates exclusively to the Exodus. We even have incomparably more information about the 40 years of wandering through the desert than the 430-year stay in Egypt. Is this a matter of chance? Of course not. The silence that the Bible keeps regarding life in Egypt is deliberate and testifies to the fact that the first compilers of the Pentateuch intentionally avoided including in the biblical canon any narratives that would have contradicted their official version of the origin of the Israelite people. This silence was an attempt to hide the fact that the Hebrews initially comprised two ethnically close, but distinct peoples – the northern group of Israel-Joseph and the southern group of Jacob-Judah; and that these two tribal groups arrived in and, more importantly, left Egypt at different times. Thus we have two dates for the Hebrews' arrival in Egypt and two different dates for their departure from the country. Moreover, the two tribal groups lived in the Nile Delta for different periods of time and played different roles in Egypt's political history.

The biblical account of the Hebrews' arrival in the Nile Delta, the peaceful life they lived there for 430 years, and their enslavement by the pharaohs and dramatic Exodus under the leadership of Moses relate only to the southern tribes of Jacob-Judah. The northern group of Israel-Joseph had a completely different experience, which was not, and could not have been properly reflected, in the Bible. These tribes, and the 'house of Joseph' in particular, were an integral part of the people that conquered Egypt – the so-called Hyksos – and shared their rise and fall. The 'house of Joseph's stay in Egypt was substantially shorter: this tribal group was forced to leave Egypt for Canaan not later than the middle of the 15th century BCE while their southern brothers from the tribal group of Jacob-Judah continued to live in the Nile Delta right up until the beginning of the 12th century BCE.

The different arrival and departure times, as well as the very different lengths of time that the two groups of Hebrew tribes lived in Egypt, made it impossible to combine the narratives of both groups into a single version such as it had been possible to create in the earlier book of Genesis. It was for this reason that the authors of Exodus thought it best to keep silent about the very extensive period of time that the Hebrews spent in Egypt. All names and events which could have helped in any way identify the locations, key moments, or active participants of this period were excised. It was only this kind of unified version of the 'Egyptian enslavement' that could join together the histories of the two tribal groups. Here we find the compilers of the Bible using the working methods that we saw in the previous chapter: it was not that they fabricated or invented anything; they merely skillfully combined the well-known legends of the time while endeavoring to fashion them into a single genealogy and a common history for the northern and southern tribes – tribes which were brought together in a single country by the hand of fate.

The Hyksos

The Western Semites began settling the Nile Delta while central Egyptian power was still strong enough to keep this process under control. An entire system of fortresses existed along the eastern border of Egypt, giving the Egyptians effective control of the roads and limiting the nomads' access from Asia into Egypt. We know of three written documents that directly or indirectly confirm the Western Semites' penetration into the Nile Delta by the 21st-20th centuries BCE, i.e. during the First Intermediate Period (2130-1938) and the beginning of the Middle Kingdom. These documents are: 'the Admonition of Ipuver', 'the Instructions for King Meri-ka-Re' and 'the Prophecy of Neferty'. All three documents unambiguously testify to the pressure that the nomadic Amorites put on the eastern border of Egypt as well as to their starting to settle in the Nile Delta. They confirm the statement in the book of Genesis that drought and famine forced the people to leave for Egypt. These documents show that what we have here is not a settled population, but nomadic tribes. But the same written sources show that the Egyptians behaved with hostility and even cruelty to Western Semites affected by a lack of water and were trying to minimize their access to the Nile Delta. However, an internal battle for power resulted in an overall weakening of Egypt during the 13th Dynasty; as a result, border controls ceased to function. From this time onwards, tribes of nomadic and semi-nomadic Amorites driven from Canaan by periodic droughts began entering Egypt and living in the Nile Delta without impediment. It cannot be said that the Egyptian pharaohs did not realize the scale of the threat that the newcomers from Asia posed, but internal strife prevented them from closing their eastern border. Moreover, this was something that by no means all the rulers would even have wanted to do. Many of the 70 pharaohs of the 13th Dynasty, in particular at the end of the dynasty's rule, were no longer Egyptians themselves, but originated from the Amorite tribal leaders and were ruling under Egyptian names. However, even those who originated from distinguished Egyptian families increasingly depended on help from the Western Semites. Thus, beginning by backing candidates for the Egyptian throne, the newcomers from Canaan gradually became the decisive military in Egypt.

The Egyptians' growing military dependence on the Western Semites soon led to the rulers of the Amorite tribes deciding to no longer resort to camouflage, but to rule Egypt themselves. 1630 BCE was the last year in the history of the 13th Dynasty and the first in the reign of the new 15th (West Semitic) Dynasty. Historians consider this year to be the end of the Middle Kingdom and the beginning of the Second Intermediate Period (1630-1523 BCE), when all control of Egypt fell into the hands of the Western Semites (the so-called Hyksos). The name 'Hyksos' was first used by Manetho, an Egyptian priest and historian who lived in the 3rd century BCE and wrote a history of Egypt in Greek. Unfortunately, his manuscripts have not survived; all that we have are extensive excerpts from his works compiled by ancient authors. Manetho was cited most frequently by the Jewish historian Josephus Flavius, who lived in the second half of the first century AD.

Manetho tells of the subjugation of Egypt by the Hyksos, an unknown people which had come from Asia. He writes:

> ...For what cause I know not, a blast of God smote us; and unexpectedly, from the regions of the East, invaders of obscure race marched in confidence of victory against our land. By main force they easily overpowered the rulers of the land, they then burned our cities ruthlessly, razed to the ground the temples of the gods, and treated all the natives with a cruel hostility, massacring some and leading into slavery the wives and children of others. Finally, they appointed as king one of their number whose name was Salitis. He had his seat at Memphis, levying tribute from Upper and Lower Egypt, and leaving garrisons behind in the most advantageous positions. Above all, he fortified the district to the east, foreseeing that the Assyrians, as they grew stronger, would one day covet and attack his kingdom. In the Saite [Sethroite] nome, he found a city very

favorably situated on the east of the Bubastite branch of the Nile, and called Avaris after an ancient religious tradition. This place he rebuilt and fortified with massive walls, planting there a garrison of as many as 240,000 heavy-armed men to guard his frontier. Here he would come in summertime, partly to serve out rations and pay his troops, partly to train them carefully in manoeuvres and so strike terror into foreign tribes (Manetho, Aegyptiaca, frag. 42, 1.75-79.2).

Since the citations from Manetho were written in Greek, the term 'Hyksos' is a Greek variant of the Egyptian words 'hekau khasut' – meaning 'foreign rulers' or, to be more precise, 'foreign Asiatic rulers'. Unfortunately, the quotes from Manetho's manuscript give us very little in terms of historical information, apart from confirmation of the fundamental fact that the Hyksos ruled over Egypt. Manetho was describing events which had happened almost 1500 years before, so the picture he paints actually reflects the conquest of Egypt not so much by the Hyksos as by the Assyrians, Babylonians, or Persians, who were much closer to him in time than the Hyksos. Manetho was as removed in time from the Hyksos period as we are today from the Huns' invasion of Rome. Archaeological data do not confirm the terrible pictures of destruction depicted by Manetho, whereas mention of the potential threat to the Hyksos from Assyria (in the 17th-16th centuries BCE) only testifies to the complete confusion in portrayals of the Hyksos in the 3rd century BCE. However, even modern historians have been unable to avoid mistakes when trying to explain the origins of the Hyksos. At first, scholars tried to associate the Hyksos with the Hittites, then with the Hurrians, and finally, they identified them as Indo-European nomadic tribes. They saw evidence of an Indo-European origin in the fact that it was the Hyksos who familiarized the Egyptians with horses and war chariots and taught them more effective methods of obtaining metals – in other words, introduced them to innovations which were considered to have been brought to the Near East by Indo-Europeans. But archaeological excavations conducted in recent decades have dispelled all doubt: the so-called Hyksos were in fact semi-nomadic Western Semites who came not from just anywhere in Asia, but specifically from Palestine. Unfortunately, these West Semitic nomads left us no written testimonies; they did not even have their own form of writing. However, linguistic analysis of their names from Egyptian sources provides unmistakable confirmation of their West Semitic and indeed Amorite origin. Could we really think that the Hittites or Hurrians arrived in Egypt en masse in the 18th-16th centuries BCE if the former were sitting tight in Anatolia at that time and the latter were in northeastern Syria? It was only much later than both the Hittites and the Hurrians started clashing with the Egyptians – and then it was not in Egypt itself, but in Syria and the land of the Amurru.

When using the term 'Hyksos', we should not forget that this was what the Egyptians called only the pharaohs and rulers of West Semitic origin. A completely different name – 'a'amu' – was used for commoners from Syria and Palestine. This is consonant with the name of the West Semitic tribes of that time (Amorites) and the name for Phoenicia and southern Syria (Amurru). The Egyptians had met the a'amu long before the rule of the Hyksos began. On the one hand, they were hired workers who came to Egypt for seasonal work, and on the other, they were the numerous slaves and captives taken during the pharaohs' campaigns in Canaan, Phoenicia, and southern Syria.

The Egyptian sources in effect confirm the accounts given in the books of Genesis and Exodus – in particular, with regard to the departure of the Amorite nomads for Egypt and their life in that country. There can be no doubt that, like the Egyptian 'a'amu' and Manetho's 'Hyksos', the biblical 'Ivri' and the 'Habiru' of Canaan were one large West Semitic ethnos. In this respect, both the southern and the northern Hebrew tribes were merely a small part of the large ethnos which dominated in Canaan, Phoenicia, southern Syria, and subsequently in the Nile Delta as well.

By combining biblical and ancient Egyptian sources and by taking into account the latest archaeological data we are able to reconstruct an approximate picture of the Hyksos' conquest of Egypt and the arrival of the Hebrew tribes in the Nile Delta. This picture will be incomplete if we leave out Canaan, because those who subordinated Egypt not only came from Canaan, but had also lived there for a lengthy period of time. Here we have in mind the semi-nomadic Amorite tribes who came from northwestern Mesopotamia to southern Syria, Phoenicia, and northern/central Canaan in approximately the 23rd century BCE. This large group of tribes also included nomads from the northern Hebrew tribes, who subsequently came to be known as 'Israel'. The arrival of a large mass of nomads led to the collapse of the entire system of Canaanite city states. Some of the cities were destroyed; others were deserted by their inhabitants, who evidently left for regions in the south of Canaan, which had suffered least from the invasion. Archaeological data testify to the quick and violent nature of the destruction of the entire urban culture of Western Palestine of the Early Bronze Age (3050-2300 BCE). They also provide evidence that this culture was replaced by a wholly different one.

The new culture of the semi-nomadic tribes predominated in northern and central Canaan for three centuries, from the 23rd to the 20th century BCE. Throughout this period, semi-nomadic tribes and small agricultural communities preponderated in Palestine. Similar processes occurred on the Lebanese coast and in southern Syria. Unlike these regions, southern Palestine and Transjordan hardly suffered at all. Archaeologists have traced their full continuity with the previous Canaanite city culture. It is likely that the southern and eastern regions served as places of refuge for the former population of Western

Palestine. 'The Story of Sinuhe', a well-known ancient Egyptian document from the 20th century BCE, fully confirms the domination of the semi-nomadic peoples in northern and central Canaan. Sinuhe was an Egyptian high official at the court of the Pharaoh who ran away from his country during the difficult time of the interregnum. He left us a detailed description of northern and central Palestine, where he lived for many years. From this it follows that semi-nomadic tribes lived everywhere in Retenu, as the Egyptians called Palestine. Although he lived in these regions for many years, Sinuhe never once mentions seeing or visiting any large city there – which is hardly surprising since, judging by the archaeological data, all large cities had already been long since destroyed or abandoned by their inhabitants.

The main reason for the destruction of the Canaanite cities of the Early Bronze Age was therefore not sporadic military campaigns undertaken by the Egyptians or climate change of any kind, but an invasion from the north by a large mass of semi-nomadic Amorite tribes. The latter came to Canaan from southern Syria and the Lebanese coast, where they had arrived after having traveled from northwest Mesopotamia, the original native land of all the Western Semites. At approximately this time another powerful wave of Amorite tribes headed in a south-easterly direction along the river valleys of the Tigris and Euphrates. Many Mesopotamian cities experienced the same fate as the cities of Canaan. However, in terms of territory and population, Mesopotamia clearly surpassed Canaan and southern Syria, so the Amorites very quickly intermingled with the local population and adopted their culture. Here this period of chaos and ruin turned out to be much shorter, lasting only approximately 100 years (2230-2130 BCE).

Unlike Mesopotamia, Canaan experienced the arrival of a second wave of Amorite tribes in approximately the 20th century BCE. The coming involved those nomadic Western Semites who for some reason could not live in Mesopotamia and decided to join their fellow tribesmen in Canaan. This group of tribes was led by the biblical patriarch Abraham and included not only southern Hebrew tribes, but also their closest relatives – the future Edomites, Moabites, and Ammonites – and the ancestors of the Midianites and of the peoples of the desert who traced their origins to Abraham. In contrast to the wave of Amorite nomads who came to southern Syria and northern/central Canaan in the 23rd century BCE, the second tribal wave occupied the part of Palestine that remained vacant, i.e. in the south and in Transjordan. Their arrival in Canaan was relatively peaceful or at least involved far less destruction and shock than the first wave. Thus, both chronologically and geographically, the Hebrew tribes were for a long time far removed from each other. The northern tribes found themselves in central Palestine as early as the 23rd century BCE while the southern tribes only came to the south of this country in the 20th century BCE.

In Egypt

However, Canaan too did not serve all the nomadic Amorites as their final resting place. Later, the majority of them moved further, to the Nile Delta in the south-west. Climatic conditions in the Nile Delta – above all, the abundance of water in all seasons – were more suitable for semi-nomadic cattle breeders than Canaan with its periodic droughts and consequent famines. Significantly, the book of Genesis compares the Egyptian land to the 'garden of the Lord' (Genesis 13:10). Most likely, the first groups of semi-nomadic Amorites came to the Nile Delta precisely because of the drought and famine in Canaan. Soon enough, the West Semitic nomads came increasingly frequently to Egypt and stayed for increasingly longer periods of time. This was how the a'amu became a permanent presence in the Nile Delta.

Arrival of West Semitic nomads in Egypt. A wall-painting in the tomb of the governor of the Oryx nome, Khnumhotep II, at Beni Hasan. 19th century BCE.

By the 20th century BCE ancient Egyptian sources were already voicing alarm regarding the pressure exerted by the a'amu on the country's eastern border. In essence, the book of Genesis serves as confirmation that the semi-nomadic Western Semites moved to the Nile Delta due to the periodic droughts in Canaan. Abraham 'descended' into Egypt. Isaac was planning to head in the same direction, and only the intervention of God kept him back in Canaan. Joseph likewise ended up in Egypt when he was sold into slavery. Finally, Jacob and all his relatives left to go to the Nile Delta not to avoid yet another drought, but to live there fulltime. Hagar, who was Abraham's concubine and the mother of his elder son Ishmael, also originated from Egypt, most likely from the same kind of semi-nomadic Western Semites as Abraham (only from a group which came to the Nile Delta before Abraham). Abraham's return to Canaan is merely evidence that, at that time, i.e. approximately the 20th century BCE, the Egyptians still exerted quite effective control over their eastern border and were not allowing the semi-nomadic Amorites to live for long in the Nile Delta.

The period during which the West Semitic pharaohs (Hyksos) ruled is the most obscure and mysterious in the history of ancient Egypt. We still have no written texts, inscriptions, or bas-reliefs deriving from the Hyksos; we know nothing about the pyramids or burial tombs of their pharaohs or their high officials, not to mention wall frescos or sculptures. But the shroud of mystery and darkness covering the period when the West Semitic pharaohs ruled is no accident. The rule of the Amorite foreigners was even in most ancient times considered by the Egyptians to be disgraceful and humiliating. Therefore, after the Hyksos had been driven out, the Egyptian pharaohs systematically and methodically endeavored to obliterate all traces of the Amorites having ruled over Egypt and to erase from memory anything that had to do with the Hyksos. Following orders given by the pharaohs of the New Kingdom, absolutely everything in the country which could have in any way served as a reminder of the Hyksos and their rule was destroyed. For this reason there is little hope today that a Hyksos written monument that could shed light on this dark period of history will ever be discovered. The only thing that remains for archaeologists to do is to study the remains of the Hyksos material culture in the Nile Delta and, above all, in the capital, Avaris. But here too there are considerable difficulties. The vindictive Egyptians completely destroyed the capital, burning it to the ground along with the Hyksos settlements in the Nile Delta. The surviving written and material monuments from this period belong to the enemies of the Hyksos – the pharaohs of the 17th Dynasty from Thebes, who were initially the vassals of the Amorites, but later became their principal adversaries. Indeed, the pharaohs of the 17th and then the 18th Dynasties did everything to ensure that no one among subsequent generations would know anything about the Hyksos or their deeds. It is interesting that the darkest period in Egyptian history, the Hyksos period, chronologically coincided with the most mysterious part of the Bible dealing with the Hebrews' stay in Egypt. In both cases any memory of events which took place during this time was deliberately erased. The pharaohs of the New Kingdom attempted to consign to oblivion the shame of being ruled over by foreigners; and the compilers of the Bible tried to force their readers to forget the fact that the sons of Jacob and Israel had arrived in and left Egypt at different times and indeed had different histories up until their unification in the United Monarchy.

Manetho clearly made a mistake when he depicted the arrival of the Hyksos as an 'invasion' that was 'sudden' and 'unexpected' for the Egyptians. What actually happened was completely different: the infiltration of the semi-nomadic Amorite tribes was gradual and peaceful and took place over the course of several centuries. Most likely, this process even took place with the agreement of the Egyptian authorities, at least to begin with. Egypt's unification and strengthening during the Middle Kingdom led to some of the Amorite tribes being driven out back to southern Canaan and to the fortification of Egypt's eastern border. Indirect evidence of this is found in the biblical narrative concerning Abraham's stay in Egypt. The episode which tells of Abraham's wife Sarah being put into the 'pharaoh's' harem is only an artistic transposition of real migrations made by the semi-nomadic Amorites. Thus the second half of the 20th century and the entire 19th century BCE were an interruption in the settlement of the Nile Delta by Western Semites. The situation changed only towards the middle of the 18th century BCE. The new weakening of the central authority in Egypt and the decline in the country's military power coincided with the end of the 12th Dynasty. The 13th Dynasty was typified by continual changes of power, with each pharaoh hardly having time to replace his predecessor. Civil wars raged and separatism intensified among the nomes. Guarding the eastern frontier was no longer of interest to anyone. It was during this period that the Amorite tribes once again began settling the Nile Delta in large numbers. In the eastern part of the Nile Delta an enormous fortified city emerged. This was Avaris, which subsequently became the capital of the Western Semites while they were in Egypt. Avaris was three times larger than Hazor, the largest city at the time in Palestine. The city's rapid growth and large size testify to the enormous influx of Amorite tribes into the Nile Delta as well as to the fact that these semi-nomads were now beginning to settle. We have reason to suppose that by the 17th century BCE the majority of the nomadic Amorites from Canaan and southern Syria had concentrated in the Nile Delta and that they far outnumbered the local Egyptian population, which evidently quickly intermarried with the Western Semites.

During the rule of the numerous pharaohs of the 13th Dynasty, the legal status and political role of the Amorites who had settled in the Nile Delta change substantially. From being newcomers with no rights who lived in Egypt at the discretion of the Pharaoh, they became full residents of the Delta with an ever-growing influence on the internal politics of Egypt. Without the military support of the leaders of the Amorite tribes, no candidate for the position of Pharaoh could count on success. By the end of the rule of the 13th Dynasty several pharaohs were Egyptian in name only, being in actual fact descended from the Amorite rulers. The drastic weakening of central power resulted in Egypt once again disintegrating into separate nomes whose rulers were sole masters of their regions. Eventually, the complete chaos and confusion in Egyptian politics constituted what was in effect an invitation to the Amorite tribal rulers of the Nile Delta to seize power.

Thus it was that a new and purely Amorite Dynasty of pharaohs emerged – the 15th (1630-1523 BCE), usually referred to as the Hyksos Dynasty. However, the Amorite rulers – the Hyksos – came to power not as foreign conquerors, but as Egyptians of West Semitic origin who used the symbolism, language, culture, and rituals of Egypt. Moreover, in their foreign and domestic policy they represented the interests of Egypt and not of any other country. This was the principal difference that distinguished the rule of the Hyksos from the later reigns of the Assyrians, Babylonians, and the Persians.

The Amorite rulers, most of whom had been born in Egypt and were not the first generation of their families to live in the country, considered themselves to be not conquerors of Egypt, but Egyptian pharaohs; they ruled in accordance with the local customs and in the interests of the local population. They identified themselves with Egypt, which they considered their own country. The name 'hekau khasut' – 'foreign Asiatic rulers' ('Hyksos' in Greek) – was conferred upon them by their enemies, the Theban pharaohs of Upper Egypt, who were traditional rivals of the rulers from Lower Egypt.

The Hebrews and the 'King-Shepherds'

The question of the place and role of the Hebrew tribes among the Hyksos is of great importance. From the ethnic point of view, the two formed a single whole; both were semi-nomadic Amorite tribes. The main difference between the Amorites in Egypt was the political role played by their tribal leadership; and this role depended, in turn, on the size of the tribes and the time of their arrival in Egypt. Having established themselves in the Nile Delta earlier than their fellow tribesmen, the largest groups of Amorites occupied the top rung in the Hyksos hierarchy, and it was these same Amorites from whom the Hyksos pharaohs derived. The less numerous Amorite tribes and in particular those who came to Egypt later, during the rule of the Hyksos, played a lesser role and depended on the protection of their relatives who were part of the Hyksos hierarchy.

This principle extended to the Hebrew tribes as well. The 'house of Joseph', forced to move to Egypt earlier than its fellow tribesmen, was able to assume a privileged position in the Hyksos kingdom. This is explained by the fact that Ephraim and Manasseh, the principal tribes comprising the 'house of Joseph', arrived in the Nile Delta before the Hyksos themselves came to power, sometime at the beginning of the 13th Dynasty, in the second half of the 18th century BCE. The 'house of Joseph' was possibly one of those Amorite rulers who were invited to take power by the pharaohs at the time when the pharaohs were still of Egyptian origin. The other northern tribes who came slightly later reinforced the position of the 'house of Joseph' and helped it secure a privileged position in the Hyksos hierarchy. Thus we may say that the 'house of Joseph' was a constituent part of the Hyksos, while its tribal elite was part of the entourage of the Hyksos pharaohs. It is probable that before their move to Egypt, Ephraim and Manasseh were one large tribe of semi-nomadic Western Semites, which we can provisionally call 'Joseph' after their legendary forefather. They divided once they were in Egypt, after a rapid increase in their numbers. The rulers, and perhaps the entire elite of the 'house of Joseph', assimilated the Egyptian culture and language and took wives from among Egyptian families of priests and high officials. The 'house of Joseph' were typical Hyksos or West Semitic rulers who had adopted the Egyptian way of life and traditions. According to the Bible, the house's legendary forefather, Joseph, led the life of an Egyptian high official, had an Egyptian name, and was married to the daughter of an influential Egyptian priest. Upon his death, he was buried in accordance with Egyptian and not West Semitic ceremonial ritual: "after they embalmed him, he was placed in a coffin in Egypt" (Genesis 50:26). As far as we can tell from the biblical description, Joseph occupied the post of supreme vizier (minister) at the court of an Egyptian pharaoh of the 13th Dynasty or at the court of the Hyksos king. We must suppose that, like Joseph himself, his descendants also led an Egyptian lifestyle. However, as later events showed, this cultural assimilation affected only the tribal rulers and their families; most commoners in these tribes remained faithful to the West Semitic traditions and language.

The 'house of Joseph' owed its special place among the Hebrew tribes not so much to its numerousness as to its privileged position in the Egypt of the Hyksos. It became protector and benefactor to all its fellow tribesmen – at first to the northern tribes and then to the southern ones as well.

The story of the southern tribes, the 'house of Jacob', in Egypt began 100 years later than the experience of the northern tribes, i.e. approximately at the end of the 17th century BCE, when the Hyksos were already rulers of the Lower Kingdom. Most probably, their arrival in Egypt occurred precisely as described in the Bible: protracted drought and famine forced them to abandon Canaan and settle peacefully in the eastern part of the Nile Delta. Moreover, all this took place with the help and protection of the 'house of Joseph'. Thus the 'house of Jacob' and the 'house of Joseph' found themselves under a single roof in Egypt. The roles that they played in the Hyksos kingdom were nevertheless completely different. If the 'house of Joseph' enjoyed a central and privileged position, the southern tribes lived humbly on the periphery of the Lower Kingdom and probably played no active part in Hyksos politics or the confrontation between the Hyksos and the Theban pharaohs. They led a quiet pastoral life under the high protection of the 'house of Joseph', thanks to whom they were able to solve all their problems in Egypt.

The Departure of the 'House of Joseph' from the Nile Delta in the 15th Century BCE

The end of the Hyksos' rule in Egypt, as was to be expected, came from the south, at the hands of the Theban rulers. Learning from the defeats of his predecessors, Theban Pharaoh Ahmose cut off in advance all paths by which the Hyksos might have received help. However, despite their numerical superiority, the Egyptians could not take Avaris by storm. Manetho, relying on ancient Egyptian sources, wrote as follows: "[The Hyksos] had built a wall surrounding this city, which was large and strong, in order to keep all their possessions and plunder in a place of strength. [The Egyptian pharaoh] attempted to take the city by force and by siege with 480,000 men surrounding it. But he despaired of taking the place by siege, and concluded a treaty with them, that they should leave Egypt, and go, without any harm coming to them, wherever they wished" (Josephus Flavius, *Against Apion*, Book 1, Section 73).

Data gathered from archaeological excavations on the site of the city of Avaris (now called Tell El-Dab'a) in large part confirm Manetho's reports of a mass exodus of the city's inhabitants from Egypt. The material culture characteristic of the Western Semites from Canaan ended abruptly with the fall of Avaris and was, after an interval, replaced with a completely different culture, Egyptian in character. The destruction suffered by Avaris contains no trace of a battle for the city or of the death of its inhabitants. The city was most likely destroyed and burnt after the mass exodus of its population. Thus ended the rule of the 15th Hyksos Dynasty in Egypt, after approximately 108 years. The Hyksos escaped to their allies and fellow tribesmen in Canaan. Fearing the restoration of Hyksos rule, Ahmose launched a campaign against southern Palestine and over the course of three years laid siege to the city of Sharuhen, where the former Hyksos rulers had firmly established themselves. The capture of Sharuhen signified an irrevocable end to the influence of the Western Semites over Egypt and the beginning of a new era in the country's history – the period of the New Kingdom. Ahmose founded a new Dynasty, the 18th, and served as its first pharaoh.

The defeat of the Hyksos changed the fate of the Amorite tribes in the Nile Delta. Some of these tribes were forced to leave immediately, together with the Hyksos rulers. However, the exodus of the Hyksos was not the simultaneous event that Manetho portrays it to be. The first to leave Egypt were those who lived in Avaris or who had sought refuge there during the siege – the army, the pharaoh's court and their families, and the inhabitants of the Hyksos capital. But most Amorites did not live in the capital or in fortified cities, but were scattered throughout the Nile Delta. Moreover, the semi-nomadic Amorites had, over the course of a lifetime, settled on the land. This is confirmed by the Bible: "Now the Israelites settled in Egypt in the region of Goshen. They acquired property there and were fruitful and increased greatly in number" (Genesis 47:27). The settled Amorite population, scattered over the perimeter of the entire Nile Delta, could never have left Egypt simultaneously, and still less together with the escaping Hyksos army and the court of the Pharaoh.

Ahmose and his successors, the pharaohs of the 18th Dynasty, were on many occasions confronted with the question of what to do with the Amorites who remained in the Nile Delta. Initially, when the New Kingdom was gaining in strength, the Amorites were still too numerous and strong to be collectively enslaved or driven out of the Nile Delta. Ahmose and his closest successors – Amenhotep I, Thutmose I, and Thutmose II – were too busy suppressing internal revolts and campaigning in Nubia and Libya to get involved in a serious conflict with the Western Semites in the Nile Delta. However, the Egyptians as a whole were negatively disposed to the continued presence of large numbers of Amorites in their country; they were afraid that the Amorites could again seize power in Egypt, as had happened during the Hyksos period, or unite with their adversaries in a time of war. The Bible also notes similar suspicions with regard to the Western Semites: "Then a new king, who did not know about Joseph, came to power in Egypt. 'Look,' he said to his people, 'the Israelites have become much too numerous for us. Come, we must deal shrewdly with them or they will become even more numerous and, if war breaks out, will join our enemies, fight against us and leave the country' (Exodus 1:8-10). The Egyptian pharaohs preferred a strategy of gradually forcing out the Western Semites. But as Egypt's strength grew, the pharaohs pursued a policy that was increasingly hostile and uncompromising towards the remaining Amorites. It was probably during the rule of Thutmose III (1479-1426 BCE) that the majority of the Western Semites were forced to leave the Nile Delta. Their departure stretched over many decades. The first to leave were the Amorite tribes whose rulers were directly linked with the Hyksos pharaohs and were part of their milieu – for instance, the Hyksos 'house of Joseph'. And vice-versa, those Amorites who lived further from Avaris and had not participated in the wars waged by the Hyksos were allowed to stay longer.

At some point in the middle of the 15th century BCE the 'house of Joseph', which consisted of the tribes of Ephraim, Manasseh, and Benjamin, left Egypt and returned to Canaan. It is possible that another northern tribe, Naphtali, left with them as well. The Bible points to the same time, telling us that the Temple of Solomon was built 480 years after the arrival of the sons of Israel from Egypt. The Temple of Solomon was erected around 960 BCE, so the approximate date we end up with for the departure of some of the northern tribes from Egypt is 1440 BCE.

But where did the Amorites go from Egypt? They headed for whence they had originally come, i.e. Canaan, southern Syria, and the Lebanese coast. The 'house of Joseph' returned to the region of Shechem, its former tribal lands. However, not everything was straightforward. During these tribes' absence from Canaan over the course of two and a half centuries, substantial changes had taken place. For example, by the middle of the 15th century BCE most of the population of this country had become settled. Those Amorite tribes who had not left to go to the Nile Delta settled on the land in Canaan itself and assimilated Canaanite urban and agricultural culture. But the most important thing was that the tribal territories of the Western Semites who had left for Egypt, including the Hebrews, were now largely occupied and had been divided up among the Canaanite and Amorite city states. Several Israelite tribes found themselves homeless upon their return to Canaan.

It was at this time that 'Habiru/Apiru' became established as a name for all Western Semites who had returned from the Nile Delta, including the Hebrews. This name was used not for semi-nomadic Amorites in general, but only for those Amorites who had lost their own tribal territory and thus become, though no choice of their own, homeless wanderers. It has to be remembered that in the Nile Delta the semi-nomadic Amorites had adopted a settled lifestyle; their return to a nomadic way of life was forced and incomplete. From the biblical texts dealing with the Exodus of the Hebrew tribes from Egypt we know how difficult and painful they found the process of returning to the nomadic life and how they strove to re-establish their previous, more comfortable and secure, settled lifestyle.

If at the beginning of the 2nd millennium BCE, the term 'Habiru' applied to semi-nomadic, non-settled Amorites, by the 15th century its meaning had clearly narrowed: it was now used only of homeless Western Semites who had lost their tribal territory. In addition to the Habiru who found themselves without a home through no choice of their own, there were also other nomadic Amorites who had retained their tribal territories because they had not gone to Egypt. This was true, for instance, of the close relatives of the southern Hebrew tribes – the Edomites, Moabites, and Ammonites. These tribes were given another name, 'Sutu', which was also the name given to more distant relatives of the Hebrews – the Midianites, Kenites, Ishmaelites, and Amalekites, desert peoples who traced their genealogy to the patriarch Abraham. Unlike the 'Sutu', who were voluntary nomads on land which was their own, the 'Habiru' were forced wanderers who had lost their tribal lands and were keen not only to repossess these lands, but to resume their settled way of life there once again.

Evidently, the majority of these Habiru in Canaan comprised the three northern tribes related to the 'house of Joseph' – Ephraim, Manasseh, and Benjamin. It is possible that they were joined by another, fourth, tribe, Naphtali. Still more Amorites found themselves in the position of Habiru in southern Syria and on the Lebanese coast. Like the Israelite tribes, they too became homeless when they found their lands occupied upon their return from Egypt. The position of the Habiru was made much more difficult by the fact that the rulers of the local city states who had 'seized' their tribal territories were vassals of the Pharaoh and under the protection of Egypt. To conquer Canaan would have been impossible due to Egypt's indisputable military superiority in the 15th-13th centuries BCE. While Egypt's hold over Canaan and Southern Syria remained intact, the most the Habiru could do was to engage in partisan warfare and to lay siege to particular cities. These actions were keenly felt by the local rulers, but were on a scale insufficient to merit a response from the Egyptian army.

Certain historians look for the ancestors of the Hebrews not among the Habiru, but among the Sutu. According to written sources at our disposal, the Sutu were West Semitic tribes of Amorite origin who lived as nomads on the semi-arid lands from southern Transjordan to northern Syria. The Egyptians termed them – or at least those of them who had settled in southern Transjordan – 'Shasu'. The Amarna letters often mention the Sutu alongside the Habiru; however, all the rulers of Canaan, Amurru, Syria, and Mesopotamia made a clear distinction between the Sutu and the Habiru – but without explaining why. The main difference seems to have been that the Sutu/Shasu did not go to Egypt, did not lead a settled life in the Nile Delta, and had nothing to do with the Hyksos. Unlike the Habiru, they were not homeless since they had managed to keep their tribal territories in Transjordan and Syria. Despite clashes with Egypt, the Sutu did not have such a deep 'historical' conflict with this country as the Habiru and were therefore not considered an anti-Egyptian power in the region. Moreover, several Sutu/Shasu tribes were even in the service of the Egyptians. It is significant that none of the rulers of Canaan or Amurru complained to the Pharaoh about contact between their rivals and the Sutu, and yet they often accused one another of alliance with the Habiru.

Another important difference was way of life. The Sutu continued their nomadic existence while the Habiru, who had already settled before they being driven out of the Nile Delta, were keen to return to their former lifestyle as soon as possible. It cannot be ruled out that by the 14th century BCE they were already leading a semi-settled lifestyle as both cattle breeders and arable farmers. However, it was Egypt's hold over Canaan and Amurru that kept them from settling on the land completely. As soon as Egyptian rule came to an end, the Habiru quickly conquered these countries and settled.

Chapter 3

The Exodus of Hebrew Tribes at the Beginning of the 12th Century BCE

Not all the Western Semites left Egypt after the expulsion of the Hyksos: some continued living in the Nile Delta. We do not know why they stayed on when the majority of their fellow tribesmen had left Egypt, but we may assume that there were two main causes. Firstly, the tribes that remained had no relation to the Hyksos and had not participated in the latter's wars with the Theban pharaohs. Secondly, they lived in the most remote regions of the Nile Delta and thus posed no threat to the population centers in Lower Egypt. It is possible that economic considerations also played a role: the pharaohs of the New Kingdom did not want to leave the Nile Delta completely empty and were planning to use the remaining Amorites for forced labor in the service of the state. Whatever the case may be, the southern Hebrew tribes or 'house of Jacob' were among those who stayed behind. In the 15th-14th centuries BCE they were probably in quite a good position; otherwise, they would have left Egypt together with their fellow tribesmen. Their situation changed markedly for the worse only when the pharaohs of the new 19th Dynasty came to power at the beginning of the 13th century BCE. In contrast to the preceding 17th and 18th Dynasties of Theban pharaohs, these new rulers originally came from the north, from the Nile Delta, the east of which – the land of Goshen – was at that time home to the Hebrew tribes. The founder of the 19th Dynasty, a former army officer who had subsequently become a minister, was a native of the region of Avaris, the former capital of the Hyksos. Upon accession to the throne, he took the name of Rameses I, but reigned for only two years, during which time he failed properly to make his mark. However, his son, Seti I, and especially his grandson, Rameses II, both achieved incomparably more. Unlike the southern pharaohs, who as a rule erected new cities and temples in Upper Egypt, the new dynasty concentrated its efforts on building in the north, in the Nile Delta region which was its original homeland. This circumstance proved fateful for the 'house of Jacob' and those Amorites who stayed on in the Nile Delta. Rameses II is famous for his feverish building activity: none of the other Egyptian pharaohs built so many cities and temples. Needing a giant labor force, he placed a heavy burden of work duties on the Western Semites living in the direct vicinity of his main building projects. It was here, in their lands, that he built a majestic new city – Piramese (meaning the 'property of Rameses') – and it was this that the southern Hebrew tribes were forced to build. The burdens of this period left such an impression on the memory of the 'house of Jacob' that they were even mentioned in the Bible: "So they put slave masters over them to oppress them with forced labor, and they built Pithom and Rameses as store cities for Pharaoh" (Exodus 1:11). It was Rameses II who was the pharaoh oppressor to whom the Bible dedicated its scant lines on Egyptian slavery. It was under Rameses II that "the Egyptians worked them ruthlessly. They made their lives bitter with hard labor in brick and mortar and with all kinds of work in the fields; in all their hard labor the Egyptians used them ruthlessly" (Exodus 1:13-14).

When Did the Biblical Exodus Happen?

Among biblical scholars the opinion prevails that the Hebrews' Exodus from Egypt took place during the rule of Rameses II, sometime in the middle or second half of the 13th century BCE. The main reason that forces us to date the Exodus precisely to this period is the stele of Pharaoh Merneptah (1207 BCE), which mentions Israel as a people which was already in Canaan at the end of the 13th century BCE. Taking into account the fact that, according to the Bible, the Hebrew tribes had spent 40 years in the desert before they could set about conquering Canaan, the date of the Exodus must be moved back to the middle of the 13th century BCE. However, this supposition does not take into account two important circumstances. First and foremost, the significance given to the Merneptah Stele in dating the Exodus is fundamentally erroneous, since in reality there was not one Exodus but two. The tribal alliance of Israel that is mentioned in the Merneptah Stele comprised only the four northern Hebrew tribes which left Egypt for Canaan in the middle of the 15th century BCE; the remaining Hebrew tribes could not have left Egypt before the beginning of the 12th century. Secondly, during the rule of Rameses II Egypt's military and political power was at its height; there was almost no chance for an entire group of tribes to depart against the Pharaoh's will. The Exodus of the four northern tribes and of the rest of the tribes happened in completely different circumstances. The 'house of Joseph', just like the majority of the Amorites, was forcibly driven out from Egypt during the period when the latter's military power was growing. The 'house of Jacob', on the other hand, was forcibly kept back by Egypt for use as slave labor. To break free from Egypt, the 'house of Jacob' had to wait for a period of national crisis. For this reason, we must look for a date for the Exodus of the southern tribes, and of the tribes which had joined them, in the years of the decline of Egypt's military might and the abrupt weakening of its central power. On this basis, the period from the end of the 19th to the beginning of the 20th Dynasty, i.e. between the final years of the reign of Queen

Tausret and the rule of Pharaoh Setnakht, is the most likely time for the biblical Exodus. This was a period of troubles in Egypt. During the course of several years the country was paralyzed by internal feuds, revolts, and court intrigues; and this was followed by the accession to the throne of the Syrian usurper, Irsu. We have evidence of the complete chaos enveloping Egypt at this time, and, even more importantly, there are mentions of an uprising of 'Asiatics' who challenged the authority of the Pharaoh. There is, unfortunately, no absolute agreement among Egyptologists as to when Queen Tausret and Pharaoh Setnakht ruled. Nevertheless, most favor dates between 1192 and 1182 BCE. It is during this period, then, that we need to look for the exact year of the Exodus of the 'house of Jacob' from Egypt.

There can be no doubt that Moses was born during the rule of the pharaoh oppressor, Rameses II. It is also clear that he was forced to flee from Egypt either at the end of Rameses II's reign or at the beginning of the rule of his son, Merneptah. Much more difficult to determine is when Moses returned. This was a period of decline in Egypt. Having reached the zenith of its power under Rameses II, it began to weaken under his successor, Merneptah. Having come to power in old age, Merneptah realized perfectly well that he had little time to accomplish large-scale projects and so devoted all his strength to retaining already conquered territories. The rapid decline of the 19th Dynasty followed his death; Egypt began to slip into serious internal political crisis. At the moment when Merneptah died, his son, the crown prince, was evidently absent from court and the throne was seized by his brother, Amenmessu. But the rule of this usurper proved very short. Merneptah's lawful successor, Seti II, ascended the throne in unclear circumstances. Guided by the desire to wreak vengeance on his brother, he not only attempted to erase all memory of the latter, but also punished everyone who had helped him. But Seti II was likewise not destined to reign for long. When he died, he was replaced, for want of a better candidate, by his sick young son, Siptah. But the latter's mother was one of the very youngest wives of the Pharaoh, so official power rested with Seti II's principal wife, Tausret, as queen regent. Upon the untimely death of Siptah, Tausret then became lawful ruler of Egypt. Real power in the country, however, belonged not so much to her, as to her all-powerful favorite – chancellor Bay, a Syrian by origin. When Queen Tausret died, the Syrian chancellor attempted to seize power and rule under the name of Irsu. The time of troubles came to an end when a new Dynasty, the 20th, was founded by Setnakht, a person of unknown origin. The rule of Setnakht, however, also lasted no longer than three years; the cause of his death is unknown. Such was the historical background to Moses' return and the Exodus of the 'house of Jacob' from Egypt.

From the book of Exodus we know that upon returning to Egypt, Moses was unable immediately to obtain his people's freedom. In order to organize and prepare for the Exodus of the Hebrew tribes, he needed several years.

He certainly could not have returned to Egypt earlier than the death of Pharaoh Merneptah, but must nevertheless have been in the country not later than the rule of the child Siptah and Queen Tausret. The famous Exodus described in the Bible happened after the death of Queen Tausret, when power had been seized by chancellor Bay and the country was caught up in a civil war. The pharaoh with whom Moses negotiated was the Syrian chancellor who became later known by the name of Irsu. The ten Egyptian plagues were mixed together with natural catastrophes and the disasters caused by internal wars. The exact moment when the Exodus occurred coincided with the time when the new pharaoh, Setnakht, had begun winning victories over his adversaries and was attempting to restore order in the country.

The Mission of Moses

We know nothing about the many years when Moses lived with the Midianites. The Bible tells us only of the most important episode in his life there, when God laid upon him a special mission to save his people from Egyptian slavery. This took place on Mount Horeb, which was regarded as a holy site not only by the Hebrews, but also by all the nomadic Western Semites, including the Midianites. This episode is extremely important in several respects. First of all, it signified God's sanctification of the role of Moses as savior and leader of his people; henceforth, no one could challenge Moses from a position of distinction, wealth, or supremacy in the tribal hierarchy since Moses had been chosen by God himself. This circumstance was extremely important for the time since Moses' position in the tribal hierarchy of the 'house of Jacob' gave him no claim to supremacy. He acted merely as chief of the tribe of Levi, which in numerical terms was inferior to the other southern tribes of Reuben, Simeon, and especially Judah. Secondly, the episode was God's sign to the 'house of Jacob' that they needed to leave Egypt and conquer the land of Canaan. There could be no withstanding this plan, for such was the will of God. It is entirely possible that among the chiefs of the Hebrew tribes and clans in Egypt there was no consensus about what to do. There were evidently those who proposed accepting enslavement and remaining in the Nile Delta to hold out for better times. Others doubted the choice of the land of Canaan as destination, realizing that conquering it would not be easy. In short, this divine injunction was needed to induce the Hebrew tribes to recognize not only Moses' claim to leadership over the 'house of Jacob', but also the necessity of leaving Egypt for Canaan. In addition, help was needed from an influential leader among the Hebrew tribes in Egypt itself, a leader who could confirm Moses' power and the divine character of the instructions given to him. Such an authority was Aaron, and it was for this reason that in referring to God's will the biblical text clearly defined the role and significance of Aaron as Moses' principal assistant, Number Two in the Exodus of the people from Egyptian slavery.

The Bible calls Aaron the brother of Moses. However here, just as in the case of the forefather Jacob-Israel, the first compilers of the Pentateuch decided to combine two different families for political considerations. Moreover, it is possible that Moses and Aaron were even from two different tribes. Indeed, who was Aaron? There is reason to think that he was head of the priestly clan of the 'house of Jacob', i.e. he was the high-priest of the southern Hebrew tribes and simultaneously closely linked with the most prominent such tribe, the tribe of Judah. According to the Bible, the brother of Aaron's wife was chief of this tribe. Furthermore, it may have been that Aaron himself came from one of the most esteemed Judahite families. The biblical version that Aaron and Moses were close relatives and had common origins in the tribe of Levi arose later, during the period of the United Monarchy, and was intended to bring together the northern Levites and the southern Aaronites.

The episode in which Moses was given his mission to save his people in Egypt had great significance from another point of view as well: it united the southern tribes' cult of Yahweh with the northern tribes' cult of El and thus paved the way for their merging. It reminded the Hebrews that the God of the 'house of Jacob' was the same as that of the 'house of Joseph' and that the Yahweh of the southern tribes was known to the forefathers Abraham, Isaac, and Jacob by the name of El or Elochim (the plural of the word El'), to whom they prayed and to whom the northern tribes in Canaan also prayed. It is not by chance that the Bible discloses the name of the Lord – Yahweh (God the Everlasting One) – for the first time in this episode. This name, designated by four Hebrew letters – the so-called tetragrammaton – was certainly known to the southern tribes even earlier. After all, even the name of Moses' mother, Yocheved, was derived from 'Yahweh'. But on this occasion it was necessary to emphasize that no one should be disturbed by the fact that the southern and northern tribes had different names for God, since in reality these names designated one and the same Lord of the 'house of Jacob' and the 'house of Joseph'. The merging of the two religious cults was the logical completion of the linking of the names of the Hebrew tribes' two forefathers, Jacob and Israel. Just as these initially distinct tribal leaders had become a single patriarch, so the two distinct religious cults of El and Yahweh merged into a single faith in a God with different names.

The growing crisis of authority and the country's general weakening not only made it possible for Moses to return to Egypt, but also allowed him to take the lead in fighting for his people's Exodus. However, until the beginning of the civil war in Egypt, Moses could put forward only the most 'harmless' and natural requests which would not call into question either the authority of the Egyptian rulers or the loyalty of the Hebrew tribes. Such were the requests for the restoration of the Western Semites' rights to conduct pilgrimages to the Mountain of God, where previously they had held ceremonial services. The Mountain of God was located in Sinai, a three-day journey from the eastern border of the Nile Delta; Moses' plan envisaged that, instead of returning to Egypt, the Hebrew tribes would flee into the mountainous regions of the Sinai or Midian, where with the help of the Midianites they could hide from the pursuing Egyptian army. It might have seemed that this was a request which the Egyptians would be unlikely to turn down, given that it concerned fulfillment of the religious duties of the 'house of Jacob' and that the Egyptians themselves worshipped both their own and other people's gods. However, as long as Queen Tausret and her favorite, chancellor Bay, retained a firm hold on power, they spurned such petitions, seeing them as an attempt to restore the Western Semites' former rights and freedoms. Obviously, the incensed leaders of the Hebrews interpreted all the natural catastrophes which befell Egypt as God's retribution for Egypt's refusal to let His people go and serve Him. The situation changed when, after the death of Queen Tausret, chancellor Bay proclaimed himself the new pharaoh, taking the name Irsu upon his accession to the throne. Many at court and especially in the army refused to recognize the Syrian usurper. Then another pretender, Setnakht, appeared and, with the support of the Egyptian army, took up arms against the former chancellor. The ensuring fight for power called the authority of Pharaoh Irsu into question. Sensing that he was losing the support of his adherents, Irsu had no choice but to change tactics and, not wishing to aggravate his position through a new conflict with the Western Semites, expressed his readiness to let them go to the Mountain of God. However, suspicious that they intended to leave Egypt forever, he forbade them to take their families with them. Subsequently, as the situation in the country deteriorated, he agreed to let their families go as well, but without taking their cattle or property. This ill suited Moses' plans since without cattle and stocks of food life in the desert would be impossible. Negotiations were again interrupted and the Hebrew leaders entered into contact with Setnakht.

The Bible especially emphasizes the fact that the Hebrews did not simply leave or independently break out of Egypt, but were sent out by the Egyptians themselves in great haste. "During the night Pharaoh summoned Moses and Aaron and said, 'Up! Leave my people, you and the Israelites! Go, worship the Lord as you have requested. Take your flocks and herds, as you have said, and go.' [...] The Egyptians urged the people to hurry and leave the country [...] So the people took their dough before the yeast was added, and carried it on their shoulders in kneading troughs wrapped in clothing [...] With the dough they had brought from Egypt, they baked cakes of unleavened bread. The dough was without yeast because they had been driven out of Egypt and did not have time to prepare food for themselves" (Exodus 12:31-34, 39).

That this was not a voluntary departure but a forced expulsion was said on more than one occasion even before the night of the Passover: "Then the Lord said to Moses, "Now you will see what I will do to Pharaoh: Because of my mighty hand he will let them go; because of my mighty hand he will drive them out of his country" (Exodus 6:1).

There is a further interesting fact that deserves attention. The Bible repeatedly and insistently mentions things of gold and silver and expensive clothing which the 'house of Jacob' takes with it out of Egypt. The first oblique mention of this comes in the prophetic dream of Abraham, the patriarch: "Know for certain that your descendants will be strangers in a country not their own, and they will be enslaved and mistreated four hundred years. But I will punish the nation they serve as slaves, and afterward they will come out with great possessions" (Genesis 15:13-14). Subsequently, Moses is told this many times over – first, in the episode when he is invested with the mission to save his people from captivity in Egypt: "And I will make the Egyptians favorably disposed toward this people, so that when you leave you will not go empty-handed. Every woman is to ask her neighbor and any woman living in her house for articles of silver and gold and for clothing, which you will put on your sons and daughters. And so you will plunder the Egyptians" (Exodus 3:21-22); then on the day before the Passover; and finally following the Passover night: "The Israelites did as Moses instructed and asked the Egyptians for articles of silver and gold and for clothing. The Lord had made the Egyptians favorably disposed toward the people, and they gave them what they asked for; so they plundered the Egyptians" (Exodus 12:35-36). On the face of it, this deed seems not merely ethically unattractive on the part of the 'house of Jacob', but also illogical from the point of view of the Egyptians: how could they give up their own precious possessions to a people whom they were themselves driving from their country? That the compilers of the Bible accentuated this event by mentioning it several times in the biblical text suggests that it did in fact happen. So, although the taking of the gold, silver, and other fine things out of Egypt constitutes a detail of secondary importance in the history of the Exodus, it can help us establish the precise time and circumstances of the departure of the tribes of Moses.

We currently have only two ancient Egyptian sources relating to the time of the rule of Pharaoh Setnakht. The first of these, the Harris Papyrus, is the largest ancient Egyptian document written during the rule of Rameses IV, Setnakht's grandson. Unfortunately, it gives only very sketchy information on the founder of the 20th Dynasty and the three years of his rule. The second source for our knowledge of this period is the stele erected by Setnakht himself on the island of Elephantin in Upper Egypt. Both of these documents tell of Setnakht's fight against disturbances and rebellions that encompassed the entire country. More interestingly, they tell of the uprising of the 'Asiatics' – as the Western Semites were then called – in Egypt. But the most intriguing thing is that both inform us of something that is many times mentioned in the Bible – the gold, silver, and copper things which the Egyptians gave up, or were supposed to give up, to the 'Asiatics'. Setnakht calls 'mutineers' those Egyptians who, after plundering Egypt, tried to reach an agreement with the 'Asiatics' with the help of the treasures that they had previously plundered. These non-biblical pieces of evidence to some extent shed light on the events of that time and on the reasons for the 'house of Jacob's hurried departure from Egypt. It is likely that during the period when chancellor Bay and Setnakht were contesting the throne, the Hebrew tribes became the decisive factor shaping the balance of forces in the region of the Nile Delta. Each of the parties involved in the struggle tried to draw the Hebrew tribes onto its side. Possibly, it was followers of Setnakht who helped the 'house of Jacob' to arm itself. For the Bible makes an unexpected admission: "The Israelites went up out of Egypt armed for battle" (Exodus 13:18). This in itself contradicts the idea that the kindness of the Pharaoh was instrumental in allowing the enslaved peoples to leave Egypt. In this way, the ruler of Egypt was forced to deal not with a crowd of unarmed slaves, but with armed and organized tribes whose stance could determine the outcome of the fight for the throne. It was necessary to send them out of Egypt as quickly as possible – at any rate, before the arrival of Setnakht's army. Having no wish to open a new front in the war, this time with the Semites, the Pharaoh's court decided to achieve its goal not through force but with the help of gold and silver. So the things of gold and silver and expensive clothes that are repeatedly mentioned by the Bible came into the possession of the Hebrew tribes as a reward for leaving Egypt without delay. This episode became part of the biblical texts only 200 years later, which explains why it underwent changes that made it illogical and ethically unattractive.

Meanwhile, the civil war in Egypt finished earlier than the Egyptians and the Hebrews expected: to seize the Nile Delta and the capital turned out to be easier and, more importantly, quicker than Setnakht himself had calculated. Irsu was overthrown and declared a mutineer and all agreements made in his name were declared invalid. With the power struggle now over, there was no longer any need for the Hebrew tribes as allies. However, the latter were once more required as an unpaid workforce. After concluding military operations in the Nile Delta, Setnakht's army threw itself into pursuit of the departing Semites. Foreseeing this, Moses led his tribes towards the desert, heading for places where the lie of the land would have made it difficult to employ the most dangerous weapon of that time, the war chariot. "When Pharaoh let the people go, God did not lead them on the road through the Philistine country, though that was shorter. For God said, "If they face war, they might change their minds and return to Egypt." So God led the people around by the desert road toward the [Sea of Reeds]" (Exodus 13:17-18). Realizing that the Egyptians were catching up with them too quickly and that he had no time to go round the Bitter Lakes, Moses decided upon a dangerous and risky maneuver: he chose to use the extreme ebb of the tide caused by a strong east wind to cross to the opposite shore of the lake over dry land or through shallow water. It is difficult to say whether this was a clever plan thought up in advance or inspiration from above at a moment of mortal danger. The crucial idea was that the muddy sea bottom would prove no obstacle to cattle and people on foot, but would be impassable for the wheels of the Egyptian war chariots. This is indeed what happened. "He made the wheels of their chariots come off so that they had difficulty driving" (Exodus 14:25). Stranded and broken, the chariots held up the progress of the Egyptian army at a dangerous moment and in a dangerous place. "At daybreak the sea went back to its place… The water flowed back and covered the chariots and horsemen—the entire army of Pharaoh that had followed the Israelites into the sea. Not one of them survived" (Exodus 14:27-28). Stripped of their main advantage – the war chariots, – the Egyptians did not dare continue the pursuit of the armed tribes and, demoralized by their losses, turned back the way they had come. Thus ended the 430-year stay of the 'house of Jacob' in Egypt. The most likely date for the Exodus is the first year of the rule of Pharaoh Setnakht.

The very initial version of the Pentateuch, which was compiled during the United Monarchy, contained an account in which both groups of Hebrew tribes left Egypt simultaneously. However, all the biblical texts that describe the preparations for the Exodus and the Exodus itself preserve absolute silence regarding the role of the northern tribes; they make no mention of either the 'house of Joseph' or the northern tribes. The first naming of the leader of the northern tribes – Joshua, son of Nun – comes during the battle with the Amalekites. It is difficult to say whether the name was inserted into this episode later or whether the battle in fact took place at a later date when the tribes of Moses had united with the 'house of Joseph'. On the contrary, not only are the southern tribes (Reuben, Simeon, and Levi) mentioned on the eve of the Exodus, but all the 'heads of their father's houses' – the clans that make up these tribes – are listed in detail. It is true, however, that our attention is drawn to something else as well: the lack of detailed information on the largest southern tribe, the tribe of Judah. What sense can we make of this? Did Judah really leave Egypt before its fellows from the 'house of Jacob'? Certainly not. The problem was that following the Exodus from Egypt, the tribe of Judah absorbed numerous Edomite and Midianite nomadic clans (Sutu), which quickly rose to leading positions within it. However, to list 'the heads of the houses of the fathers' of the tribe of Judah without the most noble Judahite families – of Kenazzite provenance, for instance, who never lived in Egypt – would have been unthinkable, so the compilers preferred not to mention this tribe at all.

The biblical description of the Exodus contains a very short, but telling phrase: "Many other people went up with them, as well as large droves of livestock, both flocks and herds" (Exodus 12:38). Who were these "many other people" who left Egypt together with the 'house of Jacob'? This is an important question if only because they were numerous and because subsequently they became part of the alliance of Hebrew tribes. Undoubtedly, these "many other people" included Egyptians too – but only those who were bound by bonds of kinship with the Semites. Forsaking Egypt for the lifeless desert brought many difficulties and deprivations and could not in any way be considered an attractive option for the Egyptians even during times of bloody troubles and civil war. The same may be said with regard to the slaves in Egypt. Unlike the West Semitic tribes, the slaves belonged to various ethnic and, moreover, racial groups, and were disunited and unarmed. No one could have driven them out of Egypt and it is improbable that slaves from Nubia, Cush, and Libya would have left of their own free will for the waterless Sinai Desert in the company of the Semites, a people who were alien to them. It is no coincidence, of course, that even Moses' fellow tribesmen reproached him on more than one occasion: "They said to Moses, "Was it because there were no graves in Egypt that you brought us to the desert to die? What have you done to us by bringing us out of Egypt? Didn't we say to you in Egypt, 'Leave us alone; let us serve the Egyptians?' It would have been better for us to serve the Egyptians than to die in the desert!" (Exodus 14:11-12). Judging by the hurriedness of the departure – or, to be more exact, the expulsion – of these people together with the 'house of Jacob', most of them occupied the same place in Egyptian society as the southern tribes, i.e. they were Western Semites just like the Hebrews themselves. We have every reason to suppose that the 'house of Jacob' was not the only one to remain in Egypt following the departure of the main body of the Amorites for Canaan and Syria. The West Semitic tribes that remained shared the fate of the 'house of Jacob' in every respect in the Nile Delta. However, they never had their own Moses or their own keepers of the tradition such as the Levites and Aaronites, who might have been able to tell of their history and lineage prior to their arrival in Egypt. Evidently, in terms of ethnic origin, they differed little from the Hebrews. We may tentatively suppose that the Western Semites who joined the 'house of Jacob' at the time of its departure from Egypt included tribes such as Issachar and Zebulun. Their founders are named as the sons of patriarch Jacob by his first wife Leah, making them part of the family tree of the southern tribes of Reuben, Simeon, Levi, and Judah. The biblical texts preceding the departure for Egypt contain no mention of the tribes of Issachar and Zebulun. The formal alliance with these tribes was formed on Mount Sinai as part of the general covenant with one God, when the 'house of Jacob' and its 'adoptive sons' took upon themselves identical obligations. However the union of the southern Hebrew tribes with these Western Semites lasted only a short period of time – from the Exodus from Egypt to the moment of unification with the northern tribal alliance of Israel. Subsequently, the southern and 'adopted' tribes went their separate ways, the latter joining the northern tribes and, following the break-up of the United Monarchy, remaining in the kingdom of Israel. This was probably no coincidence since from the point of view of geography and tribal genealogy they felt much closer to the northern rather than the southern tribes. The same goes for two other northern tribes, Gad and Asher, whose founders were held to be the sons of Jacob by Zilpah, the slave girl of his wife Leah. The fact that the primogenitors of this tribes were born to a woman of low social status is a sign of their subordinate and secondary position in the tribal hierarchy of the 'house of Jacob'. Gad and Asher also became 'adoptive sons' of Jacob during the period between the Exodus from Egypt and the arrival in Canaan. However, the lower social status of the origins of the tribes' founders is evidence that they joined the alliance as junior partners. Nevertheless, the departure of the 'house of Jacob' and its 'adoptive sons' was the final stage in the long process by which the Amorites migrated from the Nile Delta to Canaan and Syria. Unfortunately, we know only of the last stage in this process, and then only because its participants included the keepers of the biblical tradition, the Levites and Aaronites.

The Strengthening of Egypt and the Split of the Tribes of Moses

The precise route taken by Moses is almost impossible to establish today since the texts dealing with the wanderings through the desert are arranged not in strict chronological order, but by degree of importance for the first compilers of the Pentateuch. To begin with, Moses chose his route taking into account the possibility of pursuit by the Egyptians and so as to minimize the main advantage possessed by the latter – their war chariots. Subsequently, he focused more on sources of water and food for people and cattle. Here he was helped by the experience of nomadic life and the knowledge of places in Sinai and north-west Arabia that he had acquired while living with the Midianites. But the oases and springs in the desert were never vacant and Moses had to use them in such a way as not to enter into conflict with the local nomadic tribes. However, with certain of them – the Amalekites, for instance – he ended up quarrelling, while others, the Midianites, with whom he had still earlier joined in marriage, gave him a great deal of help and support.

When he brought his people out of Egypt, Moses did not intend to spend many years in the desert. Moreover, his fellow-tribesmen would never have left the Nile Delta had they known how long they would have to wander through the waterless desert. Was it really fear of the inhabitants of Canaan, as the Bible explains in the incident with the spies, that forced Moses' people to retreat? Could a single unsuccessful battle with the Amalekites and Canaanites have led to rejection of the idea of conquering Canaan for almost 40 years? Both these biblical episodes are really merely the tip of the iceberg projecting above true events that are hidden in the depths of history. They cannot be understood independently of the development of the political situation in Egypt and Canaan.

The civil war in Egypt, which allowed Moses to bring the Hebrew tribes out of the Nile Delta, finished a lot earlier than might have been expected.

In only the second year of his rule Pharaoh Setnakht dealt with his opponents and strengthened his position on the throne. Although he ruled for only one year after this, he was replaced by a worthy successor, his son, Rameses III, who became Egypt's last great pharaoh. Rameses III quickly established order in the country and, even more importantly, prepared it for the serious military trials approaching from the west and north. In the fifth year of his reign a mutiny of Libyan tribes flared up in the western part of the Nile Delta. The Libyans supposed that after several years of civil war and troubles Egypt would be rather different from the country they had known under Rameses II and Merneptah. But, as it turned out, they were mistaken. Rameses III delivered a crushing defeat to those who tried to put him to the test. However, this was only his first military examination. His main test came in the eighth year of his reign, when the Sea Peoples – a considerably more serious opponent than the Libyans – attacked Egypt from the north. The Sea Peoples consisted of various peoples of Indo-European origin whom many years of drought and famine had forced to look for a new motherland. In about 1200 BCE they devastated the powerful Hittite empire and set fire to the largest cities of northern Syria, including Alalakh and Ugarit. Their next goal was to seize the Nile Delta and Canaan. As far as we can tell, Rameses III was very well informed about the danger that threatened Egypt. He sent part of his army in good time to Gaza in the south-west of Canaan to reinforce the Egyptian garrison there and met the naval attack against the Nile Delta in full strength. His crushing of the previously unconquerable foreigners on sea and land was his greatest success and placed him on equal footing with great pharaohs such as Rameses II and Thutmose III. By the same token, Egypt demonstrated its ability not only to defend itself, but also to hold onto southern Canaan, which was under its rule. In the 11th year of his reign Rameses III once more shattered the Libyans when they attempted to challenge Egypt.

All these dramatic events did not escape the attention of Moses and the leaders of the 'house of Jacob'. They could not fail to understand that, while Egyptian power was strengthening, to conquer Canaan would be a difficult task and that they would meet opposition not merely from local peoples, but also from the Egyptian army, which had shown itself to be no less effective than previously. For as long as Egypt was ruled by a pharaoh such as Rameses III, there was no hope of success. What thought could there be of an attack on southern Canaan if Egypt was moving reinforcements to Gaza and the Sea Peoples were advancing to Palestine like a roller, destroying whatever cities in Syria and on the Lebanese coast they met on their way? Clearly, this bad news was discussed by the leaders and elders of Moses' tribes. Judging by the biblical texts, the result was serious disagreement between the leaders of the Hebrew tribes, the majority of whom considered the conquest of Canaan under such conditions unthinkable and blamed Moses and Aaron for coming up with an idea – the Exodus from Egypt and return to Canaan – that had been doomed to failure from the very start. "All the Israelites grumbled against Moses and Aaron, and the whole assembly said to them, "If only we had died in Egypt! Or in this desert! Why is the Lord bringing us to this land only to let us fall by the sword? Our wives and children will be taken as plunder. Wouldn't it be better for us to go back to Egypt?" And they said to each other, "We should choose a leader and go back to Egypt" (Numbers 14:2-4). For Moses and Aaron the situation must have been critical; they were forced to escape the wrath of the people in the Tent of Meeting, by the Tabernacle of the Covenant, a sacred religious object: "But the whole assembly talked about stoning them. Then the glory of the Lord appeared at the Tent of Meeting to all the Israelites" (Numbers 14:10). Salvation came in the form of support from their own southern tribes and their allies, the Midianites.

Another serious trial for the authority of Moses and Aaron and their union was the mutiny raised by Korah from the tribe of Levi, supported by Dathan, Abiram, and On, leaders of the tribe of Reuben. Here everything came together – terrible fatigue due to having to live in the unfamiliar desert conditions; disappointment with Moses' unfulfilled promises (to lead his people into Canaan); and, finally, dissatisfaction with the fact that the tribal hierarchy had been violated and junior partners in the 'house of Jacob' were giving orders to their seniors. To cap it all, a dangerous plague – evidently, an epidemic of some kind of serious disease – was raging in the camp of the Hebrews. Initially, the mutiny of Korah, one of the leaders of the tribe of Levi and a relative of Moses, was directed against the excessive power wielded by Aaron and the primary role played by the latter's kin in celebrating religious rites. The Levites felt hard done by and insufficiently involved in religious service. Dissatisfaction with the Aaronites affected not merely the top people in the tribe of Levi, but also the leaders and elders of other tribes and clans. Moses' attempt to calm them and protect Aaron merely poured fuel onto the fire: "and [they] rose up against Moses. With them were 250 Israelite men, well-known community leaders who had been appointed members of the council. They came as a group to oppose Moses and Aaron and said to them, "You have gone too far! The whole community is holy, every one of them, and the Lord is with them. Why then do you set yourselves above the Lord's assembly?" (Numbers 16:2-3). Seeing that the mutiny was growing, Moses tried to use force and "summoned Dathan and Abiram, the sons of Eliab", who, together with other members of the 'house of Jacob', were obliged to give support to their leader. However, Dathan and Abiram openly joined the mutineers. "But they said, "We will not come! Isn't it enough that you have brought us up out of a land flowing with milk and honey to kill us in the desert? And now you also want to lord it over us? Moreover, you haven't brought us into a land flowing with milk and honey or given us an inheritance of fields and vineyards. Will you gouge out the eyes of these men? No, we will not come!" (Numbers 16:12-14). At the most difficult moment for Moses and Aaron help probably came from the tribe of Judah, which was always ready to support the Aaronites, and likewise from the Midianites, Moses' allies. The principal mutineers were punished with a terrible death: "the earth opened its mouth and swallowed them."

This episode is a further reminder of the tribe of Reuben's claim to primacy in the 'house of Jacob' and of the contrived nature of the pretext that had deprived it of seniority. Possibly, Reuben's 'offence' was 'dug up' by the Aaronites from the epic lore of the southern tribes and inserted into the biblical text at a later date to justify the supremacy of the tribe of Judah. As time went on, the most junior partners of the 'house of Jacob', Judah and Levi, began dominating the senior ones, Reuben and Simeon, and this led to conflicts between them – at least, initially. Evidently, Moses' inability quickly to carry out his promises and the excessive influence of the Aaronites were responsible for their partners in the alliance deciding to redistribute the balance of power between the tribes. This was the background to Korah's mutiny. At the same time, the mutiny was further proof of how deep and long-lasting was the rivalry between the Aaronites and Levites, a sign of the fact that originally they had belonged not only to different families and kin, but also to different tribes in general.

The unexpected strengthening of Egypt's military might during the rule of Rameses III caused considerable complications for Moses' plans. The conquest of southern Canaan was now an impossible feat given that the Egyptians viewed these lands as their eastern border. A degree of freedom of action remained in central and northern Canaan, where there were already several northern tribes. But to break through to these parts through the lands of Egypt's vassals without triggering the intervention of the army of Rameses III did not seem possible. Part of the 'house of Jacob' – the tribes of Judah and Simeon, – having drawn closer to their Midianite and Edomite allies, preferred to wait in the oases of the desert until the Egyptians left southern Canaan. However, the majority of the tribes were impatient to head north to unite with the 'house of Joseph' and together win back the lands that had once been their tribal territory. Desiring to preserve unity, Moses tried to reconcile the interests of the two groups and to hold on for as long as possible on the border with southern Canaan, but in vain. The mutiny by Korah had shown that people no longer wanted or were no longer able to wander in the desert and that delay of any kind could lead to an uprising among the tribes and to death at their hands. It became inevitable that the 'house of Jacob' would split up. This happened not just because most of the tribes that had accompanied the 'house of Jacob' in the Exodus from Egypt belonged to the northern, Israelite, tribes and were closer to the 'house of Joseph'. This same circumstance did not, for instance, prevent the southern tribe of Reuben and the majority of Levites subsequently joining the northern tribes. The main reason for the split was, in fact, that the southern tribes of Judah and Simeon were under the influence of their more numerous allies, the Midianite and Edomite tribes. The kinship and alliance between Moses and the Midianites, and the help given by the latter in the waterless wilderness, had negative as well as positive consequences. The new allies began to prevail numerically over the old members of the tribe of Judah, and it is probable that the same threat faced the tribe of Simeon. Evidently, at some point quantity was transmuted into quality, and leadership of the tribe of Judah passed from the old tribal aristocracy into the hands of desert leaders who had had no part in the epic travails of the 'house of Jacob' in Egypt. Interestingly, during the departure from Egypt and the first months of existence in the desert, the Bible mentions Nahshon, son of Aminadav, as head of the tribe of Judah. Nahshon was brother-in-law of the high priest Aaron. However, beginning with the episode relating to the spies sent into Canaan, Caleb, son of Jephunneh and head of the Kenazzites (Edomites), is constantly named as the new leader of the tribe of Judah. Caleb and the other desert leaders imposed their own decision on the two southern tribes of Judah and Simeon – to remain in the desert they knew so well until the Egyptians left southern Canaan. This turn of events was especially unpopular with the priestly clan of the Aaronites: the transfer of power to the desert leaders deprived them of their traditional support from the old tribal aristocracy among the tribes of Judah and Simeon. The situation changed when, after the death of the extremely aged Aaron, the position of high priest was occupied by his energetic and decisive son Eleazar. The new high priest began openly to resist any form of closer relations with the Midianites, seeing any convergence as a threat both to the privileged position of his own family and to the 'house of Jacob'. Taking advantage of the fact that Moses had considerably aged and weakened, he began imposing on him his own strategy aimed at breaking off the alliance with the Midianites. In order to provoke a conflict with the latter and put Moses in an impossible position, Phinehas, son of Eleazar, killed the leader of the tribe of Simeon and his Midianite wife. It was at this moment that the Aaronites seized power from the dying Moses. Eleazar, under the cover of Moses' name, embarked on a bitter war against one of the groups of Midianite tribes, showing no mercy to either its women or the children of his rivals. Much later, the keepers of the biblical tradition from this family tried to justify the split with the Midianites, arguing that the latter had tempted the Israelites with the pagan cult of Baal of Peor, as a result of which God sent a pernicious plague in punishment of his people. From this moment forwards relations between the Hebrews and the Midianites soured, but the memory of their touching friendship during the time of Moses remained for ever.

    The split with the Midianites accelerated the break-up of the 'house of Jacob' too. The southern tribes of Judah and Simeon, who had intermarried with the numerous Midianite and Edomite clans, refused to join the 'house of Joseph' in order to conquer central and northern Canaan. Under the influence of their new relatives and allies, they preferred to stay within the borders of southern Canaan, in the oases that they knew so well, where they could wait for the Egyptians to leave. They were joined by a few Levites and the majority of Aaronites who had led the worship of Yahweh in those tribes. The other tribes, including the southern tribe of Reuben and most of the Levites, left together with Moses and Eleazar to seize central and northern Canaan. In this way, the original 'house of Jacob', which had consisted of the four southern tribes, was split: the tribes of Judah and Simeon remained for forty more years in the desert while the tribe of Reuben and the greater part of the Levites joined the northern tribes and the 'house of Joseph'.

Meanwhile, the strengthening of Egypt turned out to be short-lived, lasting only as long as Rameses III himself, who ruled for 31 years. He was replaced by his son, Rameses IV, who in spite of desperate prayers to the gods to extend his life, ruled for a mere six years. In his lifetime the military might of the Egyptians weakened considerably and the 20th Dynasty began to wane. Rameses IV did not undertake any military campaigns, but continued to use the quarries on Sinai and the copper mines in Timnah (Negev). His successor, Rameses V, ruled for an even shorter length of time – four years – and by the end of his reign Egypt had lost all its possessions in Asia, including southern Canaan. Moreover, at this time the country experienced serious internal political difficulties and perhaps even a civil war. When the next Rameses, the sixth, took over, Egypt's greatness and might vanished forever and the country's eastern border moved to the eastern edge of the Nile Delta. Even the quarries on Sinai were abandoned. In this way, forty years after the 'house of Jacob' left the Nile Delta, Egypt lost entirely and for far into the future all control over Canaan. And it was at this point that the painful wanderings of the two southern Hebrew tribes in the desert likewise came to an end. Following the example of their northern relatives, but forty years later, they began conquering southern Canaan.

Chapter 4

The Peoples of pre-Israelite Palestine

On the eve of its conquest by the Hebrew tribes, Canaan was ethnically a hotchpotch. All the peoples of this country can be divided into four main categories: 1) Western Semites; 2) the primordial pre-Semitic population of Palestine; 3) peoples of an Indo-European origin; and, finally, 4) Hurrians. Of the biblical sources the book of Genesis provides the most complete list of the peoples of Canaan. It names ten of them: "the Kenites, Kenazzites, Kadmonites, Hittites, Perizzites, Rephaites, Amorites, Canaanites, Girgashites and Jebusites" (Genesis 15:19-21). Later books of the Bible – Deuteronomy, for instance – mention only seven peoples: "the Hittites, Girgashites, Amorites, Canaanites, Perizzites, Hivites and Jebusites" (Deuteronomy 7:1). Finally, the biblical texts make separate mention of the Philistines and Maachatites.

Western Semites

The absolute majority of people living in Canaan were Western Semites. All were very close to one another and spoke in different dialects of one and the same language. The first of these peoples to arrive in Palestine, in the second half of the 4th millennium BCE, was the Canaanites; for this reason they occupied the districts that were most convenient and favorable for agriculture – the strip along the Mediterranean shore, the valley of the River Jordan, the fertile Jezreel Valley, and Shephelah, the low hills in the south west of the country. It was the Canaanites who gave their name to this country – Canaan. However, they occupied not just Palestine, but the entire coast of Lebanon and Syria. The people whom the Greeks later called Phoenicians also considered themselves to be Canaanites. The Bible gives the Canaanites another name too, calling them Sidonians after Sidon, a port in Canaan (today called Saida). This was not just a settled farming people; it was also the most developed ethnos in Palestine in terms of social, economic, and cultural activity.

The second, even larger, group of West Semitic peoples consisted of the Amorites. Unlike the Canaanites, they divided into nomadic and settled branches. The majority of the Amorite nomads were driven by prolonged droughts to move gradually into the Nile Delta, into Egypt. The settled branches of the Amorites established themselves in the interior and mountain districts of Palestine and in northern Transjordan. It was to these settled

Amorite peoples that the 'Amorites, Perizzites, Hivites, and Jebusites' mentioned in the Bible belonged. Evidently, these Amorite peoples appeared in Canaan at the same time as the northern Hebrew tribes – at any rate, before the arrival of Abraham and his tribal alliance. The Amorites lived in northern and central Transjordan, where the kingdoms of Sihon and Og were situated, and also in certain districts of inner Palestine. The Perizzites inhabited part of southwestern and central Canaan, and the Jebusites held Jerusalem or Jebus, as it was then called. The Hivites lived both in the center of the country, in Shechem, and in more southern parts, in Gibeon, Kephirah, Beeroth, and Kiriath Jearim. There were also semi-nomadic Amorite peoples who had failed to settle by the 12th century BCE. These included relatives of the 'house of Jacob' – the Moabites, Ammonites, and Edomites, who were led into Canaan by the biblical patriarch Abraham. The first two groups of tribes settled in the central part of Transjordan, while the Edomites, who were the people closest to the 'house of Jacob', inhabited the region of Mount Seir in southern Palestine. In central Negev there were camps used by another Amorite people, the Amalekites, with whom the Hebrews had extremely hostile relations. The Bible also mentions the Kenazzites as a people living in Canaan. The Kenazzites were an Edomite nomadic tribe which had joined the southern Hebrew tribe of Judah before the conquest of Canaan. The Kenazzites were one of the 'tribes of Shasu' which, as told by the ancient Egyptian sources, worshipped Yahweh. According to the Bible, as reward for loyalty to the common cause their leader, Caleb, son of Jephunneh, was distinguished first by Moses and then by Joshua, son of Nun, who gave him Hebron, the best part of southeastern Palestine. In addition to peoples who were settled or led a nomadic life in Canaan on a permanent basis, there were also tribes of Amorite nomads who occasionally ventured into this country from Sinai, north-west Arabia, and the Syrian Desert. Such were the Midianites and the Ishmaelites – peoples of the desert. Another people that periodically visited Canaan was the Kenites – those same Midianite tribes with whom Moses had intermarried when he was hiding from the Egyptians. Certain scholars have, on the basis of the Kenites' name, thought them to be clans of nomadic blacksmiths.

Among the West Semitic peoples living in Canaan there were also Habiru – Amorite tribes who had returned from Egypt following the defeat of the Hyksos pharaohs. During the centuries that they had lived in the Nile Delta their tribal lands had been occupied by other peoples, meaning that these refugees from Egypt found themselves without a home. Many Habiru in Canaan belonged to the four northern Hebrew tribes who had returned to Palestine in the 15th century BCE. However, for as long as Egypt ruled Canaan, there could no thought of regaining this lost land and the Israelites were forced to make themselves comfortable in the inconvenient and little used lands of central and northern Palestine.

Judging by the biblical texts, the Hebrews never regarded themselves as Amorites. They looked upon the latter sometimes as their allies – for instance, during the time of Abraham – and sometimes, as during the conquest of Canaan, as their enemies. They identified themselves using the name 'Ivri / Ibri', which initially sounded like 'Habiru' or 'Apiru'. Ethnically, however, all Habiru, including the Hebrews, belonged to the West Semitic tribes of Amorite origin. We should not be put off by the fact that the Israelites, being Amorites by origin, denied their connection with this ethnos and never used this name to define themselves. This kind of thing happens often. Many peoples reject the ethnonym of the largest and most well-known tribes with which they have at some time been closely linked and prefer to use other names to identify themselves. But this should not stand in the way of an understanding of the blood ties between such ethnoses. The book of Genesis gives a list of descendants of Canaan, the legendary forefather of the Canaanite peoples. Among them are the Amorites, the Jebusites, and the Hivites – i.e. peoples of Amorite origin. In this way, the Hebrew epic tradition preserves memories of the blood ties between the Canaanites and the Amorites; moreover, the Amorites are mentioned as descendants of the Canaanites. This ancient legend reflects the true picture: the Canaanites and the Amorites were initially one ethnos when they lived in their ancestral motherland in north-west Mesopotamia. Those who subsequently came to be called Canaanites were the first to leave; they went in a south-westerly direction – into Syria, Lebanon, and Palestine. Approximately 1000 years later, another part of the same ethnos, which was given the ethnonym 'Amorites', followed along the same path. It is possible that the name 'Amorites' came mainly to signify the settled part of this ethnos, while the name 'Habiru' initially applied only to nomadic Amorites. And although the Habiru did not consider themselves to be Amorites, they were undoubtedly an integral part of that people. Here we could adduce an analogy with the fellahin (peasants) and Bedouin (nomads) in Arabic countries. Among the Bedouin you still find the view that only the fellahin and not they – the Bedouin – are Arabs. Something similar existed among the settled Amorites and the semi-nomadic Habiru.

In spite of the periodic conflicts and collisions between the various Canaanite and Amorite peoples in Palestine, the only difference between them was in their level of social and economic development and lifestyle. Ethnically and linguistically, they were almost identical. Moreover, in most cases the Amorites were very quick to assimilate the Canaanite culture and religious rites.

In the 12th century BCE groups belonging to one more West Semitic people – the Arameans – began penetrating into north-east Canaan. Among them were the Girgashites and Maachatites mentioned in the Bible, who established themselves in the north of Gilead and on the Golan Heights. However, at the time of the conquest of Canaan by the Hebrew tribes, the Aramean population in Canaan was still of inconsiderable size.

Indigenous pre-Semitic Population

The most numerous people after the Western Semites were the indigenous population of Palestine, who had lived there from at least Neolithic times. Unfortunately, we know nothing of either their ethnic origins or their language. The Old Testament is the only literary source that mentions them. According to the biblical description, these ancient inhabitants of Palestine were in no way related to the Semites. They were distinguished by being far taller than the average for Semite peoples. It was their great height that made the strongest impression on the 'spies' of the 'house of Jacob' sent by Moses to 'spy out' the Promised Land. The latter reported that "We can't attack those people; they are stronger than we are [...] All the people we saw there are of great size. We saw the Nephilim there (the descendants of Anak come from the Nephilim). We seemed like grasshoppers in our own eyes, and we looked the same to them" (Numbers 13:32-34). This ancient people lived in all parts of Palestine and Transjordan. The Semites who came to Canaan had different names for their tall neighbors. The Israelites called them 'Anaks' and 'Rephaim'; the Moabites, 'Eimim'; and the Ammonites, 'Zamzumim'. In south-west Palestine, in the region of Gaza, they were known as 'Avvim'. Of these many names only one – Rephaim (Rephaites) – was in any way connected with how this people called itself; they believed their mythical forefather to be Rapha. According to the books of Judges and Joshua, the entire district of modern Hebron in the south of Palestine once belonged to the leaders of the gigantic Rephaim – Sheshai, Ahiman, and Talmai, sons of the legendary Anak; and the city of Hebron itself was founded by the same people and was previously called after the 'greatest of the Anaks', Kiriath-Arba (Judges 1:10; Joshua 14:15, 15:13-14). The same people produced the king of the Bashan region of Transjordan, Og. Another descendant of this people was the giant Goliath, who was chosen by the Philistines to fight David in single combat. However, this ancient autochthonous people very soon dissolved among the West Semitic peoples who arrived in Canaan. By the time the Israelites conquered Canaan, the Neolithic giants had become Semites in terms of language and culture. This fact confused the authors of the biblical books, which accounts for why in some cases they called this people by their old name of 'Rephaim' while in others they called them 'Amorites' or 'Canaanites'. The best example of this is the region of Hebron, whose population is described in turns as Rephaim, Amorites, and Hittites. The last mentions of the Rephaim are connected with the Philistines. In the south-west of Canaan, which was later known as Philistia, lived a large number of Rephaim who had, even before the arrival of the Sea Peoples, assimilated the language and culture of the Canaanites. The Bible specifically emphasizes that the Philistines did not touch the Rephaim and, judging by much later reports, actively exploited their outstanding physical qualities in their own army. Many of the best warriors in the Philistine army were of Rephaim origin. The book of Kings mentions among them not merely the celebrated Goliath from the city of Gath, but also the then famous warriors Yishbi and Sapha, who were also 'descendants of Rapha', this people's legendary forefather. It is difficult to say why these tall and physically strong people retreated so quickly before the Semite newcomers, but it is likely that they were considerably inferior in terms of social organization; they were also less numerous. By the time the Hebrew tribes returned from Egypt, the larger part of this autochthonous people had merged with the Western Semites who were all around them. The remnants of the Rephaim mixed with the Israelites so quickly that in the biblical Hebrew their name became a synonym for what was long past. The book of Joshua noted: "No Anakites were left in Israelite territory; only in Gaza, Gath and Ashdod did any survive" (11:22). Today the only reminder of this legendary people is the unusually tall Jews who have inherited their genes.

When describing the war of the southern Canaanite kings against the Amorite rulers of Syria, the book of Genesis provides an interesting ethnographic account of Canaan at this time. It turns out that in the east of Canaan, in Transjordan, before the Ammonites and the Moabites arrived there, the dominant presence consisted of non-Semitic peoples. These included the tall Rephaim, the Zamzumim, the Eimim and, in the very south, the Horites, who were subsequently assimilated by the Edomites. However, to the west and the south of the River Jordan, Amorite peoples were the more numerous. The Amorites controlled the Ein-Gedi oasis on the west bank of what is now the Dead Sea. Possibly, Abraham's Amorite allies – Aner, Eshkol, and Mamre – were the very same Hittites that the Bible several times mentioned when giving an account of the times of the patriarchs. The same episode, which deals with the invasion of outsiders from Syria, talks of the Amalekites as if they were the injured party, although Amalek, their forefather and a great-grandson of Abraham, should have appeared much later (Genesis 14:1-7). Either this is an historical anachronism deriving from the fact that the events of this war were recorded only 1000 years later or it is evidence that initially the Amalekites had no relation to Abraham's tribal group. If the latter is true, then it may explain the extreme hostility between the descendants of Jacob and Amalek.

Indo-Europeans
The history of the Indo-European peoples in Palestine is no less intriguing. The Bible makes frequent mention of the Hittites – initially as neighbors of the patriarch Abraham, then as a people who lived in Canaan immediately before it was conquered. But in the 20th century BCE, when Abraham was a nomad in southern Canaan, there could not have been any Indo-European Hittites living there – given that they had not yet left the borders of far-away Anatolia. On the other hand, a people that was present were the Amorite or Canaanite 'Hittites' who, according to the Hebrew epic tradition, were descended from

the mythical Canaan. The Indo-European Hittites came to Canaan much later, after the collapse of the Hittite empire around 1200 BCE. Possibly, the Hittites served the local rulers as mercenary colonists, and most were not so much Hittites as Luwians – Indo-Europeans from north Syria. The first compilers of the Pentateuch who set down the biblical texts in the 10th century BCE regrettably made no distinction between the West Semitic Hittites of the age of Abraham and the Indo-European Hittites who were their own contemporaries, so subsequently both groups began to be perceived as one and the same people.

An incomparably more important role in the life of Canaan belonged to another people of Indo-European origin – the Philistines. The Philistines appeared in the south-west of Palestine at the beginning of the 12th century BCE, i.e. shortly before the second wave of Hebrew tribes returned from Egypt. Moreover, to begin with, the Philistines came as raiders and enemies of Egypt and then as the latter's mercenaries and colonists, having been given the region of Gaza as a place in which to settle. The Philistines belonged to the so-called 'Sea Peoples' – a group of peoples of Indo-European origin who came from over the sea, from the north and north-west. We do not know the reasons why there was a mass migration of various Indo-European tribes from north to south at the end of the 13th century BCE, but we may conjecture that this was a result of natural phenomena that brought droughts and famine to the places where they had lived up to this point. It cannot be ruled out that they were forced to move south by other Indo-European peoples coming from the north. Asia Minor at this time suffered a drought so severe and prolonged that the Hittite rulers were forced to ask Egypt to send them as much grain as possible. The few literary monuments that were found on the site of the Philistine cities – for instance, inscriptions on the stamps from Ashdod – belong to so-called Minoan Linear A script. Unfortunately, this ancient system of writing, which made its first appearance on Crete, has yet to be deciphered. However, limited information on the Philistines may be gleaned from objects that are products of their material culture – their ceramic ware, for instance, which bears the distinctive marks of the Mycenaean style. This points to the Philistines' Aegean and, moreover, Achaean, origin. The Bible gives different names for the country from which the people came. In one case, it calls it Cyprus; in another, Crete. But Cyprus or Crete was only an intermediate stopping place for the Philistines' ancestors. Their most probable birthplace was Mycenae, in the south of Greece, the native city of legendary King Agamemnon. In the second half of the 13th century BCE Doric tribes invaded the Peloponnese from the north. During the course of the next century they destroyed not just Mycenae, but also the entire Achaean civilization as well. Part of the population was enslaved; the remainder emigrated to islands in the Aegean Sea, Crete, and Cyprus. In their search for a new motherland, the Achaean Greeks – and, together with them, other displaced tribes from Asia Minor – chose the Nile Delta and Canaan, which was

The Peoples of pre-Israelite Palestine

then ruled by Egypt. Bas reliefs and frescoes from the temple of Rameses III at Medinet Habu on the site of ancient Egyptian Thebes depict warriors from these peoples together with carts in which their families are sitting. What we see here is not plundering raids but a forced migration of entire peoples. But in the decisive battle with the army of Rameses III the coalition of Sea Peoples was defeated and the Philistines came to the south-west of Palestine not as conquerors but as mercenary colonists in the service of the Pharaoh. Several years later, however, following the death of Rameses III, Egypt's rule in southern Canaan came to an end and the Philistines became masters of this country's southern shore. Until the Philistines arrived, the local population in these parts consisted of Canaanites and, intermarried with the latter, Avvim, descendants of the ancient inhabitants of Palestine. The newcomers were numerically inferior, but superior in terms of military organization and quality of weaponry. It was the Philistines who brought the Iron Age to Canaan. They knew the secret of how to produce iron and used this metal to make weaponry. They seized the Canaanite cities and created their own communities there under the command of their own leaders, called 'seranim' ('tyrants'). The Philistines' country was known as the Pentapolis, i.e. the union of the five cities of Gaza, Ashkelon, Ashdod, Ekron, and Gath. The Philistines quickly assimilated with the Semite people they had conquered. They began using the Canaanite language and their gods now had Semitic names. It is significant that thoroughly Mycenean pottery is to be found only in Ashdod and Ekron – the Philistines' original settlements. Subsequently, their pottery was made in a mixed style, with the adoption of Canaanite and Egyptian motifs.

The people who came from Mycenae were only a part of the Philistines, even if the dominant part. Among them were representatives of other tribes from the Aegean and Asia Minor. In any case, the Philistines were not the only Sea People to settle in Canaan. Another Indo-European people of Aegean provenance, the Tjeker, settled on the northern coast of Palestine, in the region of the city of Dor. Finally a third Sea People, the Sherden, managed to find itself a home in the northern valleys of Canaan. Historians have at their disposal an important ancient Egyptian document dating to approximately 1100 BCE, 'The Journey of Wen-Amon', which deals with the journey of an Egyptian dignitary through Canaan to Byblos to buy cedar wood. For a time Wen-Amon stayed in Dor and was witness to the fact that the city belonged to one of the Sea Peoples, the Tjeker. From his tale it follows that the rulers of other cities on the coast of Palestine were also from Indo-European peoples from the Aegean or Asia Minor who, together with Western Semites (the Phoenicians), monopolized maritime trade in the eastern part of the Mediterranean. It has to be supposed that Wen-Amon's information on the Sea People who settled in northern Canaan was relatively reliable. The Egyptians were by this time familiar with people from these tribes, given that many of the latter had served as mercenaries in the Egyptian army from the 14th century BCE. The Amarna archive contains letters mentioning the Sherden. The latter served the Egyptian Pharaoh and, under Rameses II, took part in the battle against the Hittites at Kadesh. Later, during the rule of Pharaoh Merneptah, certain of the Sea Peoples – the Sherden, Shekelesh, Lukka, Tursha, and Avakasha – joined up with the Libyans to make a series of attacks on Egypt. But the Egyptians nevertheless learned most about the Sea Peoples during the time of Rameses III, when these peoples began to migrate en masse to the eastern Mediterranean, into Asia Minor, Syria, Canaan, and the Nile Delta. If the Lebanese and Syrian coast suffered badly from the attacks of the Sea Peoples and if some of these peoples settled in the south west of Canaan, then there is nothing surprising in their being present in north Canaan also. It cannot be ruled out that the name 'Hittites' actually indicated large numbers of immigrants from the Sea Peoples immediately prior to the conquest of Canaan.

Hurrians

Yet another ethnos in pre-Israelite Palestine was the Hurrians – a people who were unrelated to the Semites, the Indo-Europeans, or the indigenous inhabitants of Canaan. Incontrovertible evidence of their presence in the country is provided by letters in the Amarna archive mentioning rulers of Canaan with names that are of clearly Hurrian provenance. Furthermore, a large number of stamps of the kind that are characteristic of the Hurrians of Mitanni, but which were made after the latter state's destruction, have been found in Palestine. It is highly likely that the Hurrians first came to Canaan in the second half of the 16th and at the beginning of the 15th centuries BCE, during a period when the state of Mitanni was expanding more rapidly than at any other time on the one hand and there was a vacuum of power in Canaan on the other. This was a time when the Hyksos, the main power in Canaan, were trying unsuccessfully to fend off attacks by the pharaohs of Thebes and the Egyptians were still too weak to subjugate neighboring Palestine. It was at this period that both the Indo-Aryan (Maryannu) and Hurrian groups entered Canaan from Mitanni, seizing power in a number of Canaanite cities. In the Bible we sometimes find names – for instance, the Jebusite Aravenna (Arauna) – that indicate an Indo-Aryan or Hurrian provenance for their bearers. Both these groups were small in number, since we have no evidence of the presence of any large Hurrian or Indo-Aryan ethnoses in Canaan. Judging by the letters from the Amarna archive, both the former and the latter formed the ruling elite in certain Canaanite city states – which tells us that they entered Canaan by no means peacefully, but as the result of conquering certain of its cities. Later, in the 14th and 13th centuries BCE, the defeats suffered by Mitanni in the war with the Hittites and then with the Assyrians led to the appearance in Canaan of a new wave of Hurrians – this time, not conquerors but refugees.

The Hurrians were also called Hittites in the Bible. In general, the ethnonym 'Hittites', which is many times mentioned in the biblical texts, is evidently a collective name which covers not so much the Hittites themselves as various Indo-European and Hurrian groups among the population in Canaan. It is impossible to ignore an interesting fact: in spite of the frequent mentions of Hittites, no book in the Bible tells us of a Hittite ruler or city in Canaan. At the same time, we possess a large number of mentions of Amorite, Canaanite, Hivite, and Jebusite cities and rulers. There is even mention of a Rephaite ruler Og, but not a single Hittite. This is a sign that the Hittite and Hurrian presence in Canaan was well-dispersed; it consisted of colonists, mercenaries, merchants, and refugees who were scattered all over Palestine and went by the general name of 'Hittites'. Unlike the majority of local peoples who lived in dense groups, these Indo-European and Hurrian elements very quickly assimilated with the Western Semites who formed the majority of the country's population.

Some scholars see a parallel between the Hurrians who came from northern Mesopotamia and the Horites, who lived by Mount Seir in southern Palestine. The Bible tells us that Esau, the forefather of the Edomites, drove the Horites ('the cave dwellers') out from the region around Mount Seir and settled there himself in their place. But Esau lived in the 18th-17th centuries BCE and the Hurrians came to Canaan not earlier than the second half of the 16th century BCE. Moreover, it follows from the biblical text that the Horites lived in Seir long before the arrival of Esau – which rules out any link between them and the Hurrians, who at the time were living in northeastern Mesopotamia. It is likely that the Horites were part of the primordial population of Palestine, but their ethnic origins are unknown – just as it is unclear whether they were in any way related to the Rephaim. The Horites assimilated with the descendants of Esau and were an integral part of Edom. At least, the genealogy of the Amalekites given in the book of Genesis is clear confirmation of the Horites mixing with the Edomites. Subsequently, the Bible mentions the Horites again, telling us that the tribe of Simeon drove them out from the area of southern Palestine where they had settled after the conquest of Canaan. Since this implies the second half of the 12th century BCE, authentic Hurrians could also here have gone by the name of Horites. Of course, for the compilers of the Old Testament who were writing down the texts several centuries after the event, the Horites of the age of Esau and the Hurrians of the time of the conquest of Canaan had turned into one and the same people – all the more so since by that time both peoples had ceased to exist, having merged with the Western Semites who surrounded them. This was a repeat of the confusion that had happened with the Indo-European and Semitic Hittites.

Chapter 5

The Conquest of Canaan in the Light of Biblical and Archaeological Data

The Limits of Biblical Archaeology
The description of the conquest of Canaan by the Hebrew tribes is mainly given in the book of Joshua, where it is depicted as a simultaneous military campaign. Unfortunately, archaeology is unable to confirm or refute the version set out in the Bible. The problem is that many of the Canaanite cities mentioned have yet to be identified or excavated. Archaeologists continue to argue about the precise location of cities such as Horma, Libnah, Makkedah, Lasharon, Madon, Shimron-Meron, and Goiim. However, even those cities that have been identified – such as Geder, Adullam, Tapuah, Hepher, and Ahshav – have for various reasons not been excavated in the proper way. It is, of course, impossible to conduct archaeological excavations in cities such as Jerusalem or Gaza in the event that modern buildings have been erected directly on the site of ancient ruins. Other cities have been identified and excavated only for it to turn out that they have been destroyed at different times and by different conquerors. The coastal cities of Ashdod, Ashkelon, Ekron, Aphek, and Dor, for instance, were destroyed by the Sea Peoples in the 12th century BCE, while Hazor and Bethel fell to Israelite tribes in the 13th century BCE. Still other cities were burned and abandoned by their inhabitants long before Joshua's conquest. The best examples of this category of cities are Ai and Arad, which flourished during the Early Bronze Age but were destroyed at the end of the 3rd millennium BCE, their lands remaining uninhabited right up to the arrival of the Israelite tribes. On the other hand, cities such as Yokneam, Kedesh, Taanach, and Lachish were indeed destroyed by the Israelites – and, moreover, precisely during Joshua's military campaign, in the 12th century BCE. There is other evidence too that confirms the information found in the Bible. For instance, Shechem, a city in central Palestine that is of great importance for Israelite history, is never mentioned among those seized or destroyed, and there is a good reason for this: archaeological data tell us that it already belonged to the Israelite tribes or was their ally. The same goes for cities such as Jerusalem, Debir, Yarmuth, Gezer, Beth-shean, and Akko, which are mentioned as unconquered cities. As archaeologists have established, these cities contain no traces

of Israelite culture. In short, the archaeological facts partly confirm the biblical version and partly contradict it.

At the present time, archaeology furnishes us with only two unconditional conclusions. First, the Hebrew tribes' conquest of Canaan was not a simultaneous military campaign, but one that stretched over several centuries. Second, the Hebrews were not aliens in Canaan, but had been closely connected with, and were an integral part of it. Their material and spiritual culture speaks of a continuity between them and the Canaanites – and all the more so because biblical Hebrew was merely a dialect of the Canaanites' language.

Interpretation of the archaeological data is made more complicated by the fact that not all sackings of Canaanite cities in the 15th-12th centuries BCE can be attributed to Hebrew tribes. At the end of the 16th and beginning of the 15th centuries BCE the northeastern part of Canaan was attacked by Hurrian and Indo-Aryan groups associated with the state of Mitanni. At the same time, southern Canaan was subject to military expeditions organized by the pharaohs of the 18th Dynasty from Thebes, who were trying to finish once and for all with the Hyksos and their local allies. In the middle of the 15th century the Egyptian pharaoh Thutmose III conducted regular depredatory marches into Palestine, resulting in the latter's subjection to Egypt. During the course of the 13th century BCE the pharaohs of the 19th Dynasty – first Seti I, then Rameses II, and finally Merneptah – repeatedly organized punitive expeditions into Canaan in an attempt to break the resistance of the local peoples. Each expedition of this kind was accompanied by the destruction of numerous Canaanite cities. Then, at the beginning of the 12th century BCE, the Philistines invaded southwestern Canaan and seized the southern coastal cities. Other Sea Peoples – the Tjeker and Sherden – settled further north, in the region of Dor. At the same time, the cities of northeastern Canaan suffered pressure and perhaps invasion at the hands of the Arameans, a West Semitic people related to the Amorites. The Arameans are known to have settled in the region of Damascus, where they set up their own kingdom and gradually became the main opponent of the Israelite tribes in the north of the country. However, apart from invasions by foreigners, Canaan also suffered not insignificantly due to internal conflicts between its city states themselves. Evidence of these cities' frequent military conflicts is to be found in letters from the Amarna archive. Archaeologists are frequently unable to determine with any unanimity the parties responsible for the destruction of a particular city.

Three Stages of Real Conquest

The discrepancies between the outcomes of the archaeological digs and the biblical version of the conquest of Canaan are not accidental. The book of Joshua, which tells of the seizing of Canaan, was most probably compiled and set down in the 7th to 6th centuries BCE, i.e. approximately 500 years after the

The Conquest of Canaan in the Light of Biblical

events it describes. As a result of the enormous gap in time between the events themselves and their being recorded in writing, unrelated episodes from different centuries were compressed into a single, simultaneous military campaign led by a single leader. In such cases confusion and mistakes with regard to the names of individuals, peoples, and cities are inevitable. But the main problem is something else: in the book of Joshua fragments taken from three different periods when the Hebrew tribes were fighting for Canaan have been lumped together. The first period begins in the 23rd century BCE, when the nomadic Amorite tribes arrived in Palestine; among them were northern Hebrew tribes (Israel). From this time forwards, the epic tradition of the northern tribes contained narratives of the conquest of Canaanite cities. Possibly, the detailed story of the seizing of the city of Ai was taken from these legends. Later, in approximately the 20th century BCE, the biblical patriarch Abraham led another group of nomadic West Semitic tribes out of northwestern Mesopotamia; among them were the southern Hebrew tribes (Jacob). The latter's arrival in southern Palestine was more peaceful, although they too were unable to escape conflicts with the Canaanite peoples. The wars waged by the southern tribes against the ruler of Arad belong to this, the earliest period of the fight for Canaan. The first stage of conquering the country ended with the departure of the northern and then the southern tribes into the Nile Delta in Egypt, as a result of which the tribal lands they had conquered were gradually taken over by other Amorite and Canaanite peoples.

The return of the 'house of Joseph' to Canaan in the 15th century BCE marked the start of the second stage of the fight for the country. This time, what was involved was not so much conquest as re-conquest, the winning back of land that had previously belonged to the Hebrew tribes. But when Egyptian power was established in Canaan, it made impossible the return of the lost land and the northern tribes became Habiru – homeless, 'displaced persons' in their own country. They occupied regions that were vacant and ill suited to agricultural use in central and northern Palestine, where they kept cattle and fought as mercenaries for local rulers. The situation changed for the better only in the second half of the 14th and at the beginning of the 13th century BCE, when the weakening of Egypt made its rule over Canaan purely nominal. It was during this period that the Habiru started attacking, and won back, part of their former lands. However, when Egypt regained its strength in the 13th century BCE, this led to the revival of Egyptian control over Canaan and to the loss of most of the land that had been won back. Possibly, it was the military campaigns of Seti I and Rameses II during the zenith of Egyptian might that forced the several northern tribes to join together to form the tribal alliance of Israel.

The third and most important period in the fight for Canaan started at the beginning of the 12th century BCE, when internal political conflicts in Egypt deprived it of control over Canaan, on the one hand, and, on the other, allowed the tribes of Moses to leave the Nile Delta. It was at this time that the extended Israelite tribal alliance embarked on the decisive phase in the conquest of Canaan, and it was this that became the basis for the book of Joshua in the Bible. The final strengthening of Egypt under Rameses III probably had no great impact on central and northern Canaan, where the Israelite tribes continued to reinforce their positions. After the death of Rameses III, the Egyptians finally left Canaan, making it possible for the two southern tribes to return from their 40 years of wandering through the desert and start in their turn conquering the southern part of the country.

Here, in Canaan, the 'house of Jacob' united with Israel. Henceforward, Jacob was Israel and Israel, Jacob. The two groups of tribes became a single people with two parallel names. Five to six centuries later, the keepers of the tradition – the Levites and the Aaronites – linked to this third stage in the fight for Canaan a large number of narratives relating to the first and second periods, creating the impression that there had been a single, simultaneous military campaign, although there had been no such thing. For the sake of fairness, it should be noted that the fight for possession of the whole of Canaan was completed only during the rule of King David, i.e. in the first half of the 10th century BCE. In spite of this, the authors of the book of Joshua included in it all the episodes known to them relating to the conquest of the country by the Hebrew tribes from the 23rd to the 10th centuries BCE. Of course, archaeology will never be able to confirm that all these episodes took place during a single short military campaign under the leadership of Joshua. Thus the official biblical version is a result of a compilation of narratives belonging to the southern and northern tribes taken from three different periods.

Why did the 'house of Jacob' – the group of southern Hebrew tribes – join forces with Israel and not with Edom, Moab, or Ammon, who were actually closer to it? The main factor in this case was not tribal genealogy, but the fact that Israel and Jacob had historical fates and political interests in common. They were the only Habiru in Canaan, which is to say that only they had no tribal lands of their own. Jacob's relatives Edom, Moab, and Ammon had not left to go to Egypt, had not lived during the course of hundreds of years in the Nile Delta, and had not experienced either the prosperity that came during the rule of the Hyksos pharaohs or the persecutions that followed under the pharaohs of Thebes. On the other hand, this was something that the Hebrew tribes had experienced in full. The Edomites, Moabites, and Ammonites possessed old tribal lands in Transjordan which were, with rare exceptions (for instance, Sihon's seizure of part of the land of Moab) not subject to attack by their neighbors – the Amorites and Canaanites. The Hebrew tribes were in an entirely different position. Throughout the long time that they had spent in Egypt, their lands had been taken over by the Amorite and Canaanite peoples. During four centuries of life in Egypt the blood ties between the 'house of Jacob', on the one hand, and Edom, Moab, and Ammon, on the other, had grown so weak that the latter had no wish not just to help their kin but even to allow them to pass through their territory. Moreover, as we are told by the Bible, Balak, the ruler of the Moabites, looked upon the 'house of Jacob' as his potential enemy. In these conditions the only possible true ally of the southern tribes was the 'house of Joseph', which had been patron to the 'house of Jacob' in Hyksos Egypt. This is the origin of the political and military alliance of the two groups of Habiru – the houses of Jacob and Joseph, – an alliance which was later reinforced when the two groups both adopted the cult of Yahweh. From this time forwards, the name Habiru or Ibri/Ivri became the common ethnonym for both parties in the new union of Israel and Jacob. The establishment of this alliance is an interesting example of how under the influence of historical circumstances different tribal groups (admittedly within the same West Semitic ethnos) can discover that they have incomparably more in common than with tribes that are more closely related to them and with whom they have a shared genealogy. However, this shortcoming – the lack of a common tribal genealogy – was successfully compensated for during the United Monarchy, when the keepers of the tradition conflated two forefathers – Jacob and Israel – into a single shared patriarch whom they invested with two names.

Peaceful Coexistence Instead of Expulsion
The conquest of Canaan during the time of Joshua had two important features. First, it was by no means a complete conquest. The regions that were most fertile and most suitable for agriculture – such as the valley of the River Jordan and the Jezreel and coastal valleys – remained, as before, in the hands of the Canaanites. The most important interior regions in terms of economic and strategic significance and the cities in these regions – such as Jerusalem – were, as before, under the rule of the Amorite peoples. A peace agreement with the Hivites – an Amorite people from central Palestine – left their cities (Gibeon, Kephirah, Beeroth, and Kiriath-Jearim) intact. Almost the entire Mediterranean coast was outside the control of the Israelites. Being semi-nomadic, the latter possessed neither wall-breaking instruments nor experience of storming heavily fortified cities, nor chariots for fighting in the valleys. For this reason, when talking of large cities, the authors of the book of Joshua are frank in saying: "Yet Israel did not burn any of the cities built on their mounds—except Hazor, which Joshua burned" (Joshua 11: 13). The same went for the valleys: "all the Canaanites who live in the plain have iron chariots" (Joshua 17:16). At that time the Israelites had no chariots, and this for a long time prevented them from taking control of those regions that were most suitable for farming. The incomplete and partial character of the Hebrew conquest of Canaan is acknowledged by the Bible itself: "When Joshua was old and well advanced in years, the Lord said to him, "You are very old, and there are still very large areas of land to be taken over" (Joshua 13:1).

Secondly, in spite of appeals from the keepers of the tradition, the local peoples not only were not destroyed, but were not even driven off their lands. In general, the biblical texts contain overt contradictions regarding the fate of the population in cities that were conquered. On the one hand, their authors maintain that "Joshua subdued the whole region, including the hill country, the Negev, the western foothills and the mountain slopes, together with all their kings. He left no survivors" (Joshua 10:40). On the other, the Bible supplies a great deal of evidence to show that the Hebrew tribes in all regions of Canaan settled alongside the local peoples and without causing the latter any harm:

> "Judah could not dislodge the Jebusites, who were living in Jerusalem; to this day the Jebusites live there with the people of Judah" (Joshua 15:63);

> "They did not dislodge the Canaanites living in Gezer; to this day the Canaanites live among the people of Ephraim but are required to do forced labor" (Joshua 16:10);

> "Within Issachar and Asher, Manasseh also had Beth Shan, Ibleam and the people of Dor, Endor, Taanach and Megiddo, together with their surrounding settlements (the third in the list is Naphoth). Yet the Manassites were not able to occupy these towns, for the Canaanites were determined to live in that region. However, when the Israelites grew stronger, they subjected the Canaanites to forced labor but did not drive them out completely" (Joshua 17:11-13);

> "Neither did Zebulun drive out the Canaanites living in Kitron or Nahalol, who remained among them; but they did subject them to forced labor" (Judges 1:30);

> "Nor did Asher drive out those living in Acco or Sidon or Ahlab or Aczib or Helbah or Aphek or Rehob, and because of this the people of Asher lived among the Canaanite inhabitants of the land" (Judges 1:31-32);

> "Neither did Naphtali drive out those living in Beth Shemesh or Beth Anath; but the Naphtalites too lived among the Canaanite inhabitants of the land, and those living in Beth Shemesh and Beth Anath became forced laborers for them" (Judges 1:33);

"But the Israelites did not drive out the people of Geshur and Maacah, so they continue to live among the Israelites to this day" (Joshua 13:13).

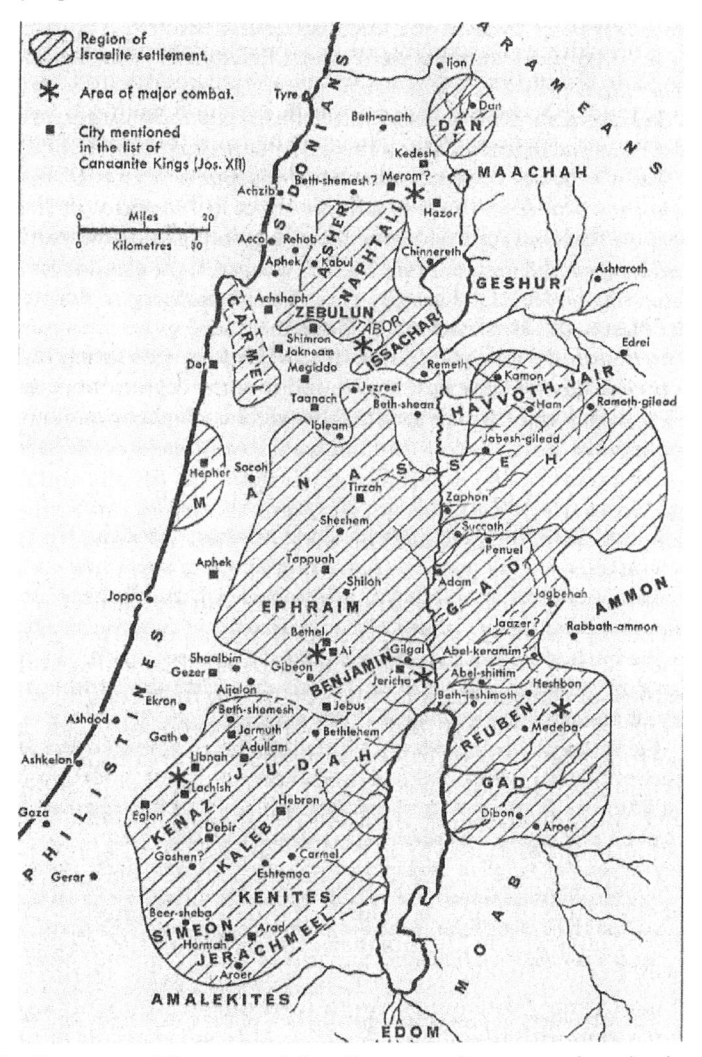

The Conquest of Canaan and the allotment of conquered territories to Hebrew tribes, as suggested by Yohanan Aharoni, The Land of the Bible.

Instances of devastation and expulsion of the inhabitants of seized cities were an exception to the rule. From the economic point of view, there was greater profit to be had from leaving the inhabitants where they were and making tributaries of them – which is what tended to happen, in fact. When the authors of the book of Joshua assert that the populations of many Canaanite cities were put to their deaths in their entirety, this is an absolutization of a number of extraordinary instances; it has a purely didactic purpose – to demonstrate how one should treat pagans. What actually happened, as the book of Judges shows, tended to be the exact opposite: "The Israelites lived among the Canaanites, Hittites, Amorites, Perizzites, Hivites and Jebusites. They took their daughters in marriage and gave their own daughters to their sons, and served their gods" (Judges 3:5-6). In this way, the Hebrew tribes not only lived in peace with the peoples they had conquered, but also quickly became assimilated with them.

Separate Wars of Joshua and Caleb

Following the death of Merneptah, the 19th Dynasty quickly faded out and Egypt weakened considerably. Currently, – at the end of the 13th and beginning of the 12th centuries BCE – the 'house of Joseph' renewed its campaign to conquer Canaan. If northern and central Canaan were conquered even partially at this time, then Joshua was not so much Moses' successor as his ally and comrade-in-arms. When Moses was fighting to get the southern tribes out of Egypt, Joshua was preparing the northern tribes for the conquest of Canaan. If this is so, then Moses could certainly have – and should have – had contact with Joshua or even plans for establishing a shared alliance with the aim of reconquering Canaan. But the two leaders could have joined forces properly only in the 1190s and 1180s BCE, at the time when the Israelite tribal alliance expanded and the biblical conquest of Canaan began. However, due to the strengthening of Egypt during the rule of Rameses III, the two southern tribes of Judah and Simeon were unable to set about winning back their lands in southern Canaan and were forced to remain in the desert for four decades. If the situation developed in accordance with this scenario, then the conqueror of southern Canaan was not Joshua at all, but Caleb, the head of the tribe of Judah, a descendant of the Kenazzites. According to the book of Judges, there were only two tribes fighting together for the south of Canaan – those of Judah and Simeon – and no mention is made of help given by the northern tribes: "Then the men of Judah said to the Simeonites their brothers, "Come up with us into the territory allotted to us, to fight against the Canaanites. We in turn will go with you into yours." So the Simeonites went with them" (Judges 1:3). The only true ally of the southern tribes was one of the Midianite tribes, the Kenites, with whom Moses had intermarried following the flight from Egypt and which had repeatedly come to his aid during his stay in the desert: "The descendants of Moses' father-in-law, the Kenite, went up from the City of Palms with the men of Judah to live among the people of the Desert of Judah in the Negev near Arad" (Judges 1:16). This fraction of the Kenites, like the Kenazzites, very quickly became part of the tribe of Judah. Such additions explain the fact that the tribe of Judah came to be so numerous, a kind of mega-tribe. Thus, if the central and northern regions of Palestine could have been conquered by Joshua in the first half of the 12th century BCE, then the south could not have been until, at the very earliest, the second half of the 12th century BCE. Consequently, the biblical stage of the conquest of Canaan, which is associated with Joshua, may have continued for almost a century. Support for this version is to be found in archaeological evidence that shows that the south of Palestine (historical Judea) was settled by Hebrew tribes at the end of the 12th and in the 11th centuries BCE, i.e. almost 100 years later than Samaria. Further proof is the Song of Deborah, the earliest surviving piece of Hebrew literature, which dates to the 12th century BCE. The Song of Deborah lists all the Hebrew tribes with the eloquent exception of the two southern tribes of Judah and Simeon. What probably happened was that at a much later time the biblical recorders joined together two leaders – Moses the lawgiver and leader of the southern tribes, and Joshua, head of the northern tribes and conqueror of Canaan, – making the latter the successor of the former.

The Fate of the Tribe of Reuben

The fact that the two southern tribes of Judah and Simeon were absent from Canaan at least until the middle of the 12th century BCE while the southern tribe of Reuben was present compels us to look again at Korah's mutiny in the desert following the Exodus of the 'house of Jacob' from Egypt. Possibly, this event had more serious consequences than the book of Exodus tells us. As we know, the dissatisfaction of some of the Levites headed by Korah was directed initially against the concentration of religious power in the hands of the Aaronites. However, due to the oppressive conditions involved in living in the desert and as a result of Moses' rejection of his former plans for conquering Canaan, the unrest very quickly transmuted into a broad and general opposition to the rule of Moses and Aaron. The malcontents were headed by the leaders of the tribe of Reuben – Dathan, Aviram, and On. Although the Bible asserts that the earth 'swallowed' the conspirators and that the latter 'disappeared without trace', it cannot be ruled out that this mutiny led to a split between the southern tribe of Reuben and the 'house of Jacob' and to the former leaving for Transjordan of its own accord. Possibly, other Amorite tribes which had joined the 'house of Jacob' when it was leaving Egypt departed together with the tribe of Reuben. There, in Transjordan, fighting for a 'place under the sun', the tribe of Reuben and its Amorite 'fellow-travelers' became members of the Israelite tribal alliance and subsequently committed themselves to sharing the fate of the northern tribes. If events did indeed develop in this way, then it becomes clear why, according to the Song of Deborah, the southern tribe of

Reuben was in Transjordan earlier than its brothers and why the book of Judges talks about the conquest of historical Judea by the two southern tribes (Judah and Simeon) only.

If you look through all the biblical commentaries on Reuben, you find that he always had a special relationship with Joseph. It was Reuben who found the mandrakes for his mother, Leah – which allowed Jacob's second but beloved wife, Rachel, to become pregnant and to give birth to Joseph. Reuben was the only brother who saved Joseph's life when his brothers had the idea of killing him. And again it was only Reuben who returned to the empty well to release Joseph, only to find that Joseph had already been sold by his brothers to the Ishmaelite merchants. Unlike his southern brothers Simeon and Levi, Reuben took no part in massacring the Hivites of Shechem, the traditional allies of the 'house of Joseph'. These narratives, which passed into the Bible from the Hebrew epic tradition, reflect the historically close and amicable links between this southern tribe and the 'house of Joseph' – links which subsequently led Reuben to join the union of northern tribes. On the other hand, within its own 'house of Jacob' the tribe of Reuben was unjustly insulted when it was deprived of the headship in spite of the fact that the latter had its right under the law on primogeniture. Moreover, Reuben lost the supremacy to Judah, the very person who had proposed selling Joseph to the Ishmaelites. As subsequent events showed, the tribe of Reuben preferred the northern tribes to the 'house of Jacob', remained with them in the kingdom of Israel, and shared their fate in everything. Admittedly, the tribe's southern origins were still felt in the beginning and it acted like an outsider among the alliance of northern tribes. As the Song of Deborah tells us, the tribe of Reuben did not come to the help of the tribes of Zebulun and Naphtali when the latter fought with the kingdom of Hazor. Evidently, Reuben was guided not so much by his relations with the northern tribes as by his own special ties with the 'house of Joseph'. It is interesting that in the same Song of Deborah the tribe of Reuben is specifically identified among all the Israelite tribes as not offering support to its brothers. For some reason it was Reuben that stirred up the most disappointment in the authors of this ancient work of poetry. While censuring in passing all who shied from offering help, the poem criticizes Reuben's position more than that of anyone else:

> "In the districts of Reuben there was much searching of heart. Why did you stay among the campfires to hear the whistling for the flocks? In the districts of Reuben there was much searching of heart" (Judges 5:15-16).

We may suppose that the closer attention given to this tribe was a consequence of the fact that it had been the first of the 'house of Jacob' to join the

Israelite tribal alliance. In order to settle properly in Transjordan, it relied upon a great deal of help from its northern fellows; however, when its own turn to help came, it then failed the test of loyalty.

The Settlement on the Land

Although modern archaeology is as yet unable to give an answer to the questions of when the Israelite tribes arrived and whence, it can with a reasonable degree of accuracy determine when they settled on the land in Canaan. This is a matter of a considerable breakthrough in biblical archaeology over recent decades. Hundreds of new settlements belonging – judging by their material culture – to the Israelites have been found. According to statistics produced by the American archaeologist Laurence Stager, during the 12th and 11th centuries BCE 633 completely new settlements with features of material culture characteristic of the Israelites appeared in Canaan. In the absolute majority of cases these were small towns which did not even have fortified walls. They were made up of four-room two-storey pillared houses of the kind that were typical for the Israelites. Their inhabitants engaged in both arable and cattle farming. Unlike their Canaanite neighbors, they did not keep pigs. All these settlements were on hills or eminences in Samaria, Judea, and Galilee, while the Canaanite cities continued to exist in the valleys. The new settlements began appearing at the start of the 12th century BCE – first in Samaria, then in Galilee, and, later still, in Judea and the Negev in the south. At approximately the same time, new settlements sprang up in Transjordan, where a similar process was evidently likewise underway with the semi-nomadic population settling on the land. The American archaeologist William Dever notes a further feature that is typical of the Israelites alone – the collar-rim store jar. This kind of ceramic ware, emphasizes Dever, is completely absent from Canaanite cities. He also points out that, judging by the archaeological finds, the inhabitants of the new settlements, unlike ordinary nomads, had already had experience of crop-growing. Dever calls the Israelites 'pioneers of terrace arable farming' and is of the opinion that it was they who first invented this way of cultivating the land in Palestine.

Moreover, the studies of objects of material culture in the new settlements have led many archaeologists (including W. Dever, I. Finkelshtein, and A. Mazar) to conclude that, for all the differences between the Israelite and Canaanite settlements, there is no evidence that the Israelites were of an 'alien' origin, i.e. their material culture reveals no important difference from that of the local Canaanite population. The archaeological data provide unanimous support for the supposition that before settling on the land, the Israelites had already been a substantial length of time in Canaan and had managed to pick up a great deal of the Canaanite culture.

Chapter 6

The Age of the Judges

The Judges and their Gods

The years following the conquest of Canaan and before the creation of the United Monarchy are usually called the period of the judges. However, 'judges' is an imprecise term for those who led the Hebrews at that time – for they were not so much judges as leaders and military commanders. The Hebrew tribes who had settled in the land of Canaan acted independently of one another during this age and tackled all problems each on their own. It is no coincidence that in characterizing this time, the Bible emphatically says that "in those days, when there was no king in Israel, each did as he pleased" (Judges 17:6). The keepers of the tradition assess the period of judges exclusively from the point of view of loyalty to the cult of Yahweh: "[…] they [Israelites] forsook him [Lord] and served Baal and the Ashtoreths. In his anger against Israel the Lord handed them over to raiders who plundered them. He sold them to their enemies all around, whom they were no longer able to resist. Whenever Israel went out to fight, the hand of the Lord was against them to defeat them, just as he had sworn to them. They were in great distress. Then the Lord raised up judges, who saved them out of the hands of these raiders. Yet they would not listen to their judges but prostituted themselves to other gods and worshiped them. Unlike their fathers, they quickly turned from the way in which their fathers had walked, the way of obedience to the Lord's commands. Whenever the Lord raised up a judge for them, he was with the judge and saved them out of the hands of their enemies as long as the judge lived; for the Lord had compassion on them as they groaned under those who oppressed and afflicted them. But when the judge died, the people returned to ways even more corrupt than those of their fathers, following other gods and serving and worshiping them. They refused to give up their evil practices and stubborn ways" (Judges 2:13-19). The keepers of the tradition emphasized, above all, the opposition between the cult of Yahweh and all other religious cults in Canaan, implying a conflict between monotheism and paganism. In actual fact, not just during the era of the judges but in later times too, there was no such conflict. Firstly, worship of Yahweh was not at this age a monotheistic religion of the kind that it became many centuries later. Secondly, not just during the time of the judges but throughout the entire period of the First Temple, the worship of Yahweh co-existed reasonably peacefully with many pagan cults. The confrontation between Yahweh and the Canaanite cults was not a fight between monotheism and paganism, but a contest for political influence and material resources. Moses' followers were unable to live up to the exalted nature of his monotheistic religious and philosophical concept, quickly abandoning it for an old, pagan, perception of their tribal faith. Moses' death brought a revival of the pagan concept of the cult of Yahweh represented by high priest Aaron at the time of the conflict arising from worship of the 'golden calf' in the desert. The books of Judges and Samuel abound with examples both of pagan rituals and beliefs contained in the religion of Yahweh and its peaceful co-existence with other pagan cults. For instance, the story of judge Ehud, who liberated his people from the sway of the Moabite King Eglon, mentions idols – the 'graven images' which stood in Gilgal. But Gilgal was not some kind of Canaanite pagan place of worship. It was the first center of the alliance of the Hebrew tribes, a site where collective circumcisions were carried out (these circumcisions were a symbol of the alliance with Yahweh) – in short, a religious center run by the Levites and Aaronites.

More striking is the behavior of the judges, the political and military leaders of the people. Gideon, who had defended the Israelite tribes from the plundering attacks of the Midianites, might have seemed to be rising up against the cult of Baal, who was worshipped not just by Gideon's family, but by his entire city. It was not for nothing that he was nicknamed 'Jerubbaal' ('Let Baal defend himself'). Gideon had originally been the bright hope of the followers of Yahweh among the northern tribes. But to the disappointment of the latter, he began attributing his victories over his enemies not to Yahweh, but to another, pagan, god. He made the pieces of golden jewellery which he had seized as plunder into "an ephod, which he placed in Ophrah, his town. All Israel prostituted themselves by worshiping it there, and it became a snare to Gideon and his family" (Judges 8:27).

Still worse in this sense was the behavior of another judge, Jephthah. Jephthah 'gave the Lord his word' that he would make a burnt offering of the first person to emerge from the door of his home if he returned victorious from battle with the Ammonites. But the first to come out to congratulate him was his only daughter. "When he saw her, he tore his clothes and cried, "Oh! My daughter! You have made me miserable and wretched, because I have made a vow to the Lord that I cannot break." "My father," she replied, "you have given your word to the Lord. Do to me just as you promised, now that the Lord has avenged you of your enemies, the Ammonites" (Judges 11:35-36). But the God of Moses not only could not demand human sacrifice; he could not even countenance such a thing. It was the pagan divinities that needed such sacrifices – for instance, the notorious Moloch, who was also worshipped by the Canaanites and to whom the latter sacrificed their children. In this way, neither Gideon's 'god' nor Jephthah's 'lord' had anything in common with Moses' Yahweh and Ten Commandments handed down to Moses on Mount Sinai. From this it follows that the words 'God' and 'Lord' – like the tetragrammaton YHWH, used in the biblical texts from the period of the judges to designate Yahweh – should not automatically be associated with the Almighty God of Moses. The 'Lord' of the majority of the judges, even if designated by the tetragrammaton YHWH, was merely one of the Canaanite divinities – probably, Baal. Possibly, in the ancient texts these pagan divinities were called by their proper names, but the compilers of the Old Testament replaced these names with 'Yahweh' or, more abstractly, 'God' or 'the Lord', dressing up the indubitable paganism of the era of the judges in a semblance of periodical enlightenment and a return to the religion of Yahweh – or, to be more exact, to the monotheistic concept of Yahweh, of which Moses had laid the foundation. It should not be forgotten that the keepers of the tradition attributed all misfortunes and vicissitudes to befall their people to the fact that the Israelites had started worshipping new, pagan, gods. Typical in this respect is the traditional leitmotif, "When they chose new gods, war came to the city gates" (Judges 5:8).

How the pagan cults flourished among the Israelites is clear from the story of Micah, head of one of the clans of the tribe of Ephraim. Setting up 'an idol and graven image' in his home, Micah turned his house into a pagan shrine and, furthermore, instructed his son to serve as a priest there. Subsequently, he appointed a Levite to command the priests in this shrine, and the Levite, without feeling the least bit embarrassed, served the pagan idol conscientiously. But the most interesting thing is that at the moment when the tribe of Dan moved from the south to the north, this Levite took the idol from the house of Micah and set it up in the temple of the city of Dan (Laish) – and at the same time founded a dynasty of local high priests: "They continued to use the idols Micah had made, all the time the house of God was in Shiloh" (Judges 18:31). It should be remembered that the temple in Dan, like the similar temple in Bethel, subsequently became in the Northern Kingdom an alternative to the Temple in Jerusalem.

The most precise characterization of the religious beliefs of the Hebrew tribes at that time is the following quotation from the book of Judges: "[...] They served the Baals and the Ashtoreths, and the gods of Aram, the gods of Sidon, the gods of Moab, the gods of the Ammonites and the gods of the Philistines. And [because] the Israelites forsook the Lord and no longer served him" (Judges 10:6). Moreover, the priests of Yahweh – the Aaronites and Levites, – like the priests of the pagan divinities, tended to regard worship as, above all, a source of income rather than a duty arising from faith. The unsavory and sacrilegious behavior, debauchery, and corruption of the priests – and especially of the sons of the high priests Eli and Samuel – made it difficult for the people to see any difference between orgies in the pagan temples and sacrifices to the

Lord. The worship of Yahweh remained the principal religion of the southern tribes only, although even in the latter case Yahweh had to coexist with other, pagan, divinities. As for the northern tribes, although they recognized the Lord of their southern brothers as the main official God of the Israelite alliance, in daily life they nevertheless continued to favor Baal and Ashtoreth.

The Israelite Tribal Confederation

In contrast to what we are told in the Bible, the Hebrew tribes returned to Canaan not simultaneously, but in three stages and during the course of approximately 300 years – from the middle of the 15th century to the second half of the 12th century BCE. This determined the history of the formation of the tribal alliance. First taking shape in Canaan in the second half of the 13th century BCE, this alliance initially consisted only of the four northern tribes. Later, in the 1190s and 1180s BCE, these four tribes were joined by another seven who had just come out of Egypt. Finally, 40 years later, the two southern tribes returned from the desert. Given this sequence of events, only ten tribes (not including the Levites) – and not 12 – could have taken part in Joshua's conquests. On the other hand, although Moses brought nine tribes, including the Levites, out of Egypt, only two of them – those of Judah and Simeon – wandered for 40 years in the desert.

The Hebrews' return to Canaan in three stages, coupled with analysis of their genealogy as given in the Bible, allows us to suppose that initially they consisted not of two but of three separate tribal groups – a northern group (Israel), a southern one (Jacob), and the Amorite tribes which had joined them at the time of their Exodus from Egypt. There can be no doubt that the core of the northern tribes was the 'house of Joseph', which consisted of the tribes of Manasseh and Ephraim. The latter were joined by the tribe of Benjamin, which, like the latter two tribes, traced its roots to the same founder, Israel. As for the northern tribe of Naphtali, it is no coincidence that the Bible traces its origins not to Rachel, the favorite wife of Jacob/Israel, but merely to her slave girl, Bilhah. This is a sign not just of the tribe's inferior status in the tribal hierarchy, but also, evidently, of the fact that it was more distantly related. We do not know at what stage the tribe of Naphtali joined up with the 'house of Joseph', but all four of these tribes had a direct relation to the Hyksos and were forced to leave Egypt after the Hyksos pharaohs had been driven out.

Another group of Amorite tribes which joined the Israelite alliance consisted of Issahar, Zebulun, Gad, and Asher. The Bible traces their genealogy to Jacob's eldest wife, Leah, and to her slave girl, Zilpah. The fate that befell these tribes in Egypt was similar to that of the 'house of Jacob'. Like the southern tribes, they arrived in the Nile Delta later and, unlike the 'house of Joseph', had no connection with the Hyksos. They likewise were held back in Egypt and experienced all the woes of living in slavery to the pharaohs of the 19th Dynasty. These tribes left

Egypt together with the southern Hebrew tribes, were with Moses at Mount Sinai and, after accepting his commandments, became part of the 'house of Jacob' and its family tree. However, unlike their two southern fellow tribes, they refused to wander the desert for 40 years and left to join up with the 'house of Joseph'. The fact that the Bible in no way links their origins with Rachel and Bilhah, the matriarchs of the northern tribes, is evidence that they had a different genealogy from the latter. The book of Genesis, which contains very old narratives from the epos of the southern and northern tribes, makes almost no mention of Naphtali, Dan, Issahar, Zebulun, Gad, and Asher during the pre-Egypt period. It is probable that the convergence with these tribes occurred in Egypt or following the departure from Egypt. Thus, in its final version the Israelite tribal confederation brought together what were three different groups of West Semitic tribes who returned to Canaan from Egypt at different times.

True unification of all 12 tribes occurred only during the period of the United Monarchy. Until then the Israelite alliance existed either in incomplete form or purely nominally. This union was actually necessary only for the conquest of Canaan; and when Canaan had been conquered, even if incompletely, under Joshua, the leaders of the tribes began to feel unhappy at the diminishment of their power in favor of the common leader. From the point of view of the authors of the Bible, the Hebrew tribes were unified by three factors – tribal kinship, worship of Yahweh, and shared history. However, the reality was somewhat different. The Hebrew tribes consisted not of one, but of three different West Semitic groups, which made their alliance unstable. Worship of Yahweh was likewise not a uniting factor. It was the principal religion only in the case of the southern tribes and partly in the case of the Amorite tribes who had come out of Egypt together with Moses. Until their departure for Egypt, and in Egypt itself too, these groups had had different histories. The main aspect that had united them earlier had been their status as Habiru/Apiru lacking a home and land following their enforced departure from Egypt. So the conquest of Canaan, even if it was only partial, disrupted the basis of their former unity. The second most important uniting factor was these tribes' dramatic memories of their stay in Egypt. But with the passing of time and as they became increasingly Canaanized, this factor too became less influential. For this reason the alliance's disintegration during the time of the judges was a natural and inevitable process. Chronologically, the period of the judges was a fairly short interval of time – between the middle of the 12th century and the end of the 11th century BCE, although, according to the Bible, it should have been much longer. The biblical version, however, was written only in the 6th century BCE, i.e. approximately 500-600 years after the era of the judges, when there was no longer any possibility of faithfully reproducing the chronological order of events and many facts had been distorted by the huge gap in time. As a result, the historical sequence of most episodes given in the book of Judges was adversely affected.

Certain judges ruled not successively, one after the other, but simultaneously. Moreover, none of the judges – not even the best known such as Gideon, Jephthah, Ehud, and Samson – ruled all of the tribes at once, but only some part of them. Judge Samuel, for instance, according to the Bible, "appointed his sons as judges for Israel", but the text goes on to explain that "they served at Beersheba" (1 Samuel 8:1-3). It is likely that Samuel ruled the tribe of Judah, but appointed his sons to rule over the tribe of Simeon. Thus he held sway only over the two southern tribes. But even during attacks by enemies, only those tribes who were under direct threat came to the defense of their brothers; the others remained indifferent to their fate. The Song of Deborah, which tells of the war of the northern tribes against kingdom of Hazor, condemns those tribes who did not come to the help of their brothers at a critical moment. The same happened when the Philistines pushed the tribe of Dan off its tribal territory. After not receiving the help it was due from the other tribes, Dan was forced to find itself new land in the very north of Canaan.

For about two and a half centuries the advance of the northern tribes was kept in check by Egyptian rule over Canaan. But when the Egyptians left and the second wave of returning Hebrew tribes arrived, the fate of Canaan was settled: it inevitably passed into the hands of the Hebrews. Although the disintegration of the Israelite tribal confederation during the age of the judges considerably weakened the Israelites' advance, it could not bring the conquest of Canaan to a halt. From this time forwards, Canaan was conquered not so much by military means as by assimilation of the Hebrews with the local peoples. The process began in the 15th century, when several northern tribes returned from Egypt to Canaan. It was then that the 'house of Joseph' drew very close to the Hivites of central Palestine, particularly in Shechem. It is no coincidence that the recently identified Israelites on the bas reliefs of Pharaoh Merneptah are almost indistinguishable in looks and dress from traditional Canaanites. Their neighbors and relatives – the Shasu nomads (Edomites, Moabites, and Ammonites) – looked different. The intermarrying of Hebrews and the Canaanite and Amorite peoples was considerably facilitated by their possession of shared West Semitic origins and a common language. The extraordinary ease with which this intermixing took place is indicated by, for instance, the case of the Israelite hero and judge Samson, who took a fancy to a Philistine girl. In spite of their different ethnic origins, different faiths, and, even more importantly, the hostility between the two peoples, Samson was able without any difficulty at all to marry the girl of his choice. If marriage between circumcised Israelites and their uncircumcised enemies, the Philistines, was so easy to arrange, then one can imagine how things stood when it came to the closely related West Semitic peoples – the Canaanites and Amorites. In time, the latter became completely intermixed with the Hebrews. The frequent mentions in the Pentateuch and the book of Joshua of the necessity of driving out the Canaanite peoples seem a mockery of the real situation. The keepers of the tradition were in fact calling for the expulsion or destruction of those who had long since become an integral part of their people. The Song of Deborah contains yet another striking example of assimilation. Listing all those who had given help to their brothers, the authors name "some [...] from Ephraim, whose roots were in Amalek" (Judges 5:14). Thus Ephraim, which was the most important northern tribe in the 'house of Joseph', contained a clan or clans deriving from Amalek, the bitter enemy of the 'house of Jacob'. The memory of these people was preserved in the name of one of the mountains on the tribal land of Ephraim. This mountain – Mount Amalek – is specially mentioned by the book of Judges as being the place where the Israelite judge Abdon, son of Hillel, a Pirathonite, was buried (Judges 12:15).

The Mystery of the Tribe of Dan

Of all the tribes that joined the Israelite alliance the most enigmatic was Dan. As already said, there is absolutely no mention of this tribe in the pre-Egypt period when the Hebrews were living in Canaan. The only exception is the official genealogy, which names the tribe's forefather, Dan, as the son of Jacob/Israel – and, moreover, the son not by one of Jacob's wives, but by the slave girl Bilhah. The second mention comes only in the list of all members of the family of the patriarch Jacob/Israel who had left for Egypt. But the mention of Dan in the official genealogy does not prove very much given that this genealogy was drawn up much later, in the time of the United Monarchy, and on the basis of the political considerations of that period. Much more important are episodes in the life of the forefathers of the tribes in the pre-Egypt period; and this is something which is completely lacking in the case of the tribe of Dan. The first information, even if completely trivial, on the tribe of Dan appears only during the time of the wandering in the desert after the Exodus from Egypt. Oholiab, son of Ahisamach from the tribe of Dan, is named as the master craftsman who helped to build and embellish the Ark of the Covenant (Exodus 35:34-35). Another, rather more important episode, tells of the son of an Egyptian man and an Israelite woman from the tribe of Dan who insulted and cursed the name of God, for which he was stoned to death (Leviticus 24:10-11). This gives us indirect proof that the tribe of Dan came out of Egypt not with the 'house of Joseph' in the 15th century BCE, but with the 'house of Jacob', together with Moses, at the beginning of the 12th century. However, unlike the other four tribes that joined Moses (Issahar, Zebulun, Gad, and Asher), the tribe of Dan was not named as one of the sons of Jacob by Jacob's eldest wife Leah and her slave girl Zilpah. The official genealogy makes Dan the son of Bilhah, the slave girl of Rachel, which is to say a member of the 'house of Joseph'. Why, then, were the Amorite tribes of Issahar, Zebulun, Gad, and Asher closer to the group of southern Hebrews than was the tribe of Dan? The answer to this is given by that same extraordinarily important episode in which the son of the Egyptian and the Israelite woman from the tribe of Dan insulted the name of the Lord. In the Bible nothing is accidental; even the most insignificant episode carries a certain historical and philosophical significance and reflects real facts, and any distortions concern merely the time at which events occurred or their evaluation. In the Pentateuch the keepers of the tradition never mentioned their ordinary fellow tribe-members, but only those who were leaders or belonged to the tribal aristocracy. For this reason, the son of the Israelite woman, who is called by name, was evidently the son of the leader of the tribe of Dan. It is notable that his father is described as an Egyptian. But it was traditional at that time for only women, not men, to be given to other families and tribes. For instance, an Egyptian woman – the daughter of the influential priest Potipherah – was given to Joseph, and not the other way around. Thus the man whom the Bible calls an Egyptian, i.e. a foreigner and a follower of a different faith, was in fact the true leader of the tribe of Dan who took a noble Israelite woman as his wife. It is not surprising that this foreign leader and his tribe did not adopt the worship of Yahweh even following the giving of the Sinai commandments. Clearly, this tribe, unlike the West Semitic tribes that had joined the alliance, found the religion of Yahweh utterly alien. Subsequently, the tribe of Dan, together with the four Amorite tribes, the southern tribe Reuben and Levites, joined the 'house of Joseph' instead of wandering for 40 years in the desert in the company of the two southern tribes Judah and Simeon. Dan's foreign origins, rejection of Yahweh, and subsequent alliance with the northern tribes, forced the keepers of the tradition to find a place for this tribe in the 'house of Joseph' as the latter's junior partner. Thus, Dan remained a member of the family of Jacob/Israel, but was reduced in status to the very bottom of the tribal hierarchy.

Another important feature that characterizes the tribe of Dan is the story of its leader Samson and his uncompromising fight against the Philistines during the time of the judges. For some reason, not a single Hebrew tribe – and, above all, Judah and Benjamin, closest neighbors of Philistines – was as hostile to the Philistines or fought against them as fiercely as the tribe of Dan, although these other tribes suffered no less at the hands of the Philistines. After settling in south-west Canaan, the Philistines did not destroy or drive out the local population – the Canaanites and the Rephaim (Avvim), an even older people. So the Semitic and pre-Semitic population remained untouched, as the Bible makes perfectly clear. Why, then, did the tribe of Dan have to leave its allotted land, which abutted the lands of the Philistines? Was it really mere chance that made the Danites chose a place for themselves next to the Philistines? Does not the reason for the intense hostility between the Philistines and the tribe of Dan lie in the latter's Indo-European or Aegean origins? It is well known that peoples that are related to one another conflict with one another more fiercely than with foreigners. It is quite possible that the name

The Age of the Judges

Samson (Hebrew: Shimshon) and the names of Samson's parents had been Semitized in the same way as Moses' Egyptian name. Samson's fight against the Philistines resembles the feats of Achaean heroes more than it does the kind of wars waged by the Israelite judges. Finally, the triumphal Song of Deborah contains an episode that throws light on the true origin of the tribe of Dan. While condemning those Israelite tribes which refused to help their brothers in the battle with Sisera, the military commander under King Jabin of Hazor, the Song of Deborah names the tribe of Dan and asks: "And Dan, why did he linger by the ships?" (Judges 5:17). This is a question that could have any specialist on ancient Jewish history stumped for an answer. How is it that an Israelite tribe of former semi-nomads who had recently settled on the land were now suddenly sailors? At that time it was only the Phoenicians and the Sea Peoples who 'lingered by the ships'. The former were Western Semites, like the Israelites, while the latter were peoples from the Aegean and Asia Minor. However, any suggestion that the tribe of Dan was of Phoenician origin can be dismissed immediately since this tribe came to Canaan from the Nile Delta. More probable is the idea that Dan originally came from Asia Minor or, rather, the Aegean. Incidentally, a Sea People by the name of 'danuna' or 'da'anu' is first mentioned in Egyptian sources during the rule of pharaohs Amenhotep III and Akhenaten in the 14th century BCE. Considerably later, during the rule of Rameses III (in the eighth year of the latter's reign), a Sea People called 'Danyen' was named among those who attacked the Egyptian army near the Nile Delta. Possibly, this is the same people to which Hittite sources gave the slightly different name of 'Daniya-wana'. Finally, Homer talks of the 'Danaeans' (another name for the Achaeans) who lived in Argolis and Argos on the Peloponnese in the south of Greece. If all these similar names are not a simple coincidence and the Israelite tribe of Dan was indeed part of this Aegean people, then this tribe probably appeared in the Nile Delta at the end of the 13th century BCE at the time when the Sea Peoples began moving en masse to the east and south east. If the Danites were directly related to the legendary 'Danaeans' of Argolis, then they were close neighbors of the Mycenaeans, who are thought by archaeologists to have comprised a considerable part of the Philistine population. It is difficult to say how the inhabitants of ancient Argos came to Egypt. Were they mercenaries and military colonizers in the service of the Pharaoh or captives who had been taken into slavery along with their families? The ancient Egyptian sources, at any rate, confirm the existence of a large number of mercenaries and military colonizers from the Sea Peoples in the Nile Delta during the rule of Rameses II and Merneptah. Later, even more captives from among these peoples appeared in the region. When Egypt was in the grip of civil war just before Pharaoh Setnakht came to power, this Sea People could have left Egypt in the same way as the Hebrew tribes of Moses. It might have been part of that same large 'rabble' mentioned by the Hebrew

Bible which caused Moses so much trouble and unpleasantness. If this was the case, then in search of a place for themselves in Canaan the Danites joined the Israelite alliance that had been created by the northern tribes. The memory of their stay in Egypt and their enforced homelessness in Canaan were factors that were stronger than ethnic kinship; it was this that united the group of Indo-Europeans with the Western Semites. Unlike the 'house of Joseph' and the 'house of Jacob', the tribe of Dan – like the four Amorite tribes that had joined the alliance (Issahar, Zebulun, Asher, and Gad) – did not practice circumcision and only agreed to undergo this ritual in Gilgal in order to become proper members of the Israelite tribal alliance. In those days the circumcision rite was not regarded as the exclusive attribute of the worship of Yahweh, but as a ceremony for solemnizing alliances with divinities or people. Thus began the process of Israelization of the Danites. Their main enemies were their old neighbors and opponents from their former motherland, the Philistines, who refused to give them access to the shore of the Mediterranean. Unable to live by arable agriculture and cattle-rearing alone, the former sailors left for the north of Canaan, where, seizing the Canaanite city of Laish (Leshem), they renamed it 'Dan' and settled. The northern shore of Canaan was controlled by the Phoenicians and the Tjeker, a people of Aegean origin, with both of whom the tribe of Dan quickly established mutual understanding. Subsequently, all the Sea Peoples who had settled in Canaan – the Danites, Tjeker, and the Philistines themselves – integrated with the Western Semites.

The biblical story regarding Dan's move from the south to the north of Canaan mentions not one of the Danites by name – not even the leaders – even though it names Micah, the head of the Ephraimite clan who gave them temporary refuge. The episode of the Danites' move makes clear that among them there was not a single Levite priest; this was yet another difference between the Danites and the other Hebrew tribes. True, the southern Levite who was later invited to serve as a priest began practicing the worship of Yahweh in their midst, but – and this is very notable – in the old pagan form which Moses had condemned.

There is another point which casts doubt on whether the tribe of Dan could have had Israelite origins. The deathbed prophecy of patriarch Jacob contains an extremely important phrase: "Dan will provide justice for his people as one of the tribes of Israel" (Genesis 49:16); this implies that Dan would come to be like all the Hebrew tribes. Nothing similar was said of any other Hebrew tribe. Why was emphasis put on Dan's becoming like all the other tribes; was this not a self-evident fact? Probably not. This underlines the significance of other words in Jacob's prophecy about Dan: "I look for your deliverance, O Lord" (Genesis 49:18). The latter was especially important since the incident in the Desert of Sinai showed how difficult it was for the leaders of the tribe of Dan to accept the God of Moses.

One may dispute whether the tribe of Dan was Semitic or Indo-European, but it cannot be denied that it was a tribe which, prior to departure from Egypt, had had no direct connection with either the 'house of Jacob' or the 'house of Joseph' and had joined the Hebrew tribes at a later date.

The Philistine Threat

After the conquests made by Joshua, the Hebrews became the dominant ethnos in Canaan, and total possession of this country was, it seemed, only a matter of time. However, in real life things rarely happen as smoothly as in theory. The Philistines, an Indo-European people which had made its appearance in the south west of Canaan at the beginning of the 12th century BCE, had an appreciable impact on the situation in this country during the two centuries that followed. Although the Philistines could hardly have outnumbered the Canaanite peoples, they possessed two important advantages. First, they were militarily much better organized and had incomparable greater military experience both as a result of the lengthy wars they had fought to keep hold of their former motherland and due to their service as mercenaries in the armies of the Egyptian pharaohs and the Hittite rulers. Secondly, they made extensive use of iron as a material in the manufacture of weapons. It cannot be said that the Western Semites, including the Israelites, had no knowledge of iron whatsoever. In fact, they had been familiar with it for many hundreds of years before the Philistines arrived. But, unlike the Philistines, they did not have any cheap method of manufacturing it. So anything that they made from iron cost them more than if it had been made from gold. Iron weaponry was much more effective than bronze and its use in battle on a mass scale gave a considerable advantage.

The Philistine threat had already been well known to both Moses and Joshua. Moses, wishing to avoid military confrontation with the Philistines, had refused to lead his people by the shortest route into Canaan (this route lay alongside the seashore through the lands of the Philistines). Joshua, as the Bible acknowledges, "was unable to drive them out". The first blow from the newcomers from overseas fell on the Israelite tribe of Dan, the Philistines' closest neighbors. Samson, the judge and leader of the Danites, devoted his life to repelling the Philistine aggression, but the tribe of Dan was unable to stand firm under pressure from its hostile neighbors and, relinquishing its tribal lands, was forced to find a new motherland in the north of Canaan. The second serious collision with the Philistines occurred during the rule of judge Shamgar, son of Anat, who "struck down six hundred Philistines with an oxgoad" (Judges 3:31). However, this was merely a probing maneuver. The Philistines' main drive for expansion came later, in the 11th century BCE. From the story of high priest Eli we know of the major battle fought with the Philistines at Eben-Ezer and Aphek, which ended with the defeat of the Israelites and the seizure of the Hebrews' shrine, the Ark of the Covenant. Judging by the directions taken by the Philistines' military maneuvers, they had greatest impact on the southern tribes of Judah and Simeon and the northern tribes of Benjamin, Ephraim, and, partly, Manasseh. It was these tribes that found themselves in the most difficult position, under attack from the Philistines in the south-west and, periodically, from Ammon and Moab and the tribes of the desert (the Midianites and the Amalekites) from Transjordan in the east. Under the last judge and high priest, Samuel, the situation became slightly more stable: the northern and southern tribes managed to successfully repel several attacks by the Philistines, although wars with the latter continued throughout the rule of Samuel. It is difficult to say what was the greater cause of these temporary successes – internal problems of some kind that afflicted the Philistines or the fact that the Israelites had struck an alliance with the other West Semitic peoples. On this subject the Bible contains the following short, but significant sentence: "And there was peace between Israel and the Amorites" (1 Samuel 7:14). Thus the conflict between the Hebrew tribes and the Amorite (and Canaanite) peoples over the land of Canaan came to an end and the Western Semites united in order to fight the enemy that represented the greatest threat, the Philistines. Perhaps, it was a pooling of resources that enabled them temporarily to halt the expansion of the Philistines. However, the decisive battles for power over Canaan still remained to be fought.

Chapter 7

The United Monarchy

The Rise of Saul and the Hegemony of the Israelites
The accelerated expansion of the Philistines in Canaan during the second half of the 11th century BCE was the main reason why the Israelite tribes came together in a new alliance. By themselves, neither the northern nor the southern Hebrew tribes would have been able to withstand Philistine Sparta, which consisted of five cities – Ashdod, Ashkelon, Gaza, Ekron, and Gath. The Israelite judges, being military commanders of at most several tribes, had reached the limit of what they could do in organizing resistance to the Philistines. Now a fundamentally new system of authority and military power was required: one which would involve all the tribes without exception – in other words, a state led by a king who would have significantly more powers than any judge. Admittedly, as subsequent history showed, economic and social conditions for the emergence of a common state for the northern and southern tribes were not yet in any way ripe, and the main motivation for union was external danger. The Bible characterizes the new needs of the time as 'the voice of the people'. Samuel, the high priest and judge, saw this as an undisguised encroachment upon his authority – authority which he was reluctant to share with anyone.

Later, the keepers of the tradition, who did not conceal their preference for a theocratic form of government, would treat the wishes of the people not as a rejection of Samuel, but as an attempt to renounce the Lord. The Philistine threat was so great, however, that Samuel was left with practically no alternative but to agree to what the tribal aristocracy was asking for – the election of a king. Naturally, the keepers of the tradition depicted these events as if it was Samuel himself who, to please the Lord God, found Saul, the first King of Israel. This, though, was wishful thinking. Judging by the facts laid out in the Old Testament, even if Samuel was the high priest of the entire union, he only had real authority over the two southern tribes, Judah and Simeon. Although he had, as a young man, for a long time served with the high priest Eli in Shiloh, he had no direct connection with the northern Levites who came from that religious center. Interestingly, after coming to power, he did not remain in Shiloh, but created his own religious center in Ramah, his birthplace. Given that he and his sons had real power only over the southern tribes and that he subsequently supported the latter's candidate for the position of king, we may suppose that he derived from the Aaronites, who had joined the tribe of Judah. In any case, it is clear from the biblical texts that he had no authority over the northern tribes. For this reason, Saul was initially elected as king by the tribal aristocracy of the northern tribes, and not by Samuel, who was subsequently forced to acknowledge Saul's supreme authority over his own, southern, tribes. In short, the role played by Samuel in electing Saul has been extremely exaggerated. Samuel was faced with an unpleasant choice: either to become the vassal of the Philistines, people who were alien to him, or to acknowledge the nominal authority of the king of the northern tribes. He chose the latter as the lesser evil.

It is difficult to say what motivated the leaders of the northern tribes when they chose Saul, who came from the smallest Israelite tribe. Perhaps this was an attempt to break free of the hegemony of the tribe of Ephraim; or perhaps it was the result of a calculation that a weak king would be the most convenient for all. Or perhaps, at this moment of high danger the main criterion was Saul's own military prowess and personal charm. It is not for nothing that the biblical text says that that Saul was "as handsome a young man as could be found anywhere in Israel, and he was a head taller than anyone else." Even Samuel, who resisted the election of the king, was compelled to acknowledge for all to hear that "There is no one like him among all the people" (1 Samuel 9:2; 10:24). The Bible notes the extraordinary modesty and shyness of the young Saul, who not only objected to being chosen as king, but even concealed himself so as not to have to take part in the celebrations of his own coronation. His extreme height was a reminder that his ancestors had intermarried with the Rephaim (Anakites), a tall race who were natives of Palestine.

However, the ceremony of Saul's election was tainted: certain of the tribal nobility refused to recognize him as their king. Of this the Bible says as follows: "But some scoundrels said, 'How can this fellow save us?' They despised him and brought him no gifts" (1 Samuel 10:27). Most probably, those who doubted Saul's right to be king included the leaders of the tribe of Ephraim, who had from the start laid claim to be the leading tribe of Israel. During the time of the judges they had threatened war against their kinsmen from the 'house of Joseph' – the tribe of Manasseh – challenging the right of the latter's leader, Gideon, to lead the Hebrew tribes. But young Saul was as yet insufficiently strong to crush those who did not acknowledge him, and he "kept silent".

The first serious test for Saul was the war with the Ammonites, who periodically laid claim to Israelite Gilead in Transjordan. Understanding that he did not yet enjoy sufficient recognition and authority among all the tribes, Saul was forced to use threats to mobilize irregular troops – a measure that was unprecedented among the free tribes, who were accustomed to doing everything in accordance with their own wishes. "He took a pair of oxen, cut them into pieces, and sent the pieces by messengers throughout Israel, proclaiming, 'This is what will be done to the oxen of anyone who does not follow Saul and Samuel.' Then the terror of the Lord fell on the people, and they came out together as one" (1 Samuel 11:7).

Describing the irregular forces raised by Saul among the tribes, the Bible makes separate mention of 'the sons of Israel' and the 'husbands of Judah'. The latter distinction is unlikely to be a historical anachronism such as the mention of Philistines during the time of Abraham. It provides us with confirmation of the initial existence of two separate tribal groups which only really embarked on the path towards unification after Saul's accession to the throne.

The convincing victory over Ammon strengthened Saul's hand and became the basis for a renewal of the alliance between the northern and southern tribes. The very fact that a second coronation ceremony was held – this time in Gilgal – was a sign of the problematic nature of both Saul's position and relations between the northern and southern tribes. Here, in Gilgal, where Joshua had for the first time put together an alliance between the Israelite tribes, there occurred a division of powers between the first king and the last judge. Saul, like Joshua before him, received military and political authority, while Samuel, like his first precursor Eleazar, was forced to make do with religious authority. Admittedly, on this occasion the alliance was indeed comprehensive. It encompassed all 12 tribes, including the two southern tribes of Judah and Simeon. In this way, Saul was in effect crowned twice – first in Mizpah, where he was elected king by the leaders of the northern tribes, and then, a year later, in Gilgal, where he received the oath of loyalty from the southern tribes. It is in view of the two different ceremonies (the ceremony involving only the northern tribes in Mizpah and the ceremony involving both the southern and northern tribes in Gilgal) that the Hebrew Bible says, "Saul reigned one year, and he had reigned two years over Israel" (1 Samuel 13:1).

However, even after the renewal of the Israelite alliance in Gilgal, Samuel did not fully accept the authority of the king. He acknowledged Saul's supreme authority over himself merely formally. He reluctantly became Saul's temporary ally, but at the same time he did everything he could to discredit Saul in the eyes of the people and the tribal aristocracy; for instance, he reproached the elders as follows: "[…] you will realize what an evil thing you did in the eyes of the Lord when you asked for a king" (1 Samuel 12:17). For his part, Saul was unable to fully take the place of Samuel, but was forced to co-exist with him as half-king, half-judge, constantly adjusting his actions to take account of the interests of the influential high priest. Samuel's strength lay in the authority and influence he wielded over the southern tribes, so without his involvement an alliance of southern and northern tribes would have been impossible.

A typical example of the ambiguous role played by the high priest was his conflict with Saul on the eve of the decisive battle with the Philistines. Samuel deliberately forced Saul's entire army to wait for him to appear in Gilgal.

"He waited seven days, the time set by Samuel; but Samuel did not come to Gilgal, and Saul's men began to scatter. So he said, "Bring me the burnt offering and the fellowship offerings" And Saul offered up the burnt offering. Just as he finished making the offering, Samuel arrived, and Saul went out to greet him. "What have you done?" asked Samuel. Saul replied, "When I saw that the men were scattering, and that you did not come at the set time, and that the Philistines were assembling at Micmash, I thought, 'Now the Philistines will come down against me at Gilgal, and I have not sought the Lord's favor.' So I felt compelled to offer the burnt offering." "You acted foolishly," Samuel said. "You have not kept the command the Lord your God gave you; if you had, he would have established your kingdom over Israel for all time. But now your kingdom will not endure." (1 Samuel 13:8-14). The unjustified absence of the high priest, followed by his demonstrative departure from Saul's camp together with some of the forces, considerably weakened and discredited the King of the Israelites before the battle with the Philistines. Furthermore, Samuel arranged things in such a way that the guilt fell on Saul. It was Saul who conducted religious rites on his own initiative and carried out a sacrifice before battle, although under the agreement that they had concluded at Gilgal, this was the exclusive prerogative of the high priest. Samuel left Saul's camp, refusing to support the King of the Israelites, but formally did not annul his alliance with him. Possibly, Saul's duplicity was also a diplomatic move aimed at the Philistines; it showed the Philistines that Samuel was not the ally of their enemy – and had Saul have lost in battle, the southern tribes would have been able to avoid their vengeance.

Saul's position was made more difficult by the fact that his army was much less well equipped than that of the Philistines. Fearing mutiny, the Philistines had forbidden the Hebrew tribes who were their dependents to use blacksmith's forges. As a result of this policy, "Not a blacksmith could be found in the whole land of Israel, because the Philistines had said, 'Otherwise the Hebrews will make swords or spears!' So all Israel went down to the Philistines to have their plow points, mattocks, axes and sickles sharpened. The price was two-thirds of a shekel for sharpening plow points and mattocks, and a third of a shekel for sharpening forks and axes and for repointing goads. So on the day of the battle not a soldier with Saul and Jonathan had a sword or spear in his hand; only Saul and his son Jonathan had them" (1 Samuel 13:19-22). This largely explains why the biblical heroes and judges struck the Philistines with weaponry which was unusual and inappropriate for military use – for instance, Samson used an ass's jaws and Shamgar, son of Anath, an ox goad.

In spite of the departure of the irregular tribal forces, the king still had with him the small but well-trained professional army which he had managed to create in the first years of his reign. Samuel was replaced with priests from Shiloh, including Ahijah, the great grandson of the high priest Eli. This incident brought to light a conflict not just between Saul and Samuel, but between two groups of priests of Yahweh – the northern Levites from Shiloh, who supported the king, and the southern Aaronites, who were represented by Samuel and were in opposition to the king. The conflict had a tribal as well political dimension. High priest Eli from Shiloh and the prophet judge Samuel represented two competing dynasties of priests; the former dynasty was oriented on the northern tribes and the latter on the southern. And although the keepers of the tradition depict Samuel as the natural and, more importantly, lawful heir to Eli, with whom he served as a young man, in reality this was a matter of competition between two groups of priests disputing the position of primacy. Samuel had managed to snatch the leadership from the priests of Shiloh only thanks to a military catastrophe which led to the Ark of the Covenant falling into the hands of the Philistines and to Eli and his sons losing their lives. In spite of the fact that they came from the southern tribes, the Levites from the religious center in Shiloh had long since, from as far back as the conquests made by Joshua, linked their fates with the northern tribes and mainly expressed the latter's interests. As for the Aaronites, after temporarily losing the support of the largest southern tribe, the tribe of Judah, they were forced to yield the religious center in Shiloh to the Levite dynasty of priests, which evidently derived from the sons of Moses.

The rout of the Philistines, an event which no one had expected, showed the advantages of the monarchical form of government and a professional army. The first king of Israel turned out to be a good general. During a short period of time he won victories against almost all the neighbors of the Hebrew tribes – Moab, Ammon, Edom, the Philistines, and the Amalekites. Saul's victories forced Samuel to make peace with him. However, a new conflict was in the offing – on this occasion, due to the Amalekites.

As a result of their geographical position, the southern tribes suffered more than anyone from attacks by these nomads based in the Negev and on Sinai. An additional factor was the old enmity between the 'house of Jacob' and Amalek, which dated back to the exodus from Egypt. It was for this reason that Samuel required of Saul's army not just that the Amalekites be routed in war, but that they be totally destroyed. However, Saul was merciful and practical: he spared the life of the defeated ruler and refrained from senselessly destroying everyone and everything. Furthermore, Saul did not yet feel entirely comfortable in the role of king and was forced to pay close attention to the moods of his soldiers. It was not for nothing that he admitted to Samuel, "I was afraid of the men and so I gave in to them" (1 Samuel 15:24). This in its turn aroused the anger of the high priest, who, passing off his own demands as the will of the Lord, rebuked the king for being merciful. And although Samuel himself killed the leader of the Amalekites, he nevertheless threatened that he would break off all relations with the king. Saul's problem was that he could not replace Samuel with another priest who would show him obedience, such as Ahijah from Shiloh. Samuel had the support of the southern tribes, and the priests from Shiloh wielded influence only over the northern tribes, who were in any case in Saul's power. The enmity between Samuel and Saul reached such a pitch that Saul even ripped Samuel's clothes. Admittedly, before they parted company altogether, the two leaders came to a kind of compromise: Samuel, as head of the southern tribes, was ready to continue to acknowledge the supreme authority of the northern king, while Saul, for his part, undertook to preserve the cult of Yahweh as the main cult of the northern tribes. Interestingly, in conversation with Samuel, King Saul told him that, "they spared the best of the sheep and cattle to sacrifice to the Lord your God" (1 Samuel 15:15). Note that he says not 'to our', but 'to your'. This phrase is thrice repeated by Saul – a reminder that the cult of Yahweh was initially the tribal faith of the southern tribes alone, while the northern tribes were more inclined to worship the Canaanite El and Baal.

At the beginning of Saul's reign the unification of the Hebrew tribes was more nominal than actual: the southern tribes (Jacob) and the northern tribes (Israel) were independent partners as opposed to integral parts of an alliance. Admittedly, the northern tribes clearly prevailed over and dominated the southern ones. It is not for nothing that the unified monarchy became known as Israel rather than Jacob. This was a time when the ethnonyms Jacob and Israel existed in parallel and signified two different groups of tribes. It was for this reason that there then arose a need for another ethnonym – *ivri* or, in the plural, *ivrim*, a term which applied to both the southern and northern tribes. At this point the biblical text begins to use, once again, this almost forgotten name, for it was the only term which made it possible to indicate the two different groups of tribes which had embarked on a course of unification. This is a sign that what had previously been a social and legal term had become a shared ethnonym for the northern and southern tribes. It was used both by the Hebrew tribes themselves and by the peoples who surrounded them. This name tended to be employed precisely at those moments when the two tribal groups were fighting together against a common enemy. For instance, at the end of the period of the judges, on the eve of the battle with the Philistines, when the latter seized the Ark of the Covenant, the Hebrew Bible twice uses the term '*ivrim*' to signify the joint forces of northern and southern tribes: "When the ark of the Lord's covenant came into the camp, all Israel raised such a great shout that the ground shook. Hearing the uproar, the Philistines asked, "What's all this shouting in the Hebrew [*ivrim*] camp?" […] Be strong, Philistines! Be men, or you will be subject to the Hebrews [*ivrim*], as they have been to you" (1 Samuel 4:5-6, 9). Later, the ethnonym *ivrim* was used by the first King of the Israelites when addressing the entire people: "Then Saul had the trumpet blown throughout the land and said, "Let the Hebrews [*ivrim*] hear!" So all Israel heard the news: 'Saul has attacked the Philistine outpost, and now Israel has become obnoxious to the

Philistines" (1 Samuel 13:3-4). In describing the fear that seized the people before the Philistines arrived, the keepers of the tradition again use the term '*ivrim*': "When the Israelites saw that their situation was critical and that their army was hard pressed, they hid in caves and thickets, among the rocks, and in pits and cisterns. Some Hebrews [*ivrim*] even crossed the Jordan to the land of Gad and Gilead" (1 Samuel 13:6-7). It is not difficult to see that in the biblical text '*ivrim*' is used to mean almost the same as 'Israel' and 'Israelites'. This tells us two things. First, that the Israelites are directly related to the *ivrim/ibrim*, i.e. to the *habiru / apiru*, as this term was originally pronounced. Second, that the ethnonym 'Jacob' quickly merged with the name 'Israel' when the name 'Israelites' automatically came to signify both groups of Hebrew tribes. The swallowing up of 'Jacob' by 'Israel' was by no means accidental, given that numerically the southern tribes were a mere third, at most, of the northern tribes.

Saul and David: Allies and Rivals

In spite of the serious conflicts between Saul and Samuel, the King of the Israelites' true rival was not the high priest, but another and still more successful military commander, David. The Bible contains two different versions of how David entered Saul's inner circle. The first is that the king, who suffered from regular depressions, discovered that David was a skillful harpist who was capable of lifting his spirits. The second, more plausible, version says that David drew attention to himself through his talents as a soldier and, above all, by his victory over the Philistine giant Goliath. It cannot, of course, be ruled out that the art of playing the harp may be combined with talent as an outstanding commander or politician. In view of the fact that under Saul the division of the army into troops from the southern and northern tribes remained, the truth is most likely that David came into the limelight as commander of detachments from the tribe of Judah. Possibly, he was to begin with in an ambiguous position – nominally subject to Saul, but in actual fact subordinate to Samuel. However, as the position of the first king of the Israelites strengthened, the detachments from the southern tribes passed under the direct command of Saul himself. Thus Saul and David were set on a course of convergence followed by inevitable divergence.

The rivalry between Saul and David rested on more serious foundations than the differences between Saul and Samuel. If the latter was, above all, a priest and prophet whose aim was to preserve his authority over the southern tribes, David was just as much a military commander as Saul and, like him, laid claim to military and political leadership over the entire alliance of the Hebrew tribes. Furthermore, if David had the support of the largest Hebrew tribe, that of Judah, Saul relied upon the smallest, that of Benjamin. As the confrontation with the Philistines grew, the leaders of the Hebrew tribes needed, above all, a strong military leader who could protect them from the danger of being enslaved by the Philistines. They were ready to choose anyone who could manifest such qualities. Objectively, the personal conflict between Saul and David also expressed contradictions between the interests of the northern and southern tribes. Each of the two sides – Jacob and Israel – tried to impose on the other its own hegemony in the alliance between them. There were two candidates for the role of king: Saul from the northern tribes and David from the southern. During a moment of fatal danger they united and acted together, but then, as the external threat receded, began to fight each other for power. The fight was initiated by Saul, who tried to exploit the strengthening of his position in order to rid himself in good time of his most dangerous rival. It was not for nothing that Saul reminded his son Jonathan that, "As long as the son of Jesse lives on this earth, neither you nor your kingdom will be established" (1 Samuel 20:31). Initially, Saul had the upper hand: using the military advantage possessed by the northern tribes, he united both groups of tribes by force, pushing to one side David – and, with David, Samuel, who stood behind him.

It was no coincidence that the first person from whom David sought help after running from the king was Samuel in Ramah. The close relations between them and the fact that Samuel, unknown to King Saul, secretly anointed David as king had their explanation in highly prosaic considerations – namely, in their coming from the same tribe. Although the Bible tells us that Samuel's father, Elkanah, came from the mountains of Ephraim, his ancestors had no connection with the northern tribes. The same biblical texts (Hebrew Bible) mention in passing that the kin of Samuel and David came from the same place, from Ephrath (Bethlehem), and that their ancestors were Ephrathians. Since David and his kin undoubtedly belonged to the tribe of Judah, this means that Samuel's ancestors must likewise have belonged to this tribe. Moreover, in view of the fact that the inhabitants of one and the same small settlement at that time were usually blood relations of one another, we may suppose that David and Samuel's ancestors were not just from the same tribe, but, quite possibly, from the same clan too (1 Samuel 1:1; 17:12). Also in favor of Samuel's coming from the south is that his sons ruled in Beer-Sheba, in central Negev.

The strengthening of Saul's authority meant that Samuel, the judge and priest of the southern tribes, and his military commander David found themselves with no useful role to play. Forced to hide, David and his detachment concealed themselves in territory belonging to their native tribe of Judah. However, the tribal aristocracy of Judah was in no hurry to support its own candidate to the throne. The rich and influential clan of the Kenazzites (the descendants of Caleb, the son of Jephunneh) demonstratively took the side of the king, while Judah's ally, the Canaanite city of Keilah, which David had saved from being laid waste by the Philistines, was ready to hand him over to Saul's army. The inhabitants of the inaccessible areas of Ziph and Maon, where David and his people were hiding, likewise expressed readiness to help

Saul track and catch the fugitives. In short, the nobility of the tribe of Judah preferred at this moment to support the strong northern king, who was capable of defending them from the Philistines, rather than to enter into conflict with him in dispute of primacy in the alliance. Thus Saul's military advantage and the refusal of the leaders of the southern tribes to provide support forced David to enter the service of the Philistines together with his detachment of soldiers. The first phase of the fight for power ended in incontrovertible victory for Saul.

The Bible contains two different versions of the episode where David could have taken advantage of the carelessness of Saul's guards to kill him, but acted nobly, refraining from doing so himself and not allowing his soldiers to kill Saul either. It is likely that something similar happened in real life and that David showed a politician's far-sightedness: he wanted to be Saul's heir, not his killer. Had he tainted himself by killing the king, he would have alienated the northern tribes and only made it more difficult for himself to attain his main objective – to become the next king of all the Hebrew tribes after Saul.

David and his detachments were by no means the only Hebrews to serve in the ranks of the Philistines. The Bible mentions other '*ivrim*' who were in the Philistine camp on the eve of the battle with Saul's army. Admittedly, the biblical text tells us that they proved unreliable in the war against their fellow tribesmen and went over to Saul's side during the battle. Being in the service of Achish, the ruler of the principal Philistine city of Gath, David and his people lived as military colonists in the border town of Ziklag, guarding Philistine land from invasion by nomadic tribes coming from the direction of the Negev and northern Sinai. These military colonists enjoyed a relatively large measure of freedom to choose objectives for their campaigns – otherwise David would not have been able to avoid clashing with his own tribe.

Saul's hunt for David on the territory of the southern tribes and David's campaigns into the Negev as the Philistines' vassal present us with interesting information regarding the relations between the tribe of Judah and their neighbors. We should note, above all, the complete lack of all mention of the southern tribe of Simeon. After arriving in Canaan, this tribe settled in the central part of the north Negev, near Beer-Sheba. However, during the time of Samuel, Saul, and David, this region was considered to be land belonging to the tribe of Judah. Evidently, by the end of the 11th century BCE the tribe of Simeon had merged completely with their surrounding kinsmen from the tribe of Judah. Given that another southern tribe, the tribe of Reuben, had joined up with the northern tribes and the tribe of Levi had split before it came to Canaan, we may fairly confidently assert that during the period of the United Monarchy the southern tribes ('the house of Jacob') were represented in effect only by the tribe of Judah. Admittedly, in terms of numbers this tribe might justifiably be considered a mega-tribe. It had swallowed up not just the tribe of Simeon and part of the tribe of Levi, but also numerous West Semitic nomads who had joined it during the 40 years of wandering in the desert. The most notable of these were the Kenazzites, the Edomite tribe from which came Caleb, the son of Jephunneh, who had headed the conquest of southern Canaan. By the end of the 11th century BCE the Kenazzites had completely integrated with the tribe of Judah, although they still remembered their Edomite origins. The rich man Nabal, who is mentioned in the Bible, was a descendant of Caleb and considered his family to be superior to that of David.

Some of the Kenites (the Midianites), who had intermarried with the family of Moses and joined the southern tribes after their exodus from Egypt, were in a similar position. They had settled in the vicinity of Arad and gradually merged with the tribe of Judah. Another part of the Kenites continued to live nomadically in both the south and the north of Canaan. The Hebrew tribes looked upon the Kenites as their allies, regarding them with special favor among the other nomadic peoples. In the first half of the 12th century BCE, during the wars of the northern tribes with the dynasty of the Jabins, who ruled over the powerful kingdom of Hazor, the Kenites, who at that time were living as nomads in Galilee, took the side of the Israelite tribes. As the Song of Deborah tells us, Jael, the wife of the leader of the Kenites, enticed Sisera, King Jabin's military commander, into her tent and killed him. Another mention of the Kenites refers to the second half of the 11th century BCE, when King Saul was fighting against the Amalekites. Among the latter there were also clans of Kenites, and Saul, not wishing to cause them any accidental harm, asked them to leave the territory of the Amalekites, whom he intended to sack. It is difficult to say whether all the Kenites joined the Hebrew tribes, but some of their number were undoubtedly part of the tribe of Judah.

The next group of West Semitic nomads who joined the tribe of Judah are called 'Maonites' in the Bible. The book of Judges names the Maonites as one of the peoples who attacked the Hebrew tribes and for some time even ruled over them. These were probably tribes of Midianite or Edomite origin who had settled to the south of the Dead Sea. Their influence is unlikely to have extended beyond the limits of the territory of the southern tribes. They inhabited the inaccessible and semi-desert districts of Ziph and Maon, where David had once hidden with his soldiers. Interestingly, the Maonites, like the Kenazzites, did not support David. Furthermore, they were the first to express a readiness to help Saul catch his enemy. The Canaanite city of Keilah, another ally of Judah, behaved towards David with just as much enmity. Evidently, these ethnic groups, which joined the tribe of Judah after its exile from Egypt, were in the conflict between Saul and David less loyal towards the latter than the Judaic clans.

It is difficult to assess the position of another group which joined Judah – the Jerahmeelites. Unlike the Kenazzites and the Kenites, the ethnic origins of the Jerahmeelites are unclear, but, given that they were also a people of the desert, we may suppose that they too were Western Semites. In any case, David, when in the service of the Philistines, endeavored to avoid causing harm not merely to his own tribe of Judah, but to the Jerahmeelites and the Kenites as well. Possibly, one of the reasons why nomadic clans such as the Kenazzites, Kenites, and Jerahmeelites joined the tribe of Judah was that they were all followers of the cult of Yahweh. Evidently, these were the very same 'Shasu Yahweh' mentioned by the ancient Egyptian documents. Furthermore, they were all part of the second wave of nomadic Amorites who were led into southern Canaan by the biblical patriarch Abraham.

When the majority of southern tribes and the clans who had joined them dissolved in the tribe of Judah, this resulted not just in a sharp increase in the latter's numbers, but also in the name of Judah becoming associated both with the southern tribes and with southern Palestine as a territory. From this time forwards the keepers of the tradition preferred using the name Judah or Judea not just to indicate the southern tribes, but also as a name for southern Palestine and to signify the latter's political and geographical situation.

There is another fact which stands out: the southern tribes – or rather, the tribe of Judah – enjoyed rather better relations with the Moab and Ammon than did the northern tribes. During the period of the judges, Ehud the Benjaminite and the 'house of Joseph' had fought against Eglon, the king of the Moabites, and his Ammonite allies. The judge Jephthah from Gilead had also been forced to fight the Ammonites. The Ammonite ruler Nahash was a bitter enemy of King Saul and the northern Transjordanian tribes, but, as we learn from the Bible, he "showed kindness" to David and helped him (2 Samuel 10:2). At a moment of mortal danger David chose Moab as a hiding place for his parents, and was helped in this by the local ruler. This alone is a sign of the very close relations between the southern tribes and Moab. The story about the Moabite woman Ruth, David's own great-grandmother, confirms not just the closeness of these two related peoples, but also the fact that they intermarried. However, the difference in relations is explained not so much by the greater ethnic closeness between the southern tribes and Moab and Ammon as by the political calculations made by both sides based on the idea that 'my enemy's enemy is my friend'. The northern tribes were more numerous and stronger than the southern tribes, so objectively they were more of a threat to the neighboring Moab and Ammon than the Judah. Moreover, relations between the Ammonites and the Moabites on the one hand and the northern tribes living in Transjordan on the other hand were poisoned by territorial disagreements, something which was not true of relations between them and Judah.

Also of interest is the fact that relations between Edom and Judah, the two peoples who were closest by blood, were worse than the relations between either of these peoples and the northern tribes. Consider just this small fact: while his fellow Benjaminites refused to hand over to Saul those who helped David flee, the Edomite Doeg had no such qualms. Further confirmation is provided by relations with the Amalekites. If the southern tribes, who were close relations of the Amalekites, considered their blood relatives to be their most bitter enemies, the northern tribes, who were ethnically far removed from the Amalekites, were on significantly better terms with them. At least, as we learn from the Bible, in Saul's army the Amalekites served as mercenaries, while Samuel demanded that they should all be killed as cursed enemies of the 'house of Jacob'. Interestingly, as soon as David's position strengthened and he became king of all the Hebrew tribes, the Ammonites' attitude towards him changed markedly and while King Nahash had helped him before, the latter's son now became his enemy. The same change came about in his relations with the Moab. There can be no doubt that territorial disputes and political plotting had a greater influence on relations between neighboring peoples than ethnic or blood relations between them.

Their role as military colonists in the service of Achish, King of the Philistines, obliged David and his people to take part in all the Philistine campaigns. This was bound, sooner or later, to result in confrontation with Saul's army and with the forces of the tribe of Judah itself. But it seems that the Philistines already had bad experiences using mercenaries from the Hebrew tribes: the latter were viewed as unreliable when they had to fight against their fellow tribesmen. The Hebrew Bible mentions an episode where in their very first serious battle some mercenary *ivrim* switched sides to fight for King Saul. This is why when Achish took David's detachment with him on the campaign against Saul, the plan met with fervent objections from the Philistine military commanders. "The commanders of the Philistines asked, 'What about these *ivrim* [Hebrews]?' Achish replied, 'Is this not David, who was an officer of Saul king of Israel? He has already been with me for over a year, and from the day he left Saul until now, I have found no fault in him.' But the Philistine commanders were angry with Achish and said, 'Send the man back, that he may return to the place you assigned him. He must not go with us into battle, or he will turn against us during the fighting. How better could he regain his master's favor than by taking the heads of our own men?" (1 Samuel 29:3-4).

The Philistines' suspiciousness helped David and his people avoid having to make a difficult choice between their own fellow tribesmen, who were hungry for their deaths, and their enemies, who had given them refuge and sustenance. The above quotation makes it clear that the ethnonym '*ivrim*' was associated not just with the northern, but also with the southern Hebrew tribes. This was the only term which applied to both Israel and Jacob simultaneously, and it was in use among both the Hebrew tribes themselves and the peoples who surrounded them. There is another thing that is clear: the *ivrim*, like the *habiru* several centuries earlier, were used as military mercenaries by all kinds of different forces. The evolution that had occurred was merely linguistic and not ethnic; what had changed was the pronunciation of this name while its referents remained the same.

However, the fact that on this occasion the *ivrim* mercenaries did not fight alongside the Philistines did not save Saul's army. The latter suffered a serious defeat in the battle at Mount Gilboa; the king and three of his sons, including Jonathan, were killed – a catastrophe which completely changed the balance of forces among the Hebrew tribes. The hegemony of the 'house of Joseph' was now finished, and for a long time to come. David's small, but battle-proven army was now the main military force on the territory of the southern tribes and lost no time in exploiting its advantage. David entered Hebron and proclaimed himself king of the southern tribes – or, to be more exact, of the tribe of Judah, in which all the members of the 'house of Jacob' (with the exception of the tribe of Reuben and part of the tribe of Levi) had already been swallowed up.

The Bible says nothing of the role of the Philistines in David's coming to rule over Judah; however, the latter could not have happened without their agreement and approval. Furthermore, the Philistines' support was at that time the main criterion for the tribal elite's choice of king. As David himself admitted, his tribe contained families that were significantly more noble and powerful – for instance, the family of Zeruiah – but his status as trusted ally of the Philistines proved decisive for the aristocracy of Judah. Nevertheless, the patronage of the Philistines was not unlimited. That their vassal should be king of Judah was undoubtedly in their interests, since it broke up the Hebrew tribes into their previous constituent parts – the northern and southern tribes – and, of course, weakened both. However, David's subsequent attempts to unite the two parts were bound to meet with resistance from the Philistines and, in the event of success, to lead to war with them – as in fact subsequently happened. The fact that David was so quickly and easily accepted as king by the elders in his own tribe was not merely a consequence of his military strength and patronage by the Philistines, but also a result of his own efforts to maintain links with the tribal aristocracy. Even while in the service of the Philistines, he had not let slip the opportunity to send to the elders of Judah part of the rich plunder he took during his campaigns against the Amalekites and other peoples of the desert.

David's Accession and the Transition of Power to the Judahites

From the moment that David was declared king of the southern tribes, he and Saul's kinsmen from the tribe of Benjamin became involved in a fight for power over the northern tribes. Eventually, after several years of negotiations with the tribal leaders and elders, Saul's cousin and military commander, Abner, gained the upper hand and managed to convince the northern tribes of the necessity of recognizing Ishbosheth, Saul's son, as the new king of Israel. For the tribal leaders of the 'house of Joseph,' the power that resided with their relatives, the Benjaminites, was a lesser evil than that of the southern tribes. The fight between the two candidates did not, however, cease at this point, but, as is usually the case, was now pursued by military means. The two armies – the armies of the northern and southern tribes (Israel and Judah) – crossed swords in the region of the town of Gibeon, on land which had originally belonged to the Hivites but was now under the control of the tribe of Benjamin. Judging from mentions made in the Bible, neither side had a military force that was very impressive. Ishbosheth's army consisted mainly of the members of his own tribe (Benjamin), while the forces of Judah were mainly made up of David's detachments with whom he had served under the Philistines. The remaining tribes adopted a policy of 'wait and see' in order, as was then common practice, to join the side of the strongest when the time was right. The Bible's description of the battle is interesting from the etymological point of view. Here we see more clearly than anywhere else how the ethnonyms 'Israel' and 'Israelites' are used exclusively of the army of the northern tribes, whose opponents are the detachments under the command of David. The battle of Gibeon, however, produced no clear winner and so negotiations between the tribes recommenced.

The calamitous position of the Hebrew tribes, who were now oppressed by the Philistines, made it more than ever necessary that there should be unity and a strong king. To tackle the Sea Peoples without help from outside would have been impossible. That the powerful Hittite empire had fallen under the blows of the Sea Peoples was no surprise; in fact, not a single city or a single state in Syria or Phoenicia had been able to resist them. The Sea Peoples' onslaught had been contained only by Ramses III, the last great pharaoh – and only at the price of straining to their limit all the forces in Egypt. But Ishbosheth did not justify the hopes of the northern tribes. He turned out to be a weak king and a sorry shadow of his heroic father. The actual ruler, however, was not even he, but Abner, his military commander, in whose hands was the real military power. Although Ishbosheth became king when he was no longer at all young, but middle-aged (over 40), his position was not enviable. He depended entirely on his powerful kinsman, and the very first attempt he made to take Abner down a peg, when Abner helped himself to Saul's former concubine without asking, led to Abner entering into secret contact with David. The conflict over Saul's woman was, however, only a formal pretext for treachery. The real reasons were, on the one hand, Ishbosheth's unpopularity and inability to unite and lead the Hebrew tribes and, on the other, the fact that David, a talented military commander and politician, was growing in strength and becoming increasingly attractive. David had fought alongside the Philistines and been in their service; no one else had his knowledge of the strengths and weaknesses of the way in which their army was organized. So there is nothing surprising in that, after two years of Ishbosheth's unimpressive rule, the leaders of the northern tribes preferred instead the southern king, David. David himself was, however, very careful in the way he presented his coming to rule over the northern tribes:

he wished not to usurp power over them but to inherit it. The condition he imposed for coming to a deal with Abner was that his wife, Michal, Saul's daughter, should be returned to him. She legitimized his position, making him heir to Saul's dynasty. It is hardly surprising that David gave orders for Ishbosheth's killers to be put to death, just as he had earlier ruthlessly punished the soldier who had dared help Saul commit suicide on the battlefield. He tried to reach an agreement with Saul's relatives and showered favors on the son of his friend Jonathan. In this way David conquered the northern tribes not through military force, but by skillful diplomacy; he gave them hope of liberation from the yoke of the Philistines; and he did not seize, but literally bought the right to inherit regal authority from Saul's relatives. If Abner had been forced to transport his candidate to Mahanaim, the political center of the northern tribes, in order to have Ishbosheth adopted as king, in David's case everything was the other way round: the elders of the Israelite tribes themselves came to David in Hebron so as to ask him to become their king.

David's next step was to unify the territories of the northern and southern tribes. The lands of the Jebusites, together with their principal city, Jerusalem (Jebus), formed a wedge jutting between Israel and Judah, in effect separating the two groups of Hebrew tribes. The Jebusites themselves were a West Semitic people who were an old neighbor and ally of the southern tribes, just as, for instance, the Hivites of Shechem were in respect of the northern tribes. The friendship between them went back to the time of the patriarch Abraham and Melchizedek, King of Shalem (Jerusalem), who formed an alliance and fought together against common enemies. The return of the 'house of Jacob' from Egypt led to a renewal of the alliance with the Jebusites. Prior to David's conquest of Jerusalem, the Bible several times mentions this city as belonging or relating to the tribe of Judah. For instance, in the episode describing David's victory over Goliath, it is said, "David took the Philistine's head and brought it to Jerusalem; he put the Philistine's weapons in his own tent" (1 Samuel 17:54). Most historians consider this to be a clear anachronism. However, the Jerusalem mentioned here is not the Judahite city, but the Jerusalem of the Jebusites, which was an ally of the southern tribes and likewise took part in warding off attacks by the Philistines.

Relations between the Jebusites and the 'house of Joseph' took an altogether different course. According to the book of Judges, the tribe of Benjamin had long since set its sights on the lands of the Jebusites and tried to seize Jerusalem during the period of Joshua's conquests. It cannot be ruled out that even prior to this, King Abdi-Heba, who ruled the city during the second half of the 14th century BCE, when complaining to the Egyptian pharaoh about the aggressive intentions of the *habiru*, had in mind the tribe of Benjamin. Subsequently, after returning from Egypt, the southern tribes and their traditional allies, the Jebusites, fought both against the Canaanites and Philistines and against the tribe of Benjamin. However, for David an alliance with the Jebusites was no longer sufficient; he wanted to turn this enclave in the center of the Hebrew tribes into his own fiefdom – one that would be in no way connected with the tribal territories of the northern or southern tribes. The very fact that this 'impregnable' city, which had supposedly been unconquerable for centuries, was taken so quickly and with such little pain, is evidence that the southern tribes did not wish either to capture their allies, the Jebusites, or to allow others to do so in their stead. It cannot be ruled out that within Jebusite Jerusalem there was an influential party of supporters of the 'house of Jacob' which eased the city's passing into the hands of David. Interestingly, no mention was made of any vengeance taken by the conquerors, massacre of those who had been besieged, or sacking of the city. The Jebusites remained where they were and quickly integrated with the tribe of Judah; in this we see a sharp distinction from the severe punishments inflicted by David on Moab and Ammon, to whom his tribe, Judah, was related by blood. The Jebusite priesthood subsequently merged with the Aaronites and the Levites. Some historians suppose that Zadok, the high priest at the court of both David and then Solomon, himself derived not from the Aaronites, but from the Jebusite priests; however, this is something that is probably impossible to either prove or refute.

The new unification of northern and southern tribes and the proclamation of David as their king led, as was only to be expected, to war with the Philistines. Henceforward, having been a protected vassal of the Philistines, David became their principal enemy. Unfortunately, the Bible contains only the most meager account of the two military campaigns which resulted in the United Monarchy's liberation from the Philistines. David hesitated as to whether to defend or attack. To begin with, he shut himself up in the newly conquered fortress of Jerusalem, but subsequently his experience as a general suggested to him the advantage of a more active strategy and he hurried to confront the enemy. Both wars with the Philistines were decided in the vicinity of Jerusalem, in the valley named after the original inhabitants of Palestine, the Valley of Rephaim. Here David exploited, as never before, his earlier service with the Philistines and his excellent knowledge of their military strategy and tactics. The first battle ended with the Philistines suffering a rout so complete and shattering that they were unable even to save their own gods. If during the time of high priest Eli the Ark of the Covenant had fallen into the hands of the Philistines, now the Philistine gods became the trophies of David's army. The second military campaign brought them even more woe than the first. The Israelite army carried out a raid deep into the enemy's rear lines and, putting the Philistines to rout, pursued the remains of their forces as far as the city of Gezer. These two victories not merely liberated the Hebrew tribes from humiliating dependence on the Philistines, but also put an end to the Philistine expansion in Canaan.

The Struggle for the Ark of the Covenant between the Northern Levites and Southern Aaronites

Victory over his most dangerous enemy strengthened David's position and made it possible for him to make Jerusalem not just the political center of the United Monarchy, but its religious center as well. For this purpose it was necessary to transport to Jerusalem the main sacred object of the cult of Yahweh – the Ark of the Covenant. Possession of the ark had not only religious significance, but political and financial implications as well. The ark and its custodians were mandatory participants in all political agreements and decisive military battles. The presence of this sacred object not only reinforced faith and authority, but also generated a considerable income for all who were involved in its care. The dynasty of priests who had responsibility for the ark received handsome donations and military trophies from the tribal leaders, but also modest offerings from all the southern and northern tribes. When the sacred object was moved from one place to another, this was a kind of signal of the translocation of the center of political and religious influence among the Hebrew tribes.

After the death of Moses and the split of the Levites, the Ark of the Covenant passed to the priestly dynasty which had joined the northern tribes. The southern tribes (Judah, Simeon, and part of the Levites), who wandered for several more decades in the desert, were parted from this sacred object for a very long time. Following Joshua's conquests in Canaan, the ark was always located in areas belonging to the northern tribes – first in Gilgal, then in Shechem, and then for a while in Bethel, before finally coming to rest in the religious center at Shiloh. At the end of the period of the judges, before the death of high priest Eli of Shiloh, the Ark of the Covenant fell into the hands of the Philistines as a war trophy. According to the Bible, the Philistines decided to return the ark out of fear that it was responsible for the epidemics and plagues of mice which had befallen them. But the most interesting thing is that they handed it over not to the Levites from the northern tribes, who had previously owned it, but to the Aaronites among the southern tribes, the rivals of the Levites. This was done deliberately, in order to bring the two groups of priests into conflict and exacerbate relations between Israel and Judah.

From what we find in the Bible it is clear that the Philistines' political intrigue was entirely successful. The Ark of the Covenant was delivered not just to Judah, but to Beth Shemesh, a town situated not far from territory that was in the possession of the northern tribes. Everything that happened subsequently may be interpreted as a fight between the Levites of the northern and Aaronites of the southern tribes over the right to possess the most important sacred object of the cult of Yahweh. The keepers of the tradition put a different interpretation on the death of so many people: "But God struck down some of the inhabitants of Beth Shemesh, putting seventy of them to death because they looked into the ark of the Lord" (1 Samuel 6:19). Evidently, the inhabitants of Beth Shemesh lacked the resources to keep hold of the ark; they had no religious center in which to store it and so turned to another Judahite city for help. "Then they sent messengers to the people of Kiriath Jearim, saying, 'The Philistines have returned the ark of the Lord. Come down and take it up to your town" (1 Samuel 6:21).

The religious center of Shiloh was literally only 30 miles away, in a northerly direction – the same religious center in which the Ark of the Covenant was supposed to be kept, but the idea of returning the holy object to its previous place occurred to no one. Even if we accept some historians' suggestion that Shiloh had by this time been destroyed, why was the ark not returned to its former possessors who had settled in other places – in the city of Nob, which was situated even closer than Shiloh? And did the religious center in Shiloh lie in ruins for long? If subsequently, at the end of the 10th century BCE, Jeroboam, King of the Israelites, sent his wife to the prophet Ahijah in Shiloh, then it seems likely that this religious center of the northern Levites had continued to exist (1 Kings 14:2).

"So the men of Kiriath Jearim came and took up the ark of the Lord. They brought it to Abinadab's house on the hill and consecrated Eleazar his son to guard the ark of the Lord" (1 Samuel 7:1). Thus the Hebrews' most holy object dating to the time of Moses passed from the northern Levites to the southern Aaronites; and, as the Philistines had planned, relations between Israel and Judah were poisoned as a result. It is not incidental that the Bible contains the following: "It was a long time, twenty years in all, that the ark remained at Kiriath Jearim, and all the people of Israel mourned and sought after the Lord" (1 Samuel 7:2). Subsequently, those who edited the Bible tried to interpret this phrase as meaning that the entire people felt a need for the true God. However, in the initial version of the Old Testament the phrase referred only to the northern tribes – to the northern Levites, who had been deprived of their sacred object.

At the end of the rule of King Saul, when he managed to extend his authority to the southern tribes, the ark was returned to the northern tribes. But Saul returned it not to Shiloh, which was in an area that belonged to the tribe of Ephraim, but to his own capital city, Gibeah, in an area controlled by his own tribe of Benjamin. It was probably at this time that a clever compromise worthy only of the future King Solomon was reached. The sacred object was returned to the northern tribes, but remained in the hands of the southern Aaronites. Only thus is it possible to interpret the fact that at the moment when King David decided to bring the Ark of the Covenant to Jerusalem, the ark, although it was in the house of Abinadab, was no longer at Kiriath-Jearim in Judah, but in

Gibeah, an area that belonged to the tribe of Benjamin. According to Hebrew Bible, "they set the ark of God on a new cart and brought it from the house of Abinadab, which was in Gibeah" (2 Samuel 6:3).

Still more interesting is something else. In order to bring the Ark of the Covenant to Jerusalem, David had to gather a large army: "David again brought together out of Israel chosen men, thirty thousand in all. He and all his men set out from Baalah of Judah to bring up from there the ark of God, which is called by the Name, the name of the Lord Almighty, who is enthroned between the cherubim that are on the ark" (2 Samuel 6:1-2). Why did David need an entire army to transport the sacred object? Would not the Levite priests and the royal guard have been sufficient on their own? The reason why all available forces were mobilized becomes comprehensible only when we consider an event which happened while the ark was being moved. The transportation of the ark was managed by Uzzah and Ahio, the sons of Abinadab, who were devoted to David. "When they came to the threshing floor of Nacon, Uzzah reached out and took hold of the ark of God, because the oxen stumbled. The Lord's anger burned against Uzzah because of his irreverent act; therefore God struck him down, and he died there beside the ark of God" (2 Samuel 6:6-7).

The king's intention to move the most important sacred object from Gibeah, in an area belonging to the northern tribes, not only sparked resistance by the northern Levites, but also led to disturbances among the local population. In spite of the fact that the cult of Yahweh was merely one of the popular cults, the northern tribes had no desire to part with the ark, which they considered to be their own. They saw the southern king's plan to take the ark back home with him as an infringement of their interests and an attempt by the southern tribes to rule over them. It was for this reason that David needed large military forces in order to ensure the ark's smooth passage to Jerusalem. But to escape confrontation still proved impossible. The dead evidently included not merely Uzzah, who headed the operation, but large numbers of ordinary participants – for otherwise David would not have postponed the ark's delivery to Jerusalem. "David was afraid of the Lord that day and said, 'How can the ark of the Lord ever come to me?' He was not willing to take the ark of the Lord to be with him in the City of David. Instead, he took it aside to the house of Obed-Edom the Gittite" (2 Samuel 6:9-10). In order to pacify the northern tribes, David, an experienced politician, decided to postpone execution of this unpopular decision. It was only three months later, when passions had quieted down, that he managed to transport the Ark of the Covenant to Jerusalem. On this occasion David tried to cheer up those who were dissatisfied by holding festivities and handing out free treats. "When those who were carrying the ark of the Lord had taken six steps, he sacrificed a bull and a fattened calf [...] Then he gave a loaf of bread, a cake of dates and a cake of raisins to each person in the whole crowd of Israelites, both men and women. And all the people went to their homes" (2 Samuel 6:13, 19).

The difficulties involved in transporting the Ark of the Covenant to Jerusalem were a timely warning to the king of the dangers which might ensue from conflicts with influential groups of priests. David's reluctance to spoil relations with the northern Levites, as with the northern tribes in general, was evidently the main reason for his refusal to build a temple for the Ark of the Covenant. In addition to rivalry between the northern Levites and the southern Aaronites there was another problem: competition between the Aaronites and the Jebusite priesthood, who were loyal to David. Both the former and the latter were keen to become the king's main support in Jerusalem. Building the temple would inevitably have forced David to favor one of the three groups of priests, and thus to diminish the importance of whichever group he did not favor and possibly to enter into conflict with them. David never forgot that he was king not of a unitary state, but of one which was probably best described as confederation since it consisted of at least two different parts that were united more in response to an external threat than through mutual desire. On this basis, he appointed not one, but two high priests – Abiathar, the head of the northern dynasty of priests and a descendant of high priest Eli, and Zadok, who represented the southern Aaronites (and perhaps the Jebusite priesthood as well). These considerations were ignored by Solomon – and the consequences were suffered by his son Rehoboam when the United Monarchy split in two. David was in an incomparably better position than Saul had been. He had no need to share his power with a high priest backed by influential tribes, as had been the case with Saul and Samuel. Furthermore, David was not only able to choose his high priest himself, but also, taking no account of the latter's opinion, to conduct religious rites and offer burnt sacrifices – something which Saul had been absolutely unable to do. In short, David was the first proper king whose powers and authority were limited and disputed by no one. However, neither David nor Saul inherited their supreme position; both were chosen by tribal leaders and elders, and for this reason, when making policy, they were compelled to constantly look to the support of those who had put them on the throne.

The Extent of David's Rule and the Discontent of the Hebrew Tribes: The Revolts of Absalom and Sheba

David's kingdom was not merely a unification of the southern and northern tribes; it encompassed the whole of Canaan and was a power which now, for the first time in the country's history, included all the historical Canaanite districts (Israel, Judah, Moab, Ammon, Edom, the Canaanite and Amorite city states and, to a certain extent, Philistia). The creation of this state was undoubtedly a positive development for Canaan. For the first time, an end was put to the ceaseless fighting between the peoples of Canaan, and the country stopped being a target for plundering and expansion on the part of its aggressive neighbors. The role of unifiers was played by the Hebrew tribes, the former Habiru, who had returned at different times to Canaan from Egypt. Numerically, these tribes constituted less than half the population of Canaan, but, since they were scattered through different parts of the country, they were intent upon unification and on prevailing over the entire territory of Canaan. Apart from one small exception, David's kingdom was a state populated by closely related West Semitic peoples who spoke in different dialects of the same language and shared ethnic and cultural roots. The unification of the country accelerated the process by which a unified people of Canaan came into being based on the Hebrew ethnos.

The Canaanite and Amorite districts of western Palestine accepted David's rule mostly of their own free will. The situation with their Transjordanian relatives – that of Moab, Ammon, and Edom – was more complicated: they had to be subordinated by force. The war with the Ammonites, who during Nahash's kingship had been allies of David, continued longest of all. After Nahash's death power in Ammon was seized by one of his sons, Hanun, an opponent of the United Monarchy. But David considered that he had a right to intervene in the dispute regarding the succession: his military commanders Joab and Abishai were grandsons of Nahash since their mother, Zeruiah, was the daughter of the King of the Ammonites. There were other Judahite families too who were directly connected to Nahash – for instance, Amasa, a general who was the son of another daughter of the Ammonite ruler. In the end, David managed to put his protégé Shobi, another son of Nahash, on the throne. However, the war with the Ammonites brought David into conflict with a more serious opponent, the Arameans. Like the Amorite tribes, who had come to Canaan 1000 years earlier, the new wave of Western Semites – the Arameans – overran Syria and Mesopotamia, where they set up their own states. The Aramean kingdoms in Syria looked upon David's growing power as a direct threat to their interests, so for them the support of Ammon was a convenient pretext for going to war with the Israelite-Judahite kingdom. To everyone's surprise, however, David's newly unified Canaan proved a formidable military power. The Aramean kingdoms of Zobah, Rehob, Maacah, Tob, and Damascus suffered a number of defeats before acknowledging David's rule. The United Monarchy thus became a regional empire with the River Euphrates as its northeastern boundary.

The Israelites' relations with the Philistines also underwent significant changes. After David had succeeded in maintaining his independence from the Philistines, he switched to an attacking strategy and seized their principal city, Gath. David's former suzerains now became his vassals. However, here, in Philistia, David adopted a gentle and flexible approach: instead of taking vengeance on his former enemies and patrons, he quickly reached an agreement with them regarding a modest level of tribute. An important factor was his old connections with the commanders of the Philistine forces, who, judging from what we are told by the Bible, did little to resist David's authority. Nevertheless, from this time forwards the Philistines no longer presented a serious military threat either for the United Monarchy or for Israel or Judah on their own when the kingdom subsequently split in two. This was probably a result not of David's campaigns, but of internal processes in the Philistine cities themselves. The alliance that had existed between them disintegrated completely, and on their own they were too weak to constitute a threat to their neighbors. Furthermore, the gradual Canaanization of the Philistines in terms of culture and physique gave them a closer resemblance to their West Semitic neighbors than to their own ancestors of Achaean and Aegean origin. By this time Philistia had, as far as David was concerned, turned into a reservoir from which he drew mercenaries to serve in his guards. The bulk of David's army in terms of numbers continued to consist of irregular military detachments from the northern and southern tribes. The various tribes refrained from mixing even when at war. Each tribe and clan sent its own detachments of armed warriors, and they retained their own order and regulations both when on the march and in battle.

However, greater significance attached to the permanent army of mercenaries which, unlike the irregular detachments fielded by the tribes of Israel and Judah, recognized the authority of the king alone and had nothing to do with the tribes. David's permanent army was considerably larger than Saul's. Under Saul the army – like most of his servants and circle of friends and supporters – had consisted mainly of his fellow tribesmen from the tribe of Benjamin; David, on the other hand, drew his soldiers and followers from all the Hebrew tribes and gave preference to mercenaries of Achaean, Aegean, and Hittite origin. The most militarily capable and experienced part of his permanent army was his own guard, which consisted of several hundred people – the so-called 'braves' and 'heroes' – who accompanied him everywhere and at all times: they had fought with Saul's army, had then hidden from it, had served with David under the Philistines, and taken part in all his military campaigns. In time David's personal guard mostly came to consist of mercenaries with origins in the Aegean or Asia Minor. The king recognized the value of their military experience and quality of organization and, most importantly, considered them more reliable and more loyal than his own fellow-tribesmen. Events entirely justified this preference.

The United Monarchy

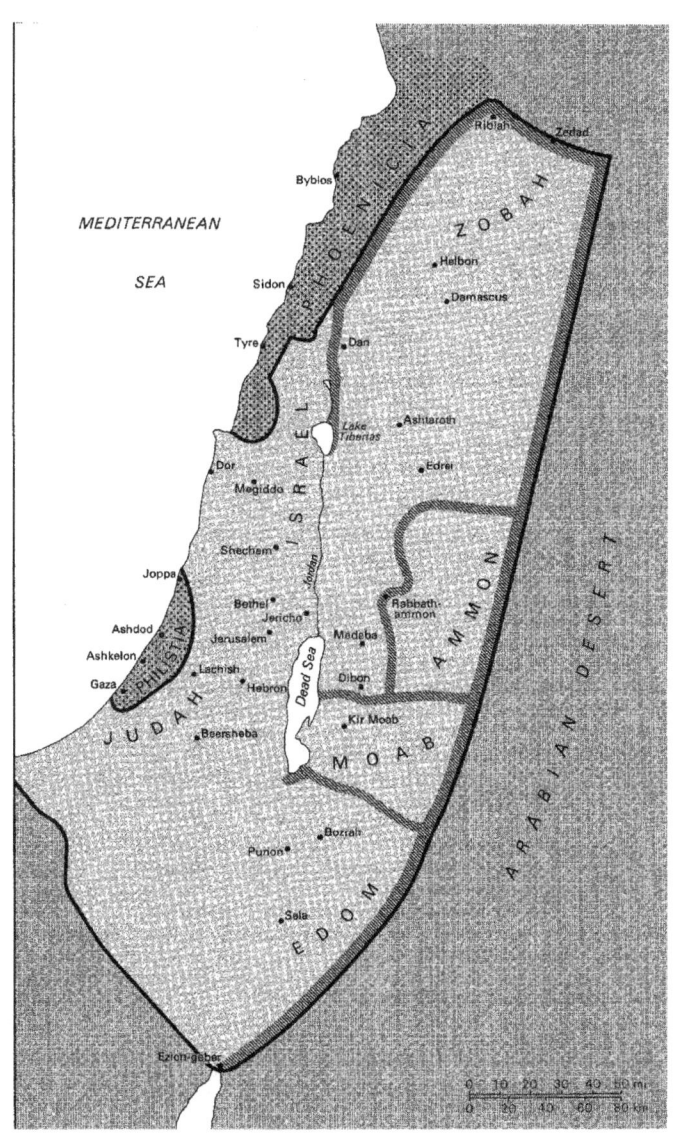

United Monarchy during the time of David and Solomon. 10th century BCE.

David's military successes were due not just to the fact that the Hebrew tribes were now united or to the king's abilities as an organizer, but also to the favorable political situation in the region during the first half of the 10th century BCE.

This was a time when Mitanni and the Hittite empire had long since ceased to exist, neighboring Egypt had lost its former power and entertained no thought of launching a military campaign in the direction of Canaan, and the Babylonian and Assyrian kingdoms in Mesopotamia had not yet turned into military giants that presented a danger to the peoples round about. The West Semitic peoples – Arameans, who had recently arrived in the area, had already achieved dominance in Syria, but were likewise not yet serious opponents for Israel.

David's continuous series of impressive successes is completely at odds with what the Bible tells us about two major mutinies against his rule. Both the mutinies were the result of dissatisfaction not among the peoples on the edges of David's kingdom who had recently joined it, but among the Hebrew tribes in the center of the country. The first and the most serious of the mutinies was organized by the king's favorite son, Absalom. The Bible says nothing of the real reasons for the conspiracy, attributing everything to Absalom's ambition and desire to wrest power from the hands of his father. However, we cannot but be struck by the scale and character of the dissatisfaction with David: it was not just the northern tribes who took up arms against him, as would have been comprehensible; rather, the main resistance came from the tribe of Judah. "And so the conspiracy gained strength, and Absalom's following kept on increasing. A messenger came and told David, 'The hearts of the men of Israel are with Absalom'" (2 Samuel 15:12-13). The irregular detachments from the northern and southern tribes took Absalom's side, and Absalom, like David before him, was 'anointed as king' in Hebron, the political center of Judah. We may suppose that among the Judahite aristocracy who were dissatisfied with David the tone was set by the Kenazzites, who at the time were the leading force in Hebron. The descendants of Caleb, son of Jephunneh considered themselves to have been unjustly treated in the kingdom of David and were impatient for the chance to get even with him. David was forced to flee from Jerusalem to Mahanaim – the capital of the northern tribes in Transjordan, where David's unsuccessful rival Ishbosheth had been crowned. Only his own guard – and the two high priests, whom he had chosen himself – remained loyal to him. Absalom took Jerusalem, the king's house, and even his concubines, without a fight.

Why was it that David, who had been such a successful king and had defended his people from the Philistines, now fell from grace in the eyes of the Hebrew tribes, including his own tribe of Judah? Whatever the skill shown by Absalom in his intrigues, his conspiracy against his father would never have enjoyed such widespread support had there not been good reasons. But what were these reasons, and why is the Bible utterly silent about them?

Judging by the biblical descriptions of the kingdom of David, the king's native Judah should have been 'swallowed up' in the Canaanite state as a whole. At the court, in the king's guard, and in the permanent army foreigners were in the majority – Cherethites, Pelethites, Achaeans (from the Sea Peoples);

Hittites and Luwians (from Asia Minor); Gathites (from the Philistine city of Gath); and Arameans. It is no coincidence that most names associated with this period belong not to Judahites, nor even to Israelites, but to foreigners. The army officer from whom David took a woman who had caught his fancy was the Hittite Uriah. The mercenary commander who remained loyal to David during the mutiny was the Gathite Ittai. Even the Ark of the Covenant was temporarily left by David not with the Levites or Aaronites for them to look after, but with Obed-Edom, a Gathite who was devoted to him. David's military commanders Joab and Abishai were grandsons of King Nahash of the Ammonites; his principal advisor and friend, Hushai the Arkite, was likewise not a Hebrew – like, incidentally, most of David's wives and concubines. Abiathar, one of his two high priests, came from the northern priestly dynasty, while Zadok, the other, was, so some historians suppose, a Jebusite. In this way, Judah was entirely without representation in the most important fields of power.

Admittedly, the abundance of foreigners, even though a cause of dissatisfaction, could not in itself have driven David's fellow-tribesmen to take up arms against their own king. For this a more weighty reason would have been needed. Such a cause was the heavy financial and economic burden which David imposed on all the Hebrew tribes, including his own. If Saul, the first king of the Israelites, himself helped to plough the land, had no palace of his own, and made do with an exceptionally modest retinue at court and with a small army consisting of his own fellow-tribesmen, David used Phoenician craftsmen to build a luxurious house for himself, kept a large court, and had a substantial army of mercenaries. Whereas Saul had conducted only defensive wars with the intention of protecting the Hebrew tribes, David launched campaigns to conquer land as far away as the Euphrates and created a true regional empire – undoubtedly at great expense. Neither during the time of the judges nor during the rule of Saul had the Hebrew tribes experienced such severe taxation and compulsory service as under David. Given his need of additional resources, it was not incidental that David resorted to the highly unpopular measure of a general census – an operation which had to be carried out not by civil servants, but by David's military commanders with the help of the entire army. In these conditions it was sufficient for Absalom to promise the tribal leaders to significantly reduce the economic burden imposed on them by his father for him to secure their full support.

However, although a skillful intriguer, Absalom was a poor strategist: after seizing power, he wasted time, allowing his father to flee and recover. David was supported by his own army of mercenaries, but also by Shobi, the ruler of the Ammonites and one of the sons of Nahash, whom David, after long wars, had put on the throne, and by two Israelite Transjordanian tribes from Gilead – the tribe of Gad and the eastern half of the tribe of Manasseh. Unlike the other Hebrew tribes, these two had their own reasons for supporting David. The people of

Gilead had long since had difficult relations with the tribe of Ephraim, the main tribe in the 'house of Joseph'. The first conflict between them had occurred during the time of Joshua, when the Gileadites had been required to take part in all military campaigns to the west of Jordan and had been forbidden to create their own religious center in Transjordan. Subsequently, judge Jephthah of Gilead had been forced into a bitter war against the Ephraimites, who disputed his authority. Even Gideon, a judge from Manasseh, the tribe that was closest to the tribe of Ephraim, had to contend with the Ephraimites' claims to primacy. It goes without saying that David's loss of the throne would have led to a strengthening of the position of the 'house of Joseph' and, above all, of its leader, Ephraim, something which would have been against the interests of Gilead. Furthermore, the Amorite tribe of Gad, which had come out of Egypt together with the southern tribes of Moses, had from the beginning periodically fluctuated in its political orientation between supporting the Israelite tribes and Ammon. The Gileadites, as the Song of Deborah bears witness, were among those who refused to come to the aid of the northern tribes in the latter's war with Jabin and Sisera. In order to force the Gileadites to choose between him and Israel, Nahash, the mighty king of the Ammonites, had threatened them with the loss of their right eyes (it was their right eyes that faced towards the Israelite tribes to the west of Jordan). In any case the Gileadites always had to take account of the position taken by their closest neighbor, Ammon.

The Transjordanian half of Manasseh, the largest northern tribe, had another, equally important, reason for supporting David against Absalom. Absalom was the son of David by his wife Maacah, the daughter of the ruler of the small Aramean kingdom of Geshur. His close blood relations with the Arameans of Geshur made it possible for Absalom to hide among them for three years when he was afraid of punishment for his murder of David's eldest son, Amnon. But the Transjordanian part of the tribe of Manasseh was the immediate neighbor of Aramean Geshur and suffered from the claims that Geshur constantly made to its territory. The members of this tribe were afraid that should Absalom win, he would dispose of their lands to the advantage of his Aramean relatives and patrons. Like the Gileadites, the tribe of Manasseh had no desire to see its relatives, the tribe of Ephraim, grow stronger. It was only natural that one of its leaders concealed Saul's grandson Mephibosheth in the hope that preservation of Saul's dynasty would prevent the Ephraimites from seizing power over the northern tribes. It is difficult to think of a better image of the relations between these two related tribes than the description given by Isaiah, the Judahite prophet: "Each will feed on the flesh of his own offspring: Manasseh will feed on Ephraim, and Ephraim on Manasseh; together they will turn against Judah" (Isaiah 9:20-21).

It is very telling that the Bible calls 'Israelites' only the army of Absalom, which consisted of irregular detachments of tribesmen from the tribes of Israel and Judah, but does not apply this term to the detachments commanded by David. The distinction was probably justified since David's main military force – his mercenaries and Ammonites – was made up of foreigners supported by detachments from the two Transjordanian tribes. There was good reason for David to prefer not to take with him the Ark of the Covenant, but to leave it with the priests in Jerusalem: he was very much aware that the procession of Levites would slow down his progress and that his foreign mercenaries would be unlikely to need this sacred object. Leaving the priests and Levites in Jerusalem allowed him to preserve his forces' maneuverability and to acquire allies and informers in the camp of Absalom. In order to cancel out his opponents' numerical superiority, David's generals, who were more experienced in military matters, compelled Absalom's army to fight in a wooded location, in the so-called Forest of Ephraim: "There Israel's troops were routed by David's men... and the forest swallowed up more men that day than the sword" (2 Samuel 18:7-8). The dense trees proved fatal for Absalom himself: catching his head on a branch, he "was left hanging in midair" and met his death.

Absalom's mutiny was part of the battle for power between the sons of David during the last years of his rule. According to the Bible, David became king when he was 30 years old and ruled for 40 years (seven and a half years over Judah on its own, and then another 33 over the United Monarchy). Thus he was approximately 70 when he died – having lived for a shorter time than many of his comrades (for instance, the military commander Joab or the high priest Abiathar). During the final years of his life he was seriously ill, and this could not have passed unnoticed among his sons and courtiers. The treacherous killing of his first son, Amnon, his son by a Canaanite woman, was merely the first step in the fight for the throne. David's illness forced the various parties that surrounded him to speed up their preparations for seizing power. This same reason also inspired his opponents from the northern tribes, who regarded the alliance with the southern tribes as a merely temporary measure dictated by external circumstance.

The fact that Absalom's mutiny was supported by David's own tribe forced him to make serious concessions to the tribal aristocracy of Judah: he alleviated their tax burden to the detriment of the northern tribes. The indignation felt by the northern tribes led to a spontaneous mutiny. "Now a troublemaker named Sheba son of Bikri, a Benjaminite, happened to be there. He sounded the trumpet and shouted, 'We have no share in David, no part in Jesse's son! Every man to his tent, O Israel!' So all the men of Israel deserted David to follow Sheba son of Bikri. But the men of Judah stayed by their king (2 Samuel 20:1-2). However, unlike the well-planned revolt organized by Absalom, the northern tribes' uprising was poorly organized, with only some of the Israelite tribes taking part. This time, numerical superiority lay with David, and he endeavored to act as quickly as possible to prevent the revolt from spreading and to keep the wavering tribal leaders from becoming involved. Although the second mutiny was on a smaller scale than the first, it was in fact much more dangerous. If Absalom's conspiracy was directed merely against David and his mercenaries, the uprising of Sheba threatened to bring about the break-up of the entire United Monarchy and a split between the northern and southern tribes (between Israel and Judah). Well aware of this, David admitted to one of his commanders: "Now Sheba son of Bikri will do us more harm than Absalom did" (2 Samuel 20:6). In distinction to the account of the mutiny led by the king's son, the Bible is completely silent about the course of Sheba's mutiny, telling us merely of its beginning and end. That the keepers of the tradition should take this approach is quite understandable given that the revolt of the northern tribes was a clear indication of the substantial difference in history and tribal origin between the two groups of Hebrew tribes and a reminder that their unification was a matter not so much of the natural order of things, but of chance, a response to an external threat. However, the first attempt by the northern tribes to rid themselves of the hegemony of the southern tribes ended in failure. Seeing that the uprising had no chance of success, the elders of the city where the mutineers were hiding executed Sheba and handed over his head to David's army.

Sheba's uprising convinced David to take a completely different view of the dynasty of Saul. Given the dissatisfaction and atmosphere of complaint among the northern tribes, the dynasty was a real threat in two respects. First, it remained a symbol of the sovereignty of the northern tribes and their former hegemony over the southern tribes. Second, it was the main rival to David's own dynasty. Saul's descendants could either cut the northern tribes off from the kingdom of David or head the United Monarchy themselves, as had been the case previously. Israel had the upper hand over Judah in all respects, especially numerically and economically, so without the northern tribes' resources in terms of people and finances David would have been unable to control all of Canaan. However, David was unsuccessful in stripping Saul's dynasty of its 'primogeniture' in the way that Jacob had stripped Esau of his. He therefore decided to physically eliminate those descendants of the first king who constituted a threat to his own dynasty. He did not have to look hard for a pretext. Three years of drought were interpreted by David's prophets as divine punishment for the crimes of the house of Saul against the Hivites of Gibeon. The king's counselors suddenly 'remembered' that the Benjaminites and, above all, Saul had violated the peace agreement concluded between the inhabitants of the city of Gibeon and Joshua two centuries earlier. An experienced politician, David did not execute the surviving descendants of Saul himself, but handed over almost all of them – two sons and five grandsons –to their enemies, the Hivites of Gibeon. He took mercy on only one of them, Mephibosheth, who was disabled and whose position was special. As a son of Jonathan, the official heir to Saul, Mephibosheth had a preferential right of accession to the throne ahead of all the other descendants of the first king. After the killing of Ishbosheth, only two of Saul's sons by his concubine Rizpah were left alive. But due to their mother's low social status they had little chance of ascending to the throne. Saul's legitimate grandsons were in a better position, but they too were only the children of his daughter. For this reason Mephibosheth, the son of Jonathan, was the most promising claimant to the throne from Saul's dynasty – in spite of the fact that he had been lame since he was a child. But David did not dare put him to death, since he was the son of his best friend, who had saved David on many an occasion and to whom he had pledged his loyalty. So David found an original way out of the situation: he granted Mephibosheth the special honor of being constantly in the king's presence and in the sight of his servants. With regard to Saul's other descendants David had no obligations – and he lost no time in exploiting this fact. His vengeance was not merely political, but personal as well. All the sons of Saul's elder daughter, Merab – who had been promised to David, but given in marriage to his richer and more influential rival, Adriel of Meholah – were put to death. The destruction of Saul's dynasty rid David of claims to power from the tribe of Benjamin, but did not protect him and his own dynasty from the growing dissatisfaction of the northern tribes.

Solomon's Palace Coup and the Change in Political Course

At the end of his life David was so ill that he practically withdrew from ruling the country. Admittedly, in describing the king's poor condition, the Bible emphasizes not his illness, but his old age: "When King David was very old, he could not keep warm even when they put covers over him" (1 Kings 1:1). Given that this is said of a person who had scarcely reached the age of 70, the cause of his ill health was more likely to be an illness of some kind than extreme decrepitude. The king's approaching death renewed with full force the battle for power between his sons. On this occasion the throne was disputed, even while David was still alive, by two candidates: Adonijah and Solomon. Each had their own group of supporters, who formed what might be seen as political parties. What was at stake was not just the personal ambitions of the two individuals, but the interests of the groups who stood behind them.

Adonijah was supported by David's best-known comrades – the priest Abiathar and Joab the commander. The former represented the interests of the northern dynasty of priests from Shiloh and those Levites who had joined the northern tribes. The latter commanded the irregular military forces of Israel and Judah. This party focused on the interests of all the Hebrew tribes and wished to continue the policies that had been characteristic of the first period in David's reign, i.e. that period when his policymaking had been well balanced and had taken account of the requirements of both the southern and northern tribes. To a certain extent, this was a national party, if such a term may be applied to society of that time. It was opposed by the followers of Solomon: the priest Zadok, the prophet Nathan, and Benaiah, the head of David's guard of mercenaries. Zadok and Nathan represented the interests of the Aaronites and the Jebusite priesthood. Benaiah and his mercenary guards were natural rivals to Joab and the tribal irregular forces. David always tried to ensure that these forces supplemented and balanced each other out, but when, due to his old age and illness, he in effect withdrew from running the country, both armies and their commanders began to compete with one another for influence over the king and his policymaking. At any event, the interests of the tribal aristocracy and the king's guard of mercenaries were directly opposed to one another. If the tribal aristocracy sought as much autonomy as possible, the king's guard was interested in strengthening the king's power and the bureaucracy. Solomon's supporters represented the interests of the southern tribes exclusively – or to be more precise, the interests of Judah, given that Solomon's party could be identified as pro-Judahite. These supporters were most in need of David's guard of mercenaries and depended on them – which suited the interests of the mercenaries themselves. Furthermore, it was in the interest of the guards, keen to preserve their privileged position, to support likewise the privileged position of Judah among the Hebrew tribes: this strengthened Judah's dependence on them and undermined the position of the irregular tribal force in the event of the latter's coming into conflict with the mercenaries. The national party, on the contrary, preferred to rely on the irregular forces of the northern and southern tribes and was afraid of excessive reinforcement of the mercenary guards. We do not know to what extent Adonijah expressed the interests of the northern tribes, but there can be no doubt that he took them into account incomparably more than did Solomon, who represented the pro-Judahite party. It cannot be ruled out that had victory gone to Adonijah, the United Monarchy would not have fallen apart following the death of Solomon.

Adonijah was his father's eldest and so, under the legal norms of the time, was considered his official heir. David himself wanted him to succeed to the kingship. At least, this supposition is backed up by what we find in the Bible: "Now Adonijah, whose mother was Haggith, put himself forward and said, 'I will be king.' So he got chariots and horses ready, with fifty men to run ahead of him. (His father had never rebuked him by asking, 'Why do you behave as you do?')" (I Kings 1:5-6). That Adonijah was the main candidate for the throne is supported by his own eloquent admission, during a conversation with Bathsheba, Solomon's mother: "'As you know,' he said, 'the kingdom was mine. All Israel looked to me as their king. But things changed, and the kingdom has gone to my brother; for it has come to him from the Lord" (1 Kings 2:15). It was Adonijah who looked after state affairs during periods when his father's illness was particularly acute, as we can see from the fact that "Adonijah conferred with Joab son of Zeruiah and with Abiathar the priest, and they gave him their support" (1 Kings 1:7). It is unlikely that, had the king not given his consent, the king's son would have dared to hold festivities for all the people to mark his accession to the throne, and it is all the more doubtful that important officials loyal to David and other sons of the king (apart from Solomon) would have allowed him to have himself hailed 'Long live King Adonijah!' had it not been known that the king's choice had settled on him.

However, another candidate for the throne proved more deft than his brother. While Adonijah was celebrating his accession not far from Jerusalem in the company of the Judahite elders and most of the important officials, dramatic events of an altogether different kind were taking place in the empty capital. Solomon's supporters had secured the support of David's mercenary guards (the main military force in the city) and carried out a palace coup, declaring their candidate the new king. Taking advantage of the helpless position of mortally ill David, they forced him to change his decision and consent to the coronation of another of his sons, Solomon. To achieve this end, they used every argument at their disposal: the prayers and reproaches of Bathsheba, David's wife and Solomon's mother; threatening warnings from the prophet Nathan; and the court intrigues of Benaiah, the head of the guard. Thus it happened that while Adonijah was celebrating, Solomon was being anointed as king. The fact that this happened while David was still alive and with his formal consent served to legitimize Solomon entirely, denying Adonijah's supporters any chance of success. Any attempt at resistance on the part of the latter would have been interpreted as mutiny and been severely put down by David's guard of mercenaries.

The new king did not have his father's magnanimity and, after coming to power, dealt severely with his brother and rival and with those who supported him. Although Adonijah managed to hide in the sanctuary of the Ark of the Covenant, he was first enticed from his hiding place with false promises and then killed under the pretext that he had not renounced his thoughts of the crown. Joab the commander, now an old man, was killed beside the altar to the Lord, where he should have been inviolable. Shimri, leader of the Benjaminites, who had once magnanimously been granted mercy by David, was forced to live exclusively in Jerusalem under the eye of the king's servants and was subsequently executed as a punishment for leaving the city for a short time. Another of David's comrades, the priest Abiathar, whose entire family had been put to death as a punishment for helping David, was forced by Solomon to retire to his fiefdom in the town of Anatot. In their comments on the latter event, the Aaronites who later redacted the Old Testament could not refrain from expressing their satisfaction with the fact that thereupon the high-priesthood passed from the northern dynasty to their southern one. It was the Aaronite redactors who put into the mouth of the dying David orders which he evidently never gave: to execute Joab and Shimri, the leader of the Benjaminites. The fact that Solomon was merely one of David's younger sons did not worry the keepers of the tradition. As far as we can tell, the 'house of Jacob' always had problems with primogeniture, so the Aaronites were used to resorting to all kinds of cunningness in order to explain how the younger son could take precedence over the elder. This began with Jacob, the patriarch and founder of the house, who used deceit to get the better of his elder brother, Esau. His example was followed by Judah, who prevailed over his elder brothers Reuben, Simeon, and Levi. There was nothing surprising in that David was the youngest among his brothers. Solomon's accession was therefore a continuation of the family tradition of the 'house of Jacob' by which younger brothers exploit various pretexts to get the better of their elder brothers.

The keepers of the tradition consider the main achievement of Solomon's reign to be the construction of the magnificent Temple in Jerusalem. However, the erection of this building did not signify a strengthening of the monotheist tendency, but in fact was directed towards an altogether different and purely political objective – to make Jerusalem, the city of the king, the country's principal religious center and to place the main state cult under its complete control. At the same time, there was a second objective – to boost the significance of Judah, the king's homeland, in the context of Solomon's kingdom, which was then still very large. The new king had no use for David's cautious approach (David had rejected the idea of building a central temple to as not to complicate relations with the influential dynasties of priests who were fighting each other for primacy). The new religious center in Jerusalem damaged the interests of the northern tribes and merely strengthened their intention to put an end to the hegemony of the southern tribes, even at the cost of a complete split with them.

The years of Solomon's rule – like, as a matter of fact, those of the reign of David – were by no means a period during which monotheism prevailed, either in the United Monarchy as a whole or in Jerusalem itself. While praising Solomon, the keepers of the tradition were forced to admit that "As Solomon grew old, his wives turned his heart after other gods, and his heart was not fully devoted to the Lord his God, as the heart of David his father had been. He followed Ashtoreth the goddess of the Sidonians, and Milkom the detestable god of the Ammonites. So Solomon did evil in the eyes of the Lord; he did not follow the Lord completely, as David his father had done. On a hill east of Jerusalem, Solomon built a high place for Chemosh the detestable god of Moab, and for Molech the detestable god of the Ammonites. He did the same for all his foreign wives, who burned incense and offered sacrifices to their gods" (1 Kings 11:4-8). Solomon's overt idolatry brought him into conflict even with the priests of the cult of Yahweh, people who were loyal to him. For this reason it is hardly surprising that the Bible has the following to say: "The Lord became angry with Solomon because his heart had turned away from the Lord, the God of Israel, who had appeared to him twice. Although he had forbidden Solomon to follow other gods, Solomon did not keep the Lord's command" (1 Kings 11:9-10). Naturally, the keepers of the tradition interpreted the country's split following Solomon's death as punishment from God for idolatry. In just the same way they explained the failures in his foreign policy that led to the loss of many lands conquered by David.

Compared with the impressive conquests made by his father, who spent most of his life at war, Solomon's foreign policy was emphatically peaceful and defensive. Solomon preferred to build fortresses and fortress walls, unlike his father, who was more accustomed to take these structures by storm and reduce them to ruins. Admittedly, the policy of peace had its price, and one which was by no means small. Almost all the 40 years of Solomon's rule constituted a series of territorial losses and retreats, which by the end of his life reduced what had been an enormous country under David to the size of a modest state situated entirely within the confines of Canaan itself. Solomon lost all of David's gains in Syria, but his largest and most dangerous miscalculation was the loss of Damascus and his allowing the Aramean Damascan kingdom to grow in strength. From this time forwards Aram-Damascus became the northern tribes' main enemy. Solomon's second most important failure was his inability quickly to deal with the mutiny in Edom led by King Adad. The Edomites, who had been routed and subjugated by David and his commander Joab, gained confidence after David's death and managed to put Solomon to a great deal of inconvenience.

Much more successful were Solomon's relations with Egypt. The Egyptians had evidently been very much concerned by the emergence of David's mighty power on their north-eastern border, and for this reason strove to form close links with his successor. Solomon's marriage to the Pharaoh's daughter was probably due not so much to Solomon's own foreign-policy successes as to the strong impression made by his father's military victories. But Solomon was most successful of all in developing relations with his small northern neighbor, the Phoenician city of Tyre – even if these relations had no great military or political significance, but were confined to the field of trade.

It is unlikely that Solomon's foreign policy may be called impressive or successful. His principal achievement was to preserve peace with his neighbors, even if this came at the cost of making concessions. The price for this relative peace had to be paid not by Solomon himself, but by his successors. Solomon saw little attraction in the lands of neighboring states or in military campaigns directed at plundering these lands. He was, though, very much interested in international trade – and it was in the latter field that he achieved his greatest successes. With the help of the Phoenician King Hiram, ruler of the city of Tyre, he built a navy at Ezion Geber, near to modern Eilat, and conducted a large number of profitable trading expeditions to exotic Ophir and Tarshish (places which have yet to be identified with certainty). It was probably only under Solomon that the United Monarchy was actively involved in international trade. An echo of the king's activities of this kind is the Bible's mention of a visit made to Jerusalem by the female ruler of the Sabbean kingdom in southern Arabia.

Solomon's domestic policy-making involved large-scale construction projects throughout the country, the creation of a large and lavish royal court, and maintenance of an expensive army of mercenaries. Solomon built not just the famous temple – which, to judge by the description of it in the Bible, could be considered one of the richest and most beautiful structures of that time – but also a palace, no less beautiful, for himself, upon which he spared no expense, inviting master craftsmen from Phoenicia and buying materials from all corners of the ancient world. He strengthened the city walls at Jerusalem and carried out extensive construction at Hazor, Megiddo, Gezer, Beth Horon, Baalath, and even at far-away Tadmor. The Bible tells us that Solomon built "store cities and the towns for his chariots and for his horses" (1 Kings 9:19). All these storehouses, barracks, and stables were necessary for his permanent army, which had "fourteen hundred chariots and twelve thousand horses..." (1 Kings 10:26). In order to understand the expense Solomon went to in order to create an army of this size, we may turn to statistics provided likewise by the Bible: "They imported a chariot from Egypt for six hundred shekels of silver, and a horse for a hundred and fifty" (1 Kings 10:29). The following example shows the contemporary buying power of this money. At the end of his life, in order to build an altar to the Lord, King David paid 50 silver shekels to the Jebusite Araunah for a large piece of land with a threshing floor and a herd of cattle near Jerusalem. In other words, the entire property of a wealthy peasant constituted merely a 12th part of the cost of a single war chariot.

An expensive army was not the only thing that Solomon spent money on; he also built his own fleet of trading ships at Ezion-Geber on the Red Sea, again hiring numerous craftsmen from Phoenicia for the purpose. Also highly expensive was Solomon's enormous court; "He had seven hundred wives of royal birth and three hundred concubines..." (1 Kings 11:3). In order to have the ability to undertake large-scale construction projects, retain a large army and fleet, and keep a lavish oriental court with an enormous harem, it was necessary to impose on the entire population of the country heavy taxes and onerous obligations regarding provision of labor. The Bible goes into considerable detail in describing these hardships: "King Solomon conscripted laborers from all Israel—thirty thousand men. He sent them off to Lebanon in shifts of ten thousand a month... Solomon had seventy thousand carriers and eighty thousand stonecutters in the hills, as well as thirty-three hundred foremen who supervised the project and directed the workers" (1 Kings 5:13-16). Furthermore, to pay for cedar and cypress trees delivered to him from the mountains of Lebanon and for the gold and craftsmen supplied by Phoenicia, Solomon gave king Hiram 20 Israelite cities in Galilee, in the north of the country. Even if all these figures given in the Bible are heavily exaggerated, this nevertheless adds up to an enormous tax burden and grueling obligations to provide labor imposed exclusively on the northern tribes and the Canaanite population. It is no surprise, then, that the lavishness of Solomon's court, the size of his army, and the scale of the construction projects carried out, in combination with the lack of concern shown for the interests of the northern tribes, sowed the seeds for the political crisis which now overtook the United Monarchy. It was only a matter of time before there would be a new mutiny by the northern tribes. On this occasion, given that Saul's dynasty had been destroyed, leadership of the northerners passed to the traditional head of the 'house of Joseph', the tribe of Ephraim. The discontented were led by one of this tribe's leaders – Jeroboam, son of Nebat. However, the uprising was put down before it had properly got underway, and Jeroboam fled to Egypt, where he remained until Solomon's death.

Contradictory Accounts about the Epoch of David and Solomon
Upon failing to find sufficient archaeological confirmation, certain historians have cast doubt upon both the military might and conquests of King David and the ambitious construction projects and economic boom during the rule of Solomon. They consider this to be overt idealization or great exaggeration on the part of the keepers of the tradition, who were writing during a later period. From the point of view of such historians, the buildings in Megiddo, Hazor, and Gezer – projects which are ascribed to Solomon – were in fact erected a century later by the Israelite king Ahab, and Judah and Jerusalem of the 10th century BCE were too under-populated and insufficiently developed economically to become the center of a large state at this point in history. As proof of this contention, they point to continuation of the Canaanite cultural stratum in the valleys of Palestine and the lack of traces of monumental structures in Jerusalem at that time.

It is indeed the case that the archaeological data relating to this period are clearly insufficient or too contradictory to confirm the information given in the Bible, which continues to remain our only documentary source for the United Monarchy. However, those who seek in David and Solomon's united state well-developed monarchy such as that of Babylonia, Assyria, or the New Kingdom in Egypt are bound to be disappointed. Canaan was always on the cultural and political periphery of ancient civilization in the Near East. The main centers of that civilization were in Mesopotamia and the Nile Valley. Monarchies that were well developed from the point of view of culture, society, and economics came into being in Canaan much later. It took until the 9th-8th centuries BCE for the Northern Kingdom (Israel) to become such a center and until the 7th-6th centuries BCE for the Southern Kingdom (Judah) to become one. Moreover, the United Monarchy of David and Solomon was the state of the Habiru tribes, who were the first in the history of Canaan to unite the entire country. These former semi-nomads properly settled on the land only in the 12th-11th centuries BCE; they were peasants, shepherds, and warriors. Craft and trade were at that time the business of the Canaanites, but not of the Habiru. Thus there was good reason for Solomon to invite all kinds of craftsmen to come from Phoenicia; he had no craftsmen – and still less, skilled craftsmen – of his own. It was the Phoenicians who became the Israelites' teachers in all types of craft, art, and trade. Furthermore, the southern Hebrew tribes who populated Judah were the less developed part of the *Habiru*; they had returned from Egypt and settled on the land later than the other Habiru. However, if we take into account the Midianite and Edomite nomadic clans who joined them, then we may define Judah as the state of the Habiru and Sutu. For this reason, the United Monarchy – and all the more so, David and Solomon's own homeland of Judah – could in no way have been considered a developed or mature state. This did not mean, however, that David's army, which included irregular detachments supplied by both the southern and the more multitudinous northern tribes, could not have conquered extensive territory up to the river Euphrates. History furnishes many examples of nomads or former nomads who took possession of enormous areas of land and held sway over peoples who were better developed than themselves from the point of view of culture or economics, although their own regions and capital cities were unimpressive. We should not forget that although the Habiru were the dominant ethnos in Canaan from the point of view of military might, they were inferior to the other Canaanite and Amorite peoples in social and cultural development. The fact that many Canaanite cities remained untouched during the United Monarchy is by no means evidence that they were not subject to or part of the kingdom. On the contrary, the Bible emphasizes that at the end of the era of the judges there was already peace between the Hebrew tribes and the local Amorite and Canaanite peoples, especially during the Philistine expansion in Canaan. The best example of this is the Canaanite city of Keilah in Judah, which was never attacked by David (instead, he defended it against the Philistines). Other examples are the Hivite cities of Shechem and Gibeon, which from the time of Joshua forwards the Israelites, far from destroying, defended from their enemies. If Moab, Ammon, Edom, and the Aramean kingdoms in Syria were incorporated in David's kingdom by force, for Canaanite and Amorite cites voluntary and peaceful alliance with the United Monarchy was more typical. In the United Monarchy these cities saw a force capable of protecting them from their enemies and of putting an end to internecine wars. Moreover, David gave them sufficient autonomy with regard to internal affairs. It is telling that in its account of the campaigns against Philistia and of the conquests of Transjordan and Syria the Bible maintains complete silence with regard to the Canaanite and Amorite neighbors. There is nothing surprising in the fact that during the United Monarchy these cities managed to avoid destruction and upheavals. The conquest of Jebusite Jerusalem was more an exception to the general rule – and

//
one due to this city's special geographical position as a wedge between areas in the possession of the southern and northern tribes.

As for the second part of the argument, i.e. the lack of traces of monumental buildings relating to 10th century BCE Jerusalem, this does not really prove anything very much. It is well known that Jerusalem was on more than one occasion razed to the ground by enemies and then rebuilt by its new rulers using the foundations and stones of the buildings that had previously stood on this spot. Furthermore, Jerusalem today stands directly on the site of the ancient city of Jerusalem, which makes it impossible to carry out full-scale excavations; it is therefore too early to draw any conclusions about the lack of traces of monumental structures built at that time.

Interestingly, all the local peoples of Canaan whose expulsion was called for by the Pentateuch and the book of Joshua as recompense for their idolatry in actual fact not only remained safely where they were, but also (for the most part, peacefully) became part of the United Monarchy. This was the case with the Canaanites, Amorites, Hivites, Jebusites, Perizzites, Girgashites, and Hittites. Even the Amalekites, the bitter enemies of the 'house of Jacob', continued to live nomadically in the Negev as if nothing had happened. It seems likely that all the calls to drive out the idolaters were added to the Bible at a much later date, in the 6th-5th centuries BCE when the final redaction of the Old Testament was being carried out. But the majority of these people had by then already entirely intermarried with the Hebrew tribes. If that is the case, then what was the purpose of inserting such severe demands into an account of the past? The only possible purpose was to influence the present and the future and to protect the as yet unconsolidated monotheistic faith from the influence of pagan religions as a result of intermarriage with other peoples. We have very reason to suppose that, in spite of the cruelty characteristic of that age, ethnic processes in Canaan were shaped not by the expulsion or destruction of closely related West Semitic peoples, but by their convergence and intermarriage. Unlike in later times, wars during this era were conducted not in order to physically eradicate or drive out peoples, but in order to plunder and exploit them. The differences in religious faiths were likewise not an obstacle to tribes and peoples becoming assimilated. The extremely distressing accounts of how David treated the Edomites, Ammonites, and Moabites were probably extreme exaggeration added to the biblical text during the times of the imprisonment in Babylon or even later. Offended by the traitorous behavior of their relatives, the keepers of the tradition included these passages in the books of the Kings and Samuel as an edifying example of how to treat bad neighbors and idolaters. In any case, these episodes completely contradict both events that had occurred before and events that came afterwards. It is difficult to accept the assertion that "Joab and all the Israelites stayed there for six months, until they had destroyed all the men in Edom" (1 Kings 11:16). If this was indeed the case, then how was it that these long since eliminated Edomites continued to live in Edom and, moreover, occupied southern Judah after the destruction of the First Temple? The same goes for the Ammonites, whom David led out of Rabbah, consigning them "to labor with saws and with iron picks and axes, and he made them work at brickmaking. David did this to all the Ammonite towns" (2 Samuel 12:31). It is hardly likely that after this the Ammonites would have selflessly made haste to help David when the latter was fleeing from Jerusalem, escaping his own son Absalom. It is just as difficult to believe that, after defeating the Moabites, he would have "made them lie down on the ground and measured them off with a length of cord. Every two lengths of them were put to death, and the third length was allowed to live" (2 Samuel 8:2). Here we are talking of the same David, the great-grandson of a Moabite woman, who hid his parents from King Saul with the Moabites since he trusted them above all and was in good relations with them. Moreover, the very fact that the book of Ruth is included in the biblical canon is evidence not just of intermarriage between the Moabites and the Judahites, but also of admission of a special relationship between the Moabites and the southern tribes. These acts of cruelty were not a mass phenomenon, but vengeance wreaked by David on specific groups of his opponents among the peoples of Transjordan; for didactic reasons, however, the keepers of the tradition generalized these events out of all proportion.

The Bible's account of the last years of David's reign mentions Araunah the Jebusite, on whose land the king built an altar to mark the end of the plague. This name is clearly not Semitic in origin, but is more likely to be Indo-Aryan, although the Jebusites were Western Semites. Here we find confirmation of the fact that Aryan and Hurrian groups among the population managed to penetrate into and settle in various parts of Canaan – most likely during the period when the Hyksos had already lost control of this country and the Egyptians had yet to seize it.

In our understanding of the ethnic make-up of Canaan during the United Monarchy there is a further problem relating to the location of Geshur and the Geshurites. As we know, one of the wives of King David and the mother of the mutinous Absalom was Maacah, the daughter of Talmai, the ruler of Geshur. The Bible on the one hand places Geshur in Aram, i.e. in the north-east of the country, and on the other hand talks of the Geshurites as one of the hostile peoples of the desert who, together with the Amalekites, lived in Negev and on Sinai (2 Samuel 15:8; 1 Samuel 27:8). Evidently, this was a mistake which proved impossible to correct in good time since this part of the Old Testament was compiled and redacted in the 6th-5th centuries BCE when the Geshurites did not yet exist as a distinct people. In any case, they were a small West Semitic people who merged with their larger neighbors.

It was probably during the rule of David and Solomon that the initial version of the first four books of the Pentateuch was written. Their authors evidently made use of the few written texts left by Moses and his successors – the first keepers of the tradition – as well as of oral narratives taken from the epic tradition of both the southern and northern tribes. The political interests of the United Monarchy required that the necessity of the unification of the two principal partners in the alliance – Israel and Judah – be justified and that Judah's leading role be legitimized. The new state and its kings needed not merely a magnificent court, but also a history of their own that would be an integral part of their image for both the inhabitants of the country and for the world outside. Furthermore, the keepers of the tradition themselves – the Levites and the Aaronites – had an interest in sanctifying the roots of the cult of Yahweh and of connecting the latter with fundamental strata in the history of both the southern and the northern tribes. For this reason, the first compilers of the Pentateuch were faced with a task of some difficulty – to create a unified history and genealogy for two different groups of Hebrew tribes; and this task they carried out brilliantly. They managed with extraordinary skill to connect the narratives of two groups: the patriarchs of the southern tribes (Abraham, Isaac, and Jacob) became simultaneously the forefathers of the northern tribes; and the founder of the northern tribes, Israel, merged with the patriarch of the southern tribes, Jacob. The 'house of Joseph' became part of Jacob's large family. The shared genealogy necessitated that the history of both these groups likewise be unified. It was this that gave rise to the idea of their simultaneous departure for Egypt, their joint stay in Egypt during the course of four centuries, and their joint exodus under the leadership of Moses. In this new history Joshua, the head of the northern tribes, was successor to Moses, the leader of the southern tribes, and his conquests in Canaan were the joint achievement of both tribal groups. On the other hand, the receipt of the commandments handed down on Mount Sinai and Moses' monotheism became the joint inheritance of both the southern and northern tribes. This symbiosis of the cultural and historical legacy of the two different groups enriched each of them – just as it enriched the spiritual life of all humanity – but it has proved a stumbling block for modern historians and archaeologists. For where today's historians look for the historical path taken by a single people are in fact concealed two distinct histories and two peoples.

Later, after the break-up of the United Monarchy, this initial unified version of the history of the Hebrew tribes served as the basis for two sources of the modern biblical texts – the Yahwist source (J) in the Southern Kingdom and the Elohist source (E) in the northern. The same initial version was known to the authors of the third and later biblical source – the so-called Deuteronomist (D), who created the following books: Deuteronomy (the last part of the Pentateuch), Joshua, Samuel, and Kings. This paved the way for a unique historical, literary, religious and philosophical work which has no equal in either the ancient world or the modern.

Chapter 8

The Divided Monarchy

The Secession of Northern Tribes

The United Monarchy did not exist for long – for a mere 100 years or so. Of this period David and Solomon ruled for approximately 40 years each, and Saul for about 20-25 years. According to the Bible (there are no other sources for this period), the union between the southern and northern tribes ended with the death of Solomon, in approximately 928 BCE, whereupon Solomon's son Rehoboam set off for Shechem, intending to secure the backing of the elders there for his kingship. At Shechem representatives of the northern tribes asked him to reduce the tax burden imposed on them by his father. Rehoboam reflected for three days on this request. Experienced advisors who had been in the service of his father tried to persuade him that he should make concessions to the leaders of the northern tribes; however, his friends considered it out of the question to make concessions of any kind. In the end, it was the latter's opinion that prevailed, and Rehoboam haughtily declared that he would not only not reduce the level of tribute and obligations to be paid, but would increase it still further: "My father made your yoke heavy; I will make it even heavier. My father scourged you with whips; I will scourge you with scorpions.'… When all Israel saw that the king refused to listen to them, they answered the king: 'What share do we have in David, what part in Jesse's son? To your tents, O Israel!" (1 Kings 12:14-16).

Thus it was that the northern and southern tribes again went their own separate ways and the historical fates of Israel and Judah were again divided. According to one of the versions in the Bible, Rehoboam, "after listening to the word of the Lord", conveyed to him by the prophet Shemaiah, renounced his intention to force the mutinous Israelites into submission. However, according to another version, "There was continual warfare between Rehoboam and Jeroboam" (1 Kings 12:24; 14:30). Evidently, the truth lay somewhere in the middle of these diametrically opposite assertions. Rehoboam could not have failed to try to suppress the revolt of the northern tribes using military means, but the latter's numerical advantage was so great that the Judahite king very soon gave up all attempts to restore his authority by means of force. At the same time, the hostile relations between the two former allies continued for the entire period of 17 years during which Rehoboam was on the throne. This is what was meant by the second version given in the Bible.

Everything that we know from the Bible about the dissolution of the United Monarchy amounts to no more than small fragments of the history of that time. Additionally, these fragments were recorded only in the 7th -5th centuries BCE, i.e. 300-500 years after the events themselves, when the compilers of the texts already knew the sad end that had befallen both kingdoms (first the northern and then the southern). Knowledge of these outcomes allowed the compilers – and subsequently the redactors of the book of Kings – to structure their account in such a way as to make it maximally didactic as edification for future generations. The main principle applied in selection of the ancient texts and their editing was not historical, but religious. The authors were interested not so much in history as in the possibility of using examples taken from history to denounce idolatry, preach monotheism, and likewise get their own back on the opponents of the cult of Yahweh in both the northern and Southern Kingdoms. This means that the task confronting us is not easy: we must reconstruct the events of that time on the basis of a very limited number of fragments, taking account of the fact that these fragments are more didactic than historical in character.

Above all, we cannot escape noting the fact that Rehoboam, unlike David and Solomon, had to come to Shechem, the principal city of the northern tribes, in order to secure the elders' agreement to his kingship. His grandfather David, as we know, did not need to travel anywhere for his coronation; on the contrary, the leaders of the northern tribes themselves came to him in Hebron to ask him to be their king. Nor did Rehoboam's father, Solomon, have any need to present himself to the Israelites; his kingship was affirmed in Jerusalem in accordance with a decision taken by David. In this respect Rehoboam was in a far weaker position – one which was much closer to that of the first king of the Israelites, Saul, who had been dependent on the approval of the tribal leaders. It is hardly coincidental that his experienced advisors recommended him to be a 'servant to these people' – i.e. to the elders of the northern tribes, seeing in this the only possibility of avoiding a split. Thus the monarchical power which had been absolute and unrestricted under David and Solomon once more became conditional and limited, as it had been under Saul. All this must make us suspect that the negotiations at Shechem in fact occurred not before, but after the mutiny of the northern tribes, since their representatives spoke with the new king from a position of strength, forcing him to present himself to them in person at Shechem and to undergo what would have been for an oriental despot a humiliating ceremony of having his regal status confirmed. The fact that the Ephraimite Jeroboam, who was considered a runaway criminal under Solomon, had managed to return from Egypt and was present at the talks as one of the leaders of the northerners only confirms the supposition that the meeting involving the king occurred after the northern tribes had already risen in revolt. Rehoboam was compelled to agree to these talks because his previous attempts to use force had been unsuccessful – and this in turn explains why he listened to the prophet Shemaiah and decided not to go to war with the Israelites.

It is also extremely probable that, out of sympathy for the closely related Davidic dynasty, the Aaronites who redacted the biblical texts depicted Rehoboam's unenviable position in a more favorable light and attributed the split between the northern and southern tribes to mistakes made by the young king and his friends. But Rehoboam could hardly be called young: when he ascended to the throne, he was already 41 years old. It is another matter that he was unable to significantly reduce the pressure of taxation on the northern tribes since this would have meant renouncing his lavish court and the greater part of his army of mercenaries or transferring the unbearable burden of taxation to his own tribe of Judah. Both the latter options were unacceptable to him. The Israelites were evidently keen that the alliance between northerners and southerners should be recreated in the form of a confederative state of the kind that had existed during the first period of Saul's rule.

At the moment when the United Monarchy split the tribe of Benjamin supported not the northern tribes to which it was closely related and not even the 'house of Joseph', of which it was part, but Judah and the dynasty of David, i.e. the main rivals of Saul's dynasty. This paradox is confirmation of the serious conflict that existed within the 'house of Joseph' between the tribe of Ephraim, which always laid claim to the role of leader, and the tribes of Manasseh and Benjamin, which were afraid of their ambitious kinsmen becoming excessively strong. This reveals to us the identity of the 'troublemakers' who had been reluctant to recognize the authority of the Benjaminite Saul. We can say that in all probability they were Ephraimites. In the light of this fact it becomes clear why one of the leaders of the tribe of Manasseh – Machir, the son of Ammiel – had supported King David when the northern tribes who acknowledged the authority of Absalom moved against him.

Would it have been possible to avoid dissolution of the United Monarchy? Probably not. The fact that during the 200 years when they existed separately (928-722 BCE), Israel and Judah never again made any attempt to unite, even during times when relations between them were at their best, is evidence of the objective and inevitable character of this split. After all, what was it that the southern and the northern tribes had in common? Were they closely related by blood? Probably not. From the point of view of blood relations, the 'house of Jacob's cursed enemy Amalek was much closer to it than the 'house of Joseph'. The story of the two tribal groups sharing patriarchs and of the 12 sons of Jacob, the founders of the southern and northern tribes, emerged during the United Monarchy for entirely understandable political reasons. Why did the 'house of Jacob' unite with the 'house of Joseph', rather than with Edom, Moab, or Ammon, who were closer to it? There can only be one answer to this question: the northern and southern tribes, after returning from Egypt to Canaan, found themselves in the position of Habiru, i.e. were in effect homeless, dispossessed of the tribal territory that had once been theirs. Thus it was their lengthy stay in Egypt and then their enforced homelessness in Canaan that were the political and social factors which forced the two different tribal groups to unite, along with those Amorite tribes which joined them on their way out of Egypt. Memories of the vicissitudes of fate in Egypt were of such importance to both groups that even after the dissolution of the United Monarchy in both separate kingdoms (Judah and Israel) the principal festive occasion continued to be Passover, the celebration of the Exodus from Egypt.

However, it is not sentimental memories of the past that unite people, but the entirely material interests of the present – which is why, after the northern and then the southern tribes managed to conquer part of Canaan and acquire their own territory there, their alliance naturally fell apart. Neither during the time of Joshua nor during the period of the judges was there ever a constant alliance between the northern and southern tribes. The Israelite tribal alliance that we know of was an alliance not of 12, but of 10 tribes: the 'house of Joseph', which was already in Canaan, and those Amorite tribes, including the southern tribe of Reuben, which Moses had brought out of Egypt. The two southern tribes of Judah and Simeon first joined the alliance only during the United Monarchy.

The main motivation for the alliance between the northerners and southerners was the expansion of the Philistines, something which they were unable to withstand each on their own. After the external danger had receded, the northern tribes began to find that their alliance with the southern tribes – or rather the latter's hegemony over them – weighed heavily up on them, as is evidenced both by Sheba's uprising during the last years of David's rule and by Jeraboam's attempt at a similar mutiny during the kingship of Solomon. The southern Davidic dynasty clearly impinged upon the interests of the northern tribes by imposing upon them and the local peoples of Canaan a large number of taxes and obligations regarding provision of labor (while the tribe of Judah had a privileged status and was free of the obligation to pay if not all, then most taxes and dues). The position of the northern tribes deteriorated still further during the rule of Solomon, who engaged in extensive and expensive construction projects throughout the country. The famous temple in Jerusalem, the palace of Solomon himself, the numerous defensive fortifications, and the barracks and storehouses were built mainly at the expense of the northern tribes, who also had to support Solomon's lavish court and his large army of mercenaries. Merely for help in building the Temple in Jerusalem and for decorating his palace Solomon gave Hiram, King of the city of Tyre, '20 cities in the land of Galilee'. This was undoubtedly done against the wishes of the Israelites themselves and must in part have reinforced their discontent with the rule of the southern king. The interests of the northerners were likewise impinged upon by Solomon's foreign policy. Solomon mainly concentrated on defending the south of the country; he, for example, did not spare resources for the war with the Edomite ruler Adad, but looked with indifference upon the growing Aramean threat from the north. His passivity on the country's northern frontiers resulted in the Aramean kingdom of Damascus being allowed to gain in strength and become the northern tribes' principal enemy. Had Solomon's military power and authority been weaker, the union of the northern and southern tribes would have collapsed during his rule.

Possibly, the alliance would have been more viable had it been headed by representatives of the northern tribes such as the tribes of the 'house of Joseph', rather than by the southern Davidic dynasty. However multitudinous the southern tribe of Judah, it was still a clear minority among the Hebrew tribes. Had Saul's northern dynasty managed to stay in power, it would have had a better chance of maintaining a balanced approach to policy-making than the Davidic dynasty. Saul's dynasty successfully expressed the interests of both the northern tribes as a whole and the 'house of Joseph' in particular. At the same time, since it was represented by the smallest tribe, it was compelled to take account of the interests of the other tribes, on relations with whom its fate depended entirely. Furthermore, the Benjaminites were not merely the most southern of the northern tribes, but also proximate neighbors of Judah, and for this reason they tended to take more account of Judahite interests. Possibly, it was these considerations which lay behind the leaders of the Hebrew tribes' decision to choose Saul.

Economically and socially, Israel was much more developed than Judah. The northern and central areas of Canaan which Israel occupied were densely populated agricultural regions with numerous towns and cities. On the contrary, the southern parts of the country which belonged to Judah were much more thinly populated and their inhabitants were mainly involved in cattle rearing. Here there were far fewer cities and those that did exist, with the exception of Jerusalem, were smaller than cities in the north and center of the country. This contrast in development between the north and south of Canaan was mainly explained by the difference in natural conditions. The regions that were most fertile and suitable for agriculture were in the northern part of Canaan, which possessed more abundant rainfall and the main sources of water, while the south of the country consisted of mountainous, arid regions that were more suited to cattle-rearing than to agriculture. The contrast in population size was equally great: the northern tribes were about twice as populous as the southern tribes. But Israel's numerical superiority over Judah was a matter of more than this. The Israelite tribes constituted merely the ruling minority among the population of the Northern Kingdom. The Mediterranean coast, Galilee, and the Jezreel and Jordan valleys were mainly populated with Canaanite and Amorite peoples, who further increased the difference between Israel and Judah. Of course, there were the same peoples living in Judah, but in relatively small numbers due to the difficult natural conditions. For this reason the southern Hebrew tribes constituted a larger proportion of the total population in Judah than did the northern tribes in Israel, but it is likely that they still made up less than half the total. Archaeological information on the density of the population of Canaan at that time gives us reason to suppose that the population of Israel was at least 5-6 times that of Judah. In the light of such a large difference between the two parts of the United Monarchy, the actual hegemony of the southern over the northern tribes was unnatural and could not last.

The differences between Israel and Judah amounted to more than just the difference in levels of social and economic development and the lack of direct kinship. There is good reason to suppose that these tribal groups were even distinct from one another from the point of view of anthropology. For instance, among the northern tribes there was a tendency for brachycephaly, whereas the southern tribes had a tendency for dolichocephaly. And yet both groups had identical ethnic roots, originally came from northwestern Mesopotamia, the common homeland of the Semites, and should have been anthropologically identical. Where then did the southern Hebrew tribes get their dolichocephaly? It is very likely that this happened in Egypt. As is well known, the ancient Egyptians were very noticeably dolicephalic and even limited intermarriage with them could have led to the emergence of the same characteristics in the Hebrews. Given that the southern tribes spent 430 years in Egypt and the northern tribes not more than 250, we may state with certainty that the 'house of Jacob' had far greater opportunity for intermarriage with the Egyptians than did the 'house of Joseph'. We should note that according to the book of Exodus, the Hebrews lived together with the Egyptians. There was good reason for Moses to give orders that the houses of his fellow tribesmen should be marked with the blood of sacrificial animals in order that the 'angel of death' should strike down only the Egyptians' firstborn. Had the Hebrew tribes lived separately from the Egyptians, there would have been no need to distinguish their houses from those of the Egyptians. Nor can we rule out that some of the nomadic groups who joined the southern tribes during their wandering through the desert were dolichocephalic. In any case it is clear that the by no means identical historical paths followed by the two Hebrew groups led to the accumulation of certain anthropological differences between them.

Generally, the historical paths taken by the 'house of Joseph' and the 'house of Jacob' displayed more differences than similarities. After leaving their native lands – the upper courses of the Tigris and the Euphrates – the two houses immediately went different ways: the former set off in a south-western direction, into Syria and Canaan, and the latter in a south-eastern one, into Mesopotamia. If the northern tribes came to Canaan in the 23rd century BCE, the southern ones arrived not earlier than the 20th century, having had time to pass through the whole of Mesopotamia and to stay in its most southern parts, in Sumer. If the ancestors of the Israelites took possession of the northern and central parts of Canaan by force, the forefathers of the Judahites settled in the southern, semi-desert regions of the country in a more or less peaceful fashion. The 'house of Joseph' and the 'house of Jacob' left for Egypt at different times and returned to Canaan at different times. If the 'house of Joseph' was among the Hyksos conquerors of Egypt, sharing in the latter's victories and defeats, the 'house of Jacob' arrived peacefully in the Nile Delta and had nothing in common with the Hyksos. Admittedly, in Egypt both these tribal groups had very similar experiences: they began by flourishing under the patronage of the Pharaohs, but subsequently suffered oppression. Their departure from Egypt was similarly tough, and their return to Canaan, the land which they had left long ago, was equally difficult. For two and half centuries (from the 15th to 12th centuries BCE) they were separated from one another: the 'house of Jacob' was in slavery in Egypt, while the 'house of Joseph' became homeless Habiru in Canaan. The years of trouble and the sunset of the New Kingdom in Egypt made it possible for Moses to lead the Hebrews out of the Nile Delta and for Joshua to conquer part of Canaan for them. The 'house of Joseph' and the 'house of Jacob' properly came together for the first and last time only in the United Monarchy, the state which brought together the northern and southern Habiru, and this was mainly as a result of the Philistine threat. It was then too that the keepers of the tradition – the Levites and the Aaronites – merged the family trees and narratives of the northern and southern tribes to create a single story. Thus the southern patriarchs Abraham and Isaac became ancestors of the 'house of Joseph' too and Israel, the name of the forefather of the northern tribes, came to signify likewise Jacob, the ancestor of the southern tribes. But the two peoples could not co-exist for long in the same harness, and especially when the junior partner was commanding the senior. The union fell apart, and fell apart for ever.

130   Israel and Judah: How Two Peoples Became One

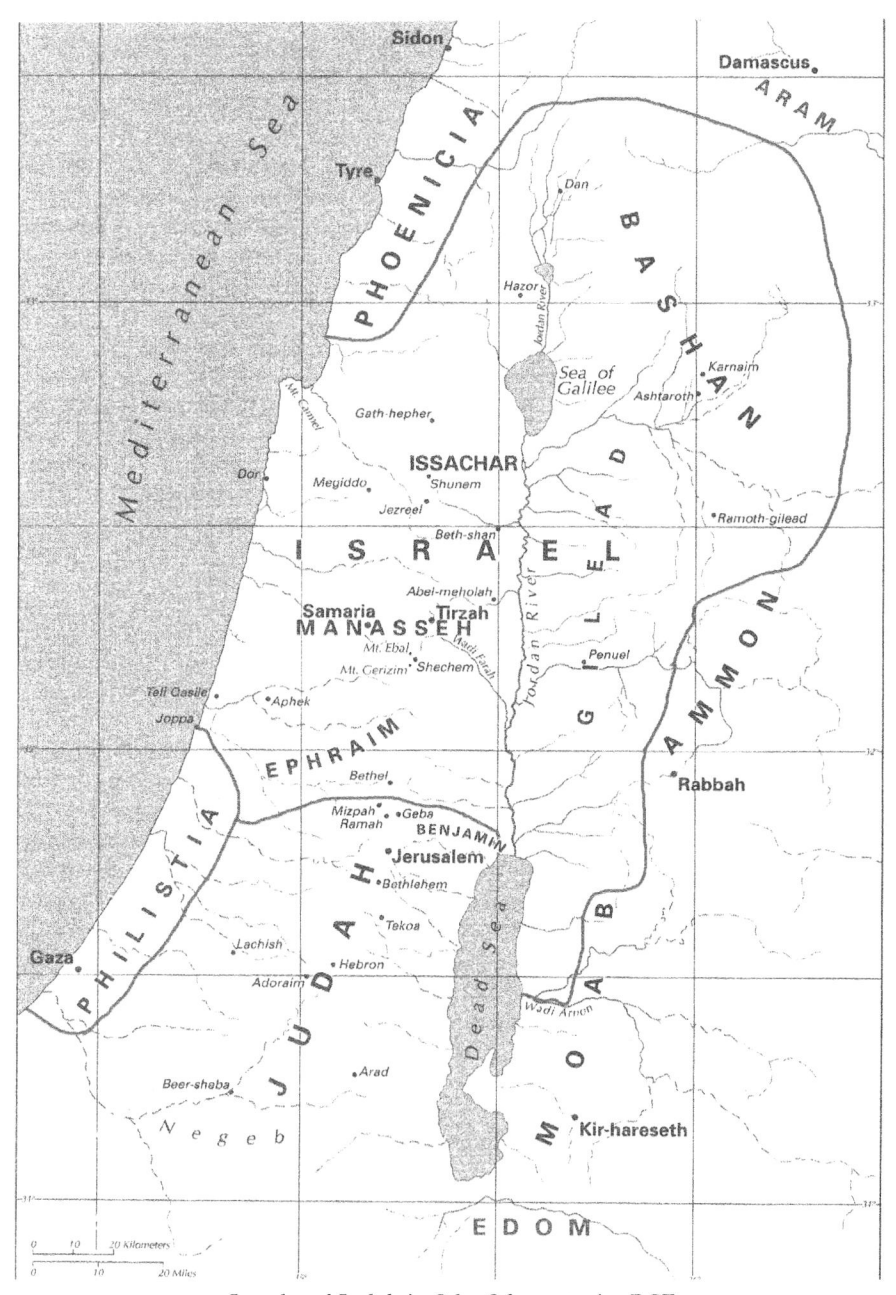

Israel and Judah in 9th - 8th centuries BCE.

The Divided Monarchy

The break-up of the alliance resulted in the formation of two unequal kingdoms: the Israelite kingdom, which was the largest and most militarily powerful, and the Judahite, which was considerably smaller and weaker. The two kingdoms were separate states of the northern and southern Hebrew tribes. Rehoboam, the son of Solomon, was fated to become the first king of Judah, while the first king of Israel was Jeroboam, one of the leaders of Ephraim's tribe. Jerusalem, the capital of the United Monarchy, remained the principal city of Judah, while Jeroboam took as his residence Shechem, the largest city in central Canaan, which had been the stronghold of the 'house of Joseph' since before the conquests made by Joshua.

However, the split between the Hebrew tribes had serious consequences not just for these tribes themselves, but for the whole of Canaan. After dividing, Israel and Judah were unable to keep hold of Transjordan for long; and the kinsmen of the southern tribes, Edom, Moab, and Ammon, gradually re-established their independence. Thus, instead of a single United Monarchy, Canaan now had five small states of Amorite origin. If we add to these the cities of Philistia, which after the break-up of the United Monarchy became completely independent, then we see that what had until recently been a united Canaan had now broken apart into six centers of power which were constantly fighting among themselves. The largest of these centers was Israel, which controlled the most developed northern and central parts of the country. After Israel in terms of importance and military power came Judah, Philistia, Moab, Ammon, and Edom. The temporary strengthening of particular centers and weakening of others led to periodic wars between them and to changes in ownership of territories, returning Canaan to the chronic instability which has been so characteristic of the entire history of this country. The main problem, however, was that following the break-up of the United Monarchy, Canaan once again became vulnerable to invasion by foreigners. Remarkably, during the rule of Solomon, neither Egypt in the south nor the Aramean states in the north had dared to attack the United Monarchy. But five years later, following the division of the country, the Egyptian pharaoh Sheshonq I (the biblical Shishak) plucked up the courage to carry out a plundering raid on Judah and Israel, given that separately these kingdoms were no longer strong enough to resist him. In just the same way the Arameans from the neighboring kingdom of Damascus started attacking the northern districts of Israel almost immediately after the breakup of the alliance between the southern and northern tribes.

Why did Canaan, unlike the great river civilizations of Egypt and Mesopotamia, almost never constitute a single whole? Why was it always divided into warring states and tribes, although the absolute majority of these had common ethnic roots and a common culture? One of the most important factors keeping these related peoples apart was probably the different natural conditions in which they lived. The relatively small area of land occupied by Canaan comprises neighboring regions which are utterly different in terms of climate, soil, and terrain. Galilee, for instance, has abundant rainfall and water resources, while the Negev is arid and semi-desert. The sun-baked Judean Hills in the south and snowy Mount Hermon in the north loom over the Jordan Rift Valley, which is the deepest rift on the Earth. The picturesque freshwater Lake Kinnereth (Sea of Galilee), which teems with fish, is the utter opposite of the saltiest and most lifeless lake in the world, the Dead Sea. Fertile valleys such as the Shephelah, the Jezreel Valley, and the Jordan Valley offered ideal conditions for agriculture, while the greater part of Transjordan and the south of the country were suitable only for cattle rearing. If the shore regions were open and easily traversable, many interior regions of Judea, Moab, and Ammon were considered difficult to access. All these diverse conditions existed within a very small territory which was only a little larger than the Nile Delta. It was this diversity of relief and climate that determined the different ways in which its population lived economically and socially, while the fact that the terrain was so difficult to cross helped preserve the distinct peoples which lived there.

The second important factor which served to separate the related peoples of Canaan was that their development had taken very different paths. Although the Canaanites and the Amorites were two groups of peoples who shared the same ethnic roots, the routes which they had taken through history were far from identical. The Canaanites first appeared in Canaan 1000 years before the Amorites and, by occupying the valleys that were most suited to agriculture, were able to secure the lead in social, economic, and cultural development. There are noticeable differences to be seen between the Amorite peoples of Canaan too. Some, such as the Hivites, Perizzites, Jebusites, and the Amorites of Hazor, settled on the land; others continued for a long time to live nomadically. But even among the nomadic Amorites there were substantial differences. Some – the northern Hebrews (Israel), and the southern Hebrews (Jacob), for instance – departed for Egypt and lived there for hundreds of years; others, such as the Shasu (Sutu), continued to live as nomads on their tribal lands in Transjordan (subsequently forming the tribes of Ammon, Moab, and Edom). These Shasu also included the semi-nomadic Amorites from the 'kingdom of Sihon' mentioned in the Bible.

Thus, in spite of having a common language and origin, many Canaanite and Amorite peoples followed historical paths which were just as different from one another as geographical regions such as Galilee and the Negev. Differences in both the natural environment and histories of the peoples of Canaan made it impossible for this country to unite. Only the foreign rule exercised by Egypt, Assyria, and Babylon was capable of uniting divided Canaan; however, price paid for this 'unification' was excessively high. Neighboring Syria and Phoenicia, which were likewise split up into a number of small states, were in a similar position: they united only under the rule of foreign conquerors. Even the histories of the Egyptian and Mesopotamian civilizations, though, offer numerous examples confirming the importance of natural conditions. For instance, although the climate and terrain of Upper and Lower Egypt contained substantially less variation than those found in Galilee and the Negev, these parts of the same Nile river civilization were also subject to rivalry and antagonism which resulted in Egypt periodically splitting into two kingdoms. The same may be said of the area between the rivers Tigris and Euphrates. The natural and historical differences between southern, central, and northern Mesopotamia resulted in constant fighting between the different states – first, between Sumer and Akkad and then between Babylonia, Assyria, and Mitanni. If the populations of Sumer and Mitanni were unrelated to the Semites, most inhabitants of the two neighboring Mesopotamian kingdoms, Assyria and Babylonia – the two states that were most hostile to one another – belonged to the same group of Semitic peoples. The Egyptians of Upper and Lower Egypt were likewise ethnically close to one another, which did not, however, prevent them going to war against one another as they fought for control of the country.

Unlike in Judah, political authority in Israel was notable for being chronically unstable. Whereas, following the break-up of the United Monarchy and before the destruction of the First Temple, i.e. during the course of almost three and a half centuries, Judah was ruled by the same Davidic dynasty, Israel had no single ruling dynasty. Throughout the two centuries of the Northern Kingdom's existence, 19 kings sat on Israel's throne, but only two of them, Omri and Jehu, managed to found dynasties which ruled for any length of time. The dynasty founded by Omri produced four kings, and that of Jehu five. The remaining rulers were unable to found their own dynasties, and their sons were deposed almost immediately after ascending the throne. It was generally the case that the Israelite kings were successful military commanders who managed to exploit circumstances in order to seize power. Their principal problem was how to hold on this power and to protect their heirs from other military commanders who were just as power-hungry as themselves.

The lack of an established dynasty and the resulting instability of supreme power in the Northern Kingdom had objective causes. Unlike homogeneous Judah, which was mainly represented by a single large tribe, Israel consisted of ten Hebrew tribes who contested the supreme power among themselves. Even tribes as important as those of Ephraim and Manasseh were not influential enough to monopolize power in the Northern Kingdom. For this reason, unlike the tribe of Judah in the Southern Kingdom, not one of the northern tribes possessed the 'critical weight' which would have allowed them to set the tone in Israel. Furthermore, it was the Northern Kingdom that was particularly heavily populated by the Canaanite and Amorite peoples, who had remained there and prospered following all the conquests made by Joshua. As these peoples assimilated culturally and physically with the Israelite tribes, they also began to require their share in the governing of the Northern Kingdom. There is another thing too that we should not forget: by the time the United Monarchy split up, only Judah possessed an established royal dynasty, the Davidic dynasty. David's elimination of the descendants of King Saul in effect left the northern tribes headless, making it difficult first for them to choose a king and then for power to be transferred in a smooth way. Finally, Judah remained for a long time a more patriarchal and less developed and dynamic state, so all political processes and changes occurring in the country happened more slowly and less dramatically than in neighboring Israel.

The Religious Break-up

Having put an end to the rule of the Davidic dynasty on the territory of the northern tribes, the king of Israel was in a hurry to rid himself of the religious influence of the Aaronites of the Temple in Jerusalem. To this end, he created two Israelite religious centers – one in the south of the country, in Bethel, and the other in the north, in Dan, where he installed the golden calves. There can be no doubt that these were pagan cults that had no relation to the monotheism of Moses; it is likely that the calves in question were similar to the golden calf which the high priest Aaron had created in the Desert of Sinai. They resembled the traditional Canaanite cult of Baal, which was widespread at that time among the northern tribes and their Canaanite neighbors. At best, this may be seen as a return to the pagan concept of the early cult of Yahweh against which Moses fought. Although certain historians try to argue that the golden calves were set up only so that the spirit of God could rest upon them, i.e. as a throne for invisible and impalpable God himself, such sophistries are hardly convincing. To compare the golden calves at Bethel and Dan with the cherubim of the Ark of the Covenant is inappropriate in the present case, especially given that Jeroboam, the king of the Israelites, himself said of these calves: "Here are your gods, Israel, who brought you up out of Egypt" (1 Kings 12:28).

Bronze statuette of a bull from Samarian uplands.

Admittedly, criticism of the pagan cults in the Northern Kingdom was expressed by the keepers of the tradition at a later time, when the idea of monotheism had put down firm roots. Moreover, the main critics of the northerners' pagan cults were the Aaronites of the Southern Kingdom, who in that remote age had themselves been far from true monotheism. The Bible tells us that at the time when the golden calves were set up in Israel, idolatry was just as widespread in Judah: "Judah did evil in the eyes of the Lord. By the sins they committed they stirred up his jealous anger more than those who were before them had done. They also set up for themselves high places, sacred stones and Asherah poles on every high hill and under every spreading tree" (1 Kings 14:22-23). King Rehoboam of Judah was no less of an idolater than the mercilessly criticized King Jeroboam. The Bible admits that Rehoboam "committed all the sins his father had done before him; his heart was not fully devoted to the Lord his God, as the heart of David his forefather had been" (1 Kings 15:3). In talking about the idolatry of the Judahite king, the keepers of the tradition hint heavily that his mother was an Ammonite. This circumstance, however, not only does not excuse Rehoboam, but also casts a shadow on his father Solomon, for the omniscient king could not have been ignorant of the Torah's prohibition against marrying Ammonites and Moabites due to the incest which they had committed. If Solomon himself did not think it necessary to comply with this prohibition, then no such prohibition existed at that time (it must have been added at a much later date). But esteemed Solomon was merely following the example of his more righteous father, David, who was married to both a Canaanite woman, Ahinoam, and to a woman from Geshur, Maacah, although he should have known that the religious law not merely forbad intermarriage with these peoples, but actually ordered that they should be chased out of Canaan as punishment for their idolatry. There is every reason to suppose that the stringent prohibition of any kind of kinship with the peoples of Canaan and the absolute intolerance of idolatry came not from the lawgiver Moses, who was himself married to a Midianite, but from traditionalists living in the post-Babylonian period. It was the latter who, when redacting the Old Testament, added uncompromising requirements of which both the kings and the Levites had known nothing during the time in question.

There was another cause of the extreme hostility felt by the Levites towards the Israelite king Jeroboam: he appointed priests for his new religious centers not from among the Levites, but "from all sorts of people" (1 Kings 13:33). This policy affected most of all the northern Levites associated with the religious center at Shiloh. They had supported Jeroboam during the period of his resistance to first Solomon and then Rehoboam. They had helped him not merely due to their historical closeness to the interests of the northern tribes, but also because they had been excluded from participation in the religious rites at the Temple in Jerusalem. After Solomon ostracized Abiathar, the head of the northern dynasty of priests, the southern Aaronites deprived their rivals from Shiloh of positions of any importance at Jerusalem. It is extremely telling that the first person to predict to Jeroboam that he would become king of the northern tribes was the prophet Ahijah from Shiloh. However, the new Israelite king did not justify the hopes of the Levites and left them with nothing to do in the Northern Kingdom. From that time forwards, Jeroboam and his house were hated not just by the Aaronites of Judah, but also by the northern Levites. Some historians suppose that Jeroboam did not trust the Levites because he saw them as spreading the influence of Judah and the Davidic dynasty. However, fear of this kind is unlikely to have influenced the decision of the Israelite king. The Levites of Shiloh had been closely connected to the northern tribes since the conquests of Joshua, and their rivalry with the southern Aaronites was well known. Moreover, Jeroboam did not dismiss the main priest of the religious center at Dan, whose origins lay among the southern Levites, but left him in his position. Most probably, the Israelite king's reluctance to place control of religious services in the hands of the Levites from Shiloh was a matter not so much of any lack of trust in them as of the fact that the cult of Yahweh enjoyed little support in the Northern Kingdom. This cult, which had been imported by the southern tribes, remained the principal, although by no means the only, cult in Judah. In Israel, however, it was the Canaanite divinities which prevailed – namely, the supreme god El, Baal, the mighty god of thunder, and Asherah, the goddess of fertility. The corporations of priests in the latter cults were more influential, and Jeroboam preferred to look for support to those who had the most influence with the northern tribes. It was for this reason that the Levites from Shiloh always condemned the idolatry of the Israelite kings and fought constantly with their more successful rivals, the priests of Baal and Asherah. Their relations with the Aaronites of Judah likewise remained extremely tense right up to the fall of the Northern Kingdom.

The biblical episode telling of Jeroboam's creation of an independent religious center in Bethel contains a lengthy story about a 'man of God' who 'according to the word of the Lord' came to Bethel from Judah in order to prophesy that a little more than three centuries later the Judahite king Josiah would kill the idolatrous priests and burn their bones on this very altar. However, led astray by the local prophet – evidently a northern Levite – the 'man of God' was unable to fulfill one of the commandments of the Lord and so met his death (1 Kings 13:1-34). This story, which was added to the ancient texts in the 6th-5th centuries BCE is, on the one hand, a warning to idolaters and their priests and kings and, on the other, constitutes a veiled accusation addressed to the northern Levites, laying against them the accusation that, in helping Jeroboam split the united kingdom, they had led innocent people into sin and thus encouraged idolatry. This story was based initially on a real conflict between the northern and southern followers of Yahweh during the break-up of the United Monarchy.

Chapter 9

Israel: Successor to the 'House of Joseph'

The Historical and Ethnic Roots of the Northern Kingdom

The ancestors of the northern Hebrew tribes came to Canaan in approximately the 23rd century BCE, i.e. 300 years earlier than Abraham and the southern tribes. Like Abraham, the founding father of the southern tribes, the northern tribes came from north-west Mesopotamia; however, they had not roamed through Mesopotamia or stayed in Sumer, as their southern relatives had done, but had moved directly south-west, through Syria, into Canaan. Possibly, it was from the ancestors of the northerners that Abraham's father, Terah, learnt that the southern part of Canaan contained a sizeable amount of unoccupied land that was suitable for raising cattle – information which enabled him to take the decision to move there. Although the northern Hebrew tribes, like the southern ones, were Western Semites, they were probably not closely related to the southern tribes and, unlike the latter, did not trace their ancestry to Abraham, Isaac, and Jacob. The keepers of the tradition began associating them with the 'house of Jacob' much later, when both groups of tribes were together in the United Monarchy.

If the southern Hebrew tribes, the 'house of Jacob', were a homogeneous group consisting of four tribes (Reuben, Simeon, Levi, and Judah) sharing a common origin and history, the northern tribes, known as 'Israel', were comprised of three distinct parts. The first and most important of these was the 'house of Joseph', which consisted of three closely related tribes – Ephraim, Manasseh, and Benjamin. These were the first of the Hebrew tribes to leave for Egypt and the first to return thence to Canaan, a journey which they accomplished not later than the middle of the 15th century BCE. Unlike the majority of the Hebrew tribes, the 'house of Joseph' was among the Hyksos conquerors of Egypt, had a privileged position under the Hyksos pharaohs, and patronized the 'house of Jacob' and other Amorite tribes who arrived in the Nile Delta at a later date. Subsequently, the 'house of Joseph' was joined by another tribe, Naphtali, which possibly accompanied it on the journey back from Egypt to Canaan. These four Hebrew tribes were the 'Habiru' in Canaan known to us from the letters of the Amarna archive of the 14th century BCE. It was they who established the tribal alliance of Israel which Pharaoh Merneptah mentioned on his stele at the end of the 13th century BCE.

The second part of the northern tribes consisted of four Amorite tribes – Issachar, Zebulun, Gad, and Asher – and one presumably Indo-European (Achaean?) tribe, the tribe of Dan. These tribes left Egypt together with Moses' southern tribes at the beginning of the 12th century BCE. Unlike the two southern tribes, Judah and Simeon, they did not spend 40 years wandering the desert. Instead, together with Moses, they set out for Transjordan, where they joined the Israelite tribal alliance, whose head at that time was the leader of the 'house of Joseph', Joshua. In terms of tribal origin they felt closer to the 'house of Joseph' than to the 'house of Jacob'; moreover, their previous tribal lands were not in the south, but in the north of Canaan.

Finally, the third component of the northern tribes was the southerners themselves – the tribe of Reuben and the majority of the Levites, who belonged to the 'house of Jacob'. When the new tribes joined the Israelite alliance at the beginning of the 12th century BCE, this considerably strengthened the alliance and allowed it to start conquering part of Canaan, as Joshua duly did. We may suppose that the Israelite alliance contained only those tribes which prior to their departure for Egypt had possessed tribal lands in the central and northern parts of Canaan. A similar process occurred both on the coast of Lebanon and in southern Syria, where the Amorite tribes who had returned from Egypt were in the position of 'Habiru', i.e. homeless. Subsequently, their coming together led to the creation of the state of Amurru.

When the Hebrew tribes had come into possession of part of Canaan and settled on the land, the Israelite tribal alliance weakened and even temporarily broke up. We know this period as the time of the biblical judges, 'when each did as he pleased'. The external threat presented by the Philistines, however, not only brought the Israelite tribes back together again, but also gave them new allies – the southern tribes of Judah, Simeon, and part of the tribe of the Levites who had settled in southern Canaan after four decades of wandering the desert. The extended alliance was led by the Benjamite Saul, who became the first king initially of the northern tribes, and then of the southern tribes as well. However, Saul's defeat and death in battle with the Philistines resulted in the Hebrew tribes' subjugation to their conquerors and a new break-up of the Israelite alliance.

On this occasion, the initiative in recreating the alliance was taken by the junior partners, the southern tribes, and their military leader, David. The southern king managed to do that which the northerner Saul had been unable to do – to create a powerful united kingdom which not only defended, but also moved far to the north-east the boundaries of the Hebrew tribes. But as the southern Davidic dynasty frankly ignored the interests of the northern tribes, and the junior partner lorded over the senior one, their alliance was doomed to failure. The political interests of the tribal aristocracy turned out to be more important than tribal kinship: the southern tribe of Reuben, which had been comparatively poorly treated in the 'house of Jacob', once more preferred the northerners, while some of the clans from the northern tribe of Benjamin, who had conflicted with the Ephraimites, remained with the southerners.

The First Israelite Kings and their Policies

Jeroboam, the first proper king of the Israelites, was not a military commander, but one of the leaders of the tribe of Ephraim. His election as king satisfied the claims made by the tribe of Ephraim to the leading role both in the 'house of Joseph' and among the Israelite tribes. However, Jeroboam's prerogatives were extremely limited and could not be compared with the unconditional power enjoyed by his rival, Rehoboam, the King of Judah. In order to please the leaders and elders of the northern tribes, the new king abolished the labor obligations placed upon them by the Davidic dynasty, and substantially reduced the burden of taxation. He could not afford to keep a lavish court or a mercenary army of any great size; furthermore, he was forced to accept the not inconsiderable degree of internal autonomy enjoyed by the Israelite tribes. This 'limited' monarchy was the price to be paid for his election as king.

In foreign policy there were three serious problems with which he was confronted: a chronic conflict with Judah regarding the territory of the tribe of Benjamin; the heightened military threat from the Aram-Damascus; and an unexpected invasion by the Egyptian pharaoh Sheshonq. The first two problems were never resolved during the reign of Jeroboam. The conflict with Judah lasted a long time – half a century at least – while defeating the Arameans would have required significantly larger forces than those which Jeroboam had at his disposal. As for the attack by the Egyptian army, the Bible gives us only limited details regarding Judah and Jerusalem and tells us nothing about the Egyptians' invasion of Israel. Extremely meager information on this may be found only in Egyptian sources. Sheshonq I left a bas relief in the temple of Amon in Karnak on which he listed all the cities he had conquered in Canaan. If this list is true (it cannot be ruled out that it contains exaggerations), this means that the Egyptian invasion affected not so much Judah as Israel. During excavations conducted in 1925-1934 a fragment of Sheshonq's stele was discovered in the vicinity of Megiddo confirming the fact that this Israelite city was seized by the Egyptians. In placing the stele near Megiddo, the Egyptians were counting on an extensive occupation of the parts of Canaan which they had taken. But they were unable to repeat the successes of the pharaohs of the 18th and 19th Dynasties; their invasion turned out to be merely a one-off plundering raid.

In spite of the hopes entertained by the Levites from Shiloh, the break-up of the United Monarchy not merely failed to reinforce their position, but, on the contrary, actually weakened it. Furthermore, it also diminished the role of the cult of Yahweh in the new Northern Kingdom. However tense the relations between the northern Levites and the southern Aaronites, the very fact that the cult of Yahweh had been considered the principal cult in the United Monarchy had helped strengthen the Levites of Shiloh. Now, following the break-up of the alliance with Judah, which also worshipped Yahweh, Jeroboam was no longer bound by any obligations to either the Aaronites or the cult of Yahweh. So he returned to the traditional pagan cults taken from the Canaanites during the centuries of living together with them, and likewise to the old pagan form of the cult of Yahweh, which the ordinary people found considerably more accessible and comprehensible than the abstract monotheism of Moses. Most probably, Jeroboam did not change anything at all, but simply legalized that which already existed in the religious practice of the northern tribes – legitimized already existing cults and their priests who were of other than Levite origin. The main change was the break with the dominant role played by the Aaronites and the Levites, which had initially been a condition of the alliance with the southerners and had subsequently been imposed by Jerusalem. Although the cult of Yahweh remained, it was now no longer the principal religion but merely one of a number of cults – and it took the old pagan or semi-pagan form which was most comprehensible to ordinary people. Jeroboam's religious reforms amounted not so much to changes in the cult itself as in eliminating from it the Aaronites and Levites. This explains the extreme hostility of the keepers of the tradition, who were those same Levites and Aaronites, to Jeroboam personally and to his deeds.

The institute of regal authority required that there should also be a capital city which would be entirely in the power of the king himself and not of some tribe or other. For this reason, just as David before him had made Jebusite Jerusalem his fiefdom, so Jeroboam chose as his residence Hivite Shechem. Admittedly, he subsequently moved his capital to the small town of Tirzah, a little to the north of Shechem. Possibly, this move was a result of the conflict over the Hivite regions between the Northern and Southern Kingdoms. As is well-known, during the conquest of Canaan Joshua concluded peace with the Hivites of Gibeon and undertook not to invade their land. However, in spite of this, the northern tribe of Benjamin did not renounce its claims to the lands of the southern Hivites – Gibeon, Beeroth, Kiriath-Jearim – and during the era of the judges made several attempts to seize them. For their part, the Hivites turned for help to their traditional ally and patron, the southern tribe of Judah, which during the reign of judge Othniel had fought on their side against the Benjaminites. Although as a result of these conflicts the southern Hivite lands were in effect divided between Judah and Benjamin, they still for a long time served as a bone of contention between these tribes. During Saul's reign the Benjaminites stripped the southern Hivite cities, including the largest such city, Gibeon, of their autonomy. When David became king, he channeled the

Israel: Successor to the 'House of Joseph'

humiliation inflicted on the Hivites, using them to destroy Saul's descendants. After the break-up of the United Monarchy the southern Hivites naturally preferred to remain with Judah rather than with Israel, which was laying claim to their lands. It is likely that the Benjaminites who, according to the Bible, joined the Judahites in fighting against the northern tribes after the latter had split off were in reality not part of the tribe of Benjamin itself, but from among the southern Hivites. The extensive conflict over the Hivite lands led to tension in relations with the population of Shechem, who were mostly also of Hivite origin and sympathized with the Davidic dynasty due to the support given by the latter to the Hivites against the tribe of Benjamin. Not wishing to put his residence in danger, Jeroboam thought it best to move to Tirzah, a nearby town which was more secure, being situated on the tribal territory of the 'house of Joseph'.

Another city which Jeroboam built up was the ancient city of Penuel in Transjordan. The break-up of the United Monarchy had resulted in Ammon and Moab regaining their independence, making it necessary to reinforce the eastern border of the Israelite kingdom. Penuel closed off the entrance to the Jordan Valley from the east, and Jeroboam decided to reinforce it with all haste, fearing that neighboring Ammon might in the future join Israel's enemies, the Arameans of Damascus.

According to the book of Kings, Jeroboam ruled for 21 years, but was unable to realize his hopes of founding his own dynasty. Literally a year after ascending the throne, Jeroboam's son Nadab fell to a bloody coup organized by the commander of his own army. "Baasha son of Ahijah from the tribe of Issachar plotted against him, and he struck him down at Gibbethon, a Philistine town, while Nadab and all Israel were besieging it [...] As soon as he began to reign, he killed Jeroboam's whole family. He did not leave Jeroboam anyone that breathed, but destroyed them all [...]" (1 Kings 15:27, 29). The new king was unrelated to the 'house of Joseph'; he came from the tribe of Issachar, whose lands were near Tirzah, the then capital of Israel. This northern tribe had left Egypt together with the southern tribes of Moses and Aaron and, thanks to its large numbers and high place in the Amorite tribal hierarchy, had been 'adopted' in the desert by the 'house of Jacob'. It traced its origins back to the sons of Leah, the eldest wife of the forefather Jacob. It cannot be ruled out that the accession to the throne of a king from this tribe was facilitated by support from opponents of the hegemony of the Ephraimites. Baasha's accession demonstrated that, unlike the monopolist position of the tribe of Judah among the southern tribes, neither the 'house of Joseph' nor still less the tribe of Ephraim possessed sufficient influence to give them the exclusive right to rule among the northern tribes.

Baasha's rule was very different from that of Jeroboam. As a general, the new king relied not on agreements struck with the tribal elders, but on crude military force. This meant that he did not need approval of his actions and possessed significantly more extensive powers than his predecessor, the tribal leader Jeroboam. He considerably strengthened central authority by restricting tribal autonomy; this allowed him to expand his permanent mercenary army and to surround himself with the lavish court characteristic of an oriental despot. As a military strategist, his preference was to cover his rear in the north by signing peace with the Aram-Damascus in order to concentrate all his energy on subjecting his weaker southern neighbor, Judah. Initially, it seemed that everything was going according to plan. He managed to take from Judah all the disputed areas on land belonging to the tribe of Benjamin and, furthermore, to surround Jerusalem. In order to force the city into submission, he built Ramah, a fortress controlling the approaches to Jerusalem. The southerners' position was hopeless. But at this point military strategy gave way to politics: the Judahite king, Asa, managed to buy the good will of Damascus and draw it into the war on his side. The victorious campaign turned into a long and difficult war on two fronts.

Baasha's political miscalculations had an impact on his son Elah too, for Elah met the same sad fate as Jeroboam's son. Having only just ascended the throne, Elah was killed by his own military commander: "Zimri, one of his officials, who had command of half his chariots, plotted against him." According to the custom of the time, the new ruler destroyed all the kinsmen of the previous king: "As soon as he began to reign and was seated on the throne, he killed off Baasha's whole family. He did not spare a single male, whether relative or friend" (1 Kings 16:9,11). However, Zimri managed to cling to power for a mere seven days. After learning of the court coup in the capital, the Israelite generals, who were at that time laying siege to the cities of Philistia, hurried with their troops to Tirzah and, quickly seizing it, killed the usurper. This was followed by squabbling among the Israelite generals over which of them should occupy the throne. There were two contenders: Omri and Tibni. The army and the court were roughly equally divided in their sympathies: "Then the people of Israel were split into two factions; half supported Tibni son of Ginath for king, and the other half supported Omri" (1 Kings 16:21). A fierce civil war broke out, ending with the victory of Omri and the death of his rival.

Under the Rule of the 'House of Omri'

The Bible tells us nothing of Omri's tribal provenance; moreover, it does not even tell us his father's name, an omission which is absolutely uncharacteristic of the keepers of the tradition – and all the more so when the man in question is not just any simple person, but the King of the Israelites. We have exhaustive information on the tribal provenance and kin of Saul, David, Jeroboam, and even Baasha, i.e. of all kings who founded or tried to found their own dynasties; so the complete silence surrounding the family tree of one of the most famous kings of the Israelites seems suspicious. This has allowed a number of historians

Israel: Successor to the 'House of Joseph'

to suppose that the founder of the famous dynasty was of non-Israelite origin. Given the special attachment shown by Omri and his son Ahab to the Canaanite cult of Baal, it cannot be ruled out that the new king indeed belonged to the Canaanites or Amorites who formed the majority of the population of the Northern Kingdom. Also interesting is the fact that after Baasha the keepers of the tradition altogether ceased indicating the tribal or ethnic provenance of the successive kings of Israel, although they continued to give the names of these kings' fathers. Evidently, with the passing of time the difference both between the northern tribes themselves and between the latter and the Canaanite-Amorite population eroded to such an extent that the emphasis switched to which part of the country the new kings came from. All this is a sign of the profound cultural and physical assimilation that occurred between the Israelite tribes and the Canaanite-Amorite population. If the Canaanite and Amorite peoples underwent a process of 'Israelization', the Hebrew tribes in their turn became strongly 'Canaaanized'. Things, of course, could not have been different, given that all these West Semitic peoples had a common origin and spoke the same language.

The new king needed a new capital city. Tirzah, the creation of Jeroboam and Baasha, no longer satisfied his needs. "He bought the hill of Samaria from Shemer for two talents of silver and built a city on the hill, calling it Samaria, after Shemer, the name of the former owner of the hill" (1 Kings 16:24). This meant that the entire territory of the new capital belonged to Omri personally, which gave him clear advantages compared with what he possessed in Tirzah, which had been built and populated to meet the needs of Jeroboam and Baasha. All three capitals of the Northern Kingdom – Shechem, Tirzah, and Samaria – were situated not far from one another, an indication that it was by no means their geographical position which was the king's reason for a change of residence. Like Jeroboam before him, after the divisions and the civil wars, Omri wished to protect his residence from the general population, whose interests bound them closely to the former kings and their policies. However, the fact that Samaria, the new Israelite capital, was once more situated on the land of the 'house of Joseph' was evidence of the complete support which the new dynasty enjoyed from these influential tribes. Omri would have been unlikely to build his new residence in the midst of a hostile population.

The new king was undoubtedly the outstanding politician and general of his time. It is no coincidence that he was the first Israelite king to be mentioned in non-biblical sources. The stele of Mesha, King of Moab, names him as conqueror and enslaver of Moab, while Assyrian inscriptions of the time of King Tiglath-Pileser III call the Israelite kingdom 'the house of Omri'. This king made such a profound impression on the memories of other peoples that for many years Israel was associated in their eyes with his dynasty above all. At the same time, the Bible has surprisingly little to say about this outstanding man, the founder of one of the two true dynasties of Israelite kings. The extreme enmity felt by the Levites towards the kings of this dynasty, who were followers of the cult of Baal, can little explain anything – especially given that Omri's son, Ahab, a much more fervent follower of Baal, is nevertheless accorded incomparably more attention by the keepers of the tradition. One possible reason for this incomprehensible silence regarding Omri himself is his non-Israelite origins. Nevertheless, even during Omri's comparatively short, 12-year, reign, the Israelite kingdom was not merely able to regain stability following the coup and civil war, but also to considerably grow in military strength. Israel once more subjugated the Transjordanian states of Moab and Ammon and successfully warded off attacks by the Aram-Damascus.

Omri fundamentally changed the Israelite policy towards Judah. He renounced the enmity and wars that had been characteristic of the reigns of Jeroboam and Baasha and began establishing friendly relations with his southern neighbor. Paradoxically, the true peace with Judah constituted yet further proof of Omri's non-Israelite origins. For all the other kings, who came from Israelite tribes, tended to be openly hostile towards their southern brothers. Another new foreign-policy direction was an alliance with Ethbaal, king of the Phoenician city of Sidon. This alliance was in Israel's interests: it provided protection for Israel's rear in the north and opened up new opportunities for participation in international trade, including by sea. Omri and his son Ahab, like Solomon before them, conducted an extensive construction program and needed large numbers of highly qualified craftsmen, a resource in which the Phoenician cities were rich.

Ahab was the most famous and most successful king from this dynasty. In his domestic and foreign policy he consistently followed the course set by his father. Above all, he reinforced the alliance with Phoenicia by marrying Jezebel, daughter of the Sidonian king, Ethbaal. Support from the Phoenicians enabled him to realize his ambitious construction plans, in particular in the new capital, Samaria, and in Megiddo and Hazor. Ahab put just as much energy into improving relations with his southern neighbor, Judah. In order to reinforce the new alliance, he gave his daughter Athaliah in marriage to the son of Jehoshaphat, King of Judah, who then became not just his political ally, but a military ally as well. Both these alliances – with Phoenicia and Judah – were intended to protect Israel's rear in its confrontation with its main opponent, the kingdom of Damascus. Objectively, the opposition between Israel and Damascus was a fight for hegemony over the entire region of Syria and Palestine.

Unfortunately, all but very few of the facts that we possess concerning Ahab are taken from the Bible, whose authors were concerned not so much with the political and military issues of the time as with religious and philosophical ones. They saw Ahab's entire reign through the prism of his religious policy-making, and in particular from the point of view of his attitude to the cult of Yahweh and the northern Levites. As a pragmatist, Ahab looked not to the cult of Yahweh and the Levites, but to the cult of Baal and the latter's priests, who at the time had significantly greater influence on the population of his kingdom. There is nothing surprising in the fact that Ahab became the figure the Levites hated most and that the Bible is literally overflowing with unsparing criticism of him. "Ahab son of Omri did more evil in the eyes of the Lord than any of those before him" (1 Kings 16:30). The keepers of the tradition did not approve of Ahab's marriage to a pagan woman, the Phoenician princess Jezebel, but they were even more upset by the queen's patronage of the Canaanite cult of Baal, the principal cult in her native Phoenicia. During the years of Ahab's reign Baal became the principal religious cult of the kingdom of Israel, the second most important cult being that of Asherah, the Canaanite goddess of fertility who was regarded as Baal's spouse. "He set up an altar for Baal in the temple of Baal that he built in Samaria. Ahab also made an Asherah pole and did more to arouse the anger of the Lord, the God of Israel, than did all the kings of Israel before him" (1 Kings 16:32-33).

The then less influential cult of Yahweh and its priests, the Levites, were pushed to one side, into secondary positions, while the temple of Baal in Samaria laid claim to the same role in Israel as was played by the Temple of Jerusalem in Judah. Naturally, the Levites could not accept such a situation and spoke up if not directly against Ahab, then at least against the pagan queen. In response, Ahab began persecuting the northern Levites, who had dared to intervene in his policy-making and family affairs; and Jezebel, who regarded the Levites as personal enemies, "was killing the prophets of the Lord" (1 Kings 18:13). For the first time in the history of the northern tribes the Levites not only found themselves without patronage of any kind, but were also compelled to hide out of fear for their own lives. It was as these persecutions were taking place, that Elijah, the most famous prophet of the Northern Kingdom, began his life as a hermit.

But at this point nature intervened. As if in punishment for the persecution of the Levites, Israel was struck by a most severe drought; famine set in. This was a natural disaster which had happened in Canaan on a number of occasions in the past and had forced the ancestors of the Israelites to leave for Egypt. The drought and famine led to popular unrest and were interpreted as the Lord's punishment for the persecution of the followers of Yahweh – at least, this was the version of events that was encouraged among ordinary people by the Levites. Part of the general population and even some of the king's courtiers were dissatisfied with the monopoly enjoyed by the cult of Baal and by the dominance of the Sidonian priests. Food riots, even if only on a limited scale, broke out, and were cleverly channeled by the Levites against the priests of Baal, who had been unable to call forth rain. Afraid of bringing down the wrath of the people upon himself, Ahab refrained at this point from taking the part of the priests of Baal, and many of the latter were killed. The greatest unrest, at Mount Carmel, near today's Haifa, was headed by the prophet Elijah, who organized mass beatings of the priests of Baal and Asherah and compelled Ahab to give up persecuting the Levites. The rains which now set in completed the triumph of the followers of Yahweh, who had not only regained their former position, but also for a short time deposed the cult of Baal from its status as principal religion. The cessation of the drought and famine, however, pacified the population and brought the insurrection to an end. It was only after this that the royal family once more dared to deal harshly with the Levites as the leaders of the uprising. Many Levites were once more forced to go into hiding, and Elijah, their leader and prophet, temporarily fled to Judah.

Taking advantage of the turbulent events in Israel, Ben-Hadad, King of Aram-Damascus, invaded the country at the head of an enormous army, which included the armies of his vassals, and laid siege to Samaria. Ahab, conscious of the inequality of forces, tried to make peace with the Arameans, declaring himself prepared to become their vassal. However, seeing the difficult position which the Israelites were in, Ben-Hadad tightened the conditions he was offering, requiring an enormous tribute and Ahab's family as hostages for the future loyalty of the Israelite king. Ahab rejected these savage conditions, and the siege of Samaria was renewed. Meanwhile, irregular forces belonging to the northern tribes arrived to help the Israelite king, and Ahab decided to take the initiative by attacking the Arameans who were besieging him. The battle took place on extremely uneven ground, where the Arameans were unable to take advantage of their numerical superiority. On the other hand, the hilly terrain favored the Israelite tribal forces, which mainly consisted of foot soldiers. The Israelites' unexpected attack resulted in the utter defeat of the Arameans, the remnants of whose army fled to Damascus.

Only a year later, however, Ben-Hadad launched a new attack on Israel. On this occasion, following advice from his generals, he put the armies of the vassals under the direct command of his own generals and, most importantly, decided to conduct the decisive battle not in hilly countryside, but on the plain, where he could take full advantage of his army's numerical dominance. Battle was joined on the plain near the city of Aphek, to the east of the Sea of Galilee. As on the previous occasion, the Israelite forces consisted of two parts – the king's permanent army and tribal (regional) irregular forces. The Bible describes the battle as follows: "The Israelites camped opposite them like two small flocks of goats, while the Arameans covered the countryside […] For seven days they camped opposite each other, and on the seventh day the battle was joined. The Israelites inflicted a hundred thousand casualties on the Aramean foot soldiers in one day. The rest of them escaped to the city of Aphek" (1 Kings 20:27, 29-30). For all the Arameans' expectations, the flat terrain was of no help to them. Today, using Assyrian sources, we may suppose that the Israelites

Israel: Successor to the 'House of Joseph'

countered the Arameans' numerical superiority in cavalry and foot soldiers with their own superiority in chariots. The Israelite chariots, charioteers, and horses were considered some of the best in the ancient Near East; in fact, they were admired even by the Assyrians, who had enormous experience in military matters. After routing the Arameans near Aphek, the Israelites went on to storm the city of Aphek itself. Ben-Hadad surrendered.

Ahab, however, had no desire for vengeance. The victory over Damascus resulted not in the subjugation of his former enemy, but in an alliance with him. The reason for this unexpected turn of events lay in the emergence of another, more frightening, and more powerful opponent, Assyria. The Assyrian king, Shalmaneser III (859-824 BCE) had already invaded northern and central Syria, and there was no state in the region capable of withstanding him on its own. The extraordinary cruelty of the Assyrians and the terrible destruction which they wreaked compelled many Syrian, Phoenician, and Palestinian states to unite. Israel, Damascus, and Hamath headed an anti-Assyrian coalition comprising 12 states. The coalition successfully warded off several attacks by the Assyrian army and for a time delayed Assyria's westward progress into southern Syria, Phoenicia, and Palestine.

Unfortunately, information on these events is only available from non-biblical – or, to be more precise, Assyrian – sources. The Bible tells us nothing of the anti-Assyrian coalition, in which the leading roles were played by Israel and Aram-Damascus. In particular, the Assyrian texts provide highly interesting information on the battle of Qarqar (853 BCE), in which Israel was also a participant. According to the Assyrians, Israel confronted them with 2000 war chariots and 10,000 foot soldiers, while Damascus, another leader of the coalition, was able to field 1200 chariots and 20,000 foot soldiers. The contributions made by the remaining members of the anti-Assyrian coalition were immeasurably smaller. These are facts which speak eloquently of the considerable military and economic might of the Israelite kingdom. During the reigns of Omri and Ahab Israel clearly became one of the strongest states in Syria, Phoenicia, and Palestine and was probably in no way inferior to its traditional enemy, the kingdom of Damascus. On the basis of these facts, historians doubt the accuracy of the Bible when it tells us that during Omri's reign Damascus managed to seize a number of Israelite cities and win for itself favorable conditions for trade. As is well known, following the rout of the Arameans near Aphek, King Ben-Hadad, who had been taken prisoner by the Israelites, said to Ahab: "I will return the cities my father took from your father.' [...] 'You may set up your own market areas in Damascus, as my father did in Samaria" (1 Kings 20:34). There is a suggestion that these words found their way into the chronicles of the reign of Ahab from another period during which Israel was ruled by a different king – especially since the book of Kings was compiled centuries after the events described. It cannot be ruled out that the unsuccessful military campaign against Ramoth-Gilead, a campaign which is ascribed to Ahab, also occurred at a different time and during the reign of another king (for instance, Ahab's son Joram). Possibly, the same was also suspected by the compilers of the book of Kings themselves – which is why in most episodes they judiciously avoid naming the Israelite king.

The extreme disapproval with which the keepers of the tradition treated Ahab clearly belittled the importance of this politician and military commander. But, however negative the attitude taken to him by the authors of the Bible, it cannot be denied that his rule was a period when the kingdom of Israel demonstrated considerable economic and military might. After Ahab's death, Omri's dynasty suffered rapid decline and the Northern Kingdom weakened. Ahab's son, Ahaziah, managed to rule for less than two full years. He was seriously injured when he fell from a room on the top floor of the palace and until his death was unable to get up from his bed. His vassals, especially Moab, which had become detached from the Israelite kingdom almost immediately after Ahab's death, took advantage of his helpless situation. Also unsuccessful was Ahaziah's attempt to organize an expedition in conjunction with Judah to look for gold in Ophir. The ships intended for this journey were shattered by a storm at Ezion-Geber (in the region of today's port of Eilat), and the Judahite king refused to take part in a new expedition. His illness and the shortness of his reign prevented Ahaziah from demonstrating the qualities of a true statesman. But, judging by the little that we know of him, he endeavored to continue the policies of his father and grandfather – admittedly, though, less successfully than they. Like his father, Ahaziah favored the cult of Baal, which remained the principal cult of the Northern Kingdom. It is no coincidence that the Bible draws a direct parallel between Ahaziah and Ahab: "He served and worshiped Baal and aroused the anger of the Lord, the God of Israel, just as his father had done" (1 Kings 22:53). Ahaziah likewise presided over persecution of the Levites, and in particular of their leader, the prophet Elijah. The king's servants made a number of attempts to compel the troublesome prophet to be quiet, but did not have the courage to silence him forever, fearing popular unrest. In his turn, Elijah had no compunction about predicting the king's imminent death as a punishment for his blind faith in the pagan gods.

The premature death of the young king left him without direct male heirs, so the throne passed to his brother Joram. This last king in the dynasty of Omri lost no time in trying to improve relations with the Levites. Interestingly, the Bible acknowledges that "He did evil in the eyes of the Lord, but not as his father and mother had done. He got rid of the sacred stone of Baal that his father had made" (2 Kings 3:2). If Ahab and Ahaziah were in open conflict with the Levites and persecuted the latter's main prophet, Elijah, Joram not only did not persecute the followers of Yahweh, but even struck up close relations with their new leader, the prophet Elisha. But the cult of Baal remained, as before, the main cult in Samaria, and Elisha, although he received legitimization at

Israel: Successor to the 'House of Joseph'

the king's court, was by no means the high priest or the main prophet. So the reconciliatory gestures made by the Israelite king should not be overestimated. Nevertheless, the fact that Joram was compelled to take the Levites into account was a sign of the growth of influence of the cult of Yahweh and its priests and prophets among the population of the Northern Kingdom. In any case, the reasonably strong position enjoyed by Elisha was in strong contrast with the difficult fate suffered by to Elijah. If Elijah was forced to hide from persecutions for the larger part of his life, Elisha commanded such respect at the king's court that he could offer others his support in obtaining the patronage of the king and the latter's military commanders.

Joram's main foreign-policy problem was the endless wars with the Aram-Damascus. During the first half of his rule these wars were partly successful, but subsequently their outcomes were increasingly not in Israel's favour. Joram's reign coincided with the rules of Ben-Hadad II and Hazael, when the Aramean state was steadily increasing in strength and gradually becoming the main power in Syria and Phoenicia. In the course of this period, the balance of power between Israel and Damascus swung heavily in favor of the latter, and the Northern Kingdom switched from the active, offensive policy characteristic of the rules of Omri and Ahab to one that was purely defensive. The Arameans repeatedly laid siege to Samaria, but were unable to take it.

The conflict with the Arameans was complicated by natural disasters in the Northern Kingdom. As during the time of Ahab, the country endured a succession of years with very limited rainfall, leading to famine and mass migration to neighboring states. The Bible talks of seven years of hunger – and this is merely during Joram's 12-year rule (2 Kings 8:1). As in the time of Ahab, the Arameans ceased military actions against Israel only when Damascus was threatened by Assyria or its allies, but peace and friendship between Damascus and Israel ended just as soon as the former no longer faced a direct threat. The Bible retains indistinct mentions of the fact that the Arameans were forced to lift the siege of Samaria when they received news of foreign forces invading their own land (2 Kings 7:6-7). At that time Israel and the Assyrian state were separated by southern and central Syria, which was ruled by Damascus, so, to begin with, the Assyrian attack threated not so much Israel as Damascus and thus saved the Northern Kingdom from its aggressive neighbor.

For a certain time the Arameans stopped invading due to internal conflict in Damascus. Ben-Hadad II, who was seriously ill, was killed by his own military commander, Hazael, but the usurper then found himself up against other rivals, who disputed his claim to the throne. Taking advantage of the struggle for power in Damascus, Joram, King of Israel, made an attempt to reconquer from the Arameans part of northern Transjordan, Ramoth-Gilead, which had previously belonged to Israel. However, Hazael was able quickly to gain the upper hand over his domestic opponents and met Joram at the head of a large army. We do not know the result of the battle at Ramoth-Gilead, but we do know that the Israelite army remained there following the battle with the Arameans. Joram himself was seriously wounded and was carried back to his residence in Jezreel, the city situated in the valley of the same name.

Even before the battle near Ramoth-Gilead, Joram made an attempt to once more subjugate Moab, which had seceded from Israel following the death of Ahab. Joram invited his ally, Jehoshaphat, King of Judah, to join him in the campaign against the mutinous Moabites. The two kings were accompanied by detachments belonging to the ruler of Edom, which was then a dependant of Judah. The Bible gives this joint campaign substantial coverage due to the fact that the prophet Elisha was also present among the troops. Elisha's participation in the campaign is a sign of his official status as the king's prophet. But the prophets of Baal also participated in the campaign, whom the Israelite king counseled with in the first place (2 Kings 3:11-13). The biblical account of this military expedition is extremely contradictory and confused. The war was fraught with great difficulties. The troops suffered terrible thirst in the desert, and among the allies there were disagreements both over how to divide the plunder and over military tactics. There is another thing that is clear: in spite of the difficult climatic conditions and the fierce resistance put up by the Moabites, the allies won a series of victories over them. The Moabites were on the verge of suffering a complete defeat, given that their king was forced in desperation to sacrifice his firstborn son on the wall of his last remaining city. But what happened next was something incomprehensible. The book of Kings breaks off its account of the campaign with an unclear phrase: "The fury against Israel was great; they withdrew and returned to their own land" (2 Kings 3:27). Fortunately, there is another, non-biblical, source which can shed light on what happened. This is the stele of Mesha, that same Moabite king against whom the joint campaign was directed.

The inscriptions on the stele of Mesha date to approximately 840-830 BCE. They tell us that Moab was conquered by Omri, the King of the Israelites, and liberated in the middle of the reign of Omri's son (whose name is not given). King Mesha speaks of Moab remaining the tributary of Israel for 40 years. If this figure can be trusted, then Moab was liberated during the reign not of Omri's son Ahab, but of his grandson Joram. According to the Bible, Omri, the founder of the dynasty, ruled for 12 years; his son Ahab, for 22 years; his first grandson, Ahaziah, for less than two years; and his second grandson, Joram, for 12 years. Thus the end of the 40-year period of Moab's dependence would have coincided approximately with the middle of Joram's reign. It is probable that Joram's campaign against the Moab, recounted in the Bible, did indeed occur at this time.

But what was it that saved King Mesha from complete defeat after he sacrificed his son and heir? And what should we think of the unexpected departure of the Israelites just as they were about to accomplish a complete military triumph? The Bible attributes this to the "great fury against the Israelites", and, strangely, King Mesha offers a similar explanation: he thanks the god Chemosh for his intervention. But who was it who actually came to the help of the Moabites? Knowing the political situation at that time, it is not difficult to guess that it was probably the Arameans, who, taking advantage of Joram's departure for the land of the Moabites, invaded Israel. We shall probably never know whether this invasion took place at the initiative of Damascus itself or at the request of the king of the Moabites. But we do know that something similar had happened in this region on a number of occasions in the past. For instance, when Baasha, King of Israel, attacked Judah and tried to take Jerusalem, the Judahite king, Asa, employed rich gifts to persuade the Arameans to attack Israel and thus forced the Israelites to leave his country in haste. Something similar occurred in this case too. After receiving news of the enemy attack on his country, Joram immediately raised the siege and hurried off to confront the Arameans.

Incidentally, the biblical version contains indirect evidence of precisely such an event. "When the king of Moab saw that the battle had gone against him, he took with him seven hundred swordsmen to break through to the king of Edom, but they failed" (2 Kings 3:26). Why did the Moabites, endeavoring to turn the course of the battle, try to kill the ruler of Edom, a figure of secondary importance and a vassal of Judah, rather than the Israelite or Judahite kings, who were the true commanders of the army? The answer seems obvious: because neither the Israelite nor Judahite kings were present; they had departed in haste, leaving instead of themselves small forces under the command of the ruler of Edom. It was the latter who was ordered to finish off the Moabites, a task which he was unable to carry out. As we know from what happened subsequently, neither Joram nor his immediate descendants had the capability to subjugate Moab anew; in fact, they were all scarcely able to hold back the expansion of the Aram-Damascus. King Mesha was absolutely right when he allowed it to be understood from his stele that his hands had been completely untied with regard to the neighboring Israelite cities belonging to the Transjordanian tribe of Gad. The Israelites from this tribe were indeed left without the support of their king, whose army was busy either fighting against the Arameans or in the coalition with the Arameans against the Assyrian offensive. It is here that we find the answer to the mystery of Mesha's miraculous escape and his victories over the Israelite cities in central Transjordan. There is nothing surprising in King Mesha's keeping quiet about this important circumstance: after all, it is always difficult to boast of having support from other people. But, on the other hand, he was right in his own way when he thanked the Moabite god Chemosh for the help he had received. Why does the Bible not indicate the true reason for the Israelites' departure from Moab? Probably, the breaking off of the biblical account and its unclear end are directly bound up with the prestige of the prophet Elisha, who had predicted that "This is an easy thing in the eyes of the Lord; he will also deliver Moab into your hands" (2 Kings 3:18). However, in spite of a series of victories, the prophecy did not come true. No matter how critically the authors of the Bible treat the kings from the dynasty of Omri, Elisha's prophetic gift was for them beyond all questioning.

Some historians set the information given by Mesha's stele against the biblical account of King Joram's campaign against Moab, claiming that the more reliable (in their opinion) Moabite source refutes the version given in the Bible. However, this kind of contraposition comes from taking a too formal approach to the sources. It has to be noted that King Mesha is giving a kind of historical survey of Moab's subjugation by Israel and of the liberation of his country from the kings of Israel whereas the biblical version is merely one of the episodes in an epic that lasts almost half a century. Naturally, it is impossible to equate the whole with one of its constituent parts; these two sources do not contradict, but rather complement, one another. Moreover, neither of the two sources informs us of the true reason for the Israelites' hurried departure from Moab; they refer either to the wrath of almighty God or the kindness of a pagan divinity.

Joram turned out to be the last Israelite king of the dynasty of Omri. The wound he received in battle against the Arameans and his enforced retirement from managing affairs of state played a fatal role in his fate, helping his followers conspire against him and deprive him of both his throne and his life.

Many historians suppose that the overthrow of the dynasty of Omri had its causes in widespread social tension and the common people's dissatisfaction with having the cult of Baal forced upon them. This point of view derives from the biblical account of the battle fought by the Israelite prophets Elijah and Elisha against the pagan cults which prevailed under the kings of this dynasty, and is based on these prophets' exposure of the injustice and arbitrary rule of Ahab and Jezebel. In actual fact, the conspiracy headed by the king's military commander, Jehu, was unlikely to have differed markedly from the previous coups executed by Baasha and Zimri. The main difference may be considered to be the fact that the Levites, including Elisha himself, took an active part in it. The coup was not the result of a popular uprising or social movement; rather, it was no more than the manifestation of a battle for power between members of the ruling elite. The Levites' part in the coup merely added a religious dimension which had been absent from the previous coups. Jehu himself, unlike Omri, was of Israelite origin, but this fact is unlikely to have been of much importance during the second half of the 9th century BCE given that the process of mutual assimilation between the Hebrew tribes and the Canaanite/Amorite population was already so advanced that ethnic and cultural differences between them were now of no significance. More important considerations were the prestige of the king and the support of the army and the tribal and regional aristocracy. In this respect Joram was considerably less lucky than his father and grandfather. He likewise had to conduct numerous wars, but was significantly less successful. Under his rule Israel suffered territorial losses: Moab seceded and the Arameans seized part of northern Transjordan. The result was a reduction in revenue and military plunder. Unlike in Judah, in Israel not a single royal dynasty was able to establish itself, so every influential military commander thought himself entitled to depose any king who had lost the support of his army and courtiers. As for social and religious protests, they had been much stronger during the times of Joram's father, Ahab, but this had still not led to his losing his throne (Ahab proved a successful general and ruler). Joram for his part had improved his relations with the Levites and during his reign encountered less social and religious unrest than his father; this, however, did not save him from falling victim to a coup and bloody reprisal.

Joram's most important achievement was his maintenance of good relations, including relations of kinship, with Judah and his strengthening of the military alliance with this country. It was during the reign of Joram that the royal courts of both countries drew closest to each other, including by marriage. The Judahite throne belonged at that time to Joram's brother-in-law – Jehoram, who was married to Ahab's daughter Athaliah. The two kings – the kings of Israel and Judah – bore the same name, which was pronounced in different ways. Slightly later, the Judahite throne was occupied by Ahaziah, who was Joram's nephew. The two kingdoms became so close that historians felt entitled to ask whether Israel had not subjugated Judah and even whether Joram, the king of the Israelites, and Jehoram, the king of Judahites, were not one and the same person. Had this really been the case, the keepers of the tradition could hardly have passed over in silence such a bold maneuver by the dynasty of Omri, for which they had so much loathing given its worship of Baal. The close alliance between Israel and Judah and the close blood relations between their ruling dynasties were an ideal form of union between the northern and southern tribes. Historically speaking, both the United Monarchy and the hostilities between these tribal groups were extremes. Much more natural was a political alliance reinforced by blood ties. Possibly, this was the prevailing type of relations during the pre-Egypt period of living in Canaan and during the stay in Egypt. However, the Israelite tribal aristocracy, remembering the humiliations inflicted on it by the Davidic dynasty, regarded the close kinship between the two royal courts not so much as a political success on the part of Joram, but as a dangerous liaison with the house of David – and one which threatened its own interests.

The Reign of Jehu's Dynasty
The decisive factor for the conspirators was the king's remoteness both from the capital, Samaria, and also from his army's main forces, which were at

Ramoth-Gilead. Joram was in Jezreel, the unofficial capital of the Canaanite part of the Northern Kingdom, where he was recovering from his wounds. Joram, like his father, Ahab, preferred to spend his time not in Samaria, which was built on land belonging to the Israelite tribes, but in Canaanite Jezreel. Jehu's army marched to Jezreel with a rapidity which caught Joram, not yet recovered from his wounds, by surprise. The king not only was unaware of the preparations for the coup, but also lacked sufficient forces to defend the city. The Bible, not without pomp, notes that Joram found his death on the same field which his father, Ahab, took from Naboth of Jezreel, whom he had killed without cause. With just the same sense of rightful vengeance the keepers of the tradition write of the realization of Elijah's prophecy that Jezebel would meet a terrible end on that same 'Jezreel field'. During the course of the bloody bacchanalia the entire house of Ahab, as well as his friends and high-ranking officials, lost their lives. Jezebel met her death with great courage. The daughter of the Phoenician king, mother of the Israelite king, and grandmother of the Judahite king, she did not try to conceal herself or run away, but after painstakingly painting her face and putting on her best clothes, met the mutinous general with a contemptuous sneer: "Have you come in peace, Zimri, you murderer of your master?" (2 Kings 9:30-31). At the orders of Jehu, Ahaziah, the King of Judah, who had come to visit his kinsman Joram, was also killed.

From his position of strength Jehu addressed the frightened courtiers in Samaria, proposing that they either voluntarily hand over the heads of Ahab's 70 sons or join the latter's resistance. However, the balance of forces was so unequal – the army's support for its commander was total – that the entourage of the former king thought it best to obey the new leader. Interestingly, a message sent by Jehu to Samaria implies that power in the capital – as, incidentally, all Ahab's sons too – was in the hands of the 'princes and elders of Jezreel', who came from a region which was populated mainly with Canaanites (2 Kings 10:1-3). Possibly, this is confirmation that Omri, the founder of the dynasty, himself came from the Canaanites of the Jezreel Valley. To the massacre of all members of the overthrown royal dynasty that is usual in such cases was added the murder of the king's sons from Judah who had, completely unaware of what awaited them, come to visit their Israelite relatives. Finally, the bloody bacchanalia ended in a phenomenon that was utterly new for palace coups – the eradication of the priests of Baal and the destruction of the temple to Baal in Samaria. "They demolished the sacred stone of Baal and tore down the temple of Baal, and people have used it for a latrine to this day. So Jehu destroyed Baal worship in Israel" (2 Kings 10:27-28). Jehu invited Jehonadab, head of the Rechabites, a Yahweh-worshipping clan famous for its puritan views, to attend this beating of the 'enemies of the Lord'. In this way Jehu confirmed both his

Israel: Successor to the 'House of Joseph'

belonging to the followers of Yahweh in the Northern Kingdom and his alliance with the Levites. The keepers of the tradition saw these actions as reflecting well on the new king: "The Lord said to Jehu, 'Because you have done well in accomplishing what is right in my eyes and have done to the house of Ahab all I had in mind to do, your descendants will sit on the throne of Israel to the fourth generation" (2 Kings 10:30).

It seemed that the Levites had reason to celebrate; their victory over both their political and ideological opponents was complete. But strangely, in spite of the Levites' expectations, the temples at Bethel and Dan were not placed at their disposal. The keepers of the tradition were unable to conceal their disappointment at Jehu's decision: "However, he did not turn away from the sins of Jeroboam son of Nebat, which he had caused Israel to commit—the worship of the golden calves at Bethel and Dan" (2 Kings 10:29). It is probable that Jehu was forced to take into account the same circumstances as had influenced his remote predecessor Jeroboam. On the one hand, he had no wish to enter into conflict with those Israelite tribes on whose land these temples stood and whose priests were exercising the functions of the Levites. On the other, he was not prepared to give up the old, pagan form of the worship of Yahweh which was popular among the northern tribes and which linked this cult with the traditional Canaanite faiths. Moses' monotheism continued to be alien and incomprehensible to most ordinary people, and this was something which the new king was bound to take into consideration. It would also be naïve to think that the eradication of the priests of Baal and the destruction of their temple in Samaria spelt the end of this cult throughout the Northern Kingdom. Outside Samaria, in both Canaanite and Israelite regions, the cult of Baal continued to exist; however, its priests lost their dominant role, ceding it to the followers of Yahweh. Just as Ahab and Jezebel had been unable to eradicate the Levites, so Jehu was unable to put an end to the cult of Baal throughout the Northern Kingdom. Jehu's actions may be compared with the act of the legendary Israelite judge Gideon, who, after putting an end to worship of this Canaanite divinity, seduced the Israelites with service to other pagan gods. The Bible directly links the king's failures in the wars with the Arameans with the fact that he in effect continued the sins of Jeroboam: "Yet Jehu was not careful to keep the law of the Lord, the God of Israel, with all his heart. He did not turn away from the sins of Jeroboam, which he had caused Israel to commit. In those days the Lord began to reduce the size of Israel. Hazael overpowered the Israelites throughout their territory east of the Jordan in all the land of Gilead (the region of Gad, Reuben and Manasseh), from Aroer by the Arnon Gorge through Gilead to Bashan" (2 Kings 10:31-33).

Jehu became the founder of the most important dynasty in the history of the Northern Kingdom. He and his descendants occupied the Israelite throne for almost an entire century. Nevertheless, the Bible provides us with almost no information regarding his 28-year rule, although he came to power with full support from the Levites, i.e. the keepers of the tradition themselves, and consequently should not have been ignored by them. Almost all the information we have regarding Jehu relates to his overthrow of the dynasty of Omri and eradication of the priests of Baal. The only piece of information that we may draw from the Bible is the fact that the years of Jehu's reign coincided with the period when the Arameans were attacking Israel, and that Hazael, the most bellicose king of Damascus, managed to seize all the Transjordanian regions from the Northern Kingdom. Another source which may be used to supplement the Bible is Assyrian documents; these, however, contain only rare mentions of Israel.

Jehu and his heirs substantially changed the political course taken by the Northern Kingdom and refused to take part in the anti-Assyrian coalition. As we know, during the time of Ahab, Israel had been one of the leaders and possibly (to judge by the number of war chariots it possessed) the most important member of this coalition. Ahab's son Joram had continued his father's policy regarding Assyria. However, in spite of the extremely important contribution made by Israel to warding off Assyrian aggression, the latter during this period had affected Israel's own interests least of all. The military campaigns of Shalmaneser III had been directed, above all, against states in northern and central Syria, Phoenicia and the Aram-Damascus. Who was it who had drawn Ahab into expensive and bloody wars to defend Phoenician cities and Damascus, a kingdom which was hostile to him? Most likely, it had been his Sidonian relatives on the side of his wife, Jezebel. The Bible leaves us in no doubt that the Yahweh worshippers of the Northern Kingdom and their prophets had been categorically against Ahab's alliance with his potential enemy Ben-Hadad II, and subsequent events confirmed that Israel's own interests at that time did not require it to wage war against Assyria on the side of Phoenicia and Damascus. Jehu left the anti-Assyrian coalition, which, now that Israel was no longer taking part in it, promptly fell apart.

The considerable difference in the policies of the dynasties of Jehu and Omri was not incidental; it had its explanation in their different religious and cultural orientations. Regardless of its ethnic provenance, the dynasty of Omri was undoubtedly Canaanite in character – as can be seen from its choice of the cult of Baal, its political alliance with Phoenicia, and the fact that power was concentrated in the hands of Canaanites from the Jezreel Valley. Finally and paradoxically, the alliance and ties of kinship with the house of David were only possible because the dynasty of Omri did not have to contend with old hurts and fears felt by the tribal aristocracy of the northern tribes. In this respect the dynasty of Jehu was very different. Not only was this dynasty of Israelite origin,

Israel: Successor to the 'House of Joseph'

but also it expressed, first and foremost, the interests of the northern tribes. It was for this reason that it was in such a hurry to restore the alliance with the northern Levites, to return to worship of Yahweh, even if in the old pagan form of this cult, and to break off close relations of kinship with the house of David, of whom the Israelite tribal aristocracy was in fear. In just the same way Jehu rejected the alliance with the city states of Phoenicia. Unlike Omri and Ahab, he had no need for them: he had neither time nor money for large-scale construction or maritime trade, and militarily the Phoenician cities were too weak to be of interest.

But it was not just that there was a new direction to Israelite policy; there were also serious changes underway in Syria and Phoenicia themselves. After Hazael seized power in Damascus, this Aramean kingdom rapidly grew in strength, subjecting the whole of southern and central Syria and attempting likewise to gain control over Phoenicia and Israel. The military capability of the Northern Kingdom proved inadequate to the job of checking Damascus' expansion (Aram-Damascus possessed incomparably greater human and material resources), so Jehu decided to seek a powerful ally in the form of Assyria, the enemy of his enemy. The famous black obelisk recording the victories of the Assyrian king Shalmaneser III tells us that in the 18th year of his reign the Israelite king 'Jehu, son of Omri' brought Shalmaneser abundant tribute. On the same obelisk is engraved a scene showing Jehu or his messenger on his knees in audience with Shalmaneser III. At the same time, the Assyrian king tells us that he took tribute from the Phoenician cities of Tyre and Sidon, but says nothing of the kings of these cities and does not give their names. In another announcement, concerning his second campaign in a southern-westerly direction, three years later, Shalmaneser III talks of extracting tribute from the Phoenician cities of Tyre, Sidon, and Byblos, but no longer mentions Israel as a tributary, even though the Assyrian army still stood on the border with the Northern Kingdom. Clearly, Jehu had by this time managed to become a junior partner and ally of Assyria – otherwise he would not have been able to escape having to pay considerable tribute. It is probable that during the first campaign by the Assyrian king Jehu proved quicker than anyone else and, without waiting for the Assyrian army to approach, at his own initiative rushed to offer abundant tribute to Shalmaneser III. As far as we can judge, he was the only king in his region who was given a personal audience with the Assyrian king and won his favor. And it is for this reason that the black obelisk paid special attention to the King of Israel: the latter was regarded not so much as a tributary but as a potential ally in a region which was extremely important for Assyria. Interestingly, no Phoenician ruler who brought tribute is either shown on the obelisk or even mentioned. In this way, Jehu's strategy – to turn his enemy's enemy into his own friend – was clearly successful.

A detail of the 'Black Obelisk' showing the envoy of Israelite King Jehu prostrating himself before Assyrian King Shalmaneser III.

Initially, everything went as Jehu planned: in Shalmaneser's very first campaign against Aram-Damascus, in approximately 840 BCE, he destroyed, according to Assyrian sources, 16,000 soldiers, seized 1121 chariots, and besieged Hazael himself in Damascus. However, the Assyrian king was on this occasion unable to seize the Aramean capital and was forced to confine himself to laying waste its environs. Three years later, the Assyrians appeared once again at the walls of Damascus and again inflicted heavy losses on Hazael's army, but, as on the first occasion, were unable to seize the city. The fact that the Assyrian army, the most powerful of its time, was in one-to-one battle with the Arameans twice incapable of delivering a decisive blow to the kingdom of Damascus is clear evidence of the latter's military power and of the talents of Hazael himself as a general. Interestingly, in his inscriptions on the black obelisk, Shalmaneser III contemptuously calls Hazael a 'plebeian' and usurper' and mentions the fact that he had seized power in Damascus. And yet Jehu, who had seized the Israelite throne at approximately the same time and in similar circumstances, is respectfully called 'son of Omri' – i.e. a legitimate king from a recognized and respected dynasty – although Shalmaneser, who knew everything about Hazael, must surely have known very well the new Israelite king's true origin and the circumstances of his ascension to the throne.

As Jehu expected, Aram-Damascus, weakened by the wars with Assyria, stopped troubling Israel. However, the peace did not last long. Jehu's powerful ally confounded his plans by ceasing to put pressure on Damascus and abandoning all campaigns in a south-westerly direction, for almost the next three decades. Assyria was busy with other, more urgent matters: it had to contend with uprisings by the subjugated peoples in its rear; Shalmaneser III faced a mutiny led by his own son and heir; and there were prolonged and exhausting wars with Urartu. Delivered from the threat from Assyria, Hazael attacked Israel with new force, initiating one of the most difficult periods in the existence of the Northern Kingdom.

During the course of Jehu's reign Israel suffered significant losses of land as the Arameans gradually seized the whole of Transjordan and even Galilee. Many historians put the blame for this on the bloody coup by which Jehu came to power; on the king's intolerant religious policy, which repelled the Canaanite/Amorite population; and on the break-up of the alliance with Phoenicia and Judah. However, in eliminating his opponents, Jehu behaved in just the same way as all his predecessors who had seized the throne before him and in perfect accord with accepted practice at the time. Nor, as is clear from the criticisms made by the keepers of the tradition, was he a puritanical follower of Yahweh. As for the Phoenician cities and Judah, they were militarily weak at the time; their support could not have reversed the unfavorable balance of forces. The problem was not Jehu's personality, nor the change in the ruling dynasty; nor even was it a matter of the change of political course. The reason for the disastrous position of the Northern Kingdom lay in the changing geopolitical situation in Syria and Palestine. Although Israel remained the strongest of all the Palestinian countries (Judah, Philistia, Moab, Ammon, and Edom), it could not compete with the sharply increased might of the kingdom of Damascus. It may perhaps be argued that it is to Jehu's credit that, in spite of the serious losses of territory, he nevertheless managed to preserve Israel's independence from Aram-Damascus.

The situation deteriorated dramatically during the rule of Jehu's son Jehoahaz, whose 17-year reign coincided with a period of profound decline for the Northern Kingdom. Jehoahaz was unable to check the pressure applied by Damascus and became the latter's vassal and tributary. As was usual in such situations, the keepers of the tradition linked Jehoahaz's military failures against the Arameans with his desertion of the Lord: "He did evil in the eyes of the Lord by following the sins of Jeroboam son of Nebat, which he had caused Israel to commit, and he did not turn away from them. So the Lord's anger burned against Israel, and for a long time he kept them under the power of Hazael king of Aram and Ben-Hadad his son" (2 Kings 13:2-3). In reproaching Jehoahaz with the sins of Jeroboam, the keepers of the tradition had in mind not just the golden calves in Bethel and Dan, nor just the removal of the northern Levites from service in these temples, but also the existence of numerous pagan cults in the Northern Kingdom. Although Jehu did destroy the temple of Baal in Samaria, this did not stop other pagan cults flourishing in the Israelite capital. The Bible mentions that during the rule of Jehoahaz "the Asherah pole remained standing in Samaria" (2 Kings 13:6). The 'pole' or 'idol tree' was the symbol of Asherah, the Canaanite goddess of fertility who was considered to be the spouse of the supreme god El and was sometimes also venerated as wife of that same Baal whom Jehu, Jehoahaz's father, had disposed of.

Jehoahaz's position was more than unenviable. The Arameans not only seized the larger part of his kingdom, but also, imposing restrictions on his army, deprived him of almost all his cavalry and chariots. "Nothing had been left of the army of Jehoahaz except fifty horsemen, ten chariots and ten thousand foot soldiers, for the king of Aram had destroyed the rest and made them like the dust at threshing time" (2 Kings 13:7). If we compare Jehoahaz's 10 remaining chariots with the 2000 which Ahab had had at his disposal, then the extent of the military catastrophe which had befallen the Northern Kingdom becomes clear. The Israelite king's almost complete lack of cavalry and chariots was exploited by his eastern neighbors, the Moabites and Ammonites, whose mobile detachments periodically invaded, plundered, and laid waste the country. Later, the prophet Amos wrote of this difficult time that the Arameans of Damascus "threshed Gilead with sledges having iron teeth" and the Ammonites "ripped open the pregnant women of Gilead in order to extend [their] borders" (Amos 1:3; 1:13).

As during the time of Jehu, salvation came from the direction of Assyria, which had once again returned to a policy of conquest in Syria and Phoenicia. In 805-801 BCE the Assyrian king, Adad-nirari III, inflicted a series of serious defeats on Hazael's son Ben-Hadad III, seized Damascus, and exacted an enormous tribute. This powerful blow dealt Damascus by the Assyrians liberated Israel both from the need to pay tribute and from all dependence on the Arameans. Towards the end of his reign, Jehoahaz managed to restore his country's former alliance with Assyria, which is why Israel, unlike its neighbors, not only did not become a target for the Assyrian army's military campaigns, but continued being able to avoid having to pay tribute. Without naming the Assyrians, the Bible gives us to understand that they were sent by God himself to save Israel from the Arameans: "Then Jehoahaz sought the Lord's favor, and the Lord listened to him, for he saw how severely the king of Aram was oppressing Israel. The Lord provided a deliverer for Israel, and they escaped from the power of Aram" (2 Kings 13: 4-5).

However, Jehoahaz was not fated himself to enjoy the favorable conditions in which the Northern Kingdom now found itself. His son Jehoash was rather more lucky, presiding in the 16 years of his reign over the rapid restoration of Israel's economic and military might. Jehoash inflicted three heavy defeats on the Arameans, the most important and decisive being at Aphek, at the spot where Ahab had defeated Ben-Hadad II. As a result, he regained a substantial part of the Israelite territory previously seized by the Arameans, but was unable to properly sack Damascus. Fortunately for Jehoash, after delivering several blows to Damascus, the Assyrians halted their south-westerly expansion, finding themselves caught up for a long time to come in exhausting wars with the kingdom of Urartu and its allies in the north-east. Unlike on past occasions, this time they had the strength to put pressure on the Arameans, but were not yet ready to wage serious campaigns against Palestine and Phoenicia. It is likely that Israel remained an ally of Assyria and coordinated with the latter its actions against Damascus. The Bible describes this situation as follows: "Then Jehoash son of Jehoahaz recaptured from Ben-Hadad son of Hazael the towns he had taken in battle from his father Jehoahaz. Three times Jehoash defeated him, and so he recovered the Israelite towns" (2 Kings 13:25). From this brief piece of information it is difficult to make out where exactly the new boundary dividing Israel from the Aram-Damascus lay: either Jehoash pushed the Arameans back to the borders they had possessed when Jehu died and Jehoahaz came to power, or he managed to recover all the Israelite land and restore the frontier which had existed under Ahab.

Israel was not the only country to try to fill the political and military vacuum that had arisen following the defeats suffered by Damascus in the wars with the Assyrians. Judah, the other Hebrew kingdom, took advantage of the sudden weakening of both its opponents, Israel and Aram-Damascus, and laid claim to the role of leader of the Palestinian states. The Judahite king, Amaziah, challenged Israel's primacy and pressed upon it a war which he hoped would lead to a redistribution of territories and of political influence in Palestine. However, he clearly overestimated both the extent to which Israel had been weakened and the degree to which it was involved in wars with Damascus. At a battle near Beth-Shemesh the Israelites routed the Judahites and took their king, Amaziah, prisoner. In order to teach the aggressor a clear lesson, Jehoash gave orders for part of the city wall to be knocked down and for all the treasures of the Temple in Jerusalem to be taken as trophies. Wishing to further punish his rival, Jehoash helped the Edomites break free from the rule of Judah. The keepers of the tradition, who always sympathized with the Davidic dynasty and criticized the kings of Israel, on this occasion could find no justification for the senseless actions of the Judahite king. This victory provided fresh confirmation that, in spite of the enormous losses it had suffered in the wars with Aram-Damascus, Israel was still the most powerful kingdom among the Palestinian states.

The first years of Jehoash's rule were also marked by the death of the famous Israelite prophet Elisha. Judging by the description given in the Bible, during the rule of the dynasty of Jehu Elisha was not simply the principal court prophet, but also someone whose authority matched that of the king. The Israelite king himself wept at his deathbed, calling him his father and "the chariots and horsemen of Israel!" (2 Kings 13:14). Elisha's extremely privileged position under the dynasty of Jehu contrasts markedly with the sad fate of his teacher Elijah during the rule of the dynasty of Omri. How, given such reverence for the leader of the cult of Yahweh in the Northern Kingdom, did

Jehoash "not renounce the sins of Jeroboam" and not hand over supervision of religious services in Bethel and Dan to the northern Levites – given that, as the prophet Amos bears witness, the temple at Bethel was "the king's sanctuary and the temple of the kingdom" (Amos 7:13). Why did neither Elijah nor Elisha, fervent fighters against paganism, ever once speak up against the golden calves in these temples? The answer to this question probably lies in the character of the cult of Yahweh in the Northern Kingdom and deserves separate consideration.

Jehoash was followed by his son Jeroboam II, the fourth king from the dynasty of Jehu. According to the Bible, Jeroboam II ruled longer than any other king of Israel (41 years) and "restored the boundaries of Israel from Lebo Hamath to the Dead Sea" (2 Kings 14:25). He managed to rout the Arameans completely, seizing Damascus and annexing to Israel a large part of Syria as far as Hamath. In Transjordan he not only took back all the lands of the Israelite tribes, but also subjugated Ammon and Moab, emerging at the eastern shore of the Dead Sea. His rule marked the peak of the Northern Kingdom's might; Israel was able to expand its territory as far as the boundaries attained by King David. We do not know what kind of relations Jeroboam II had with Judah, but it is a fact that the cities of northern Philistia became vassals of Israel. This king's successes look even more impressive if we take into account that during his rule the country was struck by serious natural disasters, including an earthquake, repeated droughts, and plagues of locusts, which resulted in famine and economic shocks (Amos 1:1; 4:6-10).

It would be a mistake to attribute Jeroboam II's brilliant military successes to the favorable political situation alone. Was this situation indeed so favorable for Israel? After all, Israel's temporary ally, Assyria, was once again busy fighting prolonged wars on its north-eastern borders and, as on previous occasions, had in effect withdrawn from southern and central Syria for a number of decades. As in the times of Jehu and Jehoahaz, Israel once again found itself facing Aram-Damascus on its own. Admittedly, in 773 BCE the Assyrian king Shalmaneser IV undertook a campaign against Damascus, but this ended extremely badly for him; Assyria was forced to cede to the Arameans almost all of Syria – a sign of the considerable military might of the kingdom of Damascus. After this, the Assyrians helped Israel no more. In reality, the opposite was true: Assyria profited greatly from the fact that Israel drew upon itself a serious military opponent who under different circumstances might well have joined Assyria's enemies. The only circumstance that may be considered favorable for the Northern Kingdom was that a predator as frightening as Assyria was for a long time kept busy with both the wars with its northeastern neighbors and the need to deal with domestic problems such as uprisings by its subject peoples, court conspiracies, and epidemics.

Israel: Successor to the 'House of Joseph'

Northern and Southern kingdoms at the time of
Israelite king Jeroboam II (788-747 BCE).

There is every reason to think that Jeroboam II was an outstanding king who transformed Israel into the principal regional power in Palestine, Syria, and Phoenicia. Unfortunately, the Bible pays him very little attention – further proof that the bearers of the tradition were interested not in history, but in theosophy, especially since Jeroboam's incontrovertible successes, given that he did not renounce the 'sins' of his predecessors, provided no edifying lessons for future generations. Admittedly, Jeroboam's court prophet was Jonah, author of one of the books of the Bible and son of Amittai from Gath-Hepher; Jonah could have left rather more detailed information regarding his king. Nevertheless, Jeroboam's rule receives a certain amount of coverage in the books of Hosea and Amos, the first prophets of the Northern Kingdom to prophesy in writing (they witnessed the last few years of Jeroboam's reign). Both prophets in effect confirm the sacking of Damascus and Israel's annexation of Syria, Moab, and Ammon. However, they have little interest in the success of Jeroboam's expansionary policy, being mostly concerned with the oppression of the poor, moral dissolution, and idolatry.

The military victories and economic prosperity under Jeroboam II had a negative side: they led to the rapid enrichment of some people and impoverishment of others, and to a deepening of social inequality in society – which in turn resulted in the corruption of morals and a growth in the influence of pagan cults. The prophet Hosea notes with bitterness that "There is no faithfulness, no love, no acknowledgment of God in the land. There is only cursing, lying and murder, stealing and adultery; they break all bounds, and bloodshed follows bloodshed [...] Old wine and new wine take away their understanding. My people consult a wooden idol, and a diviner's rod speaks to them. A spirit of prostitution leads them astray; they are unfaithful to their God" (Hosea 4:1-2; 4:11-12). The same is said by the prophet Amos, who complains that, "They sell the innocent for silver, and the needy for a pair of sandals [...] There are those who oppress the innocent and take bribes and deprive the poor of justice in the courts" (Amos 2:6; 5:12).

The prophet Hosea tells us of the spread of the cult of Baal and of views relating to this cult – views which, it might seem, should have long since been eradicated by King Jehu, but, as it turns out, were extremely widespread, and not just in regions with a Canaanite population, but in the Israelite populations as a whole. "When Ephraim spoke, people trembled; he was exalted in Israel. But he became guilty of Baal worship and died. Now they sin more and more; they make idols for themselves from their silver, cleverly fashioned images, all of them the work of craftsmen. It is said of these people, 'They offer human sacrifice and kiss the calf-idols" (Hosea 13:1-2). Interestingly, unlike the undoubtedly northern prophet Hosea, Amos, who came from Judah, reproached Israel also for 'the altars of Bethel' (Amos 3:14).

The prophets also took exception to Jeroboam II's policy of strengthening Israel's alliance with Assyria. "For they have gone up to Assyria like a wild donkey wandering alone. Ephraim has sold herself to lovers" (Hosea 8:9). These words of Hosea confirm the fact that Israel was not a tributary of Assyria, but a voluntary ally and partner. Evidently, Jeroboam II continued the Jehu dynasty's course of allying with Assyria against the kingdom of Damascus. Next in importance was the alliance with Egypt; admittedly, this was more a matter of trade and economic relations than political or military ones. Hosea is just as critical of this second alliance as of the first: "Ephraim is like a dove, easily deceived and senseless—now calling to Egypt, now turning to Assyria [...] Ephraim feeds on the wind; he pursues the east wind all day and multiplies lies and violence. He makes a treaty with Assyria and sends olive oil to Egypt" (Hosea 7:11; 12:1). Nevertheless, their condemnation of Jeroboam's alliances with Assyria and Egypt was probably due to the fact that both Hosea and Amos had witnessed the fall of the Northern Kingdom, when the Assyrians neglected their friendship with Israel and the Egyptians forgot their alliance with it.

Jeroboam's heir was his son Zechariah, who was the fifth king of the Jehu dynasty. However, Zechariah was not fated to rule for any length of time: a mere six months after ascending the throne, he was killed by conspirators. "Shallum son of Jabesh conspired against Zechariah. He attacked him in front of the people, assassinated him and succeeded him as king." In telling us this, the authors of the book of Kings emphasize that "the word of the Lord spoken to Jehu was fulfilled: 'Your descendants will sit on the throne of Israel to the fourth generation.'" (2 Kings 15:10, 12).

The murder of the king was not a traditional palace conspiracy among courtiers. The Bible tells us that the killing occurred neither in the dark crannies of the palace nor on a military campaign, as had been the case on previous occasions, but "in front of the people". Evidently, there must have been some kind of conflict with social, religious, or ethnic causes, leading to an explosion of uncontrollable passion and the unexpected murder of the king. The army on this occasion did not support the conspirators; admittedly, neither did it place on the throne any other member of the royal family – perhaps because these other members had already met the fate that is customary in such cases (they were immediately put to the sword by the new ruler). However, the murderers found support among part of the population, namely among the inhabitants of the city of Tiphsah, who refused to open the city gates to their own army. Another sign of the social or ethnic character of the conflict is the extreme ruthlessness with which the insurrection was put down. Shallum, the leader of the conspirators, managed to rule for a mere month. Menahem, son of Gadi and evidently the murdered king's military commander, "went from Tirzah up to Samaria. He attacked Shallum son of Jabesh in Samaria, assassinated him and succeeded him as king" (2 Kings 15:14). Certain historians suppose that both Shallum and Menahem, who overthrew him, were Gileadites, which is to say that they came from Israelite Transjordan. As evidence, they refer to the names of these kings' fathers, Jabesh and Gadi. The first of these names they interpret as an abbreviation of the name of the region of Jabesh-Gilead; the second, as deriving from the name of the Israelite tribe of Gad, which was based in Transjordan. However, such a frivolous interpretation of these names is hardly convincing. It is not clear why in one case the father's name is to be interpreted as a toponym and in the other as an ethnonym. But even greater confusion will result if this principle is applied to the names of all the fathers of Israelite kings, and of others as well. The biblical texts giving accounts of the 8th century BCE are usually already good at distinguishing patronyms from ethnonyms and toponyms and provide no basis for mixing the two.

The Assyrian Expansion and the Fall of Samaria

The end of the almost century-long rule of the dynasty of Jehu coincided with dramatic changes in the largest power of that time, Assyria, where there likewise occurred a change not just of kings, but of dynasties. A military coup brought to the throne the Assyrian military commander who was subsequently known as Tiglath-Pileser III (746-727 BCE). Tiglath-Pileser carried out important reforms, which led to the significant strengthening of Assyria and his authority as king and thus enabled him to break the resistance of Urartu and its allies in the north-east and renew the military campaigns against southern Syria, Phoenicia, and Palestine. The peaceful intermission which the countries of this region had been enjoying now ended; worse still, Assyria returned to the region in the guise of an even more terrible and merciless conqueror than ever before. In order to put an end to separatist tendencies among his vassals and uprisings by his subject peoples, Tiglath-Pileser III or Pul, as the Bible calls him, began turning the states conquered by Assyria into ordinary Assyrian provinces while deporting their inhabitants to remote regions. In place of the original inhabitants the Assyrians settled people from other countries they had conquered; as governors they appointed their own officials. In this way, the new policy facilitated two objectives: on the one hand, the Assyrians got rid of unreliable local rulers, and on the other they deprived the local population of the opportunity to resist. After losing their ties with their native land and finding themselves surrounded by alien peoples, the migrants became submissive to Assyria. Furthermore, the Assyrian governors were now not bound by ethnic or cultural ties to the local population, and this stifled any separatism.

Menahem did not in any significant way change the political course pursued by the Israelite kings from the dynasty of Jehu; the same, however, cannot be said of the policies of the new Assyrian ruler. Under Tiglath-Pileser III Assyria grew so strong that it no longer needed regional allies; the latter's only function was as tributaries and vassals. When the Assyrian army approached the borders of the Northern Kingdom, its former alliance with Israel was forgotten and discarded – especially since it concerned only the previous kings. Menahem, however, followed the course taken by Jehu in rejecting all attempts at confrontation with Assyria: he ceded all the Israelite lands in Syria and voluntarily paid tribute, even though the latter was an onerous burden. The Bible says as follows: "Then Pul king of Assyria invaded the land, and Menahem gave him a thousand talents of silver to gain his support and strengthen his own hold on the kingdom. Menahem exacted this money from Israel. Every wealthy person had to contribute fifty shekels of silver to be given to the king of Assyria. So the king of Assyria withdrew and stayed in the land no longer" (2 Kings 15:19-20). By paying tribute, Menahem, like all the rulers of Syria, Phoenicia, and Palestine, managed to avoid a worse fate – a hopeless and destructive war and the loss of his kingship and large amounts of land. However, the new fiscal pressure borne by the wealthiest part of the population led to dissatisfaction among the ruling elite, especially over the concessions Menahem had made to Assyria. While he was alive, his subjects did not dare – or were unable – to overthrow him, in view of the strong support that, as the former military commander, he enjoyed among the army. But his reign was short – not more than 10 years – and when his son Pekahiah, upon ascending the throne, tried to continue his father's policies, his courtiers formed a conspiracy against him and stripped him of his throne. "One of his chief officers, Pekah son of Remaliah, conspired against him. Taking fifty men of Gilead with him, he assassinated Pekahiah, along with Argob and Arieh, in the citadel of the royal palace at Samaria. So Pekah killed Pekahiah and succeeded him as king" (2 Kings 15:25).

Power was now seized by the anti-Assyrian party, which was dominated by people from Gilead (Pekah himself was probably a Gileadite). Although this was a typical palace coup involving only courtiers and the palace guard, it had very serious and damaging consequences for the future of the Northern Kingdom. Pekah radically changed Israel's foreign policy: even if not immediately, he refused to pay Assyria tribute and thus threw down a challenge to the most powerful empire of the time. Simultaneously, he entered into an alliance with Israel's principal enemy, Aram-Damascus, forming an anti-Assyrian coalition with the latter. The initial architect of this coalition – similar to that which had halted Assyria's expansion at Qarqar in 853 BCE – was Rezin, King of Aram-Damascus; but without the involvement of Israel, one of the strongest states in the region, the coalition had had no chance of success. The coup in Samaria and the coming to power of the anti-Assyrian party put new fire into Rezin's idea, and the two countries which had been antagonists, Israel and Damascus, became the basis of a new coalition against Assyria. Very soon, they were joined by cities in Philistia and Phoenicia, and likewise by

Ammon, Moab, and Edom. Further support was promised by the Syrian states and the Chaldees of Babylonia, who had already risen up against Assyrian rule. The allies were also counting on help from Egypt, which was concerned by the rapid advance of the Assyrians towards its borders. Thus there came into being a powerful bloc of states which, it might have seemed, should have been able to check the Assyrian monster. The only state not to take part in the coalition was Judah, which demonstratively occupied a neutral position. The Judahite king Ahaz not only doubted the success of this amorphous coalition, which consisted of states which had formerly been enemies of one another, but also feared a strengthening of its own close neighbors Israel and Damascus. It was at this point that the allies were compelled to resort to force. First, they were afraid of leaving in their rear a hostile army (especially since the latter could disrupt their communications with Egypt). Second, they wanted to teach a lesson to all opponents of the coalition and compel Judah to take part in it. The Israelites and the Arameans of Damascus won an easy victory over Judah's military forces and jointly laid siege to Jerusalem, while the Philistine cities which were their allies attacked the Judahites from the west and the Edomites did the same from the east. Ahaz's position was hopeless; he gathered together rich gifts and appealed directly to the Assyrian king for help, asking him to accept Judah as his vassal. Tiglath-Pileser III assented to the Judahite king's proposal and acted quickly and decisively, aiming to split up the coalition arrayed against him without giving its members time or opportunity to organize a joint defense. For this he employed both diplomacy and the policy of the stick and carrot: against some members of the coalition scare tactics were used; others were soothed and neutralized by means of promises of forgiveness and support. Nevertheless, the coalition fell apart even before any decisive battle could be fought with the Assyrians, and its organizers, Aram-Damascus and Israel, were left facing their menacing enemy on their own.

The book of Chronicles in the Bible contains an important episode relating to the Israelite campaign against Judah. The allies (the Israelites and Arameans) had failed in their plan to take Jerusalem and to replace King Ahaz with an amenable candidate who would have made Judah a member of the anti-Assyrian coalition. So they plundered the undefended part of the country and took large numbers of prisoners. "The Israelites took captive from their kinsmen two hundred thousand wives, sons and daughters. They also took a great deal of plunder, which they carried back to Samaria" (2 Chronicles 28:8). However once they were back in Samaria, the prophet Oded, a worshipper of Yahweh, convinced the generals and soldiers not to throw their brothers into slavery, but to let them go back home. "Because the Lord, the God of your fathers, was angry with Judah, he gave them into your hand. But you have slaughtered them in a rage that reaches to heaven. And now you intend to make the men and women of Judah and Jerusalem your slaves. But aren't you also guilty of sins against the Lord your God? Now listen to me! Send back your fellow countrymen you have taken as prisoners, for the Lord's fierce anger rests on you.' [...] The men designated by name took the prisoners [...] They provided them with clothes and sandals, food and drink, and healing balm. All those who were weak they put on donkeys. So they took them back to their fellow countrymen at Jericho, the City of Palms, and returned to Samaria" (2 Chronicles 28:9-11, 15). In itself this incident was an extraordinary occurrence that was altogether untypical of that severe age, given that when prisoners were taken, this was not usually with a view to their subsequent release. Of course, there is a strong temptation to interpret this episode as the birth of a feeling of ethnic and religious communality between the Israelites and the Judahites, attributing it to the growing influence of both the northern Levites in Samaria and of the followers of the cult of Yahweh in the Kingdom of Israel in general. However, to be realistic, it has to be admitted that subsequent events do not bear out such a supposition. The true explanation must lie not so much in the religious plane as in the political one. Furthermore, the soldiers could not have released the prisoners, still less helped them return home, without having received orders from their military commanders or the king. So clearly the real cause was that Pekah, King of the Israelites, wanted to make peace with Judah, especially after learning of Tiglath-Pileser III's campaign against Damascus and the imminent clash with the Assyrians. In a situation where the anti-Assyrian coalition was falling apart he had no wish to have in his rear a hostile Judah hungry for revenge – so the return of the prisoners and plunder was a goodwill gesture and an offer of peace. However, it was already too late to check the course of events.

According to Assyrian sources, in approximately 734-732 BCE Tiglath-Pileser III carried out three military campaigns into Syria, Phoenicia, and Palestine, during the course of which he suppressed resistance from mutinous vassals. First of all, he restored his control over the cities of Philistia and Phoenicia, cutting off the members of the coalition from possible support from Egypt. Then he launched an all-out attack against Israel; no one came to the latter's aid. The Assyrian invasion brought greatest suffering on Galilee and Gilead, the northern and eastern districts of the Israelite kingdom. As punishment for their persistent resistance to the Assyrians, part of the population of the land of the tribe of Naphtali was deported to Assyria. Here the Israelites were give their first real taste of the Assyrian rulers' new policy – mass deportation of peoples who failed to submit. The Bible says the following: "In the time of Pekah king of Israel, Tiglath-Pileser king of Assyria came and took Ijon, Abel Beth Maacah, Janoah, Kedesh and Hazor. He took Gilead and Galilee, including all the land of Naphtali, and deported the people to Assyria" (2 Kings 15:29).

Israelites of Ashtaroth. Bas-Relief from the palace of Tiglath-pileser at Calah.

Seeing the monstrous inequality of forces and the senselessness of resisting, a group of military commanders and courtiers headed by Hoshea organized a conspiracy against King Pekah and, killing him, appealed to Tiglath-Pileser III for peace, saying that they were ready to accept any conditions he might propose. The Bible's account of this incident is very laconic: "Then Hoshea son of Elah conspired against Pekah son of Remaliah. He attacked and assassinated him, and then succeeded him as king [...]" (2 Kings 15:30). The Assyrian inscriptions, which were made at the orders of Tiglath-Pileser III, confirm and complement the information given in the Bible, allowing us to understand that the Assyrian king personally approved Hoshea and placed upon him the duties of a vassal: "Israel (literally: "Omri-Land") ... all its inhabitants (and) their possessions I led to Assyria. They overthrew their king Pekah and I placed Hoshea as king over them. I received from them 10 talents of gold and 1000 talents of silver as their tribute and brought them to Assyria".

The peace terms imposed by the Assyrians were extremely onerous. More than 80% of Israelite territory was taken from Israel. On it four separate Assyrian

Israel: Successor to the 'House of Joseph'

provinces were created: Dor, Megiddo, Karnaim, and Gilead. Only the central part of western Palestine – or, to be more exact, the region belonging to the tribe of Ephraim and partly to Manasseh – remained under the authority of the Israelite king. The Israelites' former allies, the Arameans of Damascus, were no better off: their army had been destroyed, their capital seized, and their king, Rezin, killed. As punishment for their refractoriness, the inhabitants of Damascus were deported to the Mesopotamian city of Der (called 'Kir' in the Bible).

Hoshea represented the interests of the same forces as the dynasty of Jehu, i.e. those of the Israelite tribes who worshipped Yahweh and were in favor of compromise with Assyria. It is hardly surprising that the Bible contains the following, extremely interesting, phrase concerning Hoshea: "He did evil in the eyes of the Lord, but not like the kings of Israel who preceded him" (2 Kings 17:2). These words imply that although Hoshea was more of a follower of Yahweh than all the Israelite kings who had ruled before him, his allegiance to Yahweh was of the traditional semi-pagan kind which was insufficient for the Levite monotheists. Possibly, Hoshea went further than Jehu in his concessions to the northern Levites, but did not cede to them the temple in Bethel, and this the northern Levites regarded as "evil in the eyes of the Lord". Given that the Northern Kingdom had been reduced in size to the dimensions of the tribal lands of Ephraim and the western half of Manasseh, we may suppose not only that King Hoshea was a passionate follower of Yahweh, but also that he came from the 'house of Joseph'. It is unlikely that members of the other Israelite tribes, not to mention those of Canaanite/Amorite origin, could have found the support they needed on territory belonging to the 'house of Joseph' in those tense and tragic circumstances. Nevertheless, however much Hoshea was inclined to compromise with Assyria, not a single national party could have agreed to the occupation of four-fifths of Israelite territory. Admittedly, unlike his precursor Pekah, the new king sought a way out not in the creation of a coalition with the numerous, yet weak states of Palestine, Syria, and Phoenicia, but in an alliance with the other mighty power of the time. After the suppression of the uprising of the Chaldees of Babylonia in approximately 729 BCE, the only country that remained unoccupied by the Assyrians was Egypt. But whether Egypt had the strength and desire to overcome Assyria and forestall invasion by the latter's army was not clear. Hoshea entered into secret communications with Egypt, trying to establish its true intentions. But the court of the Israelite king was full of Assyrian spies, and the secret negotiations became known to the new Assyrian ruler, Shalmaneser V (727-722 BCE). The Bible tells us that "the king of Assyria discovered that Hoshea was a traitor, for he had sent envoys to So, king of Egypt, and he no longer paid tribute to the king of Assyria, as he had done year by year. Therefore Shalmaneser seized him and put him in prison. The king of Assyria invaded the entire land, marched against Samaria and laid siege to it for three years" (2 Kings 17:4-5).

A seal inscribed 'Belonging to Abdi, servant of Hoshea.'
Hoshea was the last king of the Northern Kingdom.

To us today, given the distance that separates us from the reality of that time, Hoshea's behavior may seem incomprehensible. What was the king – whose authority extended only over Samaria – hoping for in refusing to pay tribute to the Assyrians and thus throwing down a challenge to an empire which was at the time insuperable? Had the sad fate of his predecessor Pekah not taught him anything? And finally, how are we to explain the fact that after acting as he did, he did not conceal himself behind the walls of his capital, but hurried to the court of the Assyrian king, where he was arrested? These apparently contradictory actions of the Israelite king have to be seen in the light of the political situation of the time. During the last three decades of the 8th century BCE the earth literally burned under the feet of the Assyrian conquerors. The war over Babylon brought Assyria into conflict with its south-eastern neighbor, Elam, which in 721 BCE inflicted a painful defeat on the Assyrians. In 720 BCE the Assyrian king Sargon II, who had barely managed to suppress the uprising in Syria, had to pacify mutinous Gaza, and then fight the Egyptian forces at the borders of Sinai. He was forced to spend the next years – 717-716 BCE – in northern Syria, in order to once again subjugate Carchemish, which had declared its independence. During this period the Assyrians conducted military operations against the Phrygians in Cilicia and the Medes in Iran. Then the exhausting wars with Urartu in the north and Babylon and Elam in the south were once again renewed. After this, there came new uprisings in Syria, Philistia, and Phoenicia, and likewise wars with Judah and Egypt. So King Hoshea had good reason to suppose that the Assyrians would very soon be routed by the combined efforts of Egypt, Babylon, Elam, and Urartu; that their myriad forces would be incinerated in a blaze of insurrections by Syrian, Phoenician, and Philistine cities; and that the Israelites needed to be patient and not allow themselves to be provoked into acting before the time was right. It is likely that Hoshea was merely waiting for a convenient time and occasion to rise up against Assyria, but that this was well understood by the Assyrians themselves. It was for this reason that when domestic problems of some kind prevented the Israelite king from paying the enormous tribute on time, the Assyrians seized upon this as an opportunity to strike first against their refractory vassal. Trying to prevent the untimely conflict at any price, Hoshea set off to talk to Shalmaneser V in person. What the Assyrians wanted, however, was not explanations, but immediate war with Hoshea. Assyria was on several occasions saved by its opponents' inability to coordinate their actions – enabling the Assyrians to deal with them one by one in an order that suited their own convenience. Sensing the approach of a new series of wars with his vassals, Shalmaneser V decided to anticipate events and leave Israel without help from potential allies. The most probable of these was Egypt, which had evidently promised military support in the event of war with Assyria. However, in the middle of the 720s, when the Assyrians were in a hurry to lay siege to Samaria, the Egyptians had no thought for military expeditions into Asia, being preoccupied with their own problems. For Egypt this was a period of decline and internal divisions, but, worse, the country was being gradually conquered by its southern neighbors, the Nubians; only in the north, in the Nile Delta, was one of the Egyptian rulers, Tefnakhte, able for a time to hang on to power and check the progress of this enemy. It was probably with him that the emissaries of King Hoshea negotiated regarding an alliance against Assyria. Certain historians suppose that So, the name of the pharaoh mentioned in the Bible, was in fact the name of his capital, the city of Sais. Another version has it that this name belonged to Osorkon IV, the Egyptian ruler of another region in the Nile Delta that was geographically closer to Palestine, but incomparably weaker, being dependent on the Nubians. Whatever the case, the Nubians' northerly progress confounded all plans and left the Israelites without the help that had been promised. It cannot be ruled out that the Egyptians deliberately used promises of support to push Israel into moving against Assyria, in order to keep the latter's army in Palestine and thus win time for reinforcing their own positions. In any case, whatever the Egyptians' true intentions, when the Assyrians found out that the Egyptians were involved in negotiations with the Israelites and had promised help, conflict between Israel and Assyria became inevitable. Several years later, it is true, the Egyptians did come to the help of Gaza, which was under siege, but were routed by the Assyrians in the region of what is now Rafah. Possibly, the Egyptians were sent not by Tefnakhte, but by pharaoh Piankhy, the founder of a new 25th Dynasty of Nubian descent.

Left without help or allies, the Israelites withstood the Assyrian siege for three years. The fact that the siege of Samaria lasted so long (in spite of the involvement of the principal forces of the Assyrian army under the command of Shalmaneser V himself) is evidence both of the heroism of the defenders and of the high standard of the city's fortifications. Samaria was a first-class fortress and it is telling that the Arameans of Damascus, who lay siege to it a number of times, were not once able to take the city by storm. Three years was in that age usually considered the maximum possible length of time during which a city could hold out against attacks by an experienced army, and the Assyrians were unsurpassed masters at storming cities. So Samaria passed this difficult examination with flying colors, and much of the credit for this lay with King Ahab, who had personally chosen the site for his new capital. That Samaria resisted not merely with persistence, but truly heroically is shown by the fact that its inhabitants were deported to Assyria. Usually, the Assyrians resorted to this kind of punishment only in the case of the most fervent and embittered resistance when they themselves suffered heavy losses. During the reigns of Tiglath-Pileser III, Shalmaneser V, and Sargon II the Assyrian army captured many cities, but only a few of these were punished by the deportation of their citizens. Apart from Samaria, this extreme measure of punishment was employed against Syrian cities such as Calno, Carchemish, Hamath, Arpad, and Damascus, cities which the Assyrians likewise besieged during the course of a lengthy period and where they suffered considerable losses. In 722 BCE during the siege of Samaria the Assyrian king, Shalmaneser V, was killed. Certain historians interpret this by no means quotidian occurrence as the result of conflict among the Assyrian top echelons of power, but we have just as much reason to suppose that Shalmaneser was killed during a successful breakout by the Israelites; this then became one of the reasons why the city's inhabitants were deported en masse.

Having lost all hope of help from the Egyptians, the besieged inhabitants of Samaria looked to uprisings in other cities of the Assyrian empire or military operations by Assyria's opponents to draw away the Assyrian army and force it to raise the siege of the city. However, what actually happened was the opposite: it was the opponents of Assyria who profited from the latter's war with Israel. The armies of Elam and Babylon were able to defeat the Assyrians in 722-721 BCE only because some of the Assyrian forces had not had time to return from Samaria and King Shalmaneser V had been killed during the siege of the Israelite capital.

Israel: Successor to the 'House of Joseph'

The three-year-long siege of Samaria was completed by the new king of Assyria, Sargon II (721-705). Angered by the stubborn resistance of the inhabitants, he ordered them to be deported to three different regions of the Assyrian empire. Two of these – Gozan on the upper reaches of the Habor River and Halah in the vicinity of Nineveh – were in northern Mesopotamia, while the third was in Media in western Iran. The Bible describes these events as follows: "In the ninth year of Hoshea, the king of Assyria captured Samaria and deported the Israelites to Assyria. He settled them in Halah, in Gozan on the Habor River and in the towns of the Medes [...] The king of Assyria brought people from Babylon, Cuthah, Avva, Hamath and Sepharvaim and settled them in the towns of Samaria to replace the Israelites. They took over Samaria and lived in its towns" (2 Kings 17:6, 24). In the inscriptions executed in the palace at Khorsabad (Dur-Sharrukin) Sargon himself does not say that all the Israelites were expelled, but merely communicates the following: "I besieged and conquered Samaria (Samerina), led away as booty 27,290 inhabitants of it. I formed from among them a contingent of 50 chariots for my army [...] I made the city better than it had been before. I settled it with people from the countries which I had conquered. I installed over them an officer of mine and imposed upon them the tribute of the former king".

The Myth of the Disappearance of the Northern Tribes

The biblical account of the deportation of the inhabitants of the Northern Kingdom to Assyria is undoubtedly an exaggeration of the scale of the tragedy. For instance, the book of Kings and the books of the prophets are full of statements such as the following: "So the people of Israel were taken from their homeland into exile in Assyria, and they are still there" (2 Kings 17:23). Such statements have always been understood as implying that the Israelites were resettled in Assyria in their totality. This has given rise to a myth regarding the loss of the ten northern tribes, whose traces are still being sought to this day on the enormous space that stretches from Mesopotamia to the Japanese islands. It is not difficult to understand why the keepers of the tradition (the authors of the Bible) acted as they did: for didactic reasons and to edify future generations, they allowed themselves to overtly exaggerate the scale of the tragedy, presenting it as punishment for idolatry and for failure to obey the Lord's commandments. The biblical text very clearly defines the reason for the expulsion and its scale: "They forsook all the commands of the Lord their God and made for themselves two idols cast in the shape of calves, and an Asherah pole. They bowed down to all the starry hosts, and they worshiped Baal. They sacrificed their sons and daughters in the fire. They practiced divination and sorcery and sold themselves to do evil in the eyes of the Lord, provoking him to anger. So the Lord was very angry with Israel and removed them from his presence. Only the tribe of Judah was left" (2 Kings 17:16-18). The exaggeration of the scale of the punishment was intended to serve as a firm warning against idolatry and violating the divine commandments in the future. If from the point of view of religion and morality this exaggeration was justified, from the point of view of history its result was to mythologize the subsequent fate of the northern tribes.

The Assyrian sources that we have at our disposal give an incomparably more modest picture of the deportation of the Israelites to Assyria. For instance, Sargon II talks of only 27,290 people taken from the region of Samaria. If we add to this number the 13,500 inhabitants who had been driven out earlier from Galilee and Gilead by Tiglath-Pileser III (from the regions which belonged to the tribes of Naphtali, Zebulun, Manasseh, Gad, and Reuben), then the total number of those deported would be not more than 41,000. However, the population of the Israelite kingdom in the 8th century was at least half a million people. Consequently, we may talk of the deportation of not more than one tenth of the population of the Northern Kingdom. Even if we take as our basis the rather more modest figures given by the archaeologists Finkelstein and Silberman, who suppose that the population of the Israelite kingdom at this time was 350,000 at most, the number of those deported would still not exceed one eighth of the total population. There is no reason at all to suspect the Assyrians of artificially lowering the real figures for those taken prisoner and deported. In this respect the Assyrians had the reputation of being the most boastful conquerors of the ancient Near East (a distinction which they shared with the Egyptians). Unlike the more truthful Babylonians, who sometimes admitted their own failures, the Assyrians and the Egyptians never mentioned their defeats and always strongly exaggerated both the scale of their victories and the number of prisoners and trophies that they took. There are several figures given by the Bible which could help us form an overall view of the size of the population of the Northern Kingdom. According to the calculation made by Moses and Eleazar before the conquest of Canaan, i.e. in the 12th century BCE, the northern tribes alone (together with the tribe of Benjamin, but without the Levites) numbered 503,000 (Numbers 26:1-51). Of course, as was then accepted practice, only adult men were counted. A new census conducted during the reign of King David, i.e. in the 10th century BCE, showed that on the territory which later became the Northern Kingdom lived 800,000 men (2 Kings 24:9). Admittedly, this number included not just members of the northern tribes, but also all non-Israelite males. Finally, in the second half of the 8th century, shortly before the fall of Samaria, the Israelite king Menahem "exacted fifty shekels of silver from every wealthy person" in order to pay the tribute of 1000 talents of silver to the Assyrian king Tiglath-Pileser III (2 Kings 15:20). Knowing that 50 shekels of silver amounts to one mina, and one talent of silver contains 60 minas, it is not difficult for us to calculate that during Menahem's reign the population of the Northern Kingdom numbered at least 60,000 wealthy people. We may suppose that by 'wealthy people' the Bible meant simply relatively well-off people who could be subjected to an additional tax in order to pay the tribute to the Assyrians. Given that at that time each of these people had a large family of at least 6-7 persons, it transpires that the Israelite kingdom comprised at least 400,000 who belonged to the class of the wealthy. Of course, there were also large numbers of poor people, who were unable to pay additional taxes. Thus, independently of the archaeological data – which in themselves can be extremely controversial – we may confidently affirm that on the eve of the fall of Samaria the kingdom of Israel had a population of at least half a million. So those who were deported to Assyria were in fact only a small part of the total number of inhabitants of the Northern Kingdom.

Incidentally, the biblical sources themselves sometimes 'let the cat out of the bag' by de facto admitting a more modest scale for the deportation of the Israelites. For instance, the Judahite king Hezekiah, who ruled after the fall of the Northern Kingdom, "wrote letters to Ephraim and Manasseh, inviting them to come to the temple of the Lord in Jerusalem and celebrate the Passover to the Lord, the God of Israel" (2 Chronicles 30:1). If both these tribes had been deported in their entirety to remote Assyria, what reason did the king of Judah have for inviting them to a celebration in Jerusalem? It transpires that not only the tribes of Ephraim and Manasseh were in their accustomed places, but other northern tribes as well. "The couriers went from town to town in Ephraim and Manasseh, as far as Zebulun, but the people scorned and ridiculed them. Nevertheless, some men from Asher, Manasseh and Zebulun humbled themselves and went to Jerusalem" (2 Chronicles 30:10-11). Subsequently, even the biblical text adds that "although most of the many people who came from Ephraim, Manasseh, Issachar and Zebulun had not purified themselves, yet they ate the Passover, contrary to what was written. But Hezekiah prayed for them, saying, 'May the Lord, who is good, pardon everyone who sets his heart on seeking God—the Lord, the God of his fathers—even if he is not clean according to the rules of the sanctuary" (2 Chronicles 30:18-19). This is direct evidence of the fact that there can be no question of the northern tribes having been moved to Assyria in their entirety. There is no doubt that it was only a small part of the Israelites who were deported as Assyrian prisoners, while most remained where they were or departed to live temporarily or permanently in neighboring Judah. After the fall of Samaria the Bible often mentions "the people of Israel and Judah who lived in the towns of Judah", and "all Judah and Israel who were there with the people of Jerusalem" (2 Chronicles 31:6; 35:18). As had happened on a number of occasions in the past following invasions, many inhabitants of the Northern Kingdom found temporary refuge in the mountain ranges of northern Palestine and the Judean Hills of the Southern Kingdom. The Bible tells us of nothing of one very important event for knowledge of which we are indebted to Assyrian sources. Around 720 BCE, i.e. one and a half to two years after the fall of Samaria, its inhabitants again rose up against the Assyrians.

That year there were many Syrian, Phoenician, and Philistine cities which took action against Assyrian rule; Samaria joined them in the hope of liberation. If all its Israelite inhabitants had been deported, who was it then that rose up against the Assyrians? The new settlers from Syria and Mesopotamia had only just begun to turn up and, not having yet had time to make themselves properly at home in their new location, were not yet ready to offer resistance.

Nevertheless, it has to be admitted that although the deportation of the inhabitants of Samaria did not significantly change the demographic situation in central Palestine, from the political, economic, and cultural points of view it was a true catastrophe for the Northern Kingdom. The Assyrians had carried away with them the richest, economically active, and most cultural part of society. Israel was now headless; its body was in Palestine, while its head had been carried off to Assyria. The royal family and courtiers had been carried off into captivity, along with soldiers and their commanders, priests and prophets belonging to all cults, skillful craftsmen and rich landowners, scribes and civil servants – in short, all who represented authority, power, wealth, and knowledge in the Northern Kingdom. At the same time, the peasant farmers who formed the majority of the country's population remained where they were. The Assyrians destroyed the large cities ringed by walls, but did not touch smaller settlements and towns that had no surrounding walls. Of all the Israelite tribes the 'house of Joseph' – or rather the tribes of Ephraim and the western half of Manasseh, who were historically the leaders of the northern group of Hebrew tribes – suffered most. It should not be forgotten that Israel was a federation of northern tribes whose backbone was the Canaanite-Amorite majority in northern and central Palestine. The nerve center and brain of this heterogeneous association was the 'house of Joseph', whose dominant position in both the alliance of Israelite tribes and Palestine itself was a matter not simply of its numerical size, but also of the special role it had played in the history of Canaan and Hyksos Egypt. The blow delivered by the Assyrians was so strong that the entire association was destroyed and the northern tribes reduced to a state of permanent political disintegration. Even after the collapse of the Assyrian empire the northern tribes were unable to unite or to restore their statehood. From now on, the role of leader of both groups of Hebrew tribes passed to the southern tribe of Judah.

The Assyrians were so afraid of possible resistance by the Israelites that they settled them in three regions that were far apart from one another. The place of settlement of the first group was the city of Gozan, which was situated on the eponymous tributary of the River Habor. By an irony of fate, the Israelites' place of exile here was situated not far from Haran, the ancestral motherland of Abraham and the southern Hebrew tribes. Today the district of ancient Gozan lies on the border between Turkey and Syria, near to the modern cities of Ceylanpınar in Turkey and Ras al-Ayn in Syria. Some historians identify

Gozan in the Bible with the ruins of Tell Halaf, one of the most ancient cities in the world, which is situated on the banks of the River Habor. Gozan, like Haran was probably initially the place of settlement of the semi-nomadic Amorite tribes. Later, they were pushed out by the Aramean tribes, who perhaps also intermarried with them. Ethnically, both these peoples were related branches of the same Western Semites, so they were quite quick to assimilate with one another. In any case, by the time the Israelites appeared there, this region was already fully Arameanized.

Another district to which the inhabitants of Samaria were sent was Halah. Unlike provincial Gozan, Halah was situated in the very heart of Assyria, not far from the country's capital, Nineveh. The precise location of biblical Halah has never been identified to any degree of certainty; some people suppose that this was the ancient Assyrian city of Hallahhu, which lay to the north-east of Nineveh. If the Israelites who ended up in Gozan were surrounded by Arameans, those who were settled in Halah lived among Assyrians. Halah's favorable position – from the point of view of geography – helped this group of Israelites rapidly become drawn into the economic and social life of Assyrian society.

Finally, another, third, group of inhabitants of the Northern Kingdom was settled in the very easternmost part of Assyria, in the cities of Media, i.e. in north-west Iran. From the point of view of geography, ethnicity, and culture, these people were in the least favorable position. This region was situated furthest from their motherland and was mainly populated by Medes – an Iranian-speaking people who were very different from the Israelites (as from all Semites) in both language and culture. With respect to social, economic, and cultural factors, this district was considered the least developed in the Assyrian empire. Evidently, the Israelites were sent there not just as punishment for their resistance, but also to civilize the local population.

What subsequently happened to the Israelites who were sent to Assyria? Neither the biblical nor Assyrian sources tell us anything about this. Admittedly, there are Assyrian documents which mention the names of court dignitaries and generals whose Israelite origin is beyond dispute. It is also known that parts of the Assyrian army – e.g. detachments of chariots – were formed entirely of Israelites. However, we have no information about the fate of the tens of thousands of Israelites who were taken to Assyria. It is probable that most of them were gradually assimilated by the surrounding population. This process would have proceeded quickest in the region of Gozan, where the Israelites were surrounded by Arameans, who were, like them, Western Semites and shared common roots with them. The intermingling process occurred more slowly in Halah, where the Samarians lived side by side with Assyrians, i.e. Eastern Semites, who were much more different from them than the Arameans. At the same time, Halah's proximity to Nineveh and the country's main centers accelerated the Israelites' integration into Assyrian society and consequently their assimilation by it. The Israelites who found it most difficult to merge with the local population were those who had been taken to the Median cities in north-west Iran. It is very tempting to suppose that it was this group of Israelites who laid the foundations of the beginning of the Jewish community in Persia. However, at that time Judaism – or, to be more exact, Yahwism – was not yet the formalized monotheistic teaching which it subsequently became, closing off and protecting the Jewish communities from assimilation. In fact, this was probably only the old, semi-pagan form of the cult of Yahweh, which was very different from Moses' consistent monotheism. Furthermore, by no means all inhabitants of the Northern Kingdom were followers of even this form of Yahwism; many continued to worship various Canaanite cults such as Baal and Asherah and were consequently receptive not just to local pagan cults, but also to local culture and traditions, which in turn made their assimilation inevitable. The Assyrian captivity of the Israelites did not end as swiftly as the Babylonian exile of the Judahites; the former inhabitants of the Northern Kingdom did not have a wall-like monotheistic faith to keep them separate from the local pagan population. So in time all three groups of Israelites mostly merged with the peoples who surrounded them. Possibly, some part of them managed at a later date, still under the rule of the Assyrians, to find their way back, openly or covertly, to their motherland.

There exists an opinion that some of the Israelites returned to Palestine together with the Judahites released by Cyrus after his conquest of Babylon. Yet the biblical sources do not support this version of events. Furthermore, the great distance that then separated these two places of settlement of the Israelites and Judahites and the almost two centuries which had passed since the fall of Samaria make this hypothesis extremely unlikely. If the Israelites had indeed wanted to return to Palestine, they would not have had to wait for permission from the King of Persia or to reach an agreement with the Judahites. They could have done so immediately after Assyria had been completely routed and destroyed, leaving a vacuum of power and authority, i.e. long before the Babylonian captivity of the Judahites themselves. However, no written document contains even the slightest hint of the Israelites returning to the territory which had been the Northern Kingdom. This is probably because there was no longer anyone left to return, since the former exiles had already been absorbed in the surrounding population. This is also exactly what happened with the peoples whom the Assyrians moved into the region of Samaria: they never returned to their former motherlands because they had intermarried with the Israelites who had been left in Samaria and became an integral part of this local population.

The Bible tells us the names of the places from which the new settlers came. Three of these places – Hamath, Avva, and Sepharvaim – were in the western part of central Syria, while two – Babylon and Cuthah – were in central Mesopotamia. The inhabitants of all these cities, like the Israelites, had been expelled from their native lands as punishment for repeatedly rising up against Assyria.

The forced migrants mainly consisted of the same ethnic components that made up the population of the Northern Kingdom. For instance, the Syrian cities of Hamath, Sepharvaim, and Avva had initially been populated with Canaanites and had then been conquered by Amorites, and, finally, by Arameans. With the passing of time, all three of these related ethnoses became thoroughly intermingled to form a single West Semitic people speaking Aramean, but in terms of culture had absorbed much of the legacy of the Canaanites and Amorites. Those who came from Babylon and Cuthah differed only slightly from the inhabitants of central Syria: they too were mostly made up of Amorite and Aramean elements. Babylon had initially been founded and settled by Amorites, to whose number also belonged the most famous Babylonian king, Hammurabi II. Subsequently, this part of Mesopotamia was settled by Chaldeans, as was then the name for one of the groups of Aramean tribes who gradually took hold of Babylon, Cuthah, and neighboring cities. Admittedly, instead of the Canaanite element which was present among those who came from central Syria, the migrants from Babylon and Cuthah possessed a mixture of Akkadian (East Semitic) and Sumerian blood. This was perhaps their only slight ethnic difference from the Israelites. As for the Amorite and Canaanite components, there was a surfeit of these in the Northern Kingdom too. Furthermore, the Israelite tribes themselves came from nomadic Amorites, although they were not prepared to admit it and were for a long time the latter's enemies in the fight to possess Canaan. In short, the new settlers were ethnically very close to the inhabitants of the Northern Kingdom; their main difference from the latter was a more pronounced Aramean component and a predominantly Aramean language and culture. But the Arameans were not alien to the Israelites; they were not only the Israelites' closest neighbors, but also an integral part of the population of the north of the country (the Golan Heights and even upper Galilee). Later, during the period of the Second Temple, the Aramean language (Aramaic) began to prevail throughout almost the whole of Palestine.

Non-biblical sources speak of another group of inhabitants whom the Assyrians deported to Samaria. In one of his inscriptions, executed in the seventh year of the reign of Sargon II, the Assyrian king states as follows: "I crushed the tribes of Tamud, Ibadidi, Marsimanu, and Haiapa, the Arabs who live, far away, in the desert and who know neither overseers nor official(s) and who had not (yet) brought their tribute to any king. I deported their survivors and settled (them) in Samaria." Sargon was evidently referring to a group of Midian tribes who later became well-known as Arabs. Ethnically, they were nomadic Amorites and differed from the remaining settlers only from the point of view of culture and social characteristics. The fact that the Bible contains no mention of them is indication that their numbers were extremely small.

The Assyrians settled the inhabitants of Mesopotamian and Syrian cities not only in Samaria itself, but also throughout the region of the tribe of Ephraim and partly in the region of Manasseh, which is why the term 'Samaria' came to signify not just the capital of what had been the Northern Kingdom, but also the territory of these two tribes, territory which became a separate Assyrian province called 'Samerina'. The new settlers brought with them the pagan cults which they had followed in their motherlands. The divinities they worshipped were, for the most part, versions of the same Canaanite and Amorite gods found in the territory of the Israelite tribes. Admittedly, some pagan faiths were characteristic only of Mesopotamia – for instance, the cult of Nergal, the god of death, the center of whose worship was the Mesopotamian city of Cuthah. It was not long before the newcomers, under the influence of the Israelites who remained in Samaria, began following the cult of Yahweh too. This process accelerated when the Assyrians permitted Israelite priests to return to the religious center at Bethel. The keepers of the tradition attribute this to the fact that the new settlers "did not worship the Lord; so he sent lions among them and they killed some of the people. It was reported to the king of Assyria: 'The people you deported and resettled in the towns of Samaria do not know what the god of that country requires. He has sent lions among them, which are killing them off, because the people do not know what he requires.' Then the king of Assyria gave this order: 'Have one of the priests you took captive from Samaria go back to live there and teach the people what the god of the land requires.' So one of the priests who had been exiled from Samaria came to live in Bethel and taught them how to worship the Lord" (2 Kings 17: 25-28).

Regardless of the causes or grounds used as justification for returning the Israelite priests, this biblical episode confirms a very important fact: the center for worship of Yahweh in Bethel was reactivated and the new settlers began professing a belief in Yahweh while simultaneously worshipping their own deities. The Bible describes this polytheism as follows: "Even while these people were worshiping the Lord, they were serving their idols" (2 Kings 17:41). Subsequently, the Aaronites from the Southern Kingdom on a number of occasions exploited the polytheism of the inhabitants of Samaria, the distinctive character of the northern Yahwism, and the fact that the Israelites had intermarried with the new settlers in order to refute the latter's right to be considered heirs to the 'house of Joseph' and so themselves to lay claim to leadership of the descendants of the Hebrew tribes. For the most part, this criticism was unjust and lacking in objectivity. In reality, during the period of the First Temple, polytheism was universal and was characteristic not just of the Samaritans and inhabitants of what had been the Northern Kingdom, but of Judah too. Most worshippers of Yahweh in the northern and Southern Kingdoms were polytheists in just the same way as the Samaritans and worshipped two or more gods at the same time. The situation in the Southern Kingdom was no better than in the Northern. While attributing the fall of Samaria to the idolatry of its inhabitants, the Bible nevertheless tells us that "even Judah did not keep the commands of the Lord their God. They followed the practices Israel had introduced" (2 Kings 17:19). As for the Aaronites' much later accusations of ethnic impurity directed against the Samaritans, they seem hardly serious, to put it mildly, when seen in the light of the Judahites' comprehensive intermarriage with the Canaanites, Jebusites, Perizzites, Kenites, and Kenazzites in southern Canaan. The main reason for the Judahites' hostility towards the Samarians was the traditional rivalry between Judah and Ephraim for hegemony over the descendants of the Hebrew tribes.

After the fall of the Northern Kingdom the 'house of Joseph' had its continuation in the Samaritans, the descendants of the tribes of Ephraim and Manasseh who had intermarried with settlers from cities in Syria and Mesopotamia. However, the alliance of the northern tribes ceased to exist, never to be revived, and the Southern Kingdom began fighting to annex the northern lands and population. Admittedly, for as long as Assyria existed and the lands of the northern tribes were five Assyrian provinces, only religious influence on these territories was possible. But following the defeat of Assyria, the Judahite king Josiah for a short time established his military and political authority in the region. Josiah destroyed all the pagan sacred places and tried to spread his religious reforms to the territory of the northern tribes. However, the arrival of the Egyptians and then of the Babylonians put an end to Judah's rule, and the lands of the northern tribes became part of the Neo-Babylonian empire.

Chapter 10

Judah: Heir to the 'House of Jacob'

Confrontation with Northern Kingdom. Incursions by Egyptian Armies

Rehoboam, son of Solomon, was the first purely Judahite king with authority only over the land of Judah itself. The 17 years during which Rehoboam ruled cannot be called a success for Judah. Rehoboam's greatest political failure was his inability to reach agreement with the northern tribes and prevent their forming the separate kingdom of Israel. The secession of the Israelites in itself turned Judah into an ordinary Palestine state and put an end to the imperial ambitions of the Davidic dynasty. Furthermore, the creation of two Hebrew kingdoms immediately led to a chronic conflict between them over the lands of the southern Hivites. This land was claimed by two Hebrew tribes – Benjamin from the north and Judah from the south. As for the southern Hivites themselves, they undoubtedly preferred Judah and invariably turned to it for help in order to withstand pressure from the Benjaminites. During the reign of Saul, the disputed land had been handed over to his fellow tribesmen, the Benjaminites, but David, upon coming to power, had returned to the Hivites their rights and territories, and moreover had done so in such a way that a considerable part of the lands of the tribe of Benjamin had come under the control of the tribe of Judah. While all the conflicting parties had been contained within the bounds of a single kingdom and under the authority of a single king, their territorial conflict had smoldered out of sight, but after the northern and southern tribes separated, it flared up with new force, with both kingdoms now laying claim to the lands of the Benjaminites and the southern Hivites.

Rehoboam's second serious failure was his defeats in the war with Israel. In justifying the king's lack of success in his relations with the northern tribes, the keepers of the tradition give us to understand that these failures were the result not of policy errors, but of the will of the Lord, who wished to punish the royal dynasty for its idolatry. "But this word of God came to Shemaiah the man of God: 'Say to Rehoboam son of Solomon king of Judah, to all Judah and Benjamin, and to the rest of the people, 'This is what the Lord says: Do not go up to fight against your brothers, the Israelites. Go home, every one of you, for this is my doing.'" So they obeyed the word of the Lord and went home again, as the Lord had ordered" (1 Kings 12:22-24).

The war between Israel and Judah was exploited by the Hebrews' external enemies: the Egyptian pharaoh Sheshonq I (Shishak) invaded Palestine with an enormous army and laid siege to cities in Judah. Facing the danger of war on two fronts, Rehoboam preferred to buy the Egyptians off. "In the fifth year of King Rehoboam, Shishak king of Egypt attacked Jerusalem. He carried off the treasures of the temple of the Lord and the treasures of the royal palace. He took everything, including all the gold shields Solomon had made" (1 Kings 14:25-26). Thus Rehoboam on the one hand saved Jerusalem and part of his country from destruction and on the other channeled the unspent energy of the invaders against his opponent, the newly created Kingdom of Israel, which subsequently suffered from Sheshonq's invasion even more than had Judah.

If the invasion of Sheshonq's army was only a short-lived event in Rehoboam's rule, military operations against the Northern Kingdom continued until his very death. It is this that explains the intensive reinforcement of cities and construction of fortresses that took place in Judah. The book of Chronicles tells us that Rehoboam "built up towns for defense in Judah: Bethlehem, Etam, Tekoa, Beth Zur, Soco, Adullam, Gath, Mareshah, Ziph, Adoraim, Lachish, Azekah, Zorah, Aijalon and Hebron. These were fortified cities in Judah and Benjamin. He strengthened their defenses and put commanders in them, with supplies of food, olive oil and wine. He put shields and spears in all the cities, and made them very strong" (2 Chronicles 11: 5-12). The fact that this list includes cities situated not just near the borders, but also in the very center of the country is evidence that the war was going badly for Rehoboam. Unlike Rehoboam, King David, who conducted successful attacking operations, was almost entirely unconcerned about fortifying the cities in the inner parts of his kingdom. Incidentally, Rehoboam's military defeats were in effect confirmed by his son Abijah. Reproaching the northern tribes for rebelling against their lord, he admitted that Rehoboam "was young and indecisive and not strong enough to resist them [Israelites]" (2 Chronicles 13:7).

Another characteristic of Rehoboam's rule was his tendency for idolatry, a trait which caused the authors of the Bible to take a negative view of his reign. For instance, the book of Chronicles asserts that "He did evil because he had not set his heart on seeking the Lord" (2 Chronicles 12:14). The book of Kings is even more critical of his reign: "Judah did evil in the eyes of the Lord. By the sins they committed they stirred up his jealous anger more than their fathers had done. They also set up for themselves high places, sacred stones and Asherah poles on every high hill and under every spreading tree. There were even male shrine prostitutes in the land; the people engaged in all the detestable practices of the nations the Lord had driven out before the Israelites" (1 Kings 14:22-24).

Rehoboam had 18 wives, of whom the most noble was considered to be Mahalat, who was the granddaughter of King David. However, among Rehoboam's 28 sons it was Abijah (Abijam), his son by his favorite wife Maacah, who became his heir. Maacah was both younger and of less noble birth than her rivals. It is interesting that the Judahite kings did not follow the laws of the Hebrew tribal hierarchy, in accordance with which the eldest son inherited everything by right of primogeniture, but were free to appoint their heirs as they wished. So the throne was often inherited not by the eldest son or the son who was most capable of managing affairs of state, nor even by the child of the eldest or most noble wife (as had been the case with Isaac), but by the son of the favorite wife. In this respect Abijah's ascent to the throne of Judah was very similar to the way in which his grandfather Solomon had come to power: Solomon was inferior to his brothers in terms of the age and nobility of birth of his mother, but was the son of David's favorite wife, Bathsheba.

In spite of the fact that Abijah reigned for only a short time, he was able to change the course of the war against Israel in Judah's favor. It is difficult to say whether these successes were a result of the Arameans of Damascus joining military operations against Israel or of Abijah's own talent as a military commander. Whatever the case, the Judahite army seized three important cities on land belonging to the tribe of Benjamin over which both kingdoms had a claim; these were Bethel, Jeshanah, and Ephrain. Of special importance was the annexation of Bethel, which was the site of the Northern Kingdom's most respected religious center and one which rivaled the Temple in Jerusalem. It cannot be ruled out that Abijah's military victories were one of the reasons for the decline of the dynasty of Jeroboam and for the deposition of the latter's son Nadab from the Israelite throne. But from the point of view of religion, Abijah differed little from his father, and the keepers of the tradition were just as dissatisfied with him as they had been with Rehoboam. It is not for nothing that the Bible notes that "He committed all the sins his father had done before him; his heart was not fully devoted to the Lord his God, as the heart of David his forefather had been" (1 Kings 15:3). This was the accepted way of speaking of those who, while not refusing to worship Yahweh, served the pagan gods with equal fervor.

For unknown reasons Abijah's rule was more than short – a mere three years. It was followed by a reign which was unusually long for that time, an entire 41 years, the reign of Abijah's son Asa. Unlike his father and grandfather, Asa was remembered by the keepers of tradition as a devoted follower of Yahweh. The biblical texts have the highest praise for him: "Asa did what was right in the eyes of the Lord, as his father David had done. He expelled the male shrine prostitutes from the land and got rid of all the idols his ancestors had made. He even deposed his grandmother Maacah from her position as queen mother, because she had made a repulsive image for the worship of Asherah.

Asa cut it down and burned it in the Kidron Valley [...] Asa's heart was fully committed to the Lord all his life" (1 Kings 15:11-14).

However, Asa also had to contend with serious military trials. The first of these was a new invasion by the Egyptian army. The book of Kings makes no mention of this, but Chronicles says as follows: "Zerah the Cushite marched out against them with an army of thousands upon thousands and three hundred chariots, and came as far as Mareshah. Asa went out to meet him, and they took up battle positions in the Valley of Zephathah near Mareshah" (2 Chronicles 14:9-10). Evidently, the invader was the Egyptian pharaoh Osorkon I, who, like Sheshonq I, was a member of the 22nd Libyan Dynasty. As is well known, the Libyan tribes of the Meshwesh who had seized power in Egypt were distinguished by their dark skin color; moreover, their pharaohs' armies used a large number of Nubian mercenaries; so it was not surprising that the new invasion by the Egyptian forces was remembered by the Judahite chroniclers as an invasion of 'Cushites'. The prophet Hanani, who was a contemporary of these events, called the invaders 'Cushites' and 'Libyans'. Subsequently, 'Cushite' came to mean not so much a Nubian as an Ethiopian or a black-skinned person in general, which is why, as the centuries passed, Zerah and his army came to be mistaken for 'Ethiopians'. Osorkon I tried to repeat the successful plundering raid on the Palestinian kingdoms made by his father, Sheshonq I. Gathering an enormous army, mainly consisting of Libyan Meshwesh and Nubians, and having secured the support of the nomadic tribes of Sinai and Midian, he invaded Palestine. Judging by the fact that he managed to reach the Judahite city of Mareshah, he must have seized cities in southern Philistine along the way. However, in Judah he suffered a disastrous defeat. The book of Chronicles describes the rout of the Egyptians as follows: "The Lord struck down the Cushites before Asa and Judah. The Cushites fled, and Asa and his army pursued them as far as Gerar. Such a great number of Cushites fell that they could not recover; they were crushed before the Lord and his forces. The men of Judah carried off a large amount of plunder. They destroyed all the villages around Gerar, for the terror of the Lord had fallen on them. They looted all these villages, since there was much plunder there. They also attacked the camps of the herders and carried off droves of sheep and goats and camels. Then they returned to Jerusalem" (2 Chronicles 14:12-15).

Pursuing their opponents as the latter retreated, the Judahite army seized the cities in southern Philistia which had previously fallen into the hands of the Egyptians and likewise caught by surprise the nomadic tribes who had been keeping Osorkon I's forces supplied with necessary provisions. It goes without saying that the Egyptians erected no triumphal stele to mark such a crushing defeat and, as usual in such cases, their sources maintain complete silence regarding this unsuccessful campaign against Judah. This episode reveals a general problem with which historians and archaeologists have to contend:

the non-biblical sources usually confirm only such information in the Bible as concerns victorious campaigns conducted by their rulers against Palestine and the Hebrew kingdoms. In the case of heavy defeats, the sources prefer to keep quiet, giving us no opportunity to check the facts given in the Bible.

The invasion by the army of Osorkon I was by no means the only problem during Asa's reign. A more serious test for him was the renewal of the war with Israel. On this occasion he was faced not with unruly hordes of Libyans and Nubians, but with an experienced and well-organized army belonging to one of the strongest states in Syria and Palestine. The biblical sources agree with one another in their description of the military operations, but not in their accounts of the dates at which these events occurred and of their duration. According to the book of Kings, "There was war between Asa and Baasha king of Israel throughout their reigns" (1 Kings 15:16). However, the book of Chronicles gives a shorter interval of time, dating the war between Israel and Judah to the end of Asa's reign, namely the 36th year of his rule (2 Chronicles 16:1). This, though, contradicts the book of Kings, which tells us that by this time Israel was ruled not by Baasha, but by the dynasty of Omri. The book of Kings is evidently the more reliable source, given that it was set down earlier, in the 7th and 6th centuries BCE, while the book of Chronicles was written much later, in the 5th and 4th centuries BCE. But of more importance is the fact that both these sources advance the same version of events – namely, one in which the Israelite king Baasha not merely managed to go on the attack, but also besieged Jerusalem.

Trying to prevent the inevitable fall of the city, the Judahite king Asa, grandson of Rehoboam, turned for help to Israel's most bitter enemy, the Aramean kingdom of Damascus, offering Damascus in payment for his salvation all the treasures he had left in his possession: "Asa then took all the silver and gold that was left in the treasuries of the Lord's temple and of his own palace. He entrusted it to his officials and sent them to Ben-Hadad son of Tabrimmon, the son of Hezion, the king of Aram, who was ruling in Damascus. 'Let there be a treaty between me and you,' he said, 'as there was between my father and your father. See, I am sending you a gift of silver and gold. Now break your treaty with Baasha king of Israel so he will withdraw from me" (1 Kings 15:18-19). The rich gifts of the Judahite king and, most importantly, the political calculations of the Arameans of Damascus themselves led to Ben-Hadad I perfidiously violating his peace treaty with Israel. Attacking the latter's northern cities, Ben-Hadad compelled the Israelites to leave Judah. Incidentally, the message sent by Asa to Ben-Hadad makes clear how Asa's father, Abijah, had won his military victories. It turns out that there had been an alliance between Aram-Damascus and Judah against Israel. Only as a result of having to engage in war on two fronts was the Northern Kingdom forced to cede a number of lands, including the important religious center of Bethel. But although the Arameans deprived Israel of victory over Judah, Israel nevertheless regained possession of some of these lands, including Bethel. This war brought to an end a prolonged period of hostility between the two countries, a period which had stretched over the rule of three Judahite kings – Rehoboam, Abijah, and Asa; it also determined the final borders between the kingdoms following the division of the United Monarchy. The southern part of the land belonging to the tribe of Benjamin remained in the possession of Judah, while the northern went to Israel. Thus the Hebrew tribes in the Southern Kingdom comprised two entire tribes (those of Simeon and Judah) and parts of two others (Levi and Benjamin).

However, the alliance with Damascus cost King Asa dear, and not just financially, but also in terms of domestic politics. The Aaronites were openly dissatisfied with the plundering of the Temple in Jerusalem. Expressing their opinion, the prophet Hanani denounced the king and predicted that he would be faced with fresh troubles as punishment for what he had done. The ranks of dissatisfied priests were swelled by that part of the population which had been forced to pay for the king's expensive policy. It is not surprising that the Bible notes that Asa did not merely imprison the prophet, but also "brutally oppressed some of the people" (2 Chronicles 16:10).

Each Judahite king had his own chronicler who tidily recorded all the most important events during his reign. Shemaiah, for instance, was Rehoboam's chronicler and Iddo was Abijah's. Some of these chronicles were used in creating the book of Kings; even more went into the book of Chronicles. However, the majority of these ancient documents have been irretrievably lost.

Alliance with Israel

Asa's heir, his son Jehoshaphat, managed to restore good relations with the Aaronites – and in fact made such progress in this respect that he earned the highest praise from them: "The Lord was with Jehoshaphat because he followed the ways of his father David before him. He did not consult the Baals but sought the God of his father and followed his commands rather than the practices of Israel" (2 Chronicles 17:3-4). Like his father before him, Jehoshaphat was indeed a true and consistent follower of Yahweh. But unlike Asa, he was a flexible and skillful politician and endeavored to maintain good relations with all influential groups among the population. In praising him, the keepers of the tradition credited him with carrying out reforms such as elimination of "the high places and Asherah poles" and teaching the Torah to the people in Judah – reforms which could never, in fact, have been carried out at this time (2 Chronicles 17:6, 9). And indeed, in the epilogue summarizing the reign of Jehoshaphat, the same book of Chronicles admits that "the high places were not removed, and the people still had not set their hearts on the God of their ancestors" (2 Chronicles 20:33).

In foreign policy, however, Jehoshaphat was much more successful. His main achievement was the peace and subsequent alliance that he established with Israel. Admittedly, at the beginning of his reign he was still very much afraid of the Northern Kingdom continuing its military action, so, as the Bible tells us, "he strengthened himself against Israel" (2 Chronicles 17:1). But there had been an important change in the foreign policy pursued by Israelite kings from the dynasty of Omri; instead of fighting with the Judahites over possession of the disputed cities in the lands belonging to the Benjaminites, they now preferred to enter into an alliance with them against a more dangerous enemy, the Arameans of Damascus. This change of policy met with a favorable response from the Southern Kingdom. Henceforward Judah had no need to worry about peace on its northern border and was able to concentrate all its military resources on protecting its interests in the south and south-west. This allowed Jehoshaphat to conquer a number of Philistine cities and to establish his authority over the Edomites and the nomadic tribes of the Negev and Midian. The Bible confirms the favorable foreign-policy situation in which Judah found itself at this time: "The fear of the Lord fell on all the kingdoms of the lands surrounding Judah, so that they did not go to war against Jehoshaphat. Some Philistines brought Jehoshaphat gifts and silver as tribute, and the Arabs brought him flocks: seven thousand seven hundred rams and seven thousand seven hundred goats" (2 Chronicles 17:10-11).

The convergence with the Israelite dynasty of Omri resulted in the creation of a military alliance between the two countries and in joint military campaigns. "So [the Israelite king] asked Jehoshaphat, 'Will you go with me to fight against Ramoth-Gilead?' Jehoshaphat replied to the king of Israel, 'I am as you are, my people as your people, my horses as your horses" (1 Kings 22:4). Jehoshaphat also took part in another Israelite campaign, this time with Ahab's son Joram, against Mesha, king of the Moabites, who had decided to secede from Israel following Ahab's death. "So at that time King Joram set out from Samaria and mobilized all Israel. He also sent this message to Jehoshaphat king of Judah: 'The king of Moab has rebelled against me. Will you go with me to fight against Moab?' 'I will go with you,' he replied. 'I am as you are, my people as your people, my horses as your horses" (2 Kings 3:6-7). But the joint campaigns with the Israelites were by no means always successful; sometimes they brought serious losses and even defeats, as was the case during the war for Ramoth-Gilead. Furthermore, they met with objections from the influential caste of priests of Yahweh, who saw a threat to themselves in the strengthening of the dynasty of Omri, who supported the cult of Baal. "Jehu the seer, the son of Hanani, went out to meet him and said to the king, 'Should you help the wicked and love those who hate the Lord? Because of this, the wrath of the Lord is on you" (2 Chronicles 19:2).

The Aaronites did not conceal their unhappiness with the policy of convergence with the dynasty of Omri. Nevertheless, Jehoshaphat persisted with this policy because the alliance with Israel had changed the balance of power in the region in favor of the Hebrew kingdoms. Admittedly, this same factor compelled their opponents likewise to unite. Judah's rejection of its former friendship with Damascus drove the Arameans into an alliance with Ammon, Moab, and Edom in the hope of using these Transjordanian kingdoms as a counterbalance to the Hebrew states. The intervention of Aram-Damascus evidently played a decisive role in saving the Moabite king Mesha when the Israelites and Judahites waged war against him. The unexpected attack launched by the Arameans against the northern parts of Israel forced the allies to interrupt their successful campaign and leave Moab in haste. In order to neutralize Judah, which had helped Israel, Damascus set up against it a coalition of three Transjordanian countries – Ammon, Moab, and Edom. Each of these kingdoms was individually weaker than Judah, but, as a coalition, they enjoyed a significant advantage over it. Each bore grudges against the Southern Kingdom: Edom was oppressed by its dependence on Judah as a vassal while Moab and Ammon saw in it the ally of their enemy, Israel, which was intent upon becoming their ruler. But the Transjordanian kingdoms also had serious problems with one another: Moab had a longstanding territorial conflict with Ammon and Edom with Moab. Only the skillful diplomacy of Aram-Damascus, and, more importantly, its rich gifts, managed to smooth over these contradictions and create an alliance of a kind which could otherwise have existed only during the time of Abraham.

A joint invasion by the armies of the Transjordanian kingdoms was the principal military danger during Jehoshaphat's reign. The news of these forces' approach struck fear into the king's court: "Some men came and told Jehoshaphat, 'A vast army is coming against you from Edom, from the other side of the Dead Sea. It is already in Hazezon Tamar' (that is, En Gedi). Alarmed, Jehoshaphat resolved to inquire of the Lord, and he proclaimed a fast for all Judah" (2 Chronicles 20:2-3). The fact that the Hebrew Bible considered it necessary to indicate that the forces of the Transjordanian kingdoms came 'from Aram', although they actually emerged from the other side of the Dead Sea, is indirect confirmation that the principal role in organizing this military campaign was played by the Arameans. It seems strange that the authors of the text say nothing of support given by the Israelites, who were then the Judahites' most important allies. Evidently, this campaign took place at a time when war was underway between Aram-Damascus and Israel, and was organized in such a way that the Hebrew kingdoms could not come to each other's aid. The biblical text presents the subsequent development of events as a miracle: "[…] the Lord set ambushes against the men of Ammon and Moab and Mount Seir who were invading Judah, and they were defeated. The Ammonites and Moabites rose up against the men from Mount Seir to destroy and annihilate them. After they finished slaughtering the men from Seir, they helped to destroy one another" (2 Chronicles 20:22-23). Thus the military coalition of the three kingdoms fell apart even before the decisive battle, and its members set to fighting with one another and gave up the idea of marching on Judah. This was a turn of events which could not but strike contemporaries as a miraculous deliverance. However, the miracle had a firm material basis. The Ammonites – a traditional ally of the southern tribes from the time of David, but just as constant an enemy of the northern tribes – were not interested in weakening the kingdom of Jehoshaphat; they wanted merely to force him to renounce his alliance with Israel. A similar position was held by the Moabites, who were mainly in conflict with the Northern Kingdom and with the Hebrew tribes who were part of that kingdom. Moreover, the Moabites were afraid that the weakening of Judah might strengthen their rival Edom. And it was only the Edomites, vassals of Judah, who had an interest in Jehoshaphat being completely defeated, in order that they should gain independence from their 'junior brother'. The acute divergence of interests among the participants in the campaign, when magnified by the gold and diplomacy of Jehoshaphat, led to sharp disagreements between them, which turned into mutual slaughter and destruction: "When the men of Judah came to the place that overlooks the desert and looked toward the vast army, they saw only dead bodies lying on the ground; no one had escaped" (2 Chronicles 20:24). This campaign was the first and last attempt by the Transjordanian kingdoms to join forces against Judah on the battlefield.

In general, Jehoshaphat had more success in foreign policy than his predecessors Rehoboam, Abijah, and Asa. To a large degree, this was because he conducted a far-sighted policy aimed at a close alliance with Israel – his northern neighbor and the most powerful state in Palestine at the time. Collaboration with the Northern Kingdom was not limited to the military and political fields, but involved trade as well. The Bible mentions an unsuccessful attempt at a joint sea voyage to the legendary Tarshish, which was situated somewhere in southern Arabia or in the Horn of Africa. It is probable that other, more successful trading expeditions were made, regarding which the keepers of the tradition preferred to keep quiet due to the extremely negative attitude which they took to the Israelite kings in general and to the dynasty of Omri in particular. The enmity felt by the southern followers of Yahweh for the rulers of the Northern Kingdom was so great that any attempt made by Jehoshaphat to collaborate with them was automatically criticized as amoral. For instance, the prophet Eliezer, son of Dodavahu of Mareshah, hastened to condemn Jehoshaphat just because the latter had attempted to organize a joint trading expedition with the Israelite king Ahaziah. Eliezer prophesied against Jehoshaphat, saying: "Because you have made an alliance with Ahaziah, the Lord will destroy what you have made" (2 Chronicles 20:37). However, although Jehoshaphat was a devoted follower of Yahweh, he was unable, as a practically minded politician, to turn down the opportunity for collaboration with Israel, a partnership on which Judah's prosperity depended.

Of the changes made by Jehoshaphat on the domestic front the most important were his judicial reforms. Essentially, these had two main aspects: first, judicial processes were made a separate branch of authority; second, the judicial system was expanded to include the Aaronites. It is difficult to say whether Jehoshaphat's main motivation was to put an end to abuse of the judicial system or to strengthen the role played by the priests of Yahweh, who were his active supporters. It is possible that the aim of the reform was to reinforce the influence of the laws of Moses in morality and everyday living, as opposed to the pagan standards of justice that were then in widespread use. Evidence of the latter is to be found in Jehoshaphat's advice to the judges: "He told them, 'Consider carefully what you do, because you are not judging for man, but for the Lord, who is with you whenever you give a verdict. Now let the fear of the Lord be on you. Judge carefully, for with the Lord our God there is no injustice or partiality or bribery" (2 Chronicles 19:6-7).

The legacy left by Jehoshaphat was ambiguous. On the one hand, the alliance he had built with Israel brought the country peace and economic prosperity, territorial expansion, and greater influence on neighboring peoples; on the other, Jehoshaphat had become dangerously dependent on his stronger neighbor and the latter's royal dynasty. This led to discontent among some of Jehoshaphat's courtiers and the influential priests of Yahweh. By the end of the king's life two mutually hostile parties had taken shape; they were the 'Israelite' party, which was in favor of a close alliance with the Northern Kingdom, and the 'Judahite', Yahweh-worshipping party, which was against such an alliance. Naturally, Jehoram, Jehoshaphat's eldest son and husband of Ahab's daughter represented the Israelite party at court, while other sons of the king – all or, at any rate, some of them – supported the Judahite, Yahwist camp. The fact that upon his ascent of the throne Jehoram "put all his brothers to the sword along with some of the officials of Israel" is evidence that the change of regime was accompanied by a period of political uncertainty and palace intrigues (2 Chronicles 21:4). It is very telling that the keepers of the tradition – in the present case, the Aaronites, the authors of the book of Chronicles – considered it necessary to underline that his father "had given the kingdom to Jehoram because he was his firstborn son" (2 Chronicles 21:3). But the Judahite kings were able to choose their heirs with no regard for primogeniture, as had been confirmed by the selection of Solomon and Abijah. The emphasis on the fact that Jehoshaphat "had given [Jehoram's brothers] many gifts of silver and gold and articles of value, as well as fortified cities in Judah" may well indicate that their number included sons whom he loved more or were by his favorite wives and also had a claim to the throne. Further evidence for this supposition is the message from the prophet Elijah, in which it is said that the brothers whom Jehoram killed were better than him (2 Chronicles 21:13). However, Jehoram had the support of his wife, Athaliah, daughter of the Israelite king, as well as of the Israelite party at court. Possibly also in his favor was the threat of military intervention by the Northern Kingdom. These factors played a decisive role in the fact that it was Jehoram rather than any other of Jehoshaphat's sons who was selected to be king. In any case, the destruction of all possible claimants to the throne and of many representatives of the nobility was not the usual way in which royal succession was carried out in Judah. We get the impression that either Jehoshaphat had had no time to declare an official heir or he had had to change his initial choice under pressure from the Israelite party. Something similar had happened with King David, when, under pressure from a group of courtiers, he changed his will in Solomon's favor.

The Aaronites and Levites did not conceal their frank hostility to Jehoram. They accused him of "[building] high places on the hills of Judah and [causing] the people of Jerusalem to prostitute themselves and [leading] Judah astray" (2 Chronicles 21:11). From the point of view of the worshippers of Yahweh, "He followed the ways of the kings of Israel, as the house of Ahab had done, for he married a daughter of Ahab. He did evil in the eyes of the Lord" (2 Chronicles 21:6). It is likely that both Jehoram's wife Athaliah and Jehoram himself worshipped Baal and supported the latter's priests, just as Ahab and Jezebel had done in Samaria.

The domestic troubles and infighting considerably weakened the Southern Kingdom and, as a result, led to complications in foreign relations. The first serious blow for Jehoram was the loss of Edom, Judah's traditional vassal: "In the time of Jehoram, Edom rebelled against Judah and set up its own king" (2 Kings 8:20). As far as can be judged, the war with the Edomites dragged on, producing mixed results. In open battles it was the Judahite army that had the upper hand, but the Edomites preferred partisan fighting in the desert, which they knew well: "So Jehoram went to Zair with all his chariots. The Edomites surrounded him and his chariot commanders, but he rose up and broke through by night; his army, however, fled back home" (2 Kings 8:21). Eventually, Jehoram preferred to give up the endless and expensive war for power over the Edomites; the 'senior' brother again became independent from the 'junior'.

During the war with the Edomites, Jehoram was faced with a further unpleasant surprise: the city of Libnah, a powerful fortress situated in the vicinity of Shephelah, on a strategically important road leading from Philistia to Jerusalem, revolted. "Libnah revolted at the same time, because Jehoram had forsaken the Lord, the God of his ancestors" (2 Chronicles 21:10). Libnah was one of Judah's western outposts on the border with the lands of the Philistines, and its secession from his kingdom was an extremely painful loss for Jehoram. Although, after being taken by the Hebrew tribes, Libnah had been given to the Levites to live in, its population continued to consist mostly of Amorites. The city fathers, taking advantage of Jehoram's war with the Edomites and the internal feuding in the country, opted for a change of political orientation and entered into an alliance with the Philistines, their western neighbors.

Finally, on top of all his other woes, Jehoram was struck by personal tragedy. While he was away with the Judahite army on a military campaign, detachments of Philistines and nomads from Midian penetrated into the depths of the country: "The Lord aroused against Jehoram the hostility of the Philistines and of the Arabs who lived near the Cushites. They attacked Judah, invaded it and carried off all the goods found in the king's palace, together with his sons and wives. Not a son was left to him except Ahaziah, the youngest" (2 Chronicles 21:16-17). Probably, the attackers were the Philistines and Midianites who had been tributaries of King Jehoshaphat. The weakening of the Southern Kingdom gave them the idea that they could not merely cast off their dependence as vassals, as the Edomites and Libnah had done, but also attack their former suzerain. It cannot be ruled out that behind the secession of Edom and Libnah and the attack by the Philistines and the Midianites stood the kingdom of Damascus, which was intent upon weakening Israel's closest ally. It was Aram-Damascus that helped the opponents of the Israelite party in Judah and thus pushed the country towards civil war. It was not for nothing that the Arameans courted Israelite worshippers of Yahweh, who were persecuted by the dynasty of Omri. We may suppose it to have been no coincidence that the prophet Elisha appeared in Damascus and became the personal guest of King Ben-Hadad and his military commander, Hazael. In just the same way the Arameans provided support for all King Jehoram's opponents, including for the followers of Yahweh in Judah. Jehoram's rule was a time of growing confrontation between Israel and Damascus. While the Israelites pursued alliances with the enemies of Damascus (with Assyria, for instance), the Arameans were ready to help anyone who opposed the Northern Kingdom and its allies.

In general, Jehoram's eight-year reign was extremely unsuccessful for Judah. During all these years, Judah was in a state close to civil war and lost all the territorial gains it had made during the rule of Jehoshaphat. The end of Jehoram's life was as tragic and agonizing as his reign: "After all this, the Lord afflicted Jehoram with an incurable disease of the bowels. In the course of time, at the end of the second year, his bowels came out because of the disease, and he died in great pain" (2 Chronicles 21:18-19). Thus was fulfilled the prophecy of Elijah, who had predicted a terrible death for the king in punishment for his crimes against the Lord and the killing of his own brothers.

Jehoram's heir was his only surviving son, Ahaziah. On this occasion, the transfer of authority took place calmly and without palace intrigues since there were no other claimants to the throne. However, the new king represented the same Israelite party and was as hateful to the followers of Yahweh as his father had been. Moreover, Ahaziah's coming to power marked the apogee of close relations between the two countries. Ahaziah's mother, Athaliah, was the daughter of Ahab and the sister of the then Israelite king, Joram. Ahaziah himself was a nephew of the Israelite king and a grandson of Jezebel, the latter's mother. We may say that at this moment the regal dynasties of Judah and Israel had almost merged. Naturally, the keepers of the tradition were just as hostile to the new king as they had been to his father: "He too followed the ways of the house of Ahab, for his mother encouraged him to act wickedly. He did evil in the eyes of the Lord, as the house of Ahab had done, for after his father's death they became his advisers, to his undoing" (2 Chronicles 22:3-4). Admittedly, Ahaziah's reign turned out to be exceptionally short – a mere year in length – and just as tragic as that of his father. As a devoted ally of Israel, Ahaziah, like his grandfather Jehoshaphat, took part in a joint campaign with the Israelite king, Joram, to northern Transjordan against the Aramean king, Hazael. This was a tough military campaign and it involved serious losses on the part of the allies. During one of the battles Joram was wounded and taken to his residence, the town of Jezreel, which was situated in the valley of the same name. As a true ally and close relative, Ahaziah went to visit Joram. Unfortunately, he arrived in Jezreel just at the moment when the Israelite commander Jehu came to Jezreel with his soldiers in order to kill Joram in a coup. Both Joram and Ahaziah were killed, together with numerous members of Ahaziah's family who had, like him, come to visit their injured relative.

The overthrow of the dynasty of Omri in Israel and the unexpected death of Ahaziah inspired the followers of Yahweh in Judah to go on the attack against the Baal-worshipping pro-Israel party in Jerusalem. However, Athaliah, mother of the dead king, was quicker than her opponents. Having no desire to share the terrible fate of Jezebel, she decided to seize power herself at whatever price. With the support of important figures and the palace guard, she committed a monstrous crime. She gave orders for all the king's sons, her grandsons, to be killed; and, having eliminated in this way her potential rivals, she had herself placed upon the throne. But the party of worshippers of Yahweh had no intention of surrendering. Jehosheba, wife of the high priest of the Temple in Jerusalem, managed to save one of the king's sons, the infant Joash. As the sister of King Ahaziah and the daughter of Athaliah herself, she exploited her privileged status at court in order to conceal Joash and his wet nurse in the Temple in Jerusalem with her husband, the high priest Jehoiada. "He remained hidden with them at the temple of God for six years while Athaliah ruled the land" (2 Chronicles 22:12).

The six years of Athaliah's reign were in effect a continuation of the rule of the dynasty of Omri – only not in Israel, but in Judah. During this period Judah changed its foreign policy to the direct opposite of what it had been. Previously Israel's ally, it now became the latter's enemy. On the other hand, it once more patched up relations with Aram-Damascus, the Philistine cities, and the kingdoms of Transjordan. Similarly large changes were made in domestic policy. The pro-Israel party, which supported Athaliah, became a political group fighting for the dominance of the cult of Baal. Previously, it had been in favor of a close alliance with Israel, but now, following the overthrow of the dynasty of Omri, it did everything it could to obstruct normal relations with this country. On the other hand, following Jehu's coup and his liquidation of the priests of Baal in Samaria, the camp of worshippers of Yahweh in Judah changed its extremely negative attitude to the Northern Kingdom and may even have been in secret contact with the court of the Israelite king Jehu. The years of Athaliah's rule, like those of her husband, Jehoram, and of her son Ahaziah, were a time during which the cult and priests of Baal in Judah had the upper hand and the Aaronites found themselves relegated to positions of lesser importance. This upset the *status quo* by which the principal religious cult in Judah had always been the cult of Yahweh; the latter had accompanied the southern tribes during their entire history. Of course, this situation was bound to meet with fierce resistance from the followers of Yahweh, who felt impinged upon even on their own home patch of Jerusalem. Dissatisfaction, intrigues, and conspiracies had accompanied the rule of Jehoram and, possibly, of Ahaziah as well; but especially difficult in this respect was the position of Athaliah. Unlike her husband and son, she could not hope for military support from Israel, and her ascent of the throne was an undisguised usurpation of power. Furthermore, she had no relation at all to the Davidic dynasty and must have been perceived by the Judahites as a foreign ruler who had seized power through a criminal act. She could count only on the palace guard, who were loyal to her and consisted of foreign mercenaries, and on the priests of Baal, many of whom she had brought with her from the Northern Kingdom and possibly from Phoenicia as well. Having no firm rear line to back her up, Athaliah avoided any kind of military campaign which might put her rule at risk or strengthen the military commanders, among whom the followers of Yahweh might find another Jehu.

The Growth in the Influence of the Aaronites and their Interference in Judahite Policymaking

The leader of the followers of Yahweh in Judah was the then high priest of the Temple of Jerusalem, Jehoiada. The fact that Jehoiada's wife was the king's sister and Athaliah's daughter is a sign of the importance that the pro-Israelite party of worshippers of Baal placed upon links with the head of the Aaronite priests. The intention behind this arranged marriage had been to soften the Yahwists' resistance to the influence of the dynasty of Omri and of the cult of Baal in Judah. However, Jehu's coup in Israel and Athaliah's usurpation of the Judahite throne exploded what had in any case been a fragile peace between the followers of Yahweh and Baal. For six years Jehoiada waited for a convenient moment to act while endeavoring to secure the support of the army and to mobilize the Levites. "In the seventh year Jehoiada showed his strength. He made a covenant with the commanders of units of a hundred [...] They went throughout Judah and gathered the Levites and the heads of Israelite families from all the towns [... and] came to Jerusalem" (2 Chronicles 23:1-2).

The Bible does not tell us under what pretext the high priest managed to assemble the irregular forces and the Levites and, more importantly, to bring both these contingents to Jerusalem. The fact that weapons were handed out to the irregulars and to the Levites only in Jerusalem itself, or, to be more precise, in the Temple is evidence that they had entered the capital unarmed. Evidently, in order to lull the vigilance of Athaliah and her officials, Jehoiada exploited the tradition of the festive pilgrimage or the necessity of carrying out work of whatever kind in the Temple. "Then he gave the commanders of units of a hundred the spears and the large and small shields that had belonged to King David and that were in the temple of God" (2 Chronicles 23:9,10). In the Temple in Jerusalem the Levites and irregulars, now armed, declared the juvenile Joash their new king and swore an oath of loyalty to him. Athaliah and her followers learnt of the conspiracy only when it was already too late and they were powerless to withstand it. The palace guard, likewise caught by surprise, considered it best not to intervene or cross over to the new king. Thus Joash's coronation ended with the killing of Athaliah. As in Samaria, the seizure of power in Jerusalem resulted in the plundering of the temple of Baal and the liquidation of the priests of this cult: "All the people went to the temple of Baal and tore it down. They smashed the altars and idols and killed Mattan the priest of Baal in front of the altars" (2 Chronicles 23:17). This was how the movements opposing Baal concluded in the two Hebrew kingdoms. In Israel matters were decided by Jehu's military coup; but, in Judah the change came about through an organized popular uprising headed by the Aaronites and Levites. The mass character of the anti-Baal movement in Judah was a result of the weaker position of the cult of Baal there, compared with in the Northern Kingdom, and of the stronger influence enjoyed by the followers of Yahweh. Jehoiada became the regent and trustee of seven-year-old King Joash, which meant that for the first time in Judah power was held by priests of Yahweh.

The power of the high priest was so great that it was he who, when Joash grew up, sought out two wives for him. So it is hardly surprising that the keepers of the tradition, in characterizing the king's rule under the high priest Jehoiada, took care to underline that "Joash did what was right in the eyes of the Lord all the years of Jehoiada the priest" (2 Chronicles 24:2). In effect, even when the king was grown up, Jehoiada remained the real ruler. His role and influence in Judah were so great that he became the first high priest to be "buried with the kings in the City of David" (2 Chronicles, 24:16). Interestingly, while possessing almost unlimited power, he made no attempt to destroy the pagan cults in Judah, not to mention the so-called 'high places' (places far from the Temple in Jerusalem where people worshipped Yahweh). He did not undertake religious reform of the kind carried out at a much later date by King Josiah of Judah. He confined himself to routing his main rivals – the priests of the cult of Baal in Jerusalem – following which he introduced, through Joash, a new tribute to be paid to the Temple in Jerusalem. Jehoiada's rule is interesting not so much for what he managed to do as for what he did not do, although, as high priest of Yahweh, should have done. The years of his rule are further proof that Moses' monotheism was not and, more importantly, could not have been realized in Judah in the second half of the 9th century BCE. Judahite society of that time, including the Aaronites and Levites themselves, remained far from consistent with the commandments handed down on Sinai; this is why its Yahwism could not be called a truly monotheistic religion.

After the death of high priest Jehoiada, his ward tried to liberate himself from the excessive guardianship exercised by the priests of Yahweh and from their constant interventions in his personal life. To this end, he began appointing to many of the country's important posts not Aaronites, as previously, but representatives of the Judahite nobility who had no connection with the priestly class. Instead of priests of Yahweh, Joash gave preference to priests from other cults, provoking undisguised dissatisfaction among the Aaronites, as is reflected in the following passage in the Bible: "After the death of Jehoiada, the officials of Judah came and paid homage to the king, and he listened to them. They abandoned the temple of the Lord, the God of their ancestors, and worshiped Asherah poles and idols" (2 Chronicles 24:17-18). It is doubtful that Joash rejected the cult of Yahweh; probably, he allowed himself to worship other local cults at the same time, as was the practice among most of the then population of Judah. However, feeling that they were losing the influence which they had previously enjoyed at Joash's court, the Aaronites tried to exert pressure on him by organizing popular actions against the renegade king. The dissatisfied were headed by Jehoiada's son Zechariah: "Then the Spirit of God came on Zechariah son of Jehoiada the priest. He stood before the people and said, 'This is what God says: 'Why do you disobey the Lord's commands? You will not prosper. Because you have forsaken the Lord, he has forsaken you'" (2 Chronicles 24:20). But the king did not give way to the pressure from the priests; instead he dispatched their leader, Zechariah: "But they plotted against him, and by order of the king they stoned him to death in the courtyard of the Lord's temple. King Joash did not remember the kindness Zechariah's father Jehoiada had shown him but killed his son [...]" (2 Chronicles 24:21-22). Zechariah's execution put an end to the Aaronites' overt opposition to Joash; however, the enmity they felt for the 'ungrateful' king merely grew and their resistance took forms that were concealed, but no less dangerous for Joash.

The larger part of Joash's 40-year-long reign passed relatively peacefully. Raised by priests, the king did not feel any need for military campaigns, and in any case the fight for his own independence within his own country left him with no opportunity to conduct an active foreign policy. However, the situation around Judah was deteriorating continuously. This was a time when Aram-Damascus was growing stronger at an unprecedented rate: Hazael, the king of Aram-Damascus, had managed at last to overcome Israel and now switched to conquering other Palestine and Syrian states. He needed Judah, the Philistine cities, and the kingdoms of Transjordan not as allies against Israel, but as vassals and tributaries. Carrying out a successful campaign against the Philistine cities, Hazael's army came right up close to the borders of Judah. The book of Kings tells us the following: "[...] Hazael king of Aram [...] turned to attack Jerusalem. But Joash king of Judah took all the sacred objects dedicated by his predecessors—Jehoshaphat, Jehoram and Ahaziah, the kings of Judah—and the gifts he himself had dedicated and all the gold found in the treasuries of the temple of the Lord and of the royal palace, and he sent them to Hazael king of Aram, who then withdrew from Jerusalem" (2 Kings 12:17-18). Thus the king saved his country from destruction, but could not protect himself from the wrath of those who were dissatisfied. As always happened in such cases, it was the wealthiest part of Judahite society – and especially the priests of Yahweh – who suffered most from the confiscation of gold and silver. The plundering of the Temple stretched their patience beyond breaking point and they initiated a conspiracy against the king. Taking advantage of Joash's serious illness, his courtiers killed him when he lay helpless in bed. The fact that the conspirators had the support of the Aaronites is indirectly confirmed by the following passage in the Bible: "When the Arameans withdrew, they left Joash severely wounded. His officials conspired against him for murdering the son of Jehoiada the priest, and they killed him in his bed" (2 Chronicles 24:25). The vengeance of the Aaronites, however, did not stop here: although Joash was buried in the city of David, he was stripped of the honor of being buried in the royal tomb.

The king's heir was his 25-year-old son Amaziah. The Bible says nothing of whether he was Joash's eldest son, but it cannot be doubted that his ascent to the throne, like the first years of his rule, depended entirely on his readiness to follow the recommendations of the Aaronites. At the beginning of his reign he indeed did nothing that could have disappointed the priests of Yahweh. Admittedly, they suspected – and not without good reason, as it subsequently turned out – that his compliance with them and loyalty to the cult of Yahweh were by no means sincere, but a response to the pressure of circumstances: "He did what was right in the eyes of the Lord, but not wholeheartedly" (2 Chronicles 25:2). Amaziah took his principal objective to be to punish his father's killers. However, this was no easy task: the killers had the support of influential and powerful forces connected with the Aaronites. The king could not dispatch his father's murderers immediately upon his ascent to the throne, so he patiently waited for a suitable moment. It was only later that "after the kingdom was firmly in his control, he executed the officials who had murdered his father the king." He was prevented, however, from exacting full vengeance of the kind that was accepted practice at the time: "Yet he did not put their children to death, but acted in accordance with what is written in the Law, in the Book of Moses, where the Lord commanded: 'Parents shall not be put to death for their children, nor children be put to death for their parents; each will die for their own sin" (2 Chronicles 25:3,4). It is likely that the killers' children and relatives belonged to the Aaronites, and the powerful priests did not permit the king to break the laws of Moses.

Unlike his father, Amaziah was intent upon carrying out an energetic, aggressive policy in relation to his neighbors. But for this he needed a large army and the financial resources to maintain it. To satisfy his military and fiscal needs, he carried out a census, which established that the population of Judah, including the tribe of Benjamin, comprised 300,000 men capable of carrying weapons and aged 20 or above (2 Chronicles 25:5). This means that the overall population of the Southern Kingdom at the beginning of the 8th century BCE must have been in excess of one million. In the light of current archeological data on the population density in Judah at that time, this figure seems a considerable exaggeration. It can only be explained by supposing that it found its way into the biblical text at a later date or – and this is the more probable explanation – was deliberately exaggerated by Amaziah's own chroniclers in order to enhance his kingdom's importance. The strengthening of the army and seeking out of resources needed for its maintenance were necessary, above all, in order to organize a military campaign aimed at subduing Edom once again. The Judahite kings regarded this small neighboring kingdom as their traditional vassal and saw its independence and self-sufficiency as an insult to themselves. Uncertain that his army was sufficiently strong, Amaziah hired mercenaries from the lands of the tribe of Ephraim in the kingdom of Israel. We may suppose that the very fact that Israelite forces were being hired for the Judahite army was evidence of an improvement in relations between the two Hebrew kingdoms. Of course, the Aaronites were opposed to convergence with the Northern Kingdom. The following episode is telling: "But a man of God came to him and said, 'O king, these troops from Israel must not march with you, for the Lord is not with Israel—not with any of the people of Ephraim. Even if you go and fight courageously in battle, God will overthrow you before the enemy, for God has the power to help or to overthrow.' Amaziah asked the man of God, 'But what about the hundred talents I paid for these Israelite troops?' The man of God replied, 'The Lord can give you much more than that" (2 Chronicles 25:7-9). By "man of God," the biblical texts always refer to the Levite and Aaronite prophets. Remembering the sorry fate of his father, Joash, and grandmother Athaliah, Amaziah did not dare at this moment to enter into conflict with the mighty Aaronites; his fear for his own throne outweighed any gain to be had from collaborating with the Israelites. However, this unexpected rejection of the idea of a joint campaign angered the Israelites and relations between the two kingdoms again deteriorated: "So Amaziah dismissed the troops who had come to him from Ephraim and sent them home. They were furious with Judah and left for home in a great rage" (2 Chronicles 25:10).

Remarkably, the Aaronites manifested exactly the same kind of enmity towards the dynasty of Jehu, which ruled in Israel at this time, as they had previously towards the Omrides. This was in spite of the fact that, unlike the dynasty of Omri, which was cursed by the worshippers of Yahweh, Jehu had been anointed king by the prophet Elisha himself. Furthermore, Jehu was famous for having destroyed the temple of Baal and eliminated the priests of Baal in Samaria. The Israelite king, Jehoash, who was Jehu's grandson and ruled at the same time as the Judahite king Amaziah, had great respect for the prophet Elisha and had had the latter's blessing for victory over the Arameans. Why then was it that the Aaronites, regardless of the personal characters of the Israelite kings, felt an unvarying enmity towards them, as towards the Northern Kingdom in general? The most likely cause of this enmity was the Israelites' independence from the Temple in Jerusalem and the fact that the Israelites and their Levites did not acknowledge the primacy and authority of the Aaronites. This hostility began with the conflict between Aaron and Moses, between the Aaronites and the Levites, became stronger after the Levites had established their hegemony in the north and the Aaronites in the south, and finally reached its peak when the northern tribes split from the southern tribes. The existence of two independent and competing religious centers – the Yahwist center in the south and the Elohist center in the north – was an objective expression of the interests of the two Hebrew tribal groups of different origins who had ended up living separately in the two different Hebrew kingdoms, Israel and Judah. Their convergence threatened to weaken the influence of the Aaronites since Judah, where they ruled, could lay claim only to the role of junior partner in any alliance between the two kingdoms. Naturally, the Aaronites staunchly resisted such an alliance, seeing in it a serious threat to their own interests.

In spite of the fact that the Judahite army had to march against the Edomites on its own, this military campaign was successful beyond all expectations. "He [Amaziah] was the one who defeated ten thousand Edomites in the Valley of Salt and captured Sela in battle, calling it Joktheel, the name it has to this day" (2 Kings 14:7). This victory implanted in Amaziah confidence in his own strength, reinforced his authority in Judah, and, most importantly, allowed him to break free of the guardianship of the Aaronites. Among the rich trophies which he brought from Edom were statues of the Edomites' gods and numerous religious objects. Possibly in order to spite the Aaronites, who had been annoying him for so long, or perhaps because he was truly interested in the Edomites' religion, he drew the Edomite priests close to him and began worshipping their gods. As in the case with his father, this was not a rejection of Yahweh altogether, but more probably a desire not to worship Yahweh alone. It is also possible that he was happier with a situation where the Edomite priests were entirely dependent on him, as opposed to his being dependent on the Aaronites. However, this inevitably brought Amaziah into grave conflict with the Aaronites, who, as it later turned out, did not forgive him his treachery.

In the middle of his 29-year reign Amaziah made a fatal foreign-policy mistake: he decided to go to war with Israel. In those days Israel was involved in serious and almost continuous wars against the kingdom of Damascus, as it tried to win back territories lost at earlier dates. Maybe Amaziah thought that Israel lacked the strength needed to fight on two fronts; or perhaps the Arameans, who were in need of help from an ally, had assured him of their support. In any case, the Judahite king decided to throw down a challenge to a far stronger opponent. "Then Amaziah sent messengers to Jehoash son of Jehoahaz, the son of Jehu, king of Israel, with the challenge: 'Come, let us face each other in battle.'" The Israelites, preoccupied with the war against Aram-Damascus, had no intention of testing their strength against their southern neighbor, so King Jehoash tried to reason with Amaziah: "A thistle in Lebanon sent a message to a cedar in Lebanon, 'Give your daughter to my son in marriage.' Then a wild beast in Lebanon came along and trampled the thistle underfoot. You have indeed defeated Edom and now you are arrogant. Glory in your victory, but stay at home! Why ask for trouble and cause your own downfall and that of Judah also?' Amaziah, however, would not listen, so Jehoash king of Israel attacked. He and Amaziah king of Judah faced each other at Beth Shemesh in Judah. Judah was routed by Israel, and every man fled to his home. Jehoash king of Israel captured Amaziah king of Judah, the son of Joash, the son of Ahaziah, at Beth Shemesh. Then Jehoash went to Jerusalem and broke down the wall of Jerusalem from the Ephraim Gate to the Corner Gate—a section about four hundred cubits long. He took all the gold and silver and all the articles found in the temple of the Lord and in the treasuries of the royal palace. He also took hostages and returned to Samaria" (2 Kings 14:8-14).

Amaziah's catastrophic defeat stripped him of everything that he had managed to achieve during his reign up till that point: Edom seceded from Judah and the king himself once more became compliant with the will of the Aaronites. It was only complete obedience to the priests of Yahweh that saved the king from the wrath of his people and courtiers; otherwise, it is unlikely that he would have been able to reign for another 15 years after the humiliating defeat that had been inflicted upon him by his own loss of reason. However, his first attempt to flirt with another pagan cult was his last. The scale of the conspiracy against the king was so great that he could find refuge nowhere – neither in the capital, Jerusalem, nor in the remote cities of his kingdom. The book of Chronicles describes the king's last days with laconic brevity: "From the time that Amaziah turned away from following the Lord, they conspired against him

Judah: Heir to the 'House of Jacob'

in Jerusalem and he fled to Lachish, but they sent men after him to Lachish and killed him there" (2 Chronicles 25:27).

Amaziah's place on the Judahite throne was taken by his son, for whom the biblical sources have different names. The book of Chronicles call him Uzziah, while the book of Kings gives his name as Azariah. Admittedly, the latter book uses both names – first Azariah and then Uzziah. Judging by the description of the reign of Azariah/Uzziah, this is undoubtedly one and the same person that is being talked about. It is possible that Azariah took Uzziah as a second name at a later date or that he had a double name from the very beginning. According to the biblical sources, Uzziah reigned for a very long time – 52 years in all – and his rule was a time of economic prosperity and impressive military successes for Judah, whose power during this period spread over all the southern half of Palestine, part of Transjordan, and Midian and Sinai.

Uzziah was crowned king when he was 16. If we take into account that his father had been 54 at the moment of his death, there can be no doubt that the king's heir was not one of his elder sons. The choice of Uzziah was not surprising. In his favor he had not only his youth, a factor which made him susceptible to influence, but also his origin. His mother, Jecoliah, belonged to a noble Jerusalem family which was evidently directly related to both the Davidic dynasty and the Aaronites. Like his father and even more like his grandfather, Uzziah had in effect been brought up by the Aaronites, who chose him for this very reason. The keepers of the tradition rate Uzziah's reign highly. However, they equate him with his father, Amaziah, whose loyalty to the cult of Yahweh had been inconsistent and, more importantly, not always sincere. Also telling is the phrase: "He did what was right in the eyes of the Lord, just as his father Amaziah had done [...] As long as he sought the Lord, God gave him success" (2 Chronicles 26: 4-5). We are given to understand that Uzziah did not always consult the Lord and, consequently, was likewise unable to avoid conflict with the Aaronites.

Uzziah was famous for his highly successful policy of conquest. First of all, he returned to Judah the districts of Edom which had seceded from it after Amaziah's unsuccessful war with Israel. The Bible tells us of the conquest of the city of Elath in the south of the Negev and the defeat of the Meunites (Maonites), Edomite tribes who lived to the south-west of the Dead Sea (2 Chronicles 26:2,7). Both these achievements would have been impossible without the subordination of the whole or at least the greater part of Edom. However, Uzziah's most important achievement should be considered the conquest of the Philistine cities, including the largest such city, Gath: "He went to war against the Philistines and broke down the walls of Gath, Jabneh and Ashdod. He then rebuilt towns near Ashdod and elsewhere among the Philistines" (2 Chronicles 26:6). Thus, for the first time in its history, Judah gained access to the shore of the Mediterranean. The conquest of Edom and Philistia helped Uzziah spread his authority to the nomadic tribes of the Negev, Sinai, and Midian and to gain control over the trade routes to Egypt and Arabia. The biblical text asserts that the Ammonites too paid tribute to him. If this was so, the subordination of the Ammonites could have occurred only at the end of Uzziah's reign, since until then Ammon, like Moab, was a tributary of the Israelite king Jeroboam II. It was only after the unsuccessful wars waged by the heirs of Jeroboam II against the Assyrians that Israel weakened and lost control over Transjordan. This was taken advantage of by Judah, which had grown so much stronger by the end of Uzziah's reign that it was able to subordinate Ammon too. However, territorially, access to this Transjordanian kingdom was possible only through the lands of the Moabites or Israelites, so, although the Bible says nothing of any alliance with them, we may suppose that during the reign of Uzziah there existed a kind of agreement or collaboration with both Israel and the Moabites. Evidence of friendly relations and perhaps even of an alliance between the Southern and Northern Kingdoms is the fact that Jeroboam II, who expanded his kingdom up to its previous borders under King David, did not even try to touch the land of his southern neighbor, and yet the second half of the rule of this warlike Israelite king and the zenith of his power coincided with the beginning of the reign of Uzziah. These friendly relations probably continued also during the reign of Menahem, the next Israelite king, allowing Judah to subordinate Ammon. As for Moab, it is likely that this Transjordanian kingdom was also in an alliance with Uzziah; otherwise, it would not have been able to preserve its independence at a time when its neighbor's territory was expanding.

The rapid strengthening of Judah was made possible by the enormous importance which Uzziah placed upon developing the economy, reorganizing the army, and reinforcing cities and building fortresses. This is confirmed by the Bible, which tells us in particular that "Uzziah built towers in Jerusalem at the Corner Gate, at the Valley Gate and at the angle of the wall, and he fortified them. He also built towers in the wilderness and dug many cisterns, because he had much livestock in the foothills and in the plain. He had people working his fields and vineyards in the hills and in the fertile lands, for he loved the soil [...] In Jerusalem he made devices invented for use on the towers and on the corner defenses so that soldiers could shoot arrows and hurl large stones from the walls. His fame spread far and wide, for he was greatly helped until he became powerful" (2 Chronicles 26:9-10,15). Admittedly, the size of Uzziah's army, which the book of Chronicles gives as 307,500, seems clearly exaggerated. As during the time of Amaziah, this figure has its explanation in the tendency of ancient chroniclers to exaggerate numbers in order to magnify their king and his kingdom. When, several centuries later, this figure found its way into the text of the Bible, the biblical authors no longer had any opportunity to check it.

Judah: Heir to the 'House of Jacob'

Uzziah's advancement led not just to the Aaronites' losing their influence over him, but also to his attempting to take over the powers of the high priest: "But after Uzziah became powerful, his pride led to his downfall. He was unfaithful to the Lord his God, and entered the temple of the Lord to burn incense on the altar of incense" (2 Chronicles 26:16). This was an even more dangerous challenge thrown down to the Aaronites than Joash and Amaziah's involvement with pagan cults, since on this occasion the king wished not just to restrict the influence of the Aaronites, but also to subordinate to his authority the entire corporation of priests. In the Temple of Jerusalem a serious clash occurred between the king and the priests: "Azariah the priest with eighty other courageous priests of the Lord followed him in. They confronted king Uzziah and said, 'It is not right for you, Uzziah, to burn incense to the Lord. That is for the priests, the descendants of Aaron, who have been consecrated to burn incense. Leave the sanctuary, for you have been unfaithful; and you will not be honored by the Lord God.' Uzziah, who had a censer in his hand ready to burn incense, became angry. While he was raging at the priests in their presence before the incense altar in the Lord's temple, leprosy broke out on his forehead. When Azariah the chief priest and all the other priests looked at him, they saw that he had leprosy on his forehead, so they hurried him out. Indeed, he himself was eager to leave, because the Lord had afflicted him. King Uzziah had leprosy until the day he died. He lived in a separate house—leprous, and banned from the temple of the Lord. Jotham his son had charge of the palace and governed the people of the land" (2 Chronicles 26:17-21).

Was Uzziah really struck with leprosy, or was this a clever pretext for isolating the king, removing him from power, and handing the throne over to one of his sons who was in alliance with the Aaronites? As far as we know from those same biblical sources, not one of the Israelite or Judahite kings apart from Uzziah was struck with leprosy, and yet many of them had committed substantially more serious misdeeds against the cult of Yahweh and his priests than Uzziah. For instance, King Saul not merely took upon himself the duties of Samuel, who was away in Gilgal, and carried out sacrifices and burnt incense to the Lord, but also went on to give orders for 85 entirely innocent priests to be killed, including their leader, Ahimelech. But for this rather more serious crime he was not punished with leprosy as Uzziah was. On the other hand, leprosy was the punishment handed out to the prophetess Miriam, Aaron's sister, simply for daring to challenge Moses' authority; she, however, was liberated from the disease as soon as she renounced her claims. Evidently, the threat of leprosy was used as a way of frightening those who challenged the priests and tried to take over their functions. This terrible disease – or rather, the fear of it – was the only means of keeping the army and common people from intervening in the palace conspiracy. The Aaronites were unable to deal with Uzziah as they had done with Athaliah, Joash, and Amaziah. Uzziah had the support of a mighty and loyal army, was popular among the people, and was surrounded by the aura of a conqueror and true follower of Yahweh. Whether the king suffered from a disease of the skin or not, the rumor of leprosy allowed the conspirators to get away with a covert coup and to put their preferred candidate on the throne. This was Jotham, one of the sons of Uzziah who was possibly related to the Aaronites through his mother.

In the fate of Uzziah there is much in common with the fate of Uzziah's father, Amaziah, and grandfather Joash. All three were able to take the throne and rule during their first years only thanks to the help and support they received from the Aaronites. When eventually they became stronger, each tried to rid himself of the guardianship of the priests who were advising him. Joash and Amaziah, while not rejecting the cult of Yahweh, allowed themselves to worship other religious cults, and Uzziah, while remaining a devoted follower of Yahweh, was bold enough to take upon himself the powers of the high priest; thus all three Judahite kings in one way or another entered into conflict with the Aaronites. As a result, two of them, Joash and Amaziah, were killed, and the third, Uzziah, ended up in lifelong captivity. In all three cases the conspirators were supported by the Aaronites; or, at the very least, the latter were the party most interested in the overthrow of the kings. If we take into account that Athaliah's reign was also brought to an end by the Aaronites and that the latter were the party that most opposed the rule of King Jehoram, then we see that this priestly class must be credited with enormous influence in the political life of Judah. The Levites in the Northern Kingdom did not enjoy even part of the influence which the Aaronites held in the Southern Kingdom. It is unlikely that it would be much of an exaggeration to say that even at that time real power in Judah belonged not so much to the kings as to the priests of Yahweh. Possibly, the latter became a force of such importance during the reigns of kings Asa and Jehoshaphat, who, as committed followers of Yahweh, did everything they could to strengthen the position of the Aaronites.

The first years of Jotham's actual rule coincided with the last period of what was formally the rule of his father, so in fact Jotham ruled more than the 16 years allocated to him by the Bible, and Uzziah less than the 52 years attributed to his reign. Jotham's reign should be viewed as a direct continuation of the policy of Uzziah in absolutely everything, with the exception of the fact that, unlike his father, he did not try to take upon himself the duties of the high priest. On this occasion, the Aaronites were completely satisfied with their choice, who "did what was right in the eyes of the Lord". However, even under his rule, as the keepers of the tradition admitted "the people continued their corrupt practices" – meaning that "people continued to offer sacrifices and burn incense [in the high places]", but not in the Temple in Jerusalem, as they should have done (2 Chronicles 27:2; 2 Kings 15:35). There can be no doubt that many of these 'high places' and the 'burning of incense' which took place upon them were dedicated not to the cult of Yahweh, but to pagan gods. Like his father, Jotham built a great deal and reinforced his cities and fortresses in any way he could. "Jotham rebuilt the Upper Gate of the temple of the Lord and did extensive work on the wall at the hill of Ophel. He built towns in the hill country of Judah and forts and towers in the wooded areas" (2 Chronicles 27:3-4). His greatest military success was to rout the Ammonites and turn their kingdoms into vassals of Judah: "Jotham waged war against the king of the Ammonites and conquered them. That year the Ammonites paid him a hundred talents of silver, ten thousand cors of wheat and ten thousand cors of barley. The Ammonites brought him the same amount also in the second and third years" (2 Chronicles 27:5). It cannot be ruled out that Uzziah's conquest of the Ammonites, which might have happened at the end of Uzziah's reign, was in fact the result of the military campaigns of his son Jotham.

During Jotham's reign the military and political situation around Judah underwent a marked deterioration. After a prolonged interval, Assyria returned to the region of Syria and Palestine, and its army, renewing its conquest of the Syrian and Phoenician states, rapidly approached Palestine. Faced with a shared danger, the two former enemies, Israel and Aram-Damascus, entered into a peace agreement and put together a broad anti-Assyrian coalition consisting of the Syrian, Phoenician, and Palestine states. Not desiring to be drawn into the war with Assyria, Judah refused to join this coalition and thus brought upon itself the enmity of its members. The book of Kings mentions in passing that during the years of Jotham's reign Israel and Aram-Damascus jointly attacked Judah: "In those days the Lord began to send Rezin king of Aram and Pekah son of Remaliah against Judah" (2 Kings 15:37). It is likely that a stumbling block was Judah's dominance over Ammon, which Israel and Damascus considered their zone of interest. If Jotham had joined the anti-Assyrian coalition, the disagreements would have been peacefully sorted out among allies, but Judah's refusal put it at war with Israel and Aram-Damascus. Thanks to his army, Jotham still had the strength to withstand the pressure exerted by the Israelites and Arameans, but the military situation around Judah continued to deteriorate, as Jotham's successor, Ahaz, became only too aware.

Ahaz's rule took place in a period which was very difficult and dangerous for the country. Judah found itself between a rock and a hard place: on the one hand, its borders were being approached by Assyria, which was hated by the entire ancient world; on the other, all Judah's neighbors were members of the anti-Assyrian coalition and required that Judah also join. Ahaz, like his father, Jotham, before him, did not believe that this motley coalition, consisting of countries which were hostile to one another, could withstand the Assyrian army, the mightiest army of the time, but nor did he desire confrontation with Assyria's enemies. Judah's neighbors, however, did not permit it to remain neutral for long. After failing to reach an agreement with Ahaz, Israel and Aram-Damascus decided to remove him from his throne by force and replace him with a more compliant candidate. The Judahite prophet Isaiah, who lived at this anxious time, described these events as follows: "When Ahaz son of Jotham, the son of Uzziah, was king of Judah, King Rezin of Aram and Pekah son of Remaliah king of Israel marched up to fight against Jerusalem, but they could not overpower it. Now the house of David was told, 'Aram has allied itself with Ephraim'; so the hearts of Ahaz and his people were shaken, as the trees of the forest are shaken by the wind" (Isaiah 7:1-2). Before taking refuge behind the walls of Jerusalem, Ahaz engaged in a large-scale battle with his opponents, but was unable to overcome them and suffered large losses. The book of Chronicles, the only biblical source to offer an account of this battle, gives several details: "In one day Pekah son of Remaliah killed a hundred and twenty thousand soldiers in Judah—because Judah had forsaken the Lord, the God of their ancestors. Zikri, an Ephraimite warrior, killed Maaseiah the king's son, Azrikam the officer in charge of the palace, and Elkanah, second to the king" (2 Chronicles 28:6-7).

In spite of the extreme exaggeration of the numbers of the dead, Ahaz's losses must indeed have been keenly felt if both his son and closest dignitaries fell on the field of battle. But the allies were unable to take Jerusalem: during the reigns of Uzziah and Jotham the city had been turned into a first-class fortress and had been made almost impregnable. Forced to give up the idea of storming Jerusalem, Rezin, the king of Aram-Damascus, helped the Edomites break free from Judah and seized Elath. At the same time, other allies from the anti-Assyrian coalition, the Philistines, took advantage of Ahaz's disastrous position to "[raid] towns in the foothills and in the Negev of Judah. They captured and occupied Beth-Shemesh, Aijalon and Gederoth, as well as Soko, Timnah and Gimzo, with their surrounding villages" (2 Chronicles 28:18). In his book of prophecies Isaiah says that he tried to calm Ahaz and suggest to him that it was the will of God that he should not "lose heart because of these two smoldering stubs of firewood" – Israel and Damascus – because they would soon "be too shattered to be a people" (Isaiah 7:4,8). As proof of his words, Isaiah proposed that Ahaz should ask the Lord through him for any sign he wished, but Ahaz refused to "test the Lord" and decided to turn for help to Assyria (Isaiah 7:11-12). "Ahaz sent messengers to say to Tiglath-Pileser king of Assyria, 'I am your servant and vassal. Come up and save me out of the hand of the king of Aram and of the king of Israel, who are attacking me.' And Ahaz took the silver and gold found in the temple of the Lord and in the treasuries of the royal palace and sent it as a gift to the king of Assyria. The king of Assyria complied by attacking Damascus and capturing it. He deported its inhabitants to Kir and put Rezin to death" (2 Kings 16:7-9). Subsequent events in Syria and Palestine confirmed that Ahaz had chosen the correct political course: all his enemies who were members of the anti-Assyrian coalition were either completely destroyed by Assyria or were made its vassals on terms which were significantly worse than those received by Judah. In particular, the kingdom of Damascus ceased to exist altogether and became an ordinary Assyrian province, and all that remained of the kingdom of Israel was the region of Samaria, and that was now a vassal of Assyria. Ahaz turned out to be more far-sighted than his neighbors and reaped the benefits of his foresight when the Assyrians returned to him all the lands which had been seized by his enemies.

The keepers of the tradition accused Ahaz of idolatry, reproaching him for "[following] the ways of the kings of Israel and even [sacrificing] his son in the fire, engaging in the detestable practices of the nations the Lord had driven out before the Israelites. He offered sacrifices and burned incense at the high places, on the hilltops and under every spreading tree" (2 Kings 16:3-4). The book of Chronicles, which was written much later than Kings, depicts Ahaz in rather more sinister colors. Chronicles accuses Ahaz of complete rejection of the cult of Yahweh and of contaminating and closing the Temple in Jerusalem, whereas the book of Kings, while noting the king's fascination with pagan cults, mentions only a partial reconstruction of the temple, but not its being contaminated or closed. Chronicles asserts that Ahaz "sacrificed his son in the fire", while the book of Kings talks only of imitation of the custom of "passing through the fire". The book of Chronicles is convinced that "The Lord had humbled Judah because of Ahaz [...] for he had promoted wickedness in Judah and had been most unfaithful to the Lord" and informs us of the following incriminating fact: "Ahaz gathered together the furnishings from the temple of God and cut them in pieces. He shut the doors of the Lord's temple and set up altars at every street corner in Jerusalem. In every town in Judah he built high places to burn sacrifices to other gods and aroused the anger of the Lord, the God of his ancestors" (2 Chronicles 28:19, 24-25). At the same time, Kings, the earlier and more reliable source, tells us merely that a new sacrificial altar was set up in the Temple – and that this was for sacrifices not to a pagan god, but to the Lord: "Then King Ahaz went to Damascus to meet Tiglath-Pileser king of Assyria. He saw an altar in Damascus and sent to Uriah the priest a sketch of the altar, with detailed plans for its construction. So Uriah the priest built an altar in accordance with all the plans that King Ahaz had sent from Damascus and finished it before King Ahaz returned" (2 Kings 16:10-11). According to the book of Kings, the new sacrificial altar was to be used for public services, while the old, copper, one remained in position in the Temple and was to be used by the king in person.

A clay seal impression with the inscription 'Belonging to
Ahaz [son of] Jotham king of Judah.'

Admittedly, Kings also mentions in passing a very important detail which explains the reason for the Aaronites' extreme enmity towards Ahaz: the king took upon himself the right to conduct sacrifices and burn incense, duties which should have belonged to the high priest alone, i.e. he repeated the sin of Uzziah, who had been punished with leprosy. If Chronicles tells us absolutely nothing of the Aaronites' reaction to the king's assumption of their functions, Kings makes it quite clear that the priests did not oppose the will of the king, as had been the case with Uzziah, but obediently carried out all Ahaz's commandments regarding the 'pagan' changes to the Temple. Thus Ahaz was not an apostate or villain as he is depicted by the book of Chronicles. He was a polytheist; however, while worshipping the pagan gods, he did not renounce the God of his fathers, the cult of Yahweh. He in effect took the same course as many of his predecessors, including Rehoboam, Abijah, Jehoram, Joash, and Amaziah. Under the influence of, or to please, his Assyrian patrons he went slightly further, in making the Temple in Jerusalem resemble the temples in Assyria. Confirmation of this is found in the text of the Bible, which says that Ahaz "took away the Sabbath canopy that had been built at the temple and removed the royal entryway outside the temple of the Lord, in deference to the king of Assyria" (2 Kings 16:18). But even before Ahaz the cult of Yahweh had not been a monotheistic religion; at that time it existed in parallel with other cults, over which it merely claimed primacy. Ahaz's 'crime' was that the Aaronites lost their dominant position during his reign. At the same time, no biblical source accuses Ahaz of persecuting the followers of Yahweh, as had happened in the Northern Kingdom during the reigns of Ahab and Jezebel.

What was it that drove the son of a righteous worshipper of Yahweh to serve pagan cults, and why did the Aaronites not conspire to overthrow the idolatrous king, as they had successfully done in the case of his predecessors, kings who had been guilty of lesser misdemeanors? The answer to both these questions is to be found in the character of the relations between Judah and Assyria. After becoming a vassal of Assyria, Ahaz tried to imitate the Assyrians' religious cults and customs so as to maintain the best possible relations with the Assyrian king and his retinue. This kind of behavior was rewarded with a reduction in the amount of tribute to be paid and with greater trust on the part of the rulers of the greatest empire of the ancient Near East. The agreement with the Assyrian king protected Ahaz not just from external enemies, but from internal ones as well. At that time, agreements were concluded between the kings themselves, as opposed to between countries, so Tiglath-Pileser III guaranteed his support not for Judah, but for his Judahite vassal Ahaz. It was this that restrained the Aaronites from overthrowing the king and served Ahaz as reliable protection from their wrath.

Chapter 11

Judah as the Only Hebrew Kingdom

King Hezekiah: Religious Reforms and Uprising against Assyria
Ahaz's son Hezekiah went down in his people's historical memory as a righteous king. He is known first for his religious reforms and secondly for the war with Assyria. Possibly, the first years of his reign coincided with the fall of Samaria in 722 BCE and with the removal of its inhabitants to Assyria. The fall of the kingdom of Israel could not fail to make a profound impression on Judah. No matter how tense and hostile the relations between the two Hebrew states had been at times, the memory of the period they had spent together in Egypt, their fight for Canaan, and their United Monarchy had created a feeling that these two different peoples had a shared fate. The fact that some of the southerners – the Levites and the tribe of Reuben – had joined the alliance of northern tribes and the northern tribe of Benjamin had joined the southerners had given rise to a feeling of religious and ethnic kinship between them and this had further been reinforced by the linking of their family trees. It cannot be ruled out that it was the tragic events involved in the fall of the kingdom of Israel that impelled Hezekiah to implement his religious reforms, given that they demonstrated the helplessness of entire peoples in the face of misfortune. Hezekiah saw these misfortunes as a warning from above for Judah itself, which had become mired in idolatry.

His first step was to consecrate the Temple in Jerusalem and restore the previous procedures for religious worship there. At the end of his rule Ahaz had used the Temple in Jerusalem not merely for worshipping Yahweh, but also for sacrifices to the pagan gods that had been adopted from Assyria. The book of Chronicles says the following: "In the first month of the first year of his reign, he opened the doors of the temple of the Lord and repaired them. He brought in the priests and the Levites, assembled them in the square on the east side and said: 'Listen to me, Levites! Consecrate yourselves now and consecrate the temple of the Lord, the God of your ancestors. Remove all defilement from the sanctuary. Our parents were unfaithful; they did evil in the eyes of the Lord our God and forsook him. They turned their faces away from the Lord's dwelling place and turned their backs on him […] The priests went into the sanctuary of the Lord to purify it. They brought out to the courtyard of the Lord's temple everything unclean that they found in the temple of the Lord […]" (2 Chronicles 29:3-6; 16).

The second, no less important, decision taken by Hezekiah was to incorporate the northern Levites who had come from the former kingdom of Israel into the same organization of priests as the Aaronites and southern Levites. Admittedly, the northern Levites occupied positions that were secondary compared to those of the Aaronites; on the other hand, however, for the first time since the rule of King David they were allowed to take part in religious services at Temple and were assigned positions at the royal court in Jerusalem. Nevertheless, the latent fight for primacy between the northern Levites and the Aaronites continued, as we see from the Bible. In order to avoid conflict between the Aaronites and the Levites, Hezekiah divided them into different categories, allocated all positions of responsibility in accordance with these categories, and, in order to provide for the entire class of priests materially, instituted a tithe tax (2 Chronicles 31:2-4). At the insistence of high priest Jehoiada, King Joash had established a tithe to be paid to the Temple in Jerusalem; Hezekiah now did the same in order to provide for the upkeep of the Aaronites and Levites.

Hezekiah's next step was to eliminate the pagan cults that had become widespread in Judah: from now on, the cult of Yahweh was to be not just the main religion, but the sole one. As the book of Kings says, "He removed the high places, smashed the sacred stones and cut down the Asherah poles. He broke into pieces the bronze snake Moses had made, for up to that time the Israelites had been burning incense to it. (It was called Nehushtan.)" (2 Kings 18:4). For the first time in the history of Judah, Hezekiah forbade high sacrificial tables for worshipping not just pagan gods, but also Yahweh. Henceforward all sacrifices and religious services were supposed to take place solely in the Temple in Jerusalem. This centralization made it possible to increase the Temple's income and placed all religious services in the country under the control of the priests of Yahweh. For the first time since Moses the cult of Yahweh became, even if not for long, a truly monotheistic religion. It is unsurprising, then, that, in evaluating Hezekiah, the keepers of the tradition asserted that "There was no one like him among all the kings of Judah, either before him or after him" (2 Kings 18:5).

As well as joining the northern Levite clans to the Aaronites of the Southern Kingdom, Hezekiah made every effort to spread the religious influence of Judah over the entire territory of the former kingdom of Israel, which was now divided into four Assyrian provinces. His pretext for reconciliation with the elders and religious leaders of the northerners was their shared traditional festive occasions, and, above all, the most important of these occasions – the Passover. "Hezekiah sent word to all Israel and Judah and also wrote letters to Ephraim and Manasseh, inviting them to come to the temple of the Lord in Jerusalem and celebrate the Passover to the Lord, the God of Israel" (2 Chronicles 30:1). The king placed such great importance on establishing good relations with the northern tribes that he even took the extraordinary step of delaying celebration of the Passover until the Israelites arrived (2 Chronicles 30:2-3). However, as the Bible admits, these efforts were at best only partially successful: "The couriers went from town to town in Ephraim and Manasseh, as far as Zebulun, but people scorned and ridiculed them. Nevertheless, some from Asher, Manasseh and Zebulun humbled themselves and went to Jerusalem" (2 Chronicles 30:10-11). Hezekiah's messengers encountered the strongest resistance on land belonging to the tribe of Ephraim. Although this tribe had suffered most from the removal of the population to Assyria and had been 'beheaded' in both the metaphorical and literal senses, the remaining Ephraimites, together with the migrants from Syria and Babylonia who had been moved to these parts, refused to accept the spiritual hegemony of Jerusalem. The old rivalry between the 'house of Joseph' and the 'house of Jacob' prevented the creation of even a religious alliance between northerners and southerners. And yet the military and political fall of the 'house of Joseph' gave the 'house of Jacob' hope that it could lead all the Hebrew tribes, as it had done previously under King David.

The path to this goal, however, was blocked by the Assyrians. King Hezekiah took advantage of the Assyrians' internal difficulties and of the atmosphere of universal revolt against Assyria to throw down a challenge: he refused to pay tribute or serve as Assyria's vassal. This step taken by Hezekiah, like his religious reform, was Yahwist Judah's reaction to the idolatry of Ahaz and the latter's humiliating dependence on Assyria. Furthermore, the position of dependent vassal was something with which Judah was to date unfamiliar since, in spite of numerous wars with its neighbors, the Southern Kingdom had only on several occasions been forced to buy its freedom from conquerors, and these had been one-off payments – the first time during the invasion of the Egyptian pharaoh Sheshonq I; then when the aggressor had been Hazael, the ruler of Aram-Damascus; and finally following Amaziah's unsuccessful war against King Jehoash of Israel. Only under Ahaz had the position changed radically and Judah become a permanent tributary of Assyria. So from the moment that he became king, Hezekiah desired to put an end to Judah's dependence on Assyria, and it was for this reason that he entered into secret negotiations with the rulers of other states that were subjects of the Assyrians. During these talks Judah was visited by emissaries from Marduk-apal-iddina (the biblical Merodach Baladan), the mighty leader of the Chaldeans (Aramean tribes who had settled in southern Babylonia). Hezekiah found potential allies for the fight against Assyria not just in Mesopotamia, but also in Syria, Phoenicia, and Philistia. Many of these peoples were only waiting for a convenient moment to rise up against a power that was universally hated. Finally, such an opportunity presented itself: in 705 BCE the Assyrian king Sargon II – the same king who had given orders for Samaria to be destroyed and for its inhabitants to be deported to Assyria – was ambushed and killed in northwestern Iran. The killing of the king, whose body was never found and therefore remained unburied, served as the long-awaited trigger for a general uprising against Assyria. The most serious danger for the Assyrians was the Chaldean tribes in southern Mesopotamia, who were led by Hezekiah's ally Marduk-apal-iddina II. These tribes were large, strong, and had the support of many of Mesopotamia's rulers, as well as of the army in neighboring Elam. In Palestine the anti-Assyrian uprising was led by Hezekiah himself. He was supported by the Transjordanian kingdoms and by some Philistine cities, notably Ashkelon; other cities, such as the Philistine city of Ekron, remained loyal to the Assyrians. For this reason, taking advantage of the fact that the main forces of the Assyrian army were engaged in southern and central Mesopotamia, Hezekiah seized Ekron and with the cooperation of some of its citizens imprisoned the Assyrian vassal, Padi. Hezekiah must also have undertaken other campaigns into Philistia, for the book of Kings tells us that "From watchtower to fortified city, he defeated the Philistines, as far as Gaza and its territory" (2 Kings 18:8). Over the course of several years Hezekiah drove out all the Assyrians from Palestine and disposed of their vassals.

In spite of the expectations of its opponents, Assyria did not, however, collapse under the pressure exerted by the mutiny of its subject peoples. In 705/704 BCE, following a short power struggle, the throne was occupied by Sennacherib, one of the sons of Sargon II and an experienced politician and talented military commander. During the first years of his reign Sennacherib managed to suppress the uprisings in Babylonia and Western Iran, inflicted a heavy defeat on the Elamites, the main allies of the Chaldeans, and in 701 BCE moved upon Syria, Phoenicia, and Palestine. Here, with rare exceptions, he met with no serious resistance. Some of the cities surrendered without a fight (the inhabitants of Sidon, for instance, expelled their ruler, who was an opponent of Assyria, and opened the city gates to the Assyrian army); and the resistance of other cities was quickly quelled. The Transjordanian kingdoms of Ammon, Moab, and Edom hastened to demonstrate submission to Sennacherib and to bring him tribute. The Egyptian army, which tried to come to the aid of the mutineers, suffered a crushing defeat at Elteke, on Palestine's south-western border, and Judah found itself left entirely on its own in the face of Sennacherib's enormous army. It became clear that Hezekiah had repeated the fateful mistake made by the last Israelite king, Hoshea. After underestimating the strength of the Assyrian empire and counting upon support which had been promised him, Hoshea had started a hopeless war which had ended in the fall of his kingdom. In order to imagine the fear and horror which the Assyrian monster must have provoked and the feelings which the inhabitants of the small country of Judah must have experienced when they found themselves on their own against this Assyrian war machine, we should recall the words of the prophet Isaiah regarding the behavior of the Assyrian kings (evidently, Isaiah had in mind Sargon II or Sennacherib): "As one reaches into a nest, so my hand reached for the wealth of the nations; as people gather abandoned eggs, so I gathered all the countries; not one flapped a wing, or opened its mouth to chirp" (Isaiah 10:14). The book of Kings tells us: "In the fourteenth year of King Hezekiah's reign, Sennacherib king of Assyria attacked all the fortified cities of Judah and captured them" (2 Kings 18:13). However, the Assyrians became bogged down for a long time near Lachish, a large Judahite fortress on the border with Philistia. Lachish proved difficult to take by siege; its defenders showed heroic

Judah as the Only Hebrew Kingdom

courage and inflicted appreciable losses on the Assyrians. Impressed by the fight for the city, Sennacherib subsequently gave orders for bas reliefs to be carved on the walls of his palace in Nineveh depicting the storm of Lachish.

Meanwhile, Hezekiah, who had realized the pointlessness of continuing the war, tried to make peace with the Assyrian king. "So Hezekiah king of Judah sent this message to the king of Assyria at Lachish: 'I have done wrong. Withdraw from me, and I will pay whatever you demand of me.' The king of Assyria exacted from Hezekiah king of Judah three hundred talents of silver and thirty talents of gold. So Hezekiah gave him all the silver that was found in the temple of the Lord and in the treasuries of the royal palace" (2 Kings 18:14-15). However, even after receiving the required tribute, Sennacherib did not renounce his intention of punishing the leader of the anti-Assyrian uprising in Palestine; he demanded the surrender of Jerusalem and of the king himself. As punishment for their rebelliousness and obstinate resistance, Sennacherib decided to treat Jerusalem and the Judahites just as his father, Sargon II, had treated Samaria and the Israelites – namely, by deporting the inhabitants to Assyria and settling in their place the inhabitants of other mutinous cities. Evidence of this is to be found in words spoken by Sennacherib's emissaries to the people of Jerusalem: "'Do not listen to Hezekiah. This is what the king of Assyria says: Make peace with me and come out to me. Then each of you will eat fruit from your own vine and fig tree and drink water from your own cistern, until I come and take you to a land like your own—a land of grain and new wine, a land of bread and vineyards, a land of olive trees and honey. Choose life and not death!" (2 Kings 18:31-32). In the light of these new demands from the Assyrian king, Hezekiah had no choice but to fight to the bitter end.

As the lengthy siege was about to begin, Hezekiah gave orders both for all sources of water in the environs of Jerusalem to be filled in and for water to be channeled within the city itself. "When Hezekiah saw that Sennacherib had come and that he intended to wage war against Jerusalem, he consulted with his officials and military staff about blocking off the water from the springs outside the city [...] It was Hezekiah who blocked the upper outlet of the Gihon spring and channeled the water down to the west side of the City of David" (2 Chronicles 32:2-3, 30). This information given by the Bible has transpired to be surprisingly precise: in 1880 the so-called 'Siloam inscription' was discovered; it talks of the construction of a tunnel bringing water into Jerusalem from a spring situated outside the fortress walls of that time. The 533-metre-long tunnel was carved out of the inside of a cliff and must have been a very skillful piece of engineering for its time. According to the inscription – which, unfortunately, has survived only in part – the tunnel was built in haste and, in order to speed things up, its construction proceeded from both ends simultaneously. Two groups of builders moved towards one another deep inside the stone cliff and, although they had none of the equipment and instruments needed for this operation, were able to join up with one another with amazing accuracy. The Siloam tunnel is not merely evidence of the high standard of engineering in Judah at that time; it also compels us to pay increased attention to all details in the biblical text, however unimportant or incredible they may seem. The Siloam inscription – or rather, what remains of it – is, moreover, a rare example of Hebrew writing of the late 8th century BCE.

The Siloam Tunnel. It conducted water from the Gihon spring, which was outside the city walls, into the western part of ancient Jerusalem.

One witness of the Assyrian invasion was the prophet Isaiah, thanks to whose book of prophecies we know certain details of the defense of Jerusalem.

Judah as the Only Hebrew Kingdom

Seeing before them a large, well-fortified city and remembering the self-sacrificing resistance shown by the residents of the more modest town of Lachish, the Assyrians tried to exert psychological pressure on the defenders of Jerusalem in order to get them to surrender of their own free will. To this end, the emissaries of Sennacherib, who either were Judahites by birth or had spent a long time living in Judah, deliberately refrained from speaking Aramaic, as Hezekiah's officials had asked them to do, but instead addressed themselves directly to the defenders of Jerusalem, who were on the fortress walls, in their native language – ancient Hebrew. "Tell Hezekiah: "This is what the great king, the king of Assyria, says: [...] On whom are you depending, that you rebel against me? Look, I know you are depending on Egypt, that splintered reed of a staff, which pierces the hand of anyone who leans on it! Such is Pharaoh king of Egypt to all who depend on him. But if you say to me, 'We are depending on the Lord our God'—isn't he the one whose high places and altars Hezekiah removed, saying to Judah and Jerusalem, 'You must worship before this altar in Jerusalem'? [...] "Do not listen to Hezekiah, for he is misleading you when he says, 'The Lord will deliver us.' Has the god of any nation ever delivered his land from the hand of the king of Assyria? Where are the gods of Hamath and Arpad? Where are the gods of Sepharvaim, Hena and Ivvah? Have they rescued Samaria from my hand? [...] Furthermore, have I come to attack and destroy this place without word from the Lord? The Lord himself told me to march against this country and destroy it'" (2 Kings 18:19-22, 32-34, 25).

Clearly, Sennacherib's emissaries were very well informed regarding the military weakness of Egypt, where the pharaohs of the 25th Nubian (Cushite) Dynasty were now established, and regarding Hezekiah's religious reforms, which had stirred up dissatisfaction among a part of the population, and the views of the Judahite monotheists, who saw in everything manifestations of the will of the one and all-mighty Lord. The Bible even gives the names of the messengers of the Assyrian king who appealed directly to the defenders of the city as Ravshakey, Tartan, and Rab-Saris. Admittedly, these were not proper personal names, but the titles of positions of high-ranking Assyrian dignitaries. Chronicles of the rule of the Assyrian kings make repeated mentions of officials such as 'ravshakai' or 'tartan', who were responsible for carrying out military or diplomatic missions, while the term 'tartan', for instance, was used to signify the commander of the Egyptian army which had fought the Assyrians.

According to the book of Kings, Hezekiah, depressed by what he had heard, asked the prophet Isaiah to pray for the people and ascertain the will of the Lord. When the royal dignitaries and priests came to the prophet for his answer, Isaiah commanded them to convey the following to the king: "This is what the Lord says: Do not be afraid of what you have heard—those words with which the underlings of the king of Assyria have blasphemed me. Listen! [...] When he hears a certain report, I will make him want to return to his own country, and there I will have him cut down with the sword" (2 Kings 19:6-7). Isaiah's prophecy strengthened Hezekiah's determination not to surrender to the Assyrians and to continue the defense of Jerusalem. The siege of the city lasted longer than Sennacherib had expected; furthermore, some of the latter's forces were tied down by another Judahite city, Libnah, which continued to repel the attacks of the Assyrians after the fall of Lachish. Angered by the stubborn resistance shown by the Judahites, the Assyrian king again dispatched messengers to Hezekiah, this time with a personal letter for the king. Judging by the contents of this message, the Assyrians were very well informed regarding everything which was happening at this time at the Judahite court: "Do not let the god you depend on deceive you [...] Surely you have heard what the kings of Assyria have done to all the countries, destroying them completely. And will you be delivered?" (2 Kings 19:10-11). In order to show the defenders of Jerusalem that they no longer had anyone whom they could look to for salvation, the Assyrian king gave orders for Egyptian and Nubian prisoners to be driven alongside the city walls. The book of Isaiah says that these were captives from Egypt and Cush who were led away "stripped and barefoot [...] with buttocks bared—to Egypt's shame. Those who trusted in Cush and boasted in Egypt will be dismayed and put to shame" (Isaiah 20:4-5). And again Hezekiah called to him the prophet Isaiah, requiring him to ascertain the will of the Lord, and again Isaiah foretold that the Assyrians were not destined to enter Jerusalem.

What happened subsequently is a mystery. As Isaiah had prophesied, the Assyrians were indeed unable to take Jerusalem; the Assyrian army – or what remained of it – was forced to raise the siege in a hurry and return to Assyria. The Assyrian chronicles, which generally announce only victories, maintain complete silence with regard to the unsuccessful siege of Jerusalem and the reasons for Sennacherib's hurried retreat. The Bible gives an account of these events, but one which is excessively brief: "That night the angel of the Lord went out and put to death a hundred and eighty-five thousand in the Assyrian camp. When the people got up the next morning—there were all the dead bodies! So Sennacherib king of Assyria broke camp and withdrew. He returned to Nineveh and stayed there" (2 Kings 19:35-36). We may suppose that the Assyrian army fell victim to some kind of terrible epidemic and that Sennacherib, fearing for his life, left in a hurry with the remainder of his troops for Nineveh. The Greek historian Herodotus, who lived much later than the events described here, mentions that the Assyrian army suffered from an invasion of mice, which bit through their bows and made the intended campaign against Egypt impossible. Incidentally, for the ancient Semites the mouse was a symbol of plague. But whatever the case, the misfortune that befell the Assyrians was inflicted by no human hand. The 'miracle' that occurred near Jerusalem – as the keepers of the tradition subsequently characterized it – saved Jerusalem and

Judah as the Only Hebrew Kingdom

Hezekiah from destruction, but did not liberate Judah from its position as vassal of Assyria. Furthermore, Hezekiah had to pay a heavy price in order to smooth over the conflict with the Assyrians and prevent his country being once more invaded by Sennacherib.

In general, the biblical account of the war with Assyria is confirmed and complemented by the Assyrian sources. The most serious resistance to Sennacherib during his campaign against Syria, Phoenicia, and Palestine was clearly offered by Hezekiah, so the Assyrian king pays him the most attention in his victorious report on this military expedition. "As to Hezekiah, the Jew, he did not submit to my yoke, I laid siege to 46 of his strong cities, walled forts and to the countless small villages in their vicinity, conquered (them) by means of well-stamped (earth) ramps, and battering-rams brought (thus) near (to the walls) (combined with) the attack by foot soldiers, (using) mines, breeches as well as sapper work. I drove out (of them) 200,150 people, young and old, male and female, horses, mules, donkeys, camels, big and small cattle beyond counting, and considered (them) booty. (Hezekiah) himself I made a prisoner in Jerusalem, his royal residence, like a bird in a cage. I surrounded him with earthwork in order to molest those who were leaving his city's gate. His towns, which I had plundered, I took away from his country and gave them (over) to Mitinti, king of Ashdod, to Padi, king of Ekron, and Sillibel, king of Gaza. Thus I reduced his country, but I still increased his tribute [...] Later he sent me to Nineveh, my lordly city, together with 30 talents of gold, 800 talents of silver, precious stones [...] all kinds of valuable treasures, his (own) daughters, concubines, male and female musicians. In order to deliver the tribute and to do obeisance as a slave he sent his (personal) messenger."

The Assyrian sources inform us of an important detail which is only mentioned in passing in the books of Kings and Chronicles; this relates to the devastation of Judah and the deportation of part of its population to Assyria. The archaeological evidence confirms the terrible devastation wrought by the Assyrians in the most fertile valley in Judah, Shephelah. The population of this valley, which constituted almost half of the total number of the country's residents, was reduced to a third of its former size and the majority of its cities, including the second most important Judahite city, Lachish, were left in ruins. Of course, the figure of 200,000 Judahites taken into captivity is a clear exaggeration of the kind that is very characteristic of all the Assyrians' reports of victory, but it is evidence of the deportation of a part of the Judahite population to Assyria, people of whose fate we know even less than of that of the Israelites who were deported to the same place. This means that from the end of the 8th century forwards the cities of Mesopotamia and Syria had inhabitants who came not merely from the northern Hebrew tribes, but from the southern ones as well. Moreover, we have no evidence whatever regarding their return to Palestine, unlike in the case of those who were taken into captivity in Babylonia 115 years later.

Judahite deportees being led away after the fall of
Lachish to the Assyrian King Sennacherib. 701 BCE.

The books of Kings, Chronicles, and Isaiah devote an unusually large amount of coverage to the rule of King Hezekiah. This is due to the fact that Hezekiah's reign coincided with one of the most critical moments in the history of Judah and also to his religious reforms, which led to the temporary triumph of monotheism in the country. At the same time, in spite of the abundance of information, we cannot even be sure of the exact dates of his rule, since one and the same biblical sources provide contradictory evidence. According to one version, Hezekiah came to power in 728/727; according to another, in 715 BCE. However, the problem begins earlier, with the reign of Hezekiah's father, Ahaz, who, according to the book of Kings, ascended the throne at the age of 20, ruled for 16 years, and then handed the reins of power over to his 25-year-old son, Hezekiah (2 Kings 16:2). Clearly, the 36-year-old Ahaz could not have had a 25-year-old son and must have transferred power to him considerably later, in 715 BCE. This version is supported by the Bible's statement that the Assyrian king Sennacherib initiated a war against Judah during the 14th year of Hezekiah's reign. Knowing from Assyrian sources that this happened in 701 BCE, we thus find confirmation that Hezekiah's reign must have begun in 715 BCE. We likewise know that during the siege of Jerusalem Hezekiah fell seriously ill and was close to death, but, as predicted by the prophet, recovered his health and subsequently reigned for another 15 years. Given that Hezekiah ruled for a total of 29 years, this would seem to back up the version that his reign took place at the later date.

However, the same biblical text asserts that Samaria was taken by the Assyrians in the sixth year of Hezekiah's reign and again, knowing from the Assyrian chronicles that the capital of the kingdom of Israel fell in 722/721 BCE, we have to move the beginning of the reign of this Judahite king to 728/727 BCE (2 Kings 18:10). The difficulties with determining the precise dates of Hezekiah's rule are merely a modest example of the complications that exist in general with the chronology of the reigns of most of the kings of Judah and Israel. Unfortunately, not only the biblical books themselves, but also the texts within each of them often contain contradictory information which makes it impossible to give precise dates for events. This has its explanation in the fact that they were created considerably later than the events which they describe and their authors, who had available to them ancient manuscripts which have now been lost, had no means of checking or clarifying them. In the end, the final redactors of the Bible decided to incorporate in it all the different versions without giving preference to any one of them. That is why we are today able to give only approximate dates for events in biblical history; the rule of Hezekiah is just one of numerous examples of this.

Certain historians who have conducted research into the period of Hezekiah's reign suppose that there was not one, but two wars with Assyria during his rule. The first happened approximately in 712 BCE, when Sargon II appeared at the borders of Judah in order to lay waste to the mutinous city of Ashdod and rout the Egyptian army which was trying to come to the latter's aid. It was probably then that Hezekiah managed to buy off the Assyrian king and end the conflict peacefully. The second war with the Assyrians occurred in 701 BCE, during the rule of Sennacherib, and had rather more serious consequences for Judah. According to this point of view, the accounts of these various military campaigns were in time elided, giving us the biblical account of the war with Assyria as it is now. However, the Assyrian sources with which we are familiar do not support this version and talk only of one war – of Sennacherib's campaign against Judah. Nevertheless, it has to be admitted that in certain, very badly preserved, Assyrian chronicles of the time of Sargon II, Judah is indeed mentioned as a vassal with whom Assyria had problems; so it cannot be denied that Hezekiah was trying even then to break free of Assyrian rule. But, as far as we can judge, he managed to reject in good time the idea of direct confrontation with Assyria, thus avoiding the ruination of his country. The book of Chronicles mentions, albeit not very clearly, the fact that Judah was threatened with a serious military danger which failed to materialize: "[...] the Lord's wrath was on him [Hezekiah] and on Judah and Jerusalem. Then Hezekiah repented of the pride of his heart, as did the people of Jerusalem; therefore the Lord's wrath did not come on them during the days of Hezekiah"

(2 Chronicles 32:25-26). By 'the Lord's wrath' the authors of the Bible often mean the invasion of a foreign army; so perhaps these words are an indirect confirmation of the idea that during the rule of Sargon II Judah was faced with a real threat of Assyrian invasion, and the episode with the payment of tribute dates to this time.

The overall outcome of Hezekiah's rule was not very comforting. He inherited from his 'idolatrous' father a country which, even if it was dependent on Assyria, was nevertheless prospering, and he left it in ruins and under the burden of a tribute which was even larger than previously. His attempts to break free of Assyrian power came to nothing and resulted only in the death and imprisonment of a considerable part of the population and in the plundering and devastation of Judah. Hezekiah not only failed to annex lands which had constituted the kingdom of Israel, but also lost parts of his own territory, including western Shephelah, which the Assyrians gave to Philistine cities that were their vassals. His religious reforms had very contradictory results. They made the cult of Yahweh the only 'legal', permitted, cult in the country and the Aaronites and Levites this cult's only legal priests. Thus they immeasurably strengthened the latter already mighty organization. But the forced switch to monotheism and the unification of religious faiths and service led to dissatisfaction and tension in Judah, since the numerous followers of other cults now found themselves outlawed and their priests without anything to put in their mouths. The ban on local sacrifices was a grave blow to worshippers of Yahweh in remote districts of Judah too; henceforward they were forced to spend considerable time and resources on travelling to the Temple in Jerusalem. Although in general Hezekiah's policies were unsuccessful and brought great suffering on his country, at the same time it was thanks to him that very important progress was made towards true monotheism in the religious and spiritual life of Judahite society. For the first time in the ancient Near East, and in the world in general, the idea of monotheism was realized on the scale of an entire country – and this was during an age when pagan cults and idolatry everywhere had the upper hand. No Judahite king before him, including David himself, had managed to realize the idea of monotheism as consistently and insistently as Hezekiah – so his achievements in the intellectual and spiritual transformation of society are undeniable. In short, Hezekiah's attainments concerned the spirit and faith, and it was thanks to them that he was remembered by the keepers of the tradition as a venerable and righteous king, in spite of his military and political miscalculations. Also to his credit is that his reign brought an end to the split between the Aaronites of the southern tribes and the Levites of the northern tribes, although the rivalry between these two groups within the unified caste of priests continued for a long time afterwards.

The fall of the kingdom of Israel had a serious impact on the economy and demography of Judah. Even during the reign of Hezekiah large numbers of economically active people had come from the more developed and cultural north, which had been devastated by the Assyrians; this led to Judah's rapid transformation. According to evidence possessed by Israeli archaeologists, in the decades following the fall of Samaria the population of Jerusalem grew 15 times and its land area increased by 10-12 times; new, more powerful walls were built around the city. The rapid growth also affected another large city, Lachish. Excavations have produced evidence of a sharp increase in the number of cities and agricultural settlements in both the country's most fertile valley, Shephelah, and in the drier regions south of Jerusalem. There can be no doubt that at the end of the 8th century BCE Judah was experiencing a 'demographic explosion', accompanied by rapid economic development, and that the main reason for its prospering was the influx of people from what used to be the Northern Kingdom. The invasion of the Assyrian army interrupted this process and in all respects knocked Judah backwards. Later, following the departure of the Assyrians from Judah, the country's development accelerated once again – though, unlike during the period preceding the war with Assyria, the population and economy grew not so much in the area around Shephelah, but in regions situated to the south of Jerusalem.

King Manasseh: Liberalization of Worship and Time of Peace

Hezekiah's heir was his 12-year-old son, Manasseh. The fact that the 54-year-old king was succeeded by such a young son – undoubtedly, in no way the eldest of his sons – must make us suspect that the handover of power was by no means smooth. Unfortunately, the biblical sources tell us nothing either of the identity of the young king's regent or of those who supported his claim to the throne. However, we have every reason to suppose that on this occasion the mighty Aaronites came off the worse, since the rule of Manasseh was a full retreat from everything for which Hezekiah had fought. The new king rejected the idea of monotheism and all attempts to break free from the sway of Assyria; he preferred the path of his 'idolatrous' grandfather to that of his 'righteous' father.

In their accounts of the rule of Manasseh, the books of Kings and Chronicles describe in the gloomiest colors his passion for pagan cults: "He rebuilt the high places his father Hezekiah had destroyed; he also erected altars to Baal and made an Asherah pole, as Ahab king of Israel had done. He bowed down to all the starry hosts and worshipped them" [...] In the two courts of the temple of the Lord, he built altars to all the starry hosts. He sacrificed his own son in the fire, practiced divination, sought omens, and consulted mediums and spiritists. He did much evil in the eyes of the Lord, arousing his anger" (2 Kings 21:3,5-6). As an impudent challenge to all the Aaronites and Levites, an image of Asherah, whom Manasseh worshipped, was set up in the Temple in Jerusalem. This was a clear coup directed at the worship of Yahweh and it put an end to all Hezekiah's religious reforms.

Nevertheless, the biblical books are by no means unanimous in their evaluations of Manasseh's rule. If the book of Kings depicts him as a persistent idolater throughout the course of his reign, Chronicles divides the years of his rule into two periods, with the first lasting until his imprisonment by the Assyrians upon accusations of treachery and the second beginning after his release from Assyrian captivity. Chronicles evaluates the first period just as negatively as does the book of Kings, but depicts him during the second period as a repentant sinner and talks about a revolution in his views, a rejection of idolatry, and a return to serving the Lord. In addition to idolatry, the book of Kings accuses Manasseh of the mass killing of innocent people: "Moreover, Manasseh also shed so much innocent blood that he filled Jerusalem from end to end—besides the sin that he had caused Judah to commit, so that they did evil in the eyes of the Lord" (2 Kings 21:16).

Chronicles, however, remains strangely silent about this seemingly outrageous crime. The first source, the book of Kings, was created mainly by Levites from the Northern Kingdom, whereas the authors of the second were Aaronites from the Southern Kingdom, so it has to be noted that the two groups of Yahwist priests (united by Hezekiah into a single caste) held very different views of Manasseh. This was probably a result of the different ways in which Manasseh himself treated 'his own' Aaronites' and the 'alien' Levites, a difference of treatment which Hezekiah had avoided. As a pragmatic politician, Manasseh was subsequently able to put his conflict with the Aaronites behind him, as is confirmed by this excerpt from Chronicles: "Then Manasseh knew that the Lord is God [...] He got rid of the foreign gods and removed the image from the temple of the Lord, as well as all the altars he had built on the temple hill and in Jerusalem; and he threw them out of the city. Then he restored the altar of the Lord and sacrificed fellowship offerings and thank offerings on it, and told Judah to serve the Lord, the God of Israel" (2 Chronicles 33:13, 15-16). Nothing like this is to be found in the book of Kings, which has northern Levite origins; on the contrary, this book blames Manasseh's idolatry for the subsequent destruction of Jerusalem and the Temple (2 Kings 21:11-14).

The king represented the interests of that part of the Judahite aristocracy which had links with the traditional pagan cults and was hostile to the monopolist position of the Yahwists in general and in particular of the northern Levites

Judah as the Only Hebrew Kingdom

who had settled, with the help of Hezekiah, in the Southern Kingdom. Together with the king, this group of aristocrats was prepared to look for common ground with the influential Aaronites, people who constituted a threat to their own safety, but not, under any circumstances, with the Levite newcomers. The rivalry between the Aaronites and the northern Levites within the community of priests of Yahweh made worse the position of the latter. The reconciliation that occurred between the Aaronites and Manasseh and his suite was largely made possible by infringing the interests of the northern Levites. Among the Yahwists who protested against the worship of images, it was the least protected – the northern Levites – who suffered most from persecution by the king, as is confirmed by the book of Kings (whose authors are northern Levites). The fact that this book's coverage of Manasseh's reign takes an entirely different angle from that found in Chronicles, which was written by the southern Aaronites, is in itself evidence of the serious differences between these two groups of Yahwist priests.

Manasseh ruled for 55 years, longer than all the other Judahite kings – both those who preceded him and those who came after him. The accounts given in the Bible draw a picture of a lengthy, peaceful reign on which no shadow was cast by war. The fact that Manasseh was a vassal of Assyria on the one hand protected him from all external threats and on the other bound his hands in respect of his close neighbors, who were, like him, vassals of Assyria. His giving up his claims to the lands of what had been the Kingdom of Israel was a natural consequence of his dependence on the Assyrians, although this was a source of irritation to the northern Levites, who dreamed of occupying, with the help of the Judahite kings, the leading position in their former house. In Palestine peace and stability prevailed – conditions which ideally suited the interests of economic development and population growth in Judah. The renunciation of the compulsory monotheism of Hezekiah's rule eliminated tension and dissatisfaction in Judahite society and assuaged the numerous priests of the traditional pagan cults. The king did not touch the cult of Yahweh, but stripped it of the privileged status which it had had (it was now not the country's only religion or even its main religion), and made the Temple in Jerusalem a place of worship of several different gods simultaneously. We may suppose that the tithe to be paid to the Temple in Jerusalem was either reduced or split between the priests of those cults in which people now began to worship. Thus Manasseh's counter-reforms benefitted all the pagan cults, but seriously damaged the interests of the Aaronites and particularly of the Levites from the Northern Kingdom. However, the dramatic events that subsequently occurred in the region brought important changes to the king's religious policy.

A drawing of clay seal impression from Judah, showing king of Judah handing over a bow and some arrows to a newly appointed governor.

In 681 BCE a power battle broke out in Assyria during which Sennacherib was assassinated. It so happened that the Assyrian king was killed by his own son or sons in the temple of the god Ninurta in Calah, as described in the book of the prophet Isaiah. Unexpectedly for all, the king's council, which consisted of the highest Assyrian dignitaries, chose as Sennacherib's heir one of his younger sons, Esarhaddon, whose mother probably came from Judah or Syria. The elder sons of the murdered king did not acknowledge this decision and resorted to military force in order to seize the throne. During the course of a brief, but bitter civil war Esarhaddon gained the upper hand over his opponents and Sennacherib's murderers fled to the north, to Urartu. These events badly shook Assyria's stability and gave Palestine, Syria, and Phoenicia hope of freedom from Assyrian rule. The mood of mutiny was considerably stoked by Egypt, the principal enemy of the Assyrians in the south-west. The new mutiny against Assyria was headed by the Phoenician cities of Sidon and Tyre with the support of smaller towns in Syria and Phoenicia, as well as Ashkelon in Philistia. Help was also promised by Egypt, which was then ruled by the Nubian (Cushite) pharaoh Taharqa. Egyptian emissaries and the leaders of the mutineers entered into secret negotiations with Manasseh of Judah, trying to get him to support their move against Assyria. Judah was at that time regarded as the strongest state in Palestine and Phoenicia, and its lands were a strategically important buffer between Egypt and the region of Syria and Palestine, where yet another uprising was underway. It is unlikely that such a cautious politician as Manasseh would have been in a hurry to join the anti-Assyrian coalition; however, he was in secret contact with the mutinous cities and with Egypt. The Judahite court, however – as, incidentally, all the royal palaces in the states of Syria, Palestine, and Phoenicia – was seething with Assyrian spies who had no hesitation in informing Nineveh of the behind-the-scenes meetings between Manasseh and the emissaries of the mutineers and Egyptians. Desiring to prevent the mutiny expanding and the forces of his opponents uniting, Esarhaddon hastened to land a pre-emptive blow on the mutinous Phoenician and Syrian cities. Sidon was literally razed from the face of the earth; its ruler was executed, and all its inhabitants were deported to live in Assyria. Baal, King of Tyre, surrendered and managed only by consenting to an enormous tribute to save his city from total destruction. Then, in 674 BCE, Esarhaddon sent his army to conquer Egypt, Assyria's principal enemy which was always egging on Assyria's vassals to rise up against it. It was probably at this time that on their way to Egypt, as they were passing along the borders with Judah, the Assyrians "took Manasseh prisoner, put a hook in his nose, bound him with bronze shackles and took him to Babylon" (2 Chronicles 33:11).

The Bible does not tell us how much time Manasseh spent in captivity in Assyria; however, it was clearly not long since he was not accused of mutiny but merely of unsanctioned negotiations with the mutineers. Moreover, Esarhaddon's first campaign against Egypt ended in failure and the Assyrian king needed, more than ever before, the support of Judah, which was for him an important military outpost right on the boundary with his enemy. Three years later, Esarhaddon launched a second campaign against Egypt, which was this time successful, and it cannot be ruled out that by this time the Assyrians had already returned Manasseh to Jerusalem in order that he could demonstrate his loyalty to Assyria by helping his suzerain in every way possible. But even if Manasseh remained imprisoned for longer, this could not have been for more than two years. In 669 BCE Esarhaddon suddenly died and his son Ashurbanipal, after ascending the Assyrian throne and renewing the obligations of his vassals, would have been obliged to set the king of Judah free, as was the practice at that time.

Manasseh's sufferings in captivity in Assyria served as a good lesson to him for the future, and he never repeated his mistake of entering into talks with mutineers, even when a new and broader anti-Assyrian coalition consisting of Egypt, Babylon, Elam, and a number of cities in Syria and Phoenicia came into being. This coalition suffered a crushing defeat, providing confirmation that Manasseh had been right to refuse to confront Assyria, the superpower of its time. After returning to Jerusalem, Manasseh changed not merely his foreign policy, but his domestic policy as well: he made peace with the influential

Aaronites, who represented the greatest threat to his rule, removed from the temple in Jerusalem the images which had been a particular source of irritation for the worshippers of Yahweh, and handed over the Temple itself in its entirety to the Aaronites. But the most important thing he did was to restore the primacy of the cult of Yahweh over all the other religious faiths in the country. Of course, he did not revive the puritanism of Hezekiah and the book of Chronicles notes regretfully that "the people, however, continued to sacrifice at the high places, but only to the Lord their God" (2 Chronicles 33:17).

The fact that while in captivity Manasseh experienced a spiritual revolution and subsequently changed his religious policy is indirectly confirmed by the existence of the well-known apocrypha 'Prayer of Manasseh', in which the king repents of his sins and asks the Lord for salvation. But it has to be said that in their Chronicles the Aaronites exaggerated the extent of Manasseh's repentance and rejection of the pagan cults. It was only during the reign of Manasseh's grandson Josiah that "the altars Manasseh had built in the two courts of the temple of the Lord" were removed (2 Kings 23:12). If the altars to pagan cults in the courts of the Temple in Jerusalem survived, then we may imagine how many such altars remained throughout the country as a whole. This fact in itself tells us that Manasseh's reconciliation with some of the Yahwists was not so much the result of a spiritual turnaround in response to the sufferings he had been through in captivity in Assyria as the consequence of a political deal between the king and the Aaronites.

Mindful of the lamentable outcome of all uprisings against Assyria, Manasseh, unlike his father, Hezekiah, made every effort to avoid friction with this power. The Assyrian sources twice mention the name of Manasseh – first, as one of the kings who supplied materials for the construction of Esarhaddon's luxurious palace in Nineveh and then as a ruler who helped the Assyrian king Assurbanipal conquer Egypt. Manasseh's loyalty to his obligations before Assyria was in time rewarded. He was permitted to surround Jerusalem with a higher, more powerful wall and to build new and fortify old fortresses throughout the country (2 Chronicles 33:14). It is entirely possible that during his rule Judah paid less tribute than its poorer neighbors Moab and Ammon; at any rate, this would seem to be what is suggested by an Assyrian inscription which, even though in a bad state of preservation, may be dated to approximately the time of Esarhaddon's rule.

In general, Manasseh's reign was one of the most peaceful and tranquil times in the history of Judah. Manasseh managed to restore his ruined country and lead it to new prosperity. As for the return to polytheism, of which he is accused by the biblical sources – and in particular, the book of Kings – this was inevitable given that Judahite society of that time was not yet ready for true monotheism. Continuation of the religious policy of Hezekiah carried the risk of mutinies and civil war, and the rejection of this policy was a response to its

Judah as the Only Hebrew Kingdom

bankruptcy. The same was true of foreign policy. Hezekiah's attempts to break free from his position as an Assyrian vassal had led only to the devastation of Judah, so Manasseh's reluctance to enter into conflict with Assyria was entirely justified by the further course of events and revealed him to be a wise and far-sighted politician.

The extremely negative attitude taken to Manasseh by the book of Kings has its explanation in two factors. First, the book of Kings was created considerably later than Manasseh's reign; by this time monotheism had become firmly established in Judahite society, so the religious liberalism of the earlier period was regarded as unjustified connivance with idolatry. Secondly, this unprecedentedly severe criticism was the consequence of a profound conflict between the king and the northern Levites who came from the former kingdom of Israel. It reflected the clash of interests between the old Judahite aristocracy and the newcomers from the north, who were a threat to the latter's power and revenue.

After the death of Manasseh the throne of Judah was inherited by his 22-year-old son, Amon. Amon was likewise not his 67-year-old father's eldest son, so the transfer of power was accompanied by palace plots and fighting between various clans. Judging by the policies espoused by Amon, who continued the course of religious liberalism that was so characteristic of his father, he represented the interests of the same group of the Judahite aristocracy which was linked to pagan cults and had initially supported Manasseh. We should note the evaluation of him given by the Aaronites: "He did evil in the eyes of the Lord, as his father Manasseh had done. Amon worshiped and offered sacrifices to all the idols Manasseh had made. But unlike his father Manasseh, he did not humble himself before the Lord; Amon increased his guilt" (2 Chronicles 33:22-23).

However, the Aaronites were not going to be content to once again play secondary roles, as they had for a long time done under Manasseh, and this was something which the Levites, who had been openly in conflict with Manasseh, desired still less. Moreover, the political situation in the region had changed to such an extent that Amon's domestic opponents no longer had any reason to fear a possible reaction from Assyria in response to their actions. Unlike in the time of Manasseh, the rapidly weakened Assyrian empire had great difficulty in coping with its enemies in Mesopotamia itself and could have no thought for protecting its vassals in Palestine. It is hardly surprising, then, that in the face of such serious opposition, the new king failed to make his place on the throne secure and was killed two years later: "Amon's officials conspired against him and assassinated him in his palace" (2 Chronicles 33:24). Although the biblical text tells us nothing about the reasons for, or executors of, the killing, there can be no doubt that it was in the interests of the Aaronites and Levites, and it was they who inspired the conspirators. What happened next merely confirms this supposition. In spite of what was common practice in ancient Near Eastern monarchies, the place of the murdered young king was taken not by one of his brothers, but by his small son, Josiah, a choice that was extraordinarily convenient for exercise of power by a regent. Both biblical sources – the book of Kings and Chronicles – contain an interesting phrase concerning the killing of Amon and the enthronement of Josiah: "Then the people of the land killed all who had plotted against King Amon, and they made Josiah his son king in his place" (2 Chronicles 33:25). For some reason the 'people of the land' (am ha-aretz) had been completely indifferent to the killings of kings Joash and Amaziah and to the destruction of almost the entire Davidic dynasty when Queen Athaliah had usurped power in the country, but now took exception to the conspiracy against the idolater Amon, who had not even managed to secure his place on the throne. We cannot help supposing that in reality this was a popular uprising organized by the Yahwists themselves in order on the one hand to get rid of their opponents at court, who had been intending to put their own protégé on the throne (to continue the policies of Manasseh and Amon), and on the other to pave the way for their own candidate, Josiah.

The Monotheistic Revolution of King Josiah

The start of Josiah's reign was very similar to Joash's ascent of the throne: both were crowned as minors (one at the age of six, the other at the age of eight) following the murder of their predecessor and by means of armed interventions led by Yahwists. Joash's guardian was the high priest Jehoiada; Josiah's regent was possibly the high priest Hilkiah. In both cases the real power, until these kings came of age, lay with the Aaronites. But this is where the similarities between Josiah and Joash end. In contrast to Joash, who subsequently strove to break free of the guardianship of the Yahwists and to neutralize their influence with the help of the pagan priesthood, Josiah represented the interests of the Aaronites and Levites. From the latter's point of view, he proved an ideal king who could not have been bettered in any way. "Neither before nor after Josiah was there a king like him who turned to the Lord as he did—with all his heart and with all his soul and with all his strength, in accordance with all the Law of Moses" (2 Kings 23:25).

The central idea of Josiah's policy-making and the focus of all his efforts and concerns was his famous religious reform, whose main purpose was to eradicate idolatry and turn the worship of Yahweh into the country's sole, truly monotheistic religion. Today we can be more or less exact in attributing a date to these reforms. If Josiah came to power – or, to be more precise, was placed upon the throne – sometime around 640 BCE, then, according to the book of Chronicles, "In the eighth year of his reign, while he was still young, he began to seek the God of his father David. In his twelfth year he began to purge Judah and Jerusalem of high places, Asherah poles and idols" (2 Chronicles 34:3). Given that Josiah ruled for 31 years, all his religious reforms must have taken place between 620 and 610 BCE, a very short period of time when seen in the historical perspective. Josiah, much like Hezekiah before him, began his reforms by ridding the Temple in Jerusalem of pagan cults and the latter's altars and symbols. Judging by the description of what Josiah needed to do, this Yahwist holy place had differed little, during the reign of Amon – as, incidentally, under many other kings of Judah – from other pagan temples of the time. "The king ordered Hilkiah the high priest, the priests next in rank and the doorkeepers to remove from the temple of the Lord all the articles made for Baal and Asherah and all the starry hosts. He burned them outside Jerusalem in the fields of the Kidron Valley and took the ashes to Bethel [...] He took the Asherah pole from the temple of the Lord to the Kidron Valley outside Jerusalem and burned it there. He ground it to powder and scattered the dust over the graves of the common people. He also tore down the quarters of the male shrine prostitutes that were in the temple of the Lord, the quarters where women did weaving for Asherah [...] He removed from the entrance to the temple of the Lord the horses that the kings of Judah had dedicated to the sun. They were in the court near the room of an official named Nathan-Melek. Josiah then burned the chariots dedicated to the sun" (2 Kings 23:4, 6-7, 11).

All the biblical sources are unanimous in their opinion that both the scale and depth of Josiah's religious reforms were unprecedented. "Under his direction the altars of the Baals were torn down; he cut to pieces the incense altars that were above them, and smashed the Asherah poles and the idols. These he broke to pieces and scattered over the graves of those who had sacrificed to them" (2 Chronicles 34:4). "He desecrated Topheth, which was in the Valley of Ben Hinnom, so no one could use it to sacrifice their son or daughter in the fire to Molech [...] The king also desecrated the high places that were east of Jerusalem on the south of the Hill of Corruption—the ones Solomon king of Israel had built for Ashtoreth the vile goddess of the Sidonians, for Chemosh the vile god of Moab, and for Molech the detestable god of the people of Ammon" (2 Kings 23:10,13). In general, Josiah acted exactly as his great-grandfather Hezekiah had done. However, unlike in the case of Hezekiah, his reforms were not limited to Jerusalem and Judah, but, taking advantage of the fact that Assyria had withdrawn from Palestine, encompassed territory which had formerly been the kingdom of Israel as well. In addition, Josiah not only banned the pagan cults, but used unusually cruel methods in his bid to exterminate idolatry. Not only did he destroy the altars and sacrificial high places, but he also had the priests killed and even some of their graves defiled; such things had not happened under Hezekiah. "Josiah smashed the sacred stones and cut down the Asherah poles and covered the sites with human bones. Even the altar at Bethel, the high place made by Jeroboam son of Nebat, who had caused Israel to sin— even that altar and high place he demolished. He burned the high place and ground it to powder, and burned the Asherah pole also. Then Josiah looked around, and when he saw the tombs that were there on the hillside, he had the bones removed from them and burned on the altar [...] Just as he had done at Bethel, Josiah removed all the shrines at the high places that the kings of Israel had built in the towns of Samaria and that had aroused the Lord's anger. Josiah slaughtered all the priests of those high places on the altars and burned human bones on them. Then he went back to Jerusalem" (2 Kings 23:14-16, 19-20).

Admittedly, it was only on the former territory of the Northern Kingdom that Josiah acted in such an unmerciful and violent way; in Judah he chose to refrain from physically eradicating the pagan priests, treating them in a gentler and more circumspect manner, constraining them only by a ban on the celebration of their religious rites. "He did away with the idolatrous priests appointed by the kings of Judah to burn incense on the high places of the towns of Judah and on those around Jerusalem—those who burned incense to Baal, to the sun and moon, to the constellations and to all the starry hosts" (2 Kings 23:5). It was not only worshippers of idols who were affected by Josiah's campaign of harassment; like Hezekiah, he also forbade provincial Yahwists to hold religious services and make sacrifices on the high places near their homes. Henceforward all worship of the Lord, especially sacrifices, could take place only at the Temple in Jerusalem. In order to keep the priests and their flock from violating the ban, "Josiah brought all the priests from the towns of Judah and desecrated the high places, from Geba to Beersheba [...]" (2 Kings 23:8). However, fearing competition, the Aaronites in Jerusalem did not allow the provincial priests to hold services or make sacrifices, thus causing them to lose both social standing and considerable income. "Although the priests of the high places did not serve at the altar of the Lord in Jerusalem, they ate unleavened bread with their fellow priests" (2 Kings 23:9).

One of the main foci of Josiah's religious reforms was the publication of the Torah, which outlined the principal aspects of Moses's teachings. According to the books of Kings and Chronicles, the scrolls of the Torah were found during renovation of the Temple in Jerusalem and were handed over by high priest Hilkiah to the king's scribe, Shaphan; he, in turn, read them to the king. The content of these scrolls made such a profound impression on Josiah that he ripped apart the clothes he was wearing in excitement and gave orders for the prophetess Huldah to be asked for her opinion of them (in those times it was the custom for the significance of any big and meaningful event to be discussed with prophets and clairvoyants). Huldah confirmed that the scrolls had been inspired by God and warned Josiah that idolatry would bring terrible misfortunes on Judah, adding that his repentance and meekness before the Lord would spare him of the need to witness these events. Josiah's next step was to call an assembly of all the elders in Judah and Jerusalem, where he "read in their hearing all the words of the Book of the Covenant, which had been found in the temple of the Lord. The king stood by the pillar and renewed the covenant in the presence of the Lord—to follow the Lord and keep his commands, statutes and decrees with all his heart and all his soul, thus confirming the words of the covenant written in this book. Then all the people pledged themselves to the covenant" (2 Kings 23:2-3).

Most biblical scholars today agree that the scrolls referred to above found were the book of Deuteronomy – the final part of Moses' Pentateuch. Judging by its language and style, this final book of the Torah was created by the northern Levites, and, moreover, much later than the four parts which preceded it. Most likely, the scripts read out for all to hear were not the final version of Deuteronomy which we have today, but merely part of it, even if a very substantial part. It is not known whether this book was written during the reign of Josiah and intended to sanctify his deeds or whether it had been created earlier, but was used only in Josiah's time. Whatever the case, the book became both the legislative basis for Josiah's religious reforms and an inseparable part of those reforms.

The biblical sources give different dates for the realization of the religious reforms. According to the book of Kings, Josiah commenced his reforms only after the Torah scrolls had been found – during the eighteenth year of his reign. The Chronicles, on the other hand, claims that when this book was discovered, the religious reforms were already in full swing throughout Judah. If we accept the version given by the book of Kings – the earlier and more trustworthy source – this shortens the period of the reforms to just 12 or 13 years, from 622 to 609 BCE. Such a short interval could not possibly have fundamentally transformed beliefs and traditions that had taken shape over the course of many centuries; so it is hardly surprising that the results of these reforms literally evaporated during the reigns of Josiah's successors. Both Kings and Chronicles give Josiah credit for celebrating the Passover and both agree that "Neither in the days of the judges who led Israel nor in the days of the kings of Israel and the kings of Judah had any such Passover been observed. But in the eighteenth year of King Josiah, this Passover was celebrated to the Lord in Jerusalem" (2 Kings 23:22-23). Josiah also established new procedures for celebrating the Passover that were more in line with the biblical tradition than the old procedures had been. Unfortunately, we know very little of how the Passover was celebrated before Josiah's day. Only the book of Chronicles gives a description of this festivity as it was organized a century earlier by Hezekiah; but we have reason to believe that this description was substantially tailored to fit later traditions. It is probable that in earlier times the Passover celebration combined local Canaanite traditions, which were linked to the agricultural calendar, memories of the Exodus of the Hebrew tribes from Egypt, and monotheistic elements which had been introduced by Moses. Most likely, there were different ways of celebrating Passover in the Northern and Southern kingdoms. The book of Kings mentions very briefly that after the northern and southern tribes split, Jeroboam appointed his own times and procedures for the Passover celebration and sacrifices in Bethel (1 Kings 12:32). This was a result not merely of the split between northerners and southerners, but also of the different histories of the two tribal groups.

Josiah's rule (640-609 BCE) coincided with the rapid weakening of Assyrian military power. The unending wars with neighbors and domestic quarrels led to the Assyrians losing control over Palestine, Phoenicia, and southern Syria in the mid-620s BCE. After being dependent on Assyria for almost a century, Judah once again became an independent country; and this time, the freedom came without actually having to fight for it. For a small period of time, from 620 to the 610s BCE, there was a power vacuum in the region of Syria and Palestine: Assyria had withdrawn from the area, and Egypt and Babylonia arrived there only later. Josiah exploited this circumstance in order to extend his power into the territory of what had been the kingdom of Israel. It is difficult to say whether he was successful in annexing all the lands of the northern tribes to Judah. However, there can be no doubt that he controlled central and part of northern Palestine; otherwise, he would not have been able to carry out his religious reforms there, especially using methods so authoritarian and severe that they must have required the possession of overriding political and military power. The book of Chronicles specifically lists those areas belonging to the Israelite tribes where Josiah eliminated idolatry: "In the towns of Manasseh, Ephraim and Simeon, as far as Naphtali, and in the ruins around them" (2 Chronicles 34:6). Thus, in addition to the southern tribe of Simeon which had long since become part of Judah, Josiah annexed a substantial part of what had formerly been Israel, including lower Galilee. In northern Palestine he encountered the Phoenicians; in Transjordan, Ammon and Moab; on the Golan Heights, the Arameans, who had set their sights on the lands of the northern tribes (who had been unable to re-establish their kingdom as a political entity even after Assyria's withdrawal). It is possible that during the rule of Josiah Judah had limited access to the Mediterranean coast. Although there is no mention of this in the Bible, archaeological excavations at Mesad Hashvayahu, a coastal fortress of that time, have confirmed a substantial Hebrew presence on this site.

However, local rulers were not the only ones trying to fill the political void in Palestine and southern Syria; also involved was Egypt, whose strength had been refreshed by the coming to power of the 26th or Saite Dynasty originating in the ancient Egyptian city of Sais in the Nile Delta. Psamtik I (Psammetichus), the dynasty's founder and one of the rulers in the delta of the Nile, had proved himself an obedient vassal of Assyria, in reward for which he had been appointed by Ashurbanipal to rule the whole of Egypt. But after assembling a large number of foreign mercenaries (Libyans, Ionian Greeks, Carians, Judahites, and Syrians), Psamtik had rebelled against Assyria and declared his independence. Ashurbanipal was so busy fighting endless wars against Babylon, Elam, and Media that he had neither the strength nor the time to go and deal

Judah as the Only Hebrew Kingdom

with his mutinous vassal. Thus, from the middle of the 7th century BCE Egypt once again became independent. After the Assyrians departed from Palestine and Phoenicia, Psamtik I tried to extend his power over the Mediterranean coast of these regions; he achieved only partial success. Egypt turned out to be too weak from the military point of view to subjugate the cities of Philistia and Phoenicia. The Egyptians spent decades storming Ashdod alone; according to the Greek historian Herodotus, the Egyptian army siege of the city lasted 29 years! The military failures in Philistia prevented Psamtik from imposing his rule upon Judah. Fresh confirmation of Egypt's military weakness came when the country was unexpectedly invaded by Scythian nomads. Lacking confidence in his ability to win in battle, Psamtik preferred to buy his way out of trouble. On the other hand, the Egyptians proved more successful in economics and politics: many Phoenician and Philistine cities were happy to trade with them and accept their political patronage.

In the 630-620s BCE Assyria found itself sucked into a vortex of civil wars. To begin with, the twin sons of Ashurbanipal fought over who was to inherit their father's throne; then their military commanders joined the struggle for power. At the same time, Babylonia and Media, after concluding an alliance with the Scythians, resumed their attack against Assyria. This time, the Assyrian empire, severely weakened by its internal wars, was unable to withstand the combined attacks of its external enemies and very quickly collapsed. In 612 BCE the allies occupied the two principal Assyrian cities: the old capital, Calah, and the new, Nineveh. The last Assyrian king, Sin-shar-ishkun, was burned alive in his own palace. The news of the fall of detested Assyria brought happiness to Judah. The prophet Nahum, a contemporary of these events, expressed the general mood when he wrote, "Nothing can heal you; your wound is fatal. All who hear the news about you clap their hands at your fall, for who has not felt your endless cruelty? [...] Celebrate your festivals, Judah, and fulfill your vows. No more will the wicked invade you; they will be completely destroyed [...] The Lord will restore the splendor of Jacob like the splendor of Israel, though destroyers have laid them waste and have ruined their vines" (Nahum 3:19; 1:15; 2:2). Admittedly, the remnants of the Assyrian army managed to break into the city of Haran, where they proclaimed their military commander as the new king, calling him Ashur-uballit II. However, the Babylonians and Medes quickly forced them out of Haran too. At this critical moment for Assyria, Egypt, which regarded the collapse of Assyria and consequent rapid strengthening of Babylonia and Media as against its own interests, hastened to its rescue. Pharaoh Psamtik I and his son Necho (Nekau) preferred to support Assyria, now weakened and no longer dangerous to them, in order to restrain the aggressive ambitions of its enemies. Furthermore, during the last years of its existence, Assyria had reached an agreement with Egypt to divide spheres of influence; Assyria acknowledged Egypt's interests in Palestine, Phoenicia, and Syria while the Egyptians in their turn were ready to support Assyria's claims to the whole of Mesopotamia. Yet Assyria's military defeats forced Pharaoh Necho, who succeeded his father in 610 BCE, to hurry to the banks of the Euphrates to prevent his ally's conclusive collapse.

Like many other rulers in the Syro-Palestinian region, Josiah had no wish for a resurgence of Assyria's military power. He was more inclined to support Babylonia, fearing lest the military alliance of Egypt and Assyria create a new threat to Judah's independence. At the same time, it is unlikely that he could have wished that Assyria's place be taken by other aggressive empires – by Babylonia or Media, for instance – who might aspire to supremacy in his region. Objectively speaking, therefore, he could not have been interested in supporting either side and evidently pursued a policy of neutrality. But many historians of the reign of Josiah believe that Josiah tried to prevent the Egyptians coming to the help of odious Assyria, which is why in 609 BCE the armies of Judah and Egypt fought a battle near Megiddo in northern Palestine, during which Josiah's troops were defeated and he himself was killed. However, the fact that the King of Judah died at the hands of the Egyptians is not in itself proof that this happened as a result of the battle between the two armies. The book of Kings, the most authoritative biblical source of the time, not only says nothing of this battle, but does not even mention any intention on the part of either of the parties to meet in combat (2 Kings 23:29). The book of Chronicles, a later and a less trustworthy source, mentions only Josiah's intention to fight, but again says nothing of a battle (2 Chronicles 35:20-23). Furthermore, the Egyptians themselves, who usually boasted of any victory, even when it was not theirs to boast of, for some reason on this occasion remained absolutely silent regarding their 'victory' at Megiddo. It is probable that what occurred was not a battle, but merely an encounter between the Egyptian pharaoh and the Judahite king, and that, as he returned from this meeting, Josiah was treacherously killed by Egyptian archers. Remarkably, no biblical source speaks of any kind of assembly or movement of the Judahite army to the place where the battle occurred; this is clearly atypical for descriptions of preparations for battle in such instances, especially bearing in mind that the Egyptian enemy heavily outnumbered the Judahites. Finally, the idea of forcing battle upon a clearly stronger enemy which lacked any aggressive intentions towards Judah utterly defies common sense. Most likely, Josiah came to Megiddo with a detachment of bodyguards rather than an army and his meeting with Necho concerned bilateral relations, above all, and not the war between Assyria and its enemies. During the course of these negotiations the Egyptian pharaoh, referring to his agreement with Assyria, laid claim to the role of Judah's new overlord and demanded from Judah at least minimal cooperation in military matters. Josiah rejected Necho's claims and was revealed as a potential enemy of Assyria and Egypt, causing Necho to fear that in the future Josiah could cut the supply lines at his rear and create problems

Judah as the Only Hebrew Kingdom

for the Egyptian army. Lacking the time to carry out military actions against Judah, the pharaoh gave orders for Josiah to be killed, hoping that the king's death would paralyze Egypt's enemies in Jerusalem and give him the breathing space he needed in order to come promptly to the Assyrians' aid.

The death of Josiah was an irreplaceable loss for the Aaronites and Levites. No other king of Judah or Israel had attained such a high level of understanding of true monotheism, and still less been able to realize reforms so fundamental that they could justly be called a religious revolution. This was something that had been beyond the powers of most of the Yahwist priests themselves, as was clearly shown by the regency of the high priest Jehoiada before Joash came of age. Like Moses, Josiah was far in advance of the spiritual and intellectual development of contemporary society, and clearly exceeded its level of religious consciousness. But this was not only his principal strength; it was also his weakness – for he expressed ideas that were so revolutionary for his time that they could not be properly understood or realized. The population of Judah – like any other society, even the most developed, of that time – was not yet ready to reject all forms of paganism or accept true monotheism. In spite of being conducted in the most violent and decisive manner possible, Josiah's reforms did not succeed in overturning, in the space of just a few years, the religious consciousness which had formed over the course of many centuries. This is why its effects were superficial and short-lived. Moreover, such reforms were bound to stir up indignation among the countless priests and followers of the traditional Canaanite cults such as those of Baal, Asherah or Moloch. We should not forget that most Yahwists too were at this time essentially polytheists: while acknowledging the priority of the cult of Yahweh, they worshipped the traditional pagan gods at the same time.

In its turn, the centralization of religious worship and sacrificial offerings deprived all the provincial Yahwist priests of their social status and income, giving rise to widespread discontent. Undoubtedly, the reverse side of Josiah's religious reforms was ubiquitous grumbling against the king and his policies. Even more discontent was stirred by Josiah's reforms on the territory of what had been the kingdom of Israel, where a larger population of Caananites and Amorites remained and the influence of the traditional religious cults was felt much more strongly. There is no mention of this in the Bible, but we can easily imagine the feelings of the Samaritans when Josiah's soldiers killed their priests, destroyed their temples and altars, and desecrated the graves of their much-respected prophets. As part of the 'house of Joseph', they felt even more humiliated because their new ruler, Josiah, represented the 'house of Jacob', i.e. their traditional rival in the fight for authority over the Hebrew tribes. In distinction to Josiah, their previous conquerors, the Assyrians, had never imposed their own gods and had tried not to interfere in the religious lives of their subject peoples. This is why Josiah's religious reforms, despite their undoubtedly progressive character, could only result, from the point of view of domestic policy, in discontent and social tension.

In foreign policy, however, Josiah was successful. He managed, without exacerbating relations with Assyria, to gradually break free of its dominance. He also succeeded in annexing some of the land of the northern tribes without entering any conflict with his neighbors. The only potential threat was Egypt, which had claims to Palestine and Phoenicia and was an ally of Assyria. But Josiah managed to maintain peace with Pharaoh Psamtik I during his reign (664-610 BCE); at least, we know nothing of Egypt making any attempt on the territory of Judah during these years. Psamtik proved an experienced and cautious politician with an ability to correctly weigh his opportunities; he wisely decided not to send an army of any significant size to aid Assyria in 612 BCE, when the Assyrian capital, Nineveh, was under siege by the Babylonians and Medes.

However, the situation changed during the reign of his son Necho II, who was in favor of a more aggressive foreign policy and a close alliance with Assyria. An ambitious but mediocre statesman, the new pharaoh dreamt of conquering Palestine and Syria as a means of restoring Egypt's former might and glory. He failed to understand that his Egypt was no longer the great empire that it had been during the times of Thutmose III and Ramesses II, but a dubious colossus on feet of clay, and that his military strength depended not on Egyptians, but on foreign mercenaries. He made a crucial mistake by moving to help Assyria when too much time had been allowed to pass and his ally had already ceased to exist forever. The murder of the unarmed Josiah, who had arrived for negotiations with Necho, did nothing to enhance Egypt's influence in the region; it merely frightened and repulsed many of the local rulers. As was only to be expected, the appearance of the Egyptian army on the banks of the Euphrates provided little succor to the remains of the Assyrian troops. Even together with the Egyptians, they were unable to take back the city of Haran and were later defeated by the Babylonians and Medes. Assyria lacked the strength needed in order to come to life again. The battered Egyptians withdrew to central and southern Syria, where Necho II gained a four-year breathing space in the war. This he endeavored to use to reinforce his positions in Syria and Palestine.

Between Egypt and Babylonia

Josiah's death put an end to the unbounded power of the Aaronites. Their opponents, who were associated with the traditional pagan cults, exploited the dissatisfaction of the common people with the religious reforms and put on the throne their own candidate, the 23-year-old Jehoahaz, one of the sons of Josiah. The fact that it was not the courtiers, as Josiah had wished, but the 'people of the land' who crowned Jehoahaz is an indication that the transfer of power was accompanied by popular agitation directed against the priests of Yahweh. The people now in charge were the same group of aristocrats who had previously supported kings Manasseh and Amon. The very first step taken by the new ruler was to abolish the prohibition on worshipping pagan gods. Monotheism, which had been introduced throughout the country by Josiah as a compulsory religion, failed to outlive Josiah himself. However, Jehoahaz ruled for only three months. Having established themselves in Syria and Phoenicia, the Egyptians laid claim to Palestine too and, in order to avoid war with Egypt, Jehoahaz was forced to depart for talks with Pharaoh Necho at his military headquarters at Riblah in Syria. But there he was caught by a fate which was only slightly better than that of his father, Josiah: taking advantage of the arrival of the king, who suspected nothing, the pharaoh gave orders for him to be seized and sent to Egypt, where he died suspiciously quickly – probably as a result of poisoning or another form of murder. Instead of the independent Jehoahaz, the pharaoh placed on the throne of Judah another of Josiah's sons, Eliakim, who was openly pro-Egyptian. The new king lost no time in expressing his readiness to become a vassal of Egypt and took upon himself the obligation to pay tribute. Admittedly, this tribute – 100 talents of silver and one talent of gold – was exceedingly modest compared with what the Assyrian kings had required (2 Kings 23:33). Evidently, the Egyptians were more interested in receiving military support from Judah, a country which occupied an important strategic position on the approaches to Egypt, than in squeezing it for financial resources.

The new king's ascent to the throne was accompanied by a change in his name from Eliakim to Jehoiakim. Thus the first part of his name, an echo of the supreme god El, was replaced with 'Yahweh'. And although the Bible refers to Pharaoh Necho's desire to re-name the Judahite king, the real reason for the name change was not external factors, but domestic political ones. Thanks to the book of Jeremiah we know that one of Jehoiakim's predecessors, his half-brother Jehoahaz, had also received this name upon ascending the throne, having been previously known as Shallum. Subsequently, the same happened to Jehoiakim's son, Coniah, who became Jehoiachin on ascending the throne. The taking of a new name referring to Yahweh was not incidental; it indicated a desire both to emphasize his belonging to the cult of Yahweh, which was the principal religion in Judah, and to win the support of the influential Aaronites. In general, name changes were a frequent occurrence at this time and reflected the ancient Canaanite belief that a new name could change a person's fate. This was a tactic to which people often resorted in situations where someone was gravely ill or was changing his faith or social status – for instance, when ascending the royal throne.

Jehoiakim reigned for approximately 11 years, a time of great turbulence and anxiety for Judah. The Egyptians' sway over Palestine turned out to be extremely short-lived, lasting for less than four years. In 605 BCE prince Nebuchadnezzar, the heir to the Babylonian throne, inflicted a crushing defeat on Pharaoh Necho II near the city of Carchemish in Syria. All that was left of the enormous Egyptian army was a few detachments of soldiers, and these escaped complete destruction only because Nebuchadnezzar, after receiving news of the death of his father, hastened to return to Babylon in order to occupy the royal throne which had been bequeathed him. Necho II's ambition of reviving Egypt's former greatness in Asia had been decisively crushed. The Egyptians, who had only recently entered Syria as arrogant conquerors, now hurriedly withdrew through Palestine, looking broken and sorry for themselves. The prophet Jeremiah, who witnessed these events in person, wrote of them: "They are terrified, they are retreating, their warriors are defeated. They flee in haste without looking back [...] The swift cannot flee nor the strong escape. In the north by the River Euphrates they stumble and fall [...] Daughter Egypt will be put to shame, given into the hands of the people of the north" (Jeremiah 46:5-6, 24).

The victory at Carchemish turned Babylonia into a great power and in effect the heir to Assyria. The real power in this new empire belonged to the Chaldeans – the numerous Aramean tribes which had settled in southern Mesopotamia. After the prolonged wars with the Assyrians Nabopolassar, the leader of the Chaldeans, managed in approximately 626 BCE to seize Babylon and found his own Chaldean dynasty there. Nebuchadnezzar II, his son, extended the sway of the Chaldeans to all of Mesopotamia, and after the battle of Carchemish instantly took control of the lands of Syria, Phoenicia, and Palestine. An interesting description of these new conquerors, the Chaldeans – or, to use the Hebrew word, 'kasdim' – is given by the Judahite prophet Habakkuk: "They are a feared and dreaded people; they are a law to themselves and promote their own honor. Their horses are swifter than leopards, fiercer than wolves at dusk. Their cavalry gallops headlong; their horsemen come from afar. They fly like an eagle swooping to devour; they all come intent on violence. Their hordes advance like a desert wind and gather prisoners like sand. They mock kings and scoff at rulers. They laugh at all fortified cities; by building earthen ramps they capture them" (Habakkuk 1:6-10).

King Jehoiakim likewise had no choice but to recognize the authority of the Chaldeans. However, he did that so late and reluctantly that he aroused their suspicions. As a result, like certain other rulers associated with Egypt, he was deported to Babylon, where he had to spend three entire years as a prisoner of Nebuchadnezzar II. In this respect he repeated the fate suffered by Manasseh, whom the Assyrians, suspecting him of treachery, had also held captive, likewise in Babylon. It was only after receiving pledges of his loyalty to them that the Chaldeans released Jehoiakim to go back to Jerusalem.

Judah as the Only Hebrew Kingdom

Judahite king or high-ranking official. A drawing on pottery jar from Ramat Rahel. Late 7th - early 6th century BCE.

At this time Egypt was trying to frustrate the Babylonians' plans to seize its lands and was desperately in need of allies such as Judah and Philistia, whose territories abutted its eastern border and were the only possible launching pad for an attack on Egypt from Asia. In order to make it as difficult as possible for the Babylonians to organize military campaigns against them, the Egyptians spared neither effort nor money to get Judah and the Philistine cities on their side. Jehoiakim, who owed his throne to Pharaoh Necho II, proved himself a loyal ally of Egypt and, after returning home, remained in secret contact with it. In 601 BCE Nebuchadnezzar II made his first attempt to conquer Egypt. The crucial battle with the Egyptians produced considerable bloodshed, but no clear winner and the Babylonians, unsure of their strength, retreated. Nebuchadnezzar's unsuccessful campaign and the pharaoh's promises to come to Judah's aid put an end to Jehoiakim's doubts; he openly refused to obey Babylon and to pay it tribute. Over the next two to three years the Chaldeans' main forces were occupied in Mesopotamia, so Nebuchadnezzar II attempted to deal with recalcitrant Judah with the help of his Palestinian and Syrian vassals, supporting them with part of his army. The book of Kings has the following to say of this episode: "The Lord sent Babylonian, Aramean, Moabite and Ammonite raiders against him [Jehoiakim] to destroy Judah" (2 Kings 24:2). However, neither the local vassals nor the secondary forces of the Babylonians themselves were able to overcome Judah, and in 598 BCE Nebuchadnezzar II was forced to move his army's main forces against Jerusalem. The result of this duel between little Judah and the enormous Neo-Babylonian empire was clear to all, so Jehoiakim's only remaining hope was Egypt.

The siege of Jerusalem dragged on for longer than expected: the city itself was a well-fortified fortress and its defendants' military spirit was fuelled by the belief that the Egyptian army would not fail to come to its help. This was evidently what the Babylonians themselves were afraid of, so, in order to hasten the city's fall, Nebuchadnezzar came in person to the walls of Jerusalem with additional forces. However, both the Judahites' hopes and the Babylonians' fears were in vain. After prolonged hesitation Necho II decided that his army was not ready for a new war with Babylonia and, refusing to come to the help of besieged Jerusalem, he abandoned his ally to its fate. Having no suspicion of the Egyptians' treachery, Jehoiakim continued defending Jerusalem, periodically engaging in sallies against the Babylonians. It was probably during one of these that he met his death and his body, to judge by the words of the prophet Jeremiah, fell into the hands of his enemies, who denied him a dignified burial: "Therefore this is what the Lord says about Jehoiakim son of Josiah king of Judah: 'They will not mourn for him: 'Alas, my brother! Alas, my sister!' They will not mourn for him: 'Alas, my master! Alas, his splendor!' He will have the burial of a donkey—dragged away and thrown outside the gates of Jerusalem" (Jeremiah 22:18-19).

In place of Jehoiakim the courtiers hastily declared his 18-year-old son Jehoiachin king. But, still under siege, Jerusalem's position deteriorated with each passing day. The help promised by the Egyptians never arrived. Gradually, the royal court came to the conclusion that Egypt was not going to come to Judah's rescue. The Bible contains a striking phrase concerning the time of young Jehoiachin's accession: "The king of Egypt did not march out from his own country again, because the king of Babylon had taken all his territory, from the Wadi of Egypt to the Euphrates River" (2 Kings 24:7). This is evidence of a radical change in Egypt's strategy with regard to Babylonia, a switch from attack to defense. Realizing that they could look nowhere else for salvation, the Judahite royal council took the view that to defend Jerusalem further would be senseless and, desiring to save the city and its inhabitants, decided to capitulate. In March 597 BCE the young king and his family, courtiers, and generals went out to meet the Babylonians in order to surrender the city in a peaceful fashion. This marked the end of Jehoiachin's three-month reign in Jerusalem and the beginning of his indefinite captivity in Babylon.

According to the book of Kings, the Babylonians deported 10,000 people from Jerusalem, including the royal family, court dignitaries, soldiers, craftsmen, and the wealthiest and most noble citizens. Most of these – 7000 – were elite warriors and approximately 1000 were craftsmen and smiths. Nebuchadnezzar, however, went further; he "removed the treasures from the temple of the Lord and from the royal palace [...] [He] made Mattaniah, Jehoiachin's uncle, king in his place and changed his name to Zedekiah" (2 Kings 24:13,17). It was not incidental that the Babylonian king chose Mattaniah: the latter was the brother of King Jehoahaz, whom Pharaoh Necho II had given orders to be carried off to Egypt and killed. Logically, the new king and his family should have been hostile to the Egyptians and in particular to the current Egyptian ruler, Necho II, and accordingly there should have been absolutely no chance of a fresh alliance between Judah and Egypt. However, as subsequent events showed, Nebuchadnezzar was mistaken and the mood of support for Egypt did not disappear with the change of king. Mattaniah's adoption of a new name, Zedekiah, meaning 'the Lord is my righteousness', was also not incidental. In those days, as we know from the prophet Jeremiah, the people of Judah lived in the hope of having a king, a descendant of David, who would save Judah and Israel and would be called 'Zedekianu,' 'the Lord Our Righteousness' (Jeremiah 23:5-7). Mattaniah, who knew very well the hopes of his people, naturally exploited these expectations when he ascended the throne.

The Bible has very unflattering things to say of all the four kings who followed Josiah – Jehoahaz, Jehoiakim, Jehoiachin, and Zedekiah, since they all "did evil in the eyes of the Lord". In the language of the keepers of the tradition this meant that they were not consistent worshippers of Yahweh and permitted or even gave their support to worship of other gods. This in its turn is evidence that the Aaronites had in effect lost their control over the monarchy. Admittedly, the significance of this evidence should not be exaggerated. During the last two decades preceding the fall of Jerusalem the Aaronites overcame their former disagreements with their opponents – the Judahite aristocracy associated with the traditional Canaanite cults and their priests. In this regard the book of Chronicles contains a very interesting admission which confirms reconciliation between the two hostile parties: "Furthermore, all the leaders of the priests and the people became more and more unfaithful, following all the detestable practices of the nations and defiling the temple of the Lord, which he had consecrated in Jerusalem" (2 Chronicles 36:14). During the final years of the existence of the Southern Kingdom there was conflict not so much between the worshippers of Yahweh and pagans, as between the pro-Egyptian and pro-Babylonian parties. At the end of the 7th and beginning of the 6th centuries BCE Judah again found itself between the hammer and the anvil – between the Neo-Babylonian empire, which was growing in strength, and Egypt, which, after having temporarily strengthened under the pharaohs of the Saite Dynasty, had started laying claim to dominance in Palestine, Phoenicia, and south Syria.

The country's fate and its prosperity depended on correctly choosing the strong side to support, but this was no simple matter. In 609-605 BCE, when Pharaoh Necho II enjoyed sole power over the entire Syro-Palestinian region, Egypt's preferability had seemed incontrovertible. However, following the battle of Carchemish in 605 BCE, when the Babylonians routed the Egyptians and stripped them of all the disputed territories, Babylonia had become the stronger side. Subsequently, Nebuchadnezzar II's unsuccessful attempt to subdue Egypt in 601 BCE restored a kind of balance of power between the two countries. Jerusalem preferred to look to its nearer neighbor, even if the latter was slightly weaker, rather than to one which was stronger but very remote. Egypt was closer both territorially, but also in terms of history, culture, and economics, and Judah's links with it were at the time stronger than with Babylon. Moreover, among the pharaoh's dignitaries and the mercenaries in his army there were not a few who originally came from Judah or the former kingdom of Israel, and these connections further strengthened the links between the two countries. It is also likely that the tribute asked for by the Egyptians was smaller than that demanded by the Babylonians. But the overriding consideration was that Egypt promised military assistance in the event of Judah being attacked by the Babylonians. All these factors led to the pro-Egyptian party in Jerusalem having a clear advantage over the pro-Babylonian. Both Judahite kings – Jehoaikim and Zedekiah – who ruled for the last two decades (609-587 BCE) before the fall of Jerusalem were supporters of Egypt. Jehoiakim's pro-Egyptian policy might be due to the fact that he had the Egyptians to thank for his throne, but Zedekiah's preference for the Egyptians is evidence, given that he was put on the throne by the Babylonians, that Judah was even more fundamentally interested in an alliance with Egypt.

The split into pro-Egyptian and pro-Babylonian parties affected all the political groups in Judah who were fighting for positions of power, including the Aaronites and the Levites. The book of Jeremiah tells us that Zephaniah, the assistant to the high priest of the Temple; Pashhur, the principal custodian of the Temple; and Shemaiah, a high-ranking priest from Nehelam who accompanied King Jehoiachin into exile in Babylonia, were all against Chaldean Babylon. The Yahwist prophets who were well known at that time – Ahab, Zedekiah, and Hananiah from Gibeon – preached the imminent end of the Chaldeans' rule and the return of the exiles from Babylon. They believed that Egypt, together with Media and Elam, would soon destroy the Chaldeans' military might. By sowing illusions of this kind, they in effect egged the Judahite people on towards disobedience and confrontation with the new empire.

The other, pro-Babylonian, camp consisted of the prophet Jeremiah from Anathoth, the prophet Uriah from Kiriath-Jearim, and the family of the scribe

Judah as the Only Hebrew Kingdom

Shaphan – in particular his son the high-ranking official Ahikam and grandson Gedaliah, whom the Babylonians later appointed ruler of Judah. Of course, the book of Jeremiah contains only scant and fragmentary information on the political fighting in Jerusalem on the eve of the fall of Judah; what interested Jeremiah was not history or politics, but the relations between people and God. Nevertheless, even this scant information is sufficient to make clear that the pro-Babylonian party was fairly large and representative, even if it was smaller than the pro-Egyptian party. In this respect the admission made by King Zedekiah himself is very telling. When Jeremiah tried to convince Zedekiah that the only salvation for both himself and Jerusalem lay in surrendering the city to the Babylonians without delay, Zedekiah bitterly replied: "I am afraid of the Jews who have gone over to the Babylonians, for the Babylonians may hand me over to them and they will mistreat me" (Jeremiah 38:19). If the king was afraid not of the Babylonians, but of his own fellow countrymen, then clearly a considerable percentage of the Judahite nobility was already on the side of Nebuchadnezzar and thirsted for vengeance upon Zedekiah and his allies for the persecutions which they had suffered.

That relations between political opponents tended to be brutal and unforgiving can be seen from the fate which befell Jeremiah himself. When the scroll with his prophecies was first read to King Jehoiakim, the latter took a knife and started cutting out and throwing into the fire each phrase until the entire scroll had been cut into pieces and burnt. Jeremiah was saved from the king's wrath only by the fact that he managed to hide among his friends in good time. In accordance with orders from the principal custodian of the Temple in Jerusalem, Jeremiah was beaten and put in chains while the priests asked for him to be sentenced to death; moreover, during the siege of Jerusalem he was thrown into a terrible underground prison, where he almost died. His life was saved only by the intervention of his secret supporters among the king's inner circle.

The prophet Uriah from Kiriath-Jearim, who had no such influential patrons, came off less well. According to Jeremiah, Uriah's prophesies concerning Judah and Jerusalem were in exactly the same vein as his own. When he heard Uriah's predictions, King Jehoiakim gave orders for the prophet to be killed. On hearing this, Uriah fled to Egypt, where he hoped to hide from the danger that threatened him, but the king, taking advantage of the fact that he was a vassal of Egypt, sent his people after him: "They brought Uriah out of Egypt and took him to King Jehoiakim, who had him struck down with a sword and his body thrown into the burial place of the common people" (Jeremiah 26:23).

It was not just members of the pro-Babylonian party who received severe punishments; subsequently, the victorious Babylonians dealt just as mercilessly with their opponents from the pro-Egyptian party. They seized the prophets Ahab and Zedekiah, and, as instructed by Nebuchadnezzar, roasted them on a fire (Jeremiah 29:22). But the fight between the pro-Babylonian and pro-Egyptian camps was not merely pernicious and mutually destructive. Both sides tried to influence people's minds using other, no less vivid means. The prophet Jeremiah, for instance, risked his life trying to persuade first King Jehoiakim and then King Zedekiah and the priests and inhabitants of Jerusalem of the necessity of submitting to the 'Babylonian yoke': "So do not listen to your prophets, your diviners, your interpreters of dreams, your mediums or your sorcerers who tell you, 'You will not serve the king of Babylon.' They prophesy lies to you that will only serve to remove you far from your lands [...] But if any nation will bow its neck under the yoke of the king of Babylon and serve him, I will let that nation remain in its own land to till it and to live there, declares the Lord.' I gave the same message to Zedekiah king of Judah. I said, 'Bow your neck under the yoke of the king of Babylon; serve him and his people, and you will live. Why will you and your people die by the sword, famine and plague with which the Lord has threatened any nation that will not serve the king of Babylon?" (Jeremiah 27:9-13). To more persuasively illustrate his message, Jeremiah put a wooden yoke on his neck and walked among the common people, and, thus adorned, likewise visited the Temple in Jerusalem and the house of the king, trying to impress upon everyone the need to accept the rule of Babylon, which, he said, was from God and was to last a long time – 70 years. Furthermore, he sent just such a yoke to the kings of Edom, Moab, Ammon, Tyre, and Sidon so that they too should serve the king of Babylonia into whose hands the Lord had given all the lands.

However, Jeremiah's preaching met with serious objections from another well-known prophet, Hananiah, who, again referring to the will of the Lord, tried to convince people of the exact opposite. During an act of worship in the Temple of Jerusalem, Hananiah, in the presence of other priests and the entire people, confronted Jeremiah with an altogether different prophecy: "This is what the Lord Almighty, the God of Israel, says: 'I will break the yoke of the king of Babylon. Within two years I will bring back to this place all the articles of the Lord's house that Nebuchadnezzar king of Babylon removed from here and took to Babylon. I will also bring back to this place Jehoiachin son of Jehoiakim king of Judah and all the other exiles from Judah who went to Babylon,' declares the Lord, 'for I will break the yoke of the king of Babylon" (Jeremiah 28:2-4). To back up his words, Hananiah removed the yoke from Jeremiah's neck, broke it, and declared for everyone to hear: "In the same way I will break the yoke of Nebuchadnezzar king of Babylon off the neck of all the nations within two years" (Jeremiah 28:10-11). In response, Jeremiah pointed out that prophets can only be judged only whether their prophecies come true and then, instead of the broken wooden yoke, demonstratively placed upon his neck one made of iron.

No less fierce was the fight between the pro-Babylonian and pro-Egyptian parties for the hearts and minds of those Judahites who had gone into the first

Babylonian captivity together with King Jehoiahin in 597 BCE. Jeremiah called upon the exiles not to console themselves with illusions of a rapid return, but to settled down in Babylonia and prepare in earnest for a long stay: "Build houses and settle down; plant gardens and eat what they produce. Marry and have sons and daughters; [...] Also, seek the peace and prosperity of the city to which I have carried you into exile. Pray to the Lord for it, because if it prospers, you too will prosper" (Jeremiah 29:5-7). Jeremiah claimed that the Lord would not fail to remember them and 70 years later would return them to the place from which he had driven them off. The pro-Babylonian party, however, even if it was more pragmatic and realistic, was unpopular not just in Jerusalem, but also among the exiles in Babylonia themselves. Upon receiving Jeremiah's message, the priest Shemaiah from Nehelam, one of the exiles' religious leaders, sent an indignant response to the priest Zephaniah in Jerusalem: "The Lord has appointed you priest in place of Jehoiada to be in charge of the house of the Lord; you should put any madman who acts like a prophet into the stocks and neck-irons. So why have you not reprimanded Jeremiah from Anathoth, who poses as a prophet among you? He has sent this message to us in Babylon: It will be a long time. Therefore build houses and settle down; plant gardens and eat what they produce" (Jeremiah 29:26-28).

The situation in which Zedekiah found himself was extremely difficult. It resembled the dilemma which, a little more than 100 years earlier, had confronted Hezekiah, King of Judah, and likewise Hoshea, the last king of the Israelites. Judah was suffering under the rule of Chaldean Babylon – a rule which was every bit as stifling as Assyrian rule had been at that earlier time. And just as at that earlier time, the local Syrian and Palestine rulers were tempting the king with plans for a joint uprising against their common suzerain, while the Egyptians held out the seductive promise of military aid. In the event of success Judah could regain its independence or at least exchange the oppressive Babylonian yoke for a much more bearable dependence on Egypt. However, failure could have destroyed the country and placed it in an even worse position than until now. Most of the Judahite aristocracy and most of the Aaronite priests were against Babylon and in favor of Egypt, rightly seeing Chaldean Babylon as a second Assyria – especially since in many respects its policies differed little from those of the Assyrians. Egypt seemed in all respects closer and more preferable. The pro-Babylonian party tried to show that Egypt was not an alternative to Babylon, being much weaker and moreover unreliable, and that Judah, in order to avoid catastrophe, had no choice but to accept the Chaldean yoke for the time being. Certain Yahwist prophets – Jeremiah, for instance – regarded Babylonian military might as merely an instrument by which the Lord could punish Judah for its idolatry, and for this reason thought that any attempt to resist the Babylonians was pointless or even ruinous. They saw salvation in the people's moral renaissance and its return to the Lord. But the pro-Babylonian party was in the minority, unpopular, and persecuted. The king, the people around him, and most ordinary people preferred hearing only what matched their own interests. For as long as the balance of power in the region remained clearly in Babylon's favor, Zedekiah had no choice but to continue to acknowledge its dominance; but as soon as signs appeared that Nebuchadnezzar's military might was waning, he began to waver.

In the second half of the 590s BCE Babylonia was hit by a whole series of domestic and external troubles. Above all, a mutiny against the rule of Nebuchadnezzar flared up in Babylon itself; part of the Babylonian army was involved. Almost at the same time, the forces of Elam attacked Babylonia from the east, dragging it into a fierce war with heavy bloodshed. Nebuchadnezzar had scarcely managed to deal with the mutineers and the Elamite army when his subject peoples rose up against him in his rear, in Syria. Nebuchadnezzar's problems also included tension in his relations with his former allies the Medes and Persians and his inability to conquer Egypt, so Zedekiah had serious grounds for supposing that the Babylonian empire was in difficulty and growing weak. Influenced by these events, the rulers of the Palestinian and Phoenician states began hatching plans to put together a coalition against their suzerain, Babylon. The kings of Edom, Moab, Ammon, Tyre, and Sidon entered into secret talks with Zedekiah, proposing that he should join their alliance. Judah was at this time the largest and strongest kingdom among the Palestinian and Phoenician states and possessed the largest army among them; accordingly the other states considered it extremely desirable that it should join their coalition. The main factor in Zedekiah's decision, though, was not the idea of creating an anti-Babylonian alliance from the weak states of Phoenicia and Palestine, but the position taken by Egypt. Judah was in need of proof that the Egyptians would not abandon it in a time of trouble to face Nebuchadnezzar's army on its own, as had happened in 597 BCE. Pharaoh Psamtik II, however, who ruled from 595-589 BCE, was a circumspect politician and was reluctant to enter into any obligations, although he did everything he could to get the King of Judah on his side. Feeling himself unprepared for fresh confrontation with Babylonia, Psamtik II conducted a very cautious policy in Asia. Unlike his father, Necho II, he made the focus of his attention not Syria or Palestine, but Nubia. It was here, in the south, that he organized a successful campaign against the Nubian army, which was incomparably weaker than the Babylonian and unable to withstand the Egyptian onslaught. As for Syria and Palestine, Egypt's activity in this region amounted to nothing more than organizing a peaceful visit for the pharaoh and principal priests into neighboring Judah and to certain Philistine cities, which was in itself a demonstration of Egypt's political influence on Babylonia's vassals.

The Siege of Jerusalem and the Downfall of Judah

The situation changed radically when at the beginning of 589 Apries, a new pharaoh from the Saite Dynasty, ascended the throne. The new ruler changed the focus of his foreign policy from Nubia in the south to Palestine and Phoenicia in the north-east. Like his grandfather, Necho II, Apries dreamed of extending Egypt's power over the entire Syro-Palestinian region. He paid particular attention to relations with his neighbor Judah, whose strategic importance had grown considerably following the Babylonians' total destruction of the Philistine cities of Gaza and Ashkelon and the deportation of their inhabitants to Babylonia. Unlike Psamtik II, he agreed to offer Judah a guarantee of military aid in the event that it joined the anti-Babylonian coalition. In order to prove his determination to fight the Babylonians for Palestine and Phoenicia, he sent boatloads of his soldiers to Tyre and Sidon, thereby throwing down a direct challenge to Nebuchadnezzar. These moves by Apries convinced Zedekiah that the Egyptians' intentions were serious and pushed him to split with Chaldean Babylonia. Zedekiah's decision was accelerated by the fact that he was unexpectedly called to Babylon. The Chaldeans, it turned out, were well informed not just regarding the Egyptians' visit to Judah, but also about Zedekiah's secret negotiations with their enemies. At best, the Judahite king would have had to pronounce a new oath of loyalty to Nebuchadnezzar; at worst, he faced imprisonment or agonizing death. Fears for the outcome of his trip to Babylon compelled Zedekiah to rush into his fateful choice in favor of Egypt. Nebuchadnezzar's reaction was rapid and decisive. Fearing that the mutiny would spread throughout his large empire, that very year (589 BCE) he moved his forces simultaneously against both Judah and the mutinous Phoenician cities. Tyre and Sidon were besieged; the Egyptian detachments which had been sent to help them were routed, and what remained of these forces sailed off back to Egypt. As in 598-597 BCE, the entire might of the Babylonian army descended upon Judah, which was now left alone to face it.

The best accounts of the tragic events of this time are to be found in the book of Kings and Jeremiah: "So in the ninth year of Zedekiah's reign, on the tenth day of the tenth month, Nebuchadnezzar king of Babylon marched against Jerusalem with his whole army. He encamped outside the city and built siege works all around it. The city was kept under siege until the eleventh year of King Zedekiah" (2 Kings 25:1-2). In addition to Nebuchadnezzar's army, the siege of Jerusalem involved detachments of the Babylonian king's numerous vassals from Syria and Mesopotamia. As the supporters of the pro-Babylonian party had warned, Egypt was unable or unwilling to come to Judah's aid. Pharaoh Apries sent his army or part of it to help besieged Jerusalem, but either this army was defeated or, as is more likely, it decided not to do battle with the superior Babylonian forces and hastily turned back. The prophet Jeremiah has the following to say of this: "Pharaoh's army had marched out of Egypt, and when the Babylonians who were besieging Jerusalem heard the report about them, they withdrew from Jerusalem. Then the word of the Lord came to Jeremiah the prophet: 'This is what the Lord, the God of Israel, says: Tell the king of Judah, who sent you to inquire of me, 'Pharaoh's army, which has marched out to support you, will go back to its own land, to Egypt. Then the Babylonians will return and attack this city; they will capture it and burn it down.' 'This is what the Lord says: Do not deceive yourselves, thinking, 'The Babylonians will surely leave us.' They will not!" (Jeremiah 37:5-9) Thus the fatal political miscalculation made by King Jehoakim in 598 BCE was repeated by Zedekiah in 589 BCE. Both kings placed unjustifiably large hopes in Egypt, mistakenly thinking that the forces of Egypt and Babylonia were approximately equal. This illusion of Egyptian might was maintained in every way possible by the pharaohs of the Saite Dynasty, who dreamed of extending their authority to Palestine and Syria. By liberally handing out promises of military aid, Apries, an inexperienced but vain politician, pushed the Palestinian and Phoenician kings into a clash with Babylon that was their ruin. He not only destroyed their countries, but also stripped Egypt of any influence over the region of Syria and Palestine.

Alongside Jerusalem, two other Judahite cities – Lachish and Azekah – put up the most dogged resistance to the Babylonian army. Both of these cities were mighty fortresses situated in the area of Shephelah; they guarded both the latter fertile region and the approaches to Jerusalem from the south and west. Lachish had acquired a name for its courageous defense during the invasion of King Sennacherib's Assyrian army in 701 BCE. Now, a little more than 100 years later, it was again besieged by conquerors from Mesopotamia and again became the latter's stumbling block. To date, the ruins of ancient Lachish have yielded 21 fragments from the garrison commander's correspondence with his superior in Jerusalem. Judging by this fragmentary evidence, the defenders of the Judahite cities communicated with one another by lighting fires on fortress towers. When there were no flames to be seen during the hours of darkness, this was a sign that the city had perished. For instance, it was thus that it became known that Azekah, first of these cities, fell to the Babylonians. One of the pieces from this correspondence says that at this difficult time for Judah the garrison at Lachish continued to maintain links with Egypt in the hope that the Egyptians would sooner or later come to its aid. Some excerpts from the letters contain vague echoes of the disputes which took place at that time in the army and at the court of the king. Unfortunately, most fragments of the Lachish correspondence have suffered so heavily at the hands of time and war that they are no longer legible. In general, they are of greater linguistic than historical significance – as one of very few examples of Hebrew writing of the time.

Just as poor in historically significant information, but important from the point of view of ancient Hebrew writing are fragments of letters from the town of Arad (the so-called 'ostraca'). The *ostraca* provide us with confirmation that the Judahite kings of that time, like the rulers of the neighboring states, made ready use of military mercenaries from Greece and Asia Minor ('kittim', as they were called). Many of these mercenaries served in the Judahite fortresses south of Jerusalem on the border with Edom. One of the Arad letters provides indirect confirmation of another fact which is known to us from the books of the biblical prophets – that the Edomites penetrated into southern regions of Judah. In general, the surviving fragments of the correspondence from Lachish and Arad cannot add anything new to the information given us by the Bible regarding the final years of Judah's existence. The same may be said of the chronicles of the Neo-Babylonian empire: they all, at best, merely confirm the account given in the Bible, only in a manner which is incomparably drier and more laconic.

As the situation in besieged Jerusalem became increasingly difficult, the royal court began looking for salvation in a return to the commandments of monotheistic Yahwism. In hope of repeating the miracle of the time of Hezekiah, when Jerusalem had escaped the Assyrian invasion, the king declared a strict fast and followed this up by liberating all slaves of Hebrew origin. But the general atmosphere of the time of Zedekiah, an atmosphere in which the pagan cults had flourished, was clearly very different from the period of religious puritanism under King Hezekiah, so the liberated slaves very quickly found themselves once again under the heel of their former lords. The siege of the city lasted for two years, bringing severe famine to begin with and then mass epidemics among the inhabitants. According to Jeremiah, this was a time when the Lord declared 'freedom' "to fall by the sword, plague and famine" (Jeremiah 34:17). The prophet Ezekiel describes the hopeless situation of the city's defenders in approximately the same terms: "Outside is the sword; inside are plague and famine. Those in the country will die by the sword; those in the city will be devoured by famine and plague" (Ezekiel 7:15). "By the ninth day of the fourth month the famine in the city had become so severe that there was no food for the people to eat" (2 Kings 25:3). Exhausted and weak, the inhabitants were unable any longer to withstand the onslaught of the enormous Babylonian army. "Then the city wall was broken through, and the whole army fled at night through the gate between the two walls near the king's garden, though the Babylonians were surrounding the city. They fled toward the Arabah, but the Babylonian army pursued the king and overtook him in the plains of Jericho. All his soldiers were separated from him and scattered, and he was captured. He was taken to the king of Babylon at Riblah, where sentence was pronounced on him. They killed the sons of Zedekiah before his eyes. Then they put out his eyes, bound him with bronze shackles and took him to Babylon" (2 Kings 25:4-7).

However, the tragedy of Jerusalem did not end with the capture of the city and the imprisonment of its king. Nebuchadnezzar was keen to punish the city and its inhabitants severely so that other peoples in his empire would not follow their example. In this respect the Chaldean ruler was merely abiding by Assyrian tradition, which required that mutineers be dealt with in an instructive manner and without mercy. As the book of Kings tells us, "On the seventh day of the fifth month, in the nineteenth year of Nebuchadnezzar king of Babylon, Nebuzaradan commander of the imperial guard, an official of the king of Babylon, came to Jerusalem. He set fire to the temple of the Lord, the royal palace and all the houses of Jerusalem. Every important building he burned down. The whole Babylonian army, under the commander of the imperial guard, broke down the walls around Jerusalem. Nebuzaradan the commander of the guard carried into exile the people who remained in the city, along with the rest of the populace and those who had deserted to the king of Babylon. But the commander left behind some of the poorest people of the land to work the vineyards and fields" (2 Kings 25:8-12). All the tools, religious objects, and precious things and jewelry from the Temple in Jerusalem were taken to Babylon. Then vengeance was inflicted upon the high-ranking priests and the king's courtiers and servants, and on rich and noble citizens: "The commander of the guard took as prisoners Seraiah the chief priest, Zephaniah the priest next in rank and the three doorkeepers. Of those still in the city, he took the officer in charge of the fighting men and five royal advisers. He also took the secretary who was chief officer in charge of conscripting the people of the land and sixty of his men who were found in the city. Nebuzaradan the commander took them all and brought them to the king of Babylon at Riblah. There at Riblah, in the land of Hamath, the king had them executed. [...] Nebuchadnezzar king of Babylon appointed Gedaliah son of Ahikam, the son of Shaphan, to be over the people he had left behind in Judah" (2 Kings 25:18-22).

The Babylonian Exile: its True Scope and Significance

In giving an account of the fall of Judah and Jerusalem in 586 BCE, the Bible leaves us in no doubt that the country was destroyed and the absolute majority of the Judahite population were deported to Babylonia to live. What other interpretation could we give to the words of the book of Kings that "Judah went into captivity, away from her land" or to the still more categorical assertion in the book of Chronicles that "he [Nebuchadnezzar] carried into exile to Babylon the remnant, who escaped from the sword" (2 Kings 25:21; 2 Chronicles 36:20)? However, the evidence available to us does not, in fact, support this historical myth, which has only gained in strength over the millennia. Above all, the Bible itself contains evidence of the opposite. For instance, the prophet Jeremiah, who was a witness to and a participant in this tragedy, states that "Nebuzaradan the commander of the guard left behind in the land of Judah some of the poor people, who owned nothing; and at that time he gave them vineyards and fields" (Jeremiah 39:10). Yet these so-called 'poor people' made up the majority of the population in all countries in the ancient Near East. The same fact is acknowledged by the book of Kings, although the latter adds that in Judah the Babylonians left only "some of the poor people". But the book of Kings says absolutely the same thing following the first fall of Jerusalem in 597 BCE, when it states that the King of Babylon "carried all Jerusalem into exile [...] Only the poorest people of the land were left" (2 Kings 24:14). As we already know, these 'few poor people' who remained at that time in Jerusalem included the court of King Zedekiah, his army, wealthy citizens, and the entire mass of people whom Nebuzaradan took to Babylonia following the second siege of the capital. Evidently, the phrase 'some of the poor people' is a clear exaggeration or dramatization of the onerous consequences of the fall of Jerusalem. It should not be forgotten that the Babylonians' appointment of Gedaliah as their governor in Judah was in itself evidence suggesting that a considerable part of the population had remained in Judah. It was not the custom in ancient times to appoint governors, and especially governors from among the local population, to rule over land which was desolate and unpopulated.

The book of Jeremiah contains a further extremely interesting fact: many Judahites fled, for the duration of the invasion of Nebuchadnezzar's army, to neighboring countries, returning to Judah when the Babylonians left; "When all the Jews in Moab, Ammon, Edom and all the other countries heard that the king of Babylon had left a remnant in Judah and had appointed Gedaliah son of Ahikam, the son of Shaphan, as governor over them, they all came back to the land of Judah, to Gedaliah at Mizpah, from all the countries where they had been scattered. And they harvested an abundance of wine and summer fruit" (Jeremiah 40:11-12). This means that we have reliable evidence of the fact that only a fraction of the Judahite people was deported into Babylonian exile, while the majority was left where they were by the Chaldeans themselves and a part returned to Judah when the war there came to an end.

We can try to calculate the total number of people taken off to captivity in Babylonia in 597 and 586 BCE. As we know, the book of Kings speaks of 10,000 people who went into exile together with the young king Jehoiachin following the first siege of Jerusalem. The book of Kings does not indicate the number of those imprisoned following the second siege, giving us to understand that this fate befell all or almost all of the country's inhabitants. The missing information is to be found in the book of the prophet Jeremiah: "This is the number of the people Nebuchadnezzar carried into exile: in the seventh year, 3,023 Jews [in 597 BCE]; in Nebuchadnezzar's eighteenth year, 832 people from Jerusalem [in 586 BCE]; in his twenty-third year, 745 Jews taken into exile by Nebuzaradan the commander of the imperial guard [in 582 BCE]. There were 4,600 people in all" (Jeremiah 52:28-30). As we can see, even the total number of captives given by Jeremiah is far smaller than the number indicated by the book of Kings for 597 BCE alone.

One of the most likely explanations of this divergence is that in the number of captives for 597 BCE Jeremiah fails to include 7000 soldiers – possibly because there were many foreign mercenaries among them. Notably, the well-informed historian Josephus Flavius likewise preferred not to include soldiers in the total number of those carried off to Babylonia in 597 BCE and, like Jeremiah, limited himself to giving a total of 3000. As for the figures given by Jeremiah for 586 BCE, it is unlikely that there is any reason to doubt them as he was in the best possible position to know the situation: initially, he was himself among the crowd of captives and together with them made the journey in chains from Jerusalem to Ramah, where he was set free in accordance with an order given by Nebuchadnezzar II in person. But even if we suppose that Jeremiah's figures are for some reason substantially lower than the real numbers and that the total of those carried off into captivity in Babylon in 586 BCE was not less than in 597 BCE, and even if we then include the figure of 7000 soldiers on both occasions, the total number of those removed into captivity will still not exceed 20,000. At the same time, calculations carried out by archaeologists Finkelstein and Silberman put the population of Judah at the end of the 7th and beginning of the 6th centuries BCE as, at the very least, 75,000. Accordingly, approximately one quarter of the people of Judah were taken to Babylonia – and perhaps significantly less, considering that we have compared the maximum number of prisoners with the minimum size of the population. If, on the other hand, we base our calculations solely on biblical figures, then the percentage of Judahites taken into captivity will be utterly insignificant. For instance, we could use the numbers for captives given by the prophet Jeremiah, whom we have no reason not to trust, and compare them with the results of the census of the population of Judah conducted by King Amaziah in the 8th century BCE. As we know, this census produced the figure of 300,000 men of more than 20 years in age. Even if we suppose that Jeremiah likewise counted only adult males and took no account of women and children, then the Babylonian captives would still have constituted a negligible percentage. So we have a paradoxical situation: on the one hand, the myth that the entire people of Judah were taken into exile in Babylon continues to exist on the strength of statements made by the authors of the Bible; on the other, the same biblical books contain information which not only does not support this myth, but actually refutes it.

The book of Kings tells us of one more circumstance which makes it extremely unlikely that the inhabitants of Jerusalem were deported into captivity *en masse*. This is that a whole month passed – "between the ninth day of the fourth month" and "the seventh day of the fifth month" – between the initial seizure of the capital of Judah and the arrival of detachments of Nebuzaradan's soldiers charged with the task of sending the Judahites into captivity (2 Kings 25:3-4,8). During this interval many inhabitants were able freely to leave the famine-struck and epidemic-ravaged city and to flee to safer regions of Judah or to neighboring countries. It was this that the prophet Ezekiel had in mind when he wrote of the inhabitants of Jerusalem: "The fugitives who escape will flee to the mountains. Like doves of the valleys, they will all moan, each for their own sins" (Ezekiel 7:16).

Judah as the Only Hebrew Kingdom

Finally, according to A. Mazar, we today have available to us incontrovertible archaeological evidence showing that a number of cities to the north of Jerusalem suffered no war damage and that their populations remained where they were. These were cities belonging to Judah and situated on the land of the tribe of Benjamin – for instance, Mizpah, Gibeon, and Gibeah. It is not surprising that Mizpah became the residence of the Babylonian governor Gedaliah; it had been left practically untouched by Nebuchadnezzar's army. It cannot be ruled out that their Hivite and Benjaminite provenance led the local rulers to decide to surrender voluntarily to the Babylonians. But the most surprising development has been the discovery of rich burials from the time of the Babylonian exile in the region of Jerusalem itself.

Thus the Babylonian captivity was not a catastrophe from the demographic point of view – for the absolute majority of the Judahite population remained where they were and Judah itself was not desolated, as we might think when we read the Bible. Moreover, some of the country's towns and cities – in the north, for instance – were not even destroyed. From the point of view of culture and politics, however, the Babylonian exile was indeed a disaster since those who shaped the country's politics, history, and culture and who managed its defense – i.e. the more professional, wealthy, and economically and politically active part of the population – ended up in captivity in Babylon. In the present case what happened was the same as when the Israelites were deported to Assyria following the fall of Samaria in 722 BCE: the people's 'head' went into exile, while its 'body' remained where it was. We know almost nothing of what happened in Judah itself during the half century of the Babylonian captivity because most of those who wrote the country's history (the Levites and the Aaronites) or shaped its politics (the royal court and army) and those whom the Bible calls 'the people of the land' (its wealthy citizens and landowners) were at this time outside the country's borders. The Babylonian captivity was not the first time that the Judahites had found themselves in exile; it was preceded by the Assyrian captivity of the time of Sennacherib and by imprisonment by the Arameans of Damascus during the rule of Rezin. The latter imprisonments were on a much larger scale and were more serious tragedies for the people of Judah than the famous Babylonian exile. The Assyrian chronicles tell us of the unprecedented number of Judahites – 200,000 – who were seized by Sennacherib's army; admittedly, this captivity did not affect either the royal family or the courtiers and, even more importantly, it left untouched the Aaronites and Levites, whom Hezekiah seized on this occasion in Jerusalem. The Assyrian captivity at the end of the 8th century BCE left Jerusalem untouched, affecting only the Judahite provinces and, above all, the inhabitants of Shephelah. But the Bible makes almost no mention of this event given that the captives did not include the keepers of the tradition, i.e. those who might have been able to give an account of what had happened. All this is a further reminder that we know only that part of the history of the

Israel and Judah in which the Levites and the Aaronites were directly involved. There is nothing surprising in that the early history of the northern tribes has disappeared from our field of view and we know of them only what happened after they were joined by the Levites. In just the same way – because the keepers of the tradition were not among their number – we have absolutely no information concerning the Israelites who were deported into captivity in Assyria following the fall of Samaria in 722 BCE. The priests of non-Levite origin from Bethel were never able to become a true alternative to the Levites and Aaronites. In this respect the Judahite captives in Babylonia were in luck: they had with them the keepers of the tradition, including the famous prophet Ezekiel. And although the Babylonian captivity was only short-lived, we know about it incomparably more than we do about all the other periods of captivity suffered by the Judahites and the Israelites taken together.

In spite of the apparent similarity, the Babylonian deportation of the Judahites was very different from the Israelites' exile in Assyria. First, it was much shorter, lasting for less than half a century – at least, in the case of those who were taken to Babylon in 586 BCE – while we know absolutely nothing of the Israelites' return to their country of origin. Secondly, unlike the Israelites, who were taken to three different locations at a great distance from one another, all the Judahites were settled in one and the same region near Babylon itself. And thirdly and finally, if new settlers from Mesopotamia and Syria were brought to Samaria to take the Israelites' place, Jerusalem remained empty and the lands of the captive Judahites were not occupied by people from other countries.

The Governorship of Gedaliah: an Attempt at National Revival
The destruction of Jerusalem in 586 BCE and the Babylonian captivity were not the final chord in the political history of Judah during the First Temple period. The fact that the governor appointed by the Babylonians to rule in Judah was not a member of the royal family, but a Yahwist priest in itself made the Davidic dynasty hostile to Gedaliah as a potential rival. Their hatred for him was exacerbated by the circumstance that he came not from the southern Aaronites, but from the northern Levites and they thus regarded him as a foreigner and usurper. Nebuchadnezzar II's choice of Gedaliah for this position was not, however, accidental. After the treachery of Zedekiah, who had had Nebuchadnezzar himself to thank for his throne, the king of the Babylonians lost his faith in the Davidic dynasty; nor did he trust the Aaronites, most of whom likewise belonged to the pro-Egyptian camp. Unlike the Aaronites, the northern Levites lacked deep roots in Judah and could not count on either the support of the Judahite aristocracy or help from the 'people of the land'. This made them more dependent on the Babylonians, and it was quite possibly this that pushed them towards the pro-Babylonian party. Jeremiah and his scribe, Baruch, to whom he dictated his prophecies, were also from the northern Levites. Admittedly, the

prophet himself was born in the region of the Benjaminite lands which fell into the hands of Judah following the split of the United Monarchy, so he could be equally considered 'one of their own' by both the northerners and the southerners. In general, the northern Levites were more literate and more advanced in their monotheistic interpretation of the cult of Yahweh than the southern Aaronites. However, because most of them were outsiders in Judah, they occupied secondary positions among the Yahwist priests. The fact that Gedaliah was a northern Levite by origin gave Judah greater influence over the lands of what had been the kingdom of Israel. Evidently, both in religion and in respect to the population of northern and central Palestine Gedaliah intended to conduct the same policy as kings Hezekiah and Josiah; but, unlike the latter, he had no intention of revolting against his suzerain, on whom he depended to an even greater extent than they had done.

His efforts to strengthen Judah's influence on the lands of the northern tribes began bearing their first fruit. The Bible tells us of a mass pilgrimage from Samaria, Shechem, and Shiloh – something which had previously occurred only during the reigns of Hezekiah and Josiah. It is difficult to say where these pilgrims were headed. Perhaps they were intending to visit the ruins of the Temple in Jerusalem, or perhaps they were headed for Mizpah, where Gedaliah had probably built a temporary temple. Similarly quickly, Gedaliah was able to gather at Mizpah the divisions of the Judahite army which had been scattered by the war. The prophet Jeremiah tells us that, "When all the army officers and their men who were still in the open country heard that the king of Babylon had appointed Gedaliah son of Ahikam as governor over the land and had put him in charge of the men, women and children who were the poorest in the land and who had not been carried into exile to Babylon, they came to Gedaliah at Mizpah" (Jeremiah 40:7-8). Refugees who had hidden from the war in neighboring countries returned to Judah in large numbers. The prophet Jeremiah was also among those who came to Gedaliah at Mizpah; he "stayed with him among the people who were left behind in the land" (Jeremiah 40:6). It is likely that Gedaliah would have been one of the most successful rulers of Judah and that he would have managed to revive the country and re-unify its population. However, his rule as governor was not to the liking of either the Davidic dynasty or Judah's neighbors.

Gedaliah's loyalty to his obligations to the Babylonians and his efforts to consolidate the country were leading to the revival of a strong Judah which would have dominated its Palestinian neighbors. His policy of convergence with the population of what had been the kingdom of Israel was in greatest contradiction with the interests of the northern Transjordanian kingdom of Ammon, which had since the time of King Saul laid claim to lands in central Palestine to both the east and west of the River Jordan. As we know, the formation of a powerful kingdom of Israel had forced the Ammonites not merely to renounce any claim to its lands, but also, in time, to become Israel's vassal. The fall of the kingdom of Israel and then the destruction of Assyria had revived the Ammonites' old claims. However, on this occasion they found their path blocked by Babylonia and the latter's governor, Gedaliah. Of course, Baalis, the king of the Ammonites at this time, given that he was just as much a tributary of Babylonia as all the other Palestinian rulers, had no intention of throwing down a challenge to Nebuchadnezzar single-handed. In everything that concerned Babylonia, he counted on help from Egypt, just as the Judahite kings Jehoiakim and Zedekiah had done before him. But in his confrontation with neighboring Judah, he did not expect cooperation from the region's major powers, which had little interest in disputes occurring within Palestine. For this reason, having no desire to allow his potential rival to gain in strength, he planned to use for his purposes the offended Davidides, some of whom had hidden from the invading Babylonians in his kingdom.

One of these Davidides, Ishmael, son of Nethaniah and "from the royal family and from a line of royal dignitaries", as the Bible emphatically tells us, with the help of the Ammonite king put together a conspiracy to kill Gedaliah. Initially, the conspiracy also involved the commanders of surviving divisions of the Judahite army and members of the aristocracy – in particular, those who had found refuge in Ammon. However, upon returning home, many of the latter renounced their plans to kill the Babylonian governor since they believed that Gedaliah had no intention of impinging upon their rights and interests. Furthermore, Gedaliah's policy of national consolidation and reconciliation had enabled him to melt the ice of distrust and caution felt towards him as both a placeman of the Babylonians and someone who did not come from a royal family. Although Gedaliah had been warned of the conspiracy against him, Ishmael's loyal behavior put his vigilance to sleep. The fact that a large number of people, including the governor himself, had heard of the plans to assassinate Gedaliah evidently gave rise to the belief that the conspirators had long since renounced these plans.

Biding his time until suspicions of him had died down, Ishmael struck the blow which everyone seemed to have known might occur but no one had actually expected. During a feast in Mizpah he and his co-conspirators killed Gedaliah and massacred the entire court, including the Babylonian garrison which had been sent to help the ruler. Next, they treacherously slaughtered the pilgrims who had come to Mizpah from the former kingdom of Israel. Evidently, they disliked Gedaliah's closer relations with the northerners, whom they viewed as his potential allies. It is difficult to say whether it was part of Ishmael's plans to seize power in Judah or whether he intended to stop at merely killing the 'usurper' of the power of the Davidic dynasty. Whatever the case, Gedaliah's profoundly consolidate policy had already managed to win over large numbers of supporters, including the surviving divisions of the Judahite army. The latter now intervened against the conspirators. Failing to find support among the general population, the conspirators seized large numbers of prisoners, including the daughters of the last king of Judah and tried to make good their escape to King Baalis in Ammon. However, the army detachments which remained loyal to Gedaliah caught the conspirators in the vicinity of the town of Gibeon and blocked their way to Ammon. Both sides began to prepare for battle, but the battle itself never happened. The soldiers who were in the service of the conspirators went over, together with all their prisoners, to the side of their opponents and Ishmael, together with a small number of his co-conspirators, abandoned everything and fled in secret to his patron in Ammon. Military and political command in Judah passed into the hands of one of the generals, Johanan, son of Kareah, who had been from the beginning a committed supporter of Gedaliah and opponent of Ishmael. But the situation remained extremely grave. The murder of the ruler appointed by Nebuchadnezzar II and the destruction of the Babylonian garrison were bound to incur new repressions on the part of the King of Babylon. The mission begun by Gedaliah – the mission of reviving Judah – had now to be put aside, at least for half a century, until the return of those in Babylonian captivity.

The Escape to Egypt. A New Invasion by the Chaldeans and the Destruction of Ammon, Moab and Edom

Without waiting for the arrival of the Chaldean army, the Judahite generals and the remaining aristocracy decided to leave for Egypt. The prophet Jeremiah tells us that they called upon him to ask the Lord what they should do and where they should go. But Jeremiah's answer disappointed them: "This is what the Lord, the God of Israel, to whom you sent me to present your petition, says: "If you stay in this land, I will build you up and not tear you down; I will plant you and not uproot you [...] Do not be afraid of the king of Babylon, whom you now fear. Do not be afraid of him, declares the Lord, for I am with you and will save you and deliver you from his hands [...] But if you are determined to go to Egypt and you do go to settle there, then the sword you fear will overtake you there, and the famine you dread will follow you into Egypt, and there you will die" (Jeremiah 42:9-11; 15-16). However, in both the Northern and the Southern kingdoms prophecies were only looked upon favorably when they made a good fit with decisions which had already been taken; when this was not the case, they were rejected and the prophets who made them fell out of favor and were persecuted. This was precisely what happened with the prophecy made by Jeremiah on this occasion: it was angrily rejected and the prophet himself was taken off to Egypt against his will.

Thus began another exile – this time, voluntary – in Egypt. It is possible that this migration was only on a slightly smaller scale than during the Babylonian captivity, given that it included the surviving detachments of the Judahite army, members of the nobility, and the wealthier part of the 'people of the land'. This new stay in Egypt is much less well known than the 'Babylonian exile' or the 'slavery in Egypt' because on this occasion the Judahites were not accompanied by the keepers of the tradition. We owe whatever knowledge we have of the mass departure of the Judahites for Egypt in the middle of the 580s BCE exclusively to the prophet Jeremiah, who was taken to Egypt by force. The flight into Egypt led to the formation of a large Judahite community there. We can judge the full extent of this community from prophet Isaiah's statement that five cities in Egypt would speak the 'Canaanite language'. Isaiah expresses the hope that "those who were exiled in Egypt" will return to Judah and "worship the Lord on the holy mountain in Jerusalem" (Isaiah 27:13). There is archaeological evidence to confirm the existence of large Judahite communities in Egypt at the time. For instance, the letters from the island of Elephantine are evidence that numerous Judahite mercenaries were in service there. Evidently, the detachments of Judahite soldiers who departed for Egypt following the killing of Gedaliah were very quickly absorbed into the Egyptian army, which mainly consisted of foreign mercenaries. And in general the departure of Judahites *en masse* for Egypt was made possible by the close relations which had formed between these two countries during the rules of King Zedekiah of Judah and the Egyptian pharaohs Psamtik II and Apries (called Hophra in the Bible). But, however large were the numbers of Judahites involved in the Babylonian exile and the flight into Egypt, the larger part of the Judahite population, which consisted mainly of poor farmers, remained in place in its native country.

Jeremiah, as an eyewitness of these events, draws attention to the difference between the fates of the prisoners of 597 BCE and those who were taken to Babylon in 586, when the city of Jerusalem and the Temple were destroyed. The former surrendered of their own free will, together with King Jehoiachin himself, and were therefore able to escape the sufferings and torments of a lengthy siege of the city; moreover, the Chaldeans provided them with satisfactory living conditions in Babylonia. The latter, on the other hand, having fought alongside Zedekiah to the bitter end, suffered serious losses, had to live through the most severe famine and pestilence, and were then subjected to torture and executions. Both on the way to Babylon and when settled there, they found themselves in conditions that were worse than those encountered by the prisoners of 597 BCE. Jeremiah sees the second category as including likewise those Judahites who departed for Egypt of their own free will, given that the Chaldeans' subsequent invasion of Egypt brought upon them similar suffering to that which had occurred during the siege of Jerusalem. He compares the fate of these exiles with two baskets of figs: "One basket had very good figs, like those that ripen early; the other basket had very bad figs, so bad they could not be eaten" (Jeremiah 24:2), and asserts that while the fate of the former was favorable (they lived well in Babylonia and later returned home, to Judah), the fate of the latter was unenviable: they suffered wars, hunger, and epidemics, following which only a few managed to return to their motherland. However, it should be made clear straightaway that Jeremiah's main criterion when assessing how well the exiles lived in Babylonia and Egypt was their attitude to the Lord, i.e. a religious factor. As is well known, the first category of prisoners lived together with the keepers of the tradition – the Levites and Aaronites – and quickly evolved in the direction of true monotheism, while the second category remained polytheists and combined worship of Yahweh with adoration of pagan gods. From Jeremiah's point of view, the former were 'given a heart' with which to recognize the true God, while the latter became mired in idolatry, as punishment for which they were pursued by "the sword, the plague, and famine".

The Judahite generals' fears for their safety were by no means groundless. In approximately 582 BCE the Babylonians again invaded Judah and carried off into captivity 745 people, as Jeremiah tells us. On this occasion the main blow fell not on ruined Judah, but on its rebellious neighbors – Ammon, Moab, and Edom. The first of these to suffer was the north Transjordanian kingdom of Ammon, whose king, Baalis, was accused of entering into a secret conspiracy with Egypt and of concealing enemies of Babylonia. He was probably also blamed for aiding the killers of Gedaliah. The Judahites and Samaritans looked upon the defeat of the Ammonites not without some satisfaction since they remembered well how, following the fall of the Northern Kingdom, Ammon had seized part of the lands which had belonged to the Israelite tribes in Transjordan. Of this Jeremiah said as follows: "This is what the Lord says: 'Has Israel no sons? Has Israel no heir? Why then has Molek [chief Ammonite deity] taken possession of Gad? Why do his people live in its towns? But the days are coming,' declares the Lord, 'when I will sound the battle cry against Rabbah [capital] of the Ammonites; it will become a mound of ruins, and its surrounding villages will be set on fire. Then Israel will drive out those who drove her out,' says the Lord" (Jeremiah 49:1-2). The Ammonites shared the very same fate that had befallen the Judahites: their country was destroyed and the nobler and wealthier part of their people were carried off into captivity in Babylonia. "Cry out, you inhabitants of Rabbah! Put on sackcloth and mourn; rush here and there inside the walls, for Molek will go into exile, together with his priests and officials" (Jeremiah 49:3).

A similar fate befell the more southern Transjordanian kingdom of Moab, whose ruler had also hoped in vain for help from Egypt as a means of escaping the heavy hand of the Chaldeans. But in complete contrast with their lack of compassion for Ammon, the Judahites took a sympathetic attitude to Moab. "Therefore I wail over Moab," writes Jeremiah, "for all Moab I cry out, I moan for the people of Kir Hareseth. I weep for you, as Jazer weeps, O vines of Sibmah. [...] So my heart laments for Moab like the flute [...]" (Jeremiah 48:31-32, 36). Such a sharp difference in the approach to these two neighbors is explained by the fact that of all the Transjordanian peoples the Judahites had the closest relations with the Moabites, with whom they almost never quarreled; moreover, during droughts and wars the Judahites often found refuge in Moab and the Moabites in Judah. The lands of these two peoples were divided by the waters of the Dead Sea, and this meant that there were no disputed territories between them. Judging by the descriptions given by Jeremiah, this Transjordanian kingdom suffered total devastation and desolation – to no lesser an extent than Judah – and, to cap it all, the Moabites suffered just the same kind of captivity in Babylonia as the Judahites. "Woe to you, O Moab! The people of Chemosh [the principal god of the Moabites] are destroyed; your sons are taken into exile and your daughters into captivity [...] and Chemosh will go into exile, together with his priests and officials. The destroyer will come against every town, and not a town will escape. The valley will be ruined and the plateau destroyed, because the Lord has spoken. Put salt on Moab, for she will be laid waste; her towns will become desolate, with no one to live in them" (Jeremiah 48:46, 7-9).

Nebuchadnezzar II's army also laid waste in terrible fashion the third, southernmost, Transjordanian kingdom, Edom. The Judahites had extremely problematic relations with the Edomites: on the one hand, the latter were the people that were closest to them by kin, but on the other they were a constant and jealous rival who laid claim to the legacy of their shared ancestor Isaac. It so happened that the descendants of Jacob were stronger than the heirs of Esau and frequently held sway over the latter. But during periods when Judah was weak the Edomites took revenge and seized southern parts of Judah, lands which they regarded as their own. This is what happened likewise following the fall of Jerusalem in 586 BCE, when the Edomites seized the entire south of Judah right up to Hebron. Naturally, the keepers of the tradition regarded the Chaldeans' laying waste of Edom as deserved and just punishment of their 'bad' kinsmen who rejoiced at the destruction of Judah and taken advantage of its misfortunes. The Judahite prophet Ezekiel commented on this as follows: "This is what the Sovereign Lord says: 'Because Edom took revenge on Judah and became very guilty by doing so, therefore this is what the Sovereign Lord says: I will stretch out my hand against Edom and kill both man and beast. I will lay it waste, and from Teman to Dedan they will fall by the sword" (Ezekiel 25:12-13). The treachery of Edom and its subsequent punishment is still more colorfully described by the prophet Obadiah: "You should not gloat over your brother in the day of his misfortune, nor rejoice over the people of Judah in the day of their destruction, nor boast so much in the day of their trouble [...] You should not seize their wealth in the day of their disaster [...] As you have done, it will be done to you [...]" (Obadiah 1:12,13,15).

Thus it was not just Judah, but all the Transjordanian kingdoms that were completely laid waste and devastated during the 580s BCE. It should also be said that Nebuchadnezzar had, shortly before this, utterly destroyed the Philistine cities of Gaza and Ashkelon, driving off their inhabitants to Babylonia, and had later razed the Phoenician cities of Sidon and Tyre, once again deporting their entire populations to Mesopotamia. However, it was not just the Transjordanian, Philistine, and Phoenician states, but also their neighbors in Syria – Damascus, Hamath, and Arpad – that were plundered and had their inhabitants thrown into captivity. A similar fate struck the nomadic tribes in Midian and north Arabia, where the Chaldeans laid waste to their encampments, seizing large numbers of captives and cattle. Most of Palestine, Phoenicia, and Syria was in an identically lamentable condition for almost half a century, right up until the time when Babylonia was captured by the Persians. It was only then that the Persian king, Cyrus, released all the captive peoples – the Judahites, Ammonites, Moabites, Philistines, Phoenicians, and Arameans of Syria – leaving them free to return home.

The Transformation of Judah during the First Temple Period

The destruction of Jerusalem and the Temple and the deportation to Babylonia of a small, but extremely important part of the Judahite population concluded the existence of the Southern Kingdom and the rule of the house of David, bringing to an end an entire epoch which had begun almost four centuries previously. Throughout this age, known as the First Temple period, Judah, which had initially come into being as the state of the southern Hebrew tribes – or, to be more precise, of the single mega-tribe of Judah – had experienced enormous changes. During the time of the judges and the United Monarchy regions which subsequently became part of Judah had been a rich mosaic of different ethnicities. On what was only a small piece of territory there lived dozens of peoples, tribes, and ethnic groups. The strongest of these was the southern Hebrew tribe of Judah, whose power united and gave its name to the larger portion of southern Canaan. In addition to Judah, the Hebrew tribes consisted of the small southern tribe of Simeon, which settled in the district of Beer-Sheba, and a few Levites. After the United Monarchy split, part of the northern tribe of Benjamin belonging to the 'house of Joseph' remained within the boundaries of Judah. The Hebrews in the south of Canaan were joined there by their close relatives, the Kenazzites and Maonites – Edomite tribes who had united the 'house of Jacob' before the conquest of Canaan, and also by their more distant kinsmen, the Kenites - Midianite tribes with whom Moses had intermarried. The Kenazzites and the Maonites settled to the south-west of the Dead Sea, while the Kenites settled in the district of Arad. At the same time, another related people, the Amalekites, continued to live nomadically in the Negev Desert; they, however, were openly hostile to the 'house of Jacob'.

Nevertheless, the Hebrews and their Edomite and Midianite relatives constituted a minority among the inhabitants of the country which came to be called Judah. The majority of the population consisted of Canaanite and Amorite settled peoples such as the Jebusites in the region of Jerusalem, the Hivites to the north of them, the Perizzites in the area of Shephelah, and the Hittites around Hebron (the latter are not to be confused with the Indo-European Hittites of Asia Minor). Certain Canaanite cities – Gezer, for instance – retained their independence even during the time of David thanks to alliances with the Hebrew tribes. All these peoples – the Hebrews, the Amorites, and the Canaanites, together with their related groups – belonged to the same West Semitic ethnos.

In addition to the Western Semites, Judah was also inhabited by peoples of non-Semitic origin. Such were the Rephaites (Rephaim) - the oldest inhabitants of Palestine, the Hurrianes, and the so-called 'maryannu' (groups of Indo-Aryan origin), who had penetrated into Canaan in the 16th century BCE. The latter were few in number, but were the ruling class in some Canaanite and Amorite cities. It should not be forgotten that David and Solomon, like the subsequent kings of Judah, eagerly hired large numbers of mercenaries from Achaea and Asia Minor to serve at court and in the army. Most of these mercenaries acquired families and remained forever in Judah. Like the Rephaites before them, all these groups were very quickly assimilated into the West Semitic population, infusing the latter with Achaean and Indo-European blood. Finally, the fall of the kingdom of Israel in 722 BCE released a wave of refugees and resulted in part of the Israelite population moving south, into Judah. Among those who moved to the Southern Kingdom the greater part consisted of inhabitants of Central Palestine, who had suffered most from the invasion of the Assyrians and had lived near the border with Judah; this means that they were likely to have comprised members of the 'house of Joseph' and, of course, the northern Levites.

In Judah the creation of an ethnically and culturally unified community progressed much further than in the kingdom of Israel. This was due both to the fact that the Southern Kingdom existed for 150 years longer than the Northern Kingdom and to the circumstance that Judah was considerably smaller and had a significantly lesser population than Israel. The Southern Kingdom lacked the large numbers of Canaanites and Amorites that there were in the Northern Kingdom, and if by the time of the latter's fall there were still large concentrations of Canaanites living on its territory – for instance, on the Mediterranean coast or in the Valley of Jezreel – in Judah in the 6th century BCE there were almost no such enclaves. Moreover, among the Hebrew tribes in the south the predominance of the tribe of Judah was beyond doubt, something which could not be said of the tribes of Ephraim or Manasseh in the north. The higher specific weight of the tribe of Judah and the longer period during which Judah had existed as a Hebrew state made it possible for the local peoples to be almost completely assimilated and Judaized. The result was that with the passing of time the population of the Southern Kingdom became significantly more homogeneous than in the Northern Kingdom. This circumstance played an important role in Judah's revival as a state and, conversely, impeded the renaissance of Israel in the north.

Evidence of how far the process of the formation of a unified Judahite people had advanced is to be found in the census of Babylonian prisoners who intended to return to their native land. Only a few of these people were unable to produce proof of their Judahite provenance, although at the time of the conquest of Canaan the southern Hebrew tribes had constituted less than half of the total local population. Further evidence comes from sources in the Bible. If in their account of the periods of the judges and the United Monarchy the biblical sources make frequent mention of the Canaanite and Amorite peoples and adduce non-Israelite and non-Judahite names, subsequently such mentions become increasingly infrequent until they disappear altogether. Thus all peoples on the territory of Judah, both Semitic and non-Semitic, gradually became Judahites. The wars, droughts, expulsions, and imprisonments that led to population movements accelerated their mixing and assimilation. Of course, it would be an exaggeration to claim that by the 6th century BCE the entire conglomeration of settled and nomadic ethnoses had completely merged to form a homogeneous mass called the 'Judahites'; however, there can be no doubt that the process of mixing was close to completion. At least in terms of culture and language, all these peoples were fully assimilated with one another. So the Judahites of the 6th century BCE were indeed descendants not so much of the southern Hebrew tribes as of the local autochthonous peoples of southern Canaan who had lived there prior to the arrival of the 'house of Jacob' and who made up the majority of the population. Here we can hardly fail to recall the words of the prophet Ezekiel regarding Jerusalem and its inhabitants: "Your ancestry and birth were in the land of the Canaanites; your father was an Amorite and your mother a Hittite" (Ezekiel 16:3).

The southern Hebrew tribes played a very important role: they united all these southern Canaanite ethnoses and themselves dissolved among them, giving their own name and history to a new people which was their common descendant. In this respect the Transjordanian peoples – the Edomites, Moabites, and Ammonites – were to a significantly larger extent the ethnos which the patriarch Abraham had brought into Canaan. If the tribal group of Abraham is to be called 'Hebrews', then the Edomites, Moabites, and Ammonites are incomparably more deserving of this ethnonym than the Judahites themselves because, having settled in the sparsely populated half-desert of Transjordan, the Edomites, Moabites, and Ammonites mixed incomparably less with the local Canaanite peoples than did the southern Hebrew tribes. It was this that Jeremiah had in mind when he said of the Moabites: "Moab has been at rest from youth, like wine left on its dregs, not poured from one jar to another—she has not gone into exile. So she tastes as she did, and her aroma is unchanged" (Jeremiah 48:11).

In order to understand what the 'original' Hebrews who came into Canaan together with Abraham looked like, we should take note of their closest nomadic relatives, whom the Egyptians called 'shasu' and the neighboring West Semitic peoples called 'sutu'. They are depicted on the bas reliefs on the north wall of the large temple hall in Karnak in Egypt. In all likelihood, the people shown under the general name 'shasu' on these bas reliefs are the Edomites against whom Pharaoh Seti I had conducted a number of military campaigns. In terms of anthropology, ethnic origin, and language, the Edomites, like the Moabites and Ammonites, were homogeneous with the southern Hebrew tribes. Admittedly, when the 'house of Jacob', after four centuries of settled life in the Nile Delta, returned to Canaan, the Hebrews dressed in a different way to their brothers, the nomadic 'shasu' who had continued to lead the same way of life which had once been led by Abraham. As for the northern Hebrew tribes from the 'house of Joseph', it is likely that during the time of Seti I they would have been difficult to distinguish from the Canaanites, since in their culture and the way that they dressed they had already adopted much from the latter.

The fact that Judah, Edom, Moab, and Ammon shared the same fate – crushing defeat by the Chaldeans and partial deportation into captivity in Babylon – brought these peoples closer together and accelerated their mixing. This process of assimilation proceeded most quickly in the case of the Judahites and the Moabites. According to the book of Ezra, some of the Moabites, including "the descendants of the ruler of Moab", returned from Babylonia among the Judahites, while, according to the book of Nehemiah, a certain Hashub, a descendant of the ruler of Moab who lived in Jerusalem, helped rebuild the walls around the city (Ezra 2:6; Nehemiah 3:11). It is not accidental that the book of Ruth was written at that time. The creation of this work and the mention that Ruth, a Moabite, was the great-grandmother of King David, were intended to justify the merging of the Judahites and the Moabites, in spite of the fact that the Torah forbade intermarrying with the latter people on the grounds that they had indulged in incest and refused to let the Hebrew tribes returning from Egypt pass through their lands. Notably, Nehemiah, who had been the Persian satrap in Judah for 12 years and was well known, like Ezra, for his resistance to assimilation with idolaters, names as one of the leaders of the Judahite people a certain Parosh, ruler of Moab, and, moreover, places him first among these leaders (Nehemiah 10:14). The fall of Moab and Edom made it easier for the Nabateans – ancestors of Arab nomadic tribes – to penetrate into southern Transjordan and gradually push out the Moabites and Edomites from their traditional lands and force them to move westwards, into southern Judah. The Edomites' move westwards was accompanied by a change of ethnonym: from the end of the 6th century BCE they began to be known as 'Idumeans', while southern Judah, where they had settled, was now known as 'Idumea'. Their territorial convergence with the Judahites led to their subsequent complete cultural and physical

Judah as the Only Hebrew Kingdom

assimilation with the latter. The intermixing occurred through Judaization, a process which Ruth the Moabite described as follows: "Your people will be my people and your God my God" (Ruth 1:16).

We may suppose that a similar process of assimilation took place, although on a smaller scale, in the case of the Ammonites. As the book of Nehemiah tells us, following the destruction of Jerusalem a considerable number of Judahites ended up in Ammon, and Tobiah, ruler of the Ammonites, was himself related to the Judahites (his wife and daughter-in-law came from noble Judahite families) (Nehemiah 6:17-18). Interestingly, even such a fierce opponent of the Ammonites as Nehemiah acknowledged the presence of "a good part of the sons of Ammon" – by which he meant those who were Judaized during or after the Babylonian exile.

Thus whereas during the First Temple period Hebrew tribes merged with the Canaanites and Amorites in southern Palestine, giving rise to a new ethnos – the Judahite people – the fall of Judah and of the Transjordanian kingdoms led to a marked acceleration in a different ethnic process, namely the merging of the Edomites, Moabites, and, to a certain extent, the Ammonites with the Judahites. Historical factors which had divided the once related tribes which had been led into Canaan by Abraham now helped to unify, at least in part, their descendants.

In distinction to the profound ethnic changes that occurred in Judah, the religious beliefs of the country's population changed little over the four centuries of its existence. Although the cult of Yahweh remained the main national religion, the population continued to worship other gods too, in particular those of the traditional Canaanite cults of Baal, Asherah, and Moloch. Also worshipped were the principal national divinities of neighboring peoples: Milcom, the god of the Ammonites; Chemosh, the god of the Moabites; and Qaus, god of the Edomites. During periods of dependence on Assyria and the Neo-Babylonian empire, there were in Jerusalem, as is mentioned by Judahite prophets, considerable numbers of worshippers of popular Mesopotamian gods such as Tammuz, Ishtar, or Nergal. On top of this, there were also numerous cults associated with minor local gods such as Gad, the god of Fortune, or Meni, the god of Destiny. It is hardly surprising that Jeremiah exclaims with bitterness, "You, Judah, have as many gods as you have towns" (Jeremiah 2:28). In short, throughout the course of the entire period of the First Temple Judah remained just as polytheistic as the kingdom of Israel. Attempts to introduce monotheism by force were only made during the rule of kings Hezekiah and Josiah, but they met with such dissatisfaction among the population that the heirs to these religious reformers were compelled, on ascending the throne, to renounce the reforms immediately.

In spite of what is commonly thought, the Temple in Jerusalem was a place of worship not only of Yahweh, but of other gods too – and the latter included both local, Canaanite, gods and gods adopted from Judah's neighbors. This happened equally under Solomon, who built the Temple, and under Zedekiah, the last king of Judah, and was the accepted practice not only under idolatrous kings such as Ahaz or Manasseh, but also during the rules of many members of the Davidic dynasty whom the keepers of the tradition called "unseemly in the eyes of the Lord". The Temple was completely cleansed of pagan cults only during the reigns of the king-reformers Hezekiah and Josiah. The Bible teems with examples of how the inhabitants of Judah, right up until and even after the destruction of the First Temple, continued to be polytheists. The most convincing of these biblical sources are the prophets Ezekiel and Jeremiah, who lived during the last decades of the existence of the Southern Kingdom and witnessed its religious life at first hand. Ezekiel was so struck by the scale of idolatry in contemporary Judah that he even asserted that Samaria and Sodom had not committed even half of the sins of which Jerusalem was guilty (Ezekiel 16:47,51). He likewise tells us that pagan gods were worshipped in the Temple in Jerusalem itself, that the Babylonian god Tammuz was lamented there, and of worship of the Sun. In all these ceremonies it was not just the remnants of the Canaanite and Amorite population that took part, but the Judahite nobility and elders too (Ezekiel 8:10-17). Ezekiel also tells us of an even more astonishing fact: in the Temple in Jerusalem not only were pagan gods worshipped, but the worship of Yahweh was led by foreign priests (Ezekiel 44:7-8). All this happened not under the idolatrous kings Ahaz and Manasseh, but under Jehoiakim and Zedekiah, whose behavior was indistinguishable from most of the Davidic dynasty who were "unseemly in the eyes of the Lord". We find frequent mentions of similar idolatry in Jeremiah. But it was not just the fact that "the prophets prophesied in the name of Baal" and followed worthless idols that upset Jeremiah (Jeremiah 2:8); he was equally worried by the corruption and hypocrisy among the priests of Yahweh themselves: "How can you say, 'We are wise, for we have the law of the Lord,' when actually the lying pen of the scribes has handled it falsely? The wise will be put to shame; they will be dismayed and trapped [...] From the least to the greatest, all are greedy for gain; prophets and priests alike, all practice deceit" (Jeremiah 8:8-10). Jeremiah's views were shared by other Judahite prophets and in particular by Micah, who lived much earlier, at the end of the 8th century BCE. Micah likewise condemned the people's spiritual leaders, saying of them: "Her leaders judge for a bribe, her priests teach for a price, and her prophets tell fortunes for money" (Micah 3:11); "This is what the Lord says: 'As for the prophets who lead my people astray, they proclaim 'peace' if they have something to eat, but prepare to wage war against anyone who refuses to feed them" (Micah 3:5). These prophets viewed the troubles that befell Judah as the Lord's punishment for the sins of the country's leaders: "Therefore because of you, Zion will be plowed like a field, Jerusalem will become a heap of rubble, the temple hill a mound overgrown with thickets" (Micah 3:12).

Judah as the Only Hebrew Kingdom

The biblical sources constitute unambiguous evidence that there could have been no monotheism in the First Temple period. The exception is literally a handful of years during the reigns of kings Hezekiah and Josiah. Throughout all four centuries the inhabitants of the Southern Kingdom remained polytheists who combined loyalty to the cult of Yahweh with worship of other gods; for this reason they arrived in both Babylonian captivity and exile in Egypt as polytheists. The prophet Jeremiah, whom the Judahite nobility took by force to Egypt after the murder of Gedaliah, gives us incontrovertible proof of how far the Judahites were from true monotheism. Calling upon his fellow countrymen in Egypt to renounce the worship of pagan gods, he encountered a wall of indignation and rage: "We will not listen to the message you have spoken to us in the name of the Lord! We will certainly do everything we said we would: We will burn incense to the Queen of Heaven and will pour out drink offerings to her just as we and our ancestors, our kings and our officials did in the towns of Judah and in the streets of Jerusalem" (Jeremiah 44:16-17). There is archaeological evidence confirming that even after the destruction of Jerusalem in 586 BCE the Judahites remained polytheists. The letters found on the island of Elephantine in Egypt, which were written by Judahite military mercenaries in the 5th century BCE, mention not just Yahweh, but also other gods whom the authors worshipped.

During the existence of the Southern Kingdom, the internal development and policymaking were determined by the balance of power between two influential groups, the Davidides and the Aaronites. The Davidides originally represented the aristocracy of the tribe of Judah – or rather, part of it since the Kenazzites, the Judahite tribal nobility of Edomite origin, initially opposed them and supported the northern dynasty of King Saul. However, as the Hebrews assimilated with the Canaanites and the Amorites in Southern Palestine, the Davidides began expressing the interests of the wealthier and nobler part of these peoples too. The second group, the Aaronites, was initially a special clan of priests serving the principal God of the southern Hebrew tribes, Yahweh. The Aaronites were not part of the tribe of Levi, as the biblical sources state, but had closer links with the tribe of Judah, at least at the moment of the Exodus from Egypt. The narrative that there were bonds of kinship between the two spiritual leaders of the people, Moses and Aaron, and that the Aaronites and Levites were one and the same emerged at a later date in response to political motivations which required the unification of both the Hebrew tribes and their Yahwist priests. Following David's conquest of Jerusalem, the Yahwist priesthood was swelled by an influx of Jebusite priests, who mainly took up positions that were secondary to those of the Aaronites. It is extremely likely that these Jebusite priests made up the majority of those who were subsequently called the 'Levites' of the Southern Kingdom, whereas the true descendants of the tribe of Levi were mainly to be found among the northern tribes right up to the fall of the kingdom of Israel.

The Davidides and Aaronites maintained blood ties with one another throughout the entire history of the Southern Kingdom, but at the same time they had interests that were by no means identical. The Aaronites represented the tribal religion of the principal ethnos of the Southern Kingdom, i.e. the tribe of Judah, and therefore laid claim to primacy among the local religious cults, and sometimes to the right to represent the only faith of the peoples of Judah and even to play a part in coruling with the Davidides. For their part, the Judahite aristocracy, which included many descendants of the Canaanite and Amorite peoples, had close links with the local Canaanite cults of Baal, Asherah, and Moloch and with their numerous and influential priests, and so resisted any attempts made by the Aaronites to establish a monopoly in religion. It should not be forgotten that the Judahite tribal aristocracy had itself not been homogeneous since its return to southern Canaan; it had been joined by the tribal nobility of the Kenazzites and Maonites, who were Edomites, and also by the ruling class of the Kenites, who were a Midianite tribe.

The balance of power between the Davidides and the Aaronites was often violated, resulting in drastic changes that affected every field of Judah's policy-making. When the Aaronites had the upper hand, the throne of Judah was occupied by reformers such as kings Hezekiah and Josiah or power was exercised by the high priests of Yahweh themselves (Jehoiada, for instance). On the other hand, when their rivals were the stronger party, this brought to power idolatrous kings such as Jehoram or Ahaz and Manasseh, who looked to those members of the aristocracy and priests who were not worshippers of Yahweh. Sometimes the fighting in the corridors of power took such dramatic external forms that it led to the killing of kings and priests. This is precisely what happened during the rule of kings Joash, Amaziah, and Amon. A special case was the rule of Queen Athaliah, when the supporters of the Davidides were split between those in favor of an alliance with the Israelite dynasty of Omri and those who were against such an alliance and on the side of the Aaronites. The Yahwist priests were sufficiently powerful as a caste to prevent even the strongest and most successful Davidides from depriving them of a highly important prerogative – the right to manage religious worship. Evidence of this is provided by King Uzziah's unsuccessful attempt to take over the functions of the high priest.

During the existence of the Northern Kingdom the Aaronites usually resisted closer relations with Israel, seeing in this alliance a potential threat to their own interests. In all respects the Southern Kingdom was markedly inferior to its northern neighbor, so it could only hope to be junior partner in such an alliance and in this case the Aaronites would inevitably have seen a diminishment of their influence. In the north the traditional Canaanite cults were stronger, but, more importantly, the Aaronites were frightened by the prospect of having to compete with the priests of Bethel, the most popular temple in central Palestine. However, following the fall of the kingdom of Israel the Aaronites' attitude to the northerners changed fundamentally; the Aaronites began seeking closer relations with them (admittedly, only under the aegis of Judah).

In the final two decades before the fall of the Southern Kingdom a new force – this time, external – emerged, in addition to the Davidides and Aaronites, in domestic politics in Jerusalem. Egypt and the Neo-Babylonian empire not merely fought for influence over Judah, but also placed their own candidates on the Judahite throne. One of these protégés was Jehoiakim, who was appointed by the Egyptian pharaoh; another was Zedekiah, who was chosen by the King of Babylon. Interestingly, Assyria, upon which Judah had depended for a markedly longer time – an entire century – did not once intervene in matters of succession; at least, no biblical source mentions any such thing. Judging by the books of the prophets Jeremiah and Ezekiel, during the last years of Judah's existence there was a notable convergence of the interests of the two groups, the Davidides and Aaronites, and a corresponding decline in the friction between them; the main fighting, on the contrary, now took place within each of the two parties. The Davidides split into supporters of Zedekiah and Jehoiachin, the two living kings, one of whom was in Jerusalem and the other in captivity in Babylonia. As for the Aaronites, they too were prone to internal disagreements: a succession of prophets, including Jeremiah and Ezekiel, expressed dissatisfaction with the policy of reconciliation with the pagan cults. Judah's foreign policy was a bone of equally fierce contention within each of these groups. Although the majority of Davidides and Aaronites preferred to look to Egypt for guidance, there were also a large number of skeptics who doubted the military might of the Egyptians and preferred to remain loyal to the Neo-Babylonian empire.

There was a fresh clash of interests between the two groups when Gedaliah was appointed Babylonian governor in Judah. If the Yahwist priests and prophets who remained in Judah supported Gedaliah, the Davidides regarded him as a usurper of their power and entered into a conspiracy against him. Subsequently, the paths of the two groups diverged even more. The Babylonian and then the Persian rule over Judah left the Davidic dynasty with no part to play, while the Yahwist priests – the spiritual fathers of the people – found themselves in demand. However, the Davidides were superfluous to the requirements not just of the Babylonians and Persians, who did not trust them, but of the Aaronites as well. The latter preferred to have business with the satraps, who could be relied upon for protection but did not intervene in the religious affairs of the community, rather than with the Davidides, who were incapable of guaranteeing the country's safety and stability but laid claim to spiritual as well as supreme authority. Having lost their position of power, the descendants of David were now an impediment to the Yahwist priests, who had no hesitation in taking over their position in the life of the Judahite community. The Aaronites had never had felt the need for a monarch with his expensive court and absolute authority; since the times of judge Samuel they had accepted this form of government only with great reluctance and had always found it oppressive – regarding kings as their rivals, and sometimes, when the latter gave their support to pagan cults, as their enemies. The Davidic dynasty clearly had no choice but to merge with the Aaronite ruling class or leave Judah. It is this that explains the mystery of the Davidides' disappearance. It is only natural that the keepers of the tradition – the Aaronites – should cease even mentioning the descendants of David following the return from Babylonian exile.

Chapter 12

The Levites and Aaronites – Keepers of Tradition and Memory

The Origins and Destinies of Two Priestly Groups

The small Hebrew tribe of Levi found itself playing a special role in history. The Levites became priests, keepers of historical memory and of the religious tradition of their people; but most importantly, they were the creators of the Bible, a book which had a colossal influence on the spiritual development of civilized humanity. Not only did they preserve and disseminate the cult of Yahweh, but they were also the direct heirs of Moses and his idea of monotheism. The Levites became an important link between the northern and southern Hebrew tribes and their kingdoms, Israel and Judah. No other Hebrew tribe left such a vivid footprint both in their own history and the history of the world as the Levites.

Before the Exodus from Egypt, the Levites were an ordinary Hebrew tribe belonging to the southern tribal group of Jacob. This group also included the three closely related tribes of Reuben, Simeon, and Judah. Among the four southern tribes that composed the 'house of Jacob' the tribe of Levi did not stand out in any way. In accordance with the tribal hierarchy, the Levites were regarded as the third tribe in seniority after Reuben and Simeon. Levi was also the smallest tribe of all the tribes that constituted the 'house of Jacob'. The Levites were initially closest, among other tribes, to the tribe of Simeon. In the pre-Egyptian period these two tribes – Simeon and Levi – collaborated in beating up the people of Shechem, an act which incurred the disapproval of patriarch Jacob, the head of this entire group of tribes. The Levites' special role only began during the time of Moses, the leader and lawgiver who was one of their number. Moses was taken from this Hebrew tribe when still an infant and raised at the court of the Pharaoh. He received the best education possible at the time and was considered one of the most educated and well-accomplished people of his age. Fortunately for his tribe, Moses did not become a stranger to it, as the Egyptians had hoped, but devoted all his knowledge and strength to serving his own people. He began the lengthy process of writing down the oral narratives about the origin of the 'house of Jacob', its history in Canaan, and departure for Egypt; but, most importantly, he left us the idea of monotheism. It was Moses who turned the Levites into the keepers of this idea and of the memories and traditions of their own people; and it was he who inspired them to undertake the many centuries of work that was needed to produce the unique historical, religious, philosophical, and literary creation that is the Bible.

However, the Levites were not the only keepers of the religious tradition or composers and editors of the Bible. No less a part in creating this unprecedented piece of work was played by another group of Yahwist priests, the Aaronites. According to biblical tradition, the Aaronites were the descendants of Moses' brother Aaron; in other words, they were descended from the same Levites. But analysis of relations between these two groups suggests that they were actually of different origin. The biblical sources incontrovertibly testify that the Aaronites and Levites were separate and substantially different from one other. Both before and during the Egyptian period the Aaronites were priests to the entire 'house of Jacob'. Judging by the way that the Bible depicts Aaron, he was a key figure among the Hebrew tribes in Egypt. His influence on his people extended far beyond the boundaries of what was possible for any other tribal leader. Only a high priest could have held such power during enslavement in Egypt. Thus the success of Moses' mission would have been impossible without help from Aaron.

Having spent most of his life outside Egypt and far from his fellow Hebrews, Moses was forced to communicate with them through Aaron, whom they knew better and in whom they had greater trust. Moses' God, though, was very different from Aaron's god; the episode with the golden calf clearly demonstrates the gulf between Aaron's old, pagan Yahwism and the new, monotheistic Yahwism of Moses. However, Moses had only his own tribe to support him, while Aaron enjoyed the support of the majority of the 'house of Jacob'. It is significant that after the battle following the episode with the golden calf it was Moses who had to move his tent from the common camp, not Aaron. The fact that all the Levites supported Moses and did not split between him and Aaron is evidence that the latter was not actually a blood brother of Moses or a descendant from the tribe of Levi. Had Aaron belonged to the tribe of Levi, as tradition asserts, a split would have occurred within the tribe. Moreover, given that Moses spent a lengthy time staying among the Midianites, Aaron had incomparably greater opportunity to reinforce his influence among the Levites. But nothing of the sort happened. The Bible explicitly underlines that "…all the Levites rallied to [Moses]" (Exodus 32:26). Remarkably, it was Moses who communicated with God, and it was Moses who passed on the ten commandments from the Lord, but, this notwithstanding, it was Aaron alone who carried out the functions of high priest and directed religious worship.

There are just as many contradictions in the relations between the Aaronites and the Levites. The biblical text does not conceal the fact that Aaron and his sons were separate from the Levites and held a higher position. For them the Levites were merely helpers and not a constituent part of their caste. Only the

The Levites and Aaronites – Keepers of Tradition and Memory

Aaronites could direct religious services and be priests, while the Levites were obliged to serve them and carry out security and domestic functions (Numbers 3:5-10). How could this have been possible if Aaron and Moses were really brothers and identically related to the tribe of Levi? There is another aspect that remains unclear. According to the Bible, Aaron was only three years older than Moses, but for some reason did not share the fate of his younger brother, who was parted from his family at the cruel command of the pharaoh, when the latter demanded that all Hebrew boys be killed. Finally, one minor, but nevertheless important detail is that in Exodus the prophetess Miriam is mentioned merely as the sister of Aaron; there is no mention of her being directly related to Moses. Yet Moses should have been her brother too (Exodus 15:20).

It likewise seems strange that the sons of Moses did not merely not inherit his position as ruler, but were completely unknown, notwithstanding the fact that they were his children born not to a slave or servant or the Cushite concubine who appeared later in his life, but to his lawful wife Zipporah, the daughter of the leader and high priest of the Kenites, who had helped Moses on numerous occasions. All this went against the laws and traditions of the time and required rational explanation in the Bible. The biblical text, however, maintains complete silence on the fates of Moses' sons. Had they died, it is very unlikely that this would have been concealed by the Bible; on the contrary, the Bible have been bound to mention such an event – as it did in the case of the mysterious deaths of Aaron's two sons. If this is the case, then why was it the sons of Aaron who inherited Moses' extremely important priestly responsibilities rather than his own sons? After all, no other ruler in the ancient Near East acted in this way: we know of no case in which a pharaoh, king, or mere leader of a nomad tribe disinherited his own sons and made a mere nephew his heir. The most likely explanation is the special position occupied by the Aaronites: they were descended from the traditional priestly clan within the 'house of Jacob', and only they had the right to serve as high priests and to conduct worship of Yahweh. This is why Aaron's help was essential to Moses' mission. It was only thanks to the support of the high priest and his powerful clan that Moses, in spite of his lengthy absence in Egypt, was able to establish himself as the political leader of the Hebrew tribes in such a short period of time.

The seriousness of the tensions between the Aaronites and the Levites is shown by the rebellion led by Korah, when a number of Levites made a public stand against the primacy enjoyed by the Aaronites in worship of Yahweh. The fact that this rebellion took place is itself an important argument in favor of the thesis that the Aaronites and the Levites had different provenances. Had the Aaronites really derived from the Levites, there would have been no sense at all in Korah's rebellion – given that the mutinous Levites were protesting categorically against Aaron and his relatives having a monopoly over the right to hold religious services, but had nothing against Moses or his family. If Aaron really had been the brother of Moses, how are we to explain the different attitudes taken by the Levites towards the two of them, and how are we to understand their rage against Aaron's relatives, who would then have been their very own relatives at the same time? If, as the Bible states, Aaron was the brother of Moses, then he must also have been a cousin of Korah, the leader of the mutinous Levites (Exodus 6:16-21). Clearly, Aaron and Moses, like their children, were not brothers from the same tribe; this is why the Levites protested so strongly against the Aaronites' monopoly of religious services.

Moses' goal was not merely to free his people from enslavement in Egypt, but also to reform the tribal religion of the 'house of Jacob'. He succeeded in turning the initially pagan cult of the southern Hebrew tribes into a universal monotheistic religion. However, Aaron's clan of priests had difficulty in accepting the monotheistic reformation of their old cult, so Moses put his own tribe in the service of the new religion. Wittingly or unwittingly, he created yet another class of priests which was practically a rival to the traditional clan of Aaronite priests. In order to avoid conflicts with this powerful priestly clan, Moses reached an agreement with Aaron: there was to be a division of powers between the Aaronites and Levites, giving the latter secondary functions in the worship of Yahweh. Nevertheless, conflict between the two groups of priests could not be avoided, as we see only too clearly from both the episode with the golden calf and the rebellion led by Korah. It is extremely likely that the mysterious death of Aaron's two sons due to the fact that they "[...] offered unauthorized fire before the Lord, contrary to his command" (Leviticus 10:1) was actually the result of a clash between the Levites and Aaronites.

The two parties fought not just over who was to have a leading a role in the worship of Yahweh, but also over the character of this worship. With the help of the Levites, Moses consistently upheld monotheistic Yahwism, while Aaron and his clan periodically retreated to the old, pagan interpretation of their tribal cult. Moses' problem was that he could rely only on his own tribe, one of the smallest of the Hebrew tribes; this meant that his leadership was only possible with the support of the high priest and the leaders of the other tribes, and only during his own lifetime. It comes as no surprise, then, that Moses was unable to pass on his primacy to his own sons and that after his death supreme power was inherited by Joshua, the leader of the northern tribes, while authority in religion passed to Eleazar, the head of the priestly clan of the 'house of Jacob'. The tensions between the Levites and the Aaronites were exacerbated by a division in the camp of Moses. The two southern tribes, Simeon and Judah, refused to join the northern tribes who were already in Canaan, preferring to linger in the desert with their new allies, who were nomadic tribes of Midianite and Edomite origin. However, most of the tribes left with Moses and Eleazar, Aaron's son, to conquer central and northern Canaan. Furthermore, a division occurred between both priestly groups. The split was uneven: almost all of the Levites left with Moses, while only a few Aaronites followed the high priest Eleazar. Most of the Aaronites preferred to stay with Judah, to whom they were closer, on the southern border of Canaan. It was thus that the Levites and Aaronites divided among the northern and southern tribes.

Later on, during the period of the judges, the northern Levites managed to take revenge on the Aaronites. Taking advantage of the fact that the latter, after ending up among the northern tribes, had lost the influence which they had previously enjoyed among their own, southern tribes, the northern Levites took control of the worship of Yahweh into their own hands. We have good reason to suppose that Eli, the high priest from the religious center in Shiloh, was in fact a descendant of Moses, not Aaron. The clear predominance of the northern Levites during the period of the judges only exacerbated the tension between the two bodies of priests and led to their geographical and political demarcation. The Levites were the dominant presence in the territory of the northern tribes which subsequently became part of the kingdom of Israel, while the Aaronites prevailed in the lands of the two southern tribes that formed Judah.

During the United Monarchy, when the Levites and the Aaronites were putting together the initial version of the Pentateuch, the two groups, guided by the interests of their shared kingdom, created a unified version of the Hebrews' return from Egypt and the conquest of Canaan. This version included the experiences of both sides – Joshua's conquests in central and northern Canaan, on the one hand, and the 40 years of wandering in the deserts and Caleb's conquests in the south of the country, on the other. For this reason, the compilers of the Bible united the lines of Moses and Aaron, making them brothers from the tribe of Levi. Thus they managed formally to unite the Aaronites and the Levites, the Yahwists of the southern and northern tribes – in just the same way as the southern and northern tribes had previously united to form a single kingdom. However, true unification occurred only two centuries later, after the fall of the Northern Kingdom. It was only then that the two groups of priests, originally of different origins, became one; moreover, the Aaronites yet again assumed the dominant position, while the Levites found themselves in a secondary role. This step suited the interests of both the southern Aaronites and the northern Levites. The former became heirs to the northern dynasty of high priests, while the latter at long last acquired their own home and powerful patrons. As part of the union of these two priestly groups, there was a redistribution of priestly responsibilities at the Temple in Jerusalem: the southern Aaronites conceded a number of their secondary functions to the northern Levites.

Before the reign of David the main role in the history of Yahwism was played by the northern Levites, and not at all by the southern Aaronites, as was to be the case in the future. It was the Levites who took care of the most important sacred relic, the Ark of the Covenant, and it was they who organized and managed the Yahwist centers known to us from the Bible in Gilgal, Shechem,

Mizpah, Shiloh, and Nob. As for the southern Aaronites, they were compelled to wander the deserts around southern Canaan for several decades, together with the tribes of Judah and Simeon, but without the Ark of the Covenant, which at this time was accompanying, together with the northern Levites, Joshua's conquests in Canaan. After the southern tribes settled on the land, their Aaronites created Yahwist centers of their own; these, however, were undoubtedly inferior to northern Levite centers such as Shiloh.

The Levites – like the Aaronite priests – would not have divided among themselves had a split not occurred among the tribes that left Egypt with Moses. This division among the Levites, a tribe which was in any case small, had the consequence that they ceased to exist as an independent tribe. In both tribal groups (northern and southern) they constituted a class of priests responsible for organizing worship of Yahweh; in the north they played a leading role, while in the south their role was secondary. Each tribe that left Egypt with them committed themselves to sharing with them a part of their land and income. Least of all was contributed by the 'house of Joseph', which left Egypt two and a half centuries earlier than Moses and the Levites and did not feel obliged to them in any way. This assumption finds support in the Hebrew Bible: "The Levites received no share of the land [of Manasseh and Ephraim] but only towns to live in, with pasturelands for their flocks and herds" (Joshua 14:4).

The northern Levites retained their primacy among the Yahwists of the Israelite tribes until the time of the judge and prophet Samuel. During the latter's rule religious leadership passed from the northern Levites to the southern Aaronites. In this respect great significance attaches to the story of high priest Eli of Shiloh. There is no doubt that this story was created by the southern Aaronites in order to justify their taking over the leading role in the worship of Yahweh, which before belonged to the northern dynasty of priests. The episode with the 'man of God' who came to warn Eli about forthcoming punishment for the unworthy behavior of his sons was designed to legitimize the elevation of the southern Aaronites and to show that this was due not to the tribulations of human fate, but exclusively to the will of God: "I will raise up for myself a faithful priest, who will do according to what is in my heart and mind. I will firmly establish his priestly house, and they will minister before my anointed one always" (1 Samuel 2:35). Hinting at the unenviable position in which the northern Levites found themselves both during the reign of Solomon and following the fall of the Northern Kingdom, the Bible, not without sarcasm, tells us of the sad fate of the northern priestly dynasty: "Then everyone left in your family line will come and bow down before him [the high priest of southern Aaronites] for a piece of silver and a loaf of bread and plead, 'Appoint me to some priestly office so I can have food to eat'" (1 Samuel 2:36). The same is said in the Lord's words to Samuel when he was a boy helping the high priest Eli conduct religious services. Interestingly, the southern Aaronites were unable to blame Eli himself for anything else but conniving with his sons. Nevertheless, "the guilt of Eli's house will never be atoned for by sacrifice or offering" (1 Samuel 3:14). The strictness of this verdict is explained by the fact that otherwise the southern Aaronites would have had to return the primacy to Moses' direct heirs, the northern priestly dynasty. The sons of Samuel, one of the 'faithful' Aaronite priests mentioned in the 'man of God' prophecy, actually turned out to be no better than the sons of Eli, and yet for some reason Samuel's family escaped such severe punishment. There is another remarkable fact: the 'man of God' reminds us that from among all the Israelite tribes the Lord chose the house of the forefather of Eli to be his priests, but providently does not mention his name. A later rabbinical tradition adds the name of Aaron as Eli's forefather; the Bible, however, maintains an eloquent silence on this subject. This is further reason to suppose that the southern Aaronites only acquired supremacy over the northern Levites after the enthronement of the Davidic dynasty and that this was only retrospectively justified in the Old Testament.

In Samuel's vision it is said that the Lord is "[...] about to do something in Israel that will make the ears of everyone who hears about it tingle" (1 Samuel 3:11). This impressive 'something' was that the office of high priest was to be transferred from the northern Levites to the southern Aaronites, the Ark of the Covenant was to be moved to Jerusalem, and the religious center at Shiloh was to suffer a drop in status. A factor in the transfer of primacy from the northern Levites to the southern Aaronites was the political and military situation at the time. The defeat of the army of the northern tribes in the battle of Ebenezer, the seizure of the Ark of the Covenant by the Philistines, and the probable destruction of the religious center in Shiloh by the latter all led to the high priesthood passing to a southern Aaronite, Samuel, while the northern Levites had no choice but to settle temporarily in Nob and remain forever without Yahwism's most important relic. Subsequently, the Philistines returned the Ark of the Covenant not to its rightful owners, the Levites of Shiloh, but to the Aaronites of the southern tribes; this, as the Philistines had hoped, sparked clashes between the two priestly groups and tensions between the Hebrew tribes. It might have been expected that the strengthening of Saul, the northern king, would restore the Levites to their former position; history, however, had other ideas. Saul ordered the Ark of the Covenant to be moved from Kiriath-Jearim, which was situated in the territory of the southern tribe of Judah, again not to the Levites, but to his own residence in Gibeah, in the region occupied by his own tribe of Benjamin. Offended by this, the Levites helped David during his flight from Saul, thus sealing the latter's displeasure with them. As a punishment for their helping David, Saul executed 85 Levite priests and destroyed their center in Nob. Abiathar, the surviving son of the head of the northern priestly dynasty, had no other option but to join David. Thus was formed an unexpected and purely temporary alliance between the northern Levites and the claimant to the throne from among the southern tribes.

There was another reason for Saul's discontent with the priestly dynasty of the northern Levites: Saul's family and clan were closely connected with the cult of Baal. Some members of his family – for instance, his son Ishbaal (Ish-bosheth) had names that incorporated the name of the pagan god. As his power grew, Saul increasingly had no need for the support of the Yahwists and more and more favored the cult of Baal, whose priests provided him with every possible kind of support. His main rival, David, was known as a faithful Yahwist and could count on help from both the southern Aaronites and the northern Levites. Aware of this, Saul did not trust the Levites and suspected them of sympathizing with the Yahwist David, although the latter was descended from the southern tribes.

The first Israelite king, Saul, who represented the northern tribes, agreed to unite with the southern tribes on terms that were very similar to the agreement between Moses and Aaron. Saul was to possess supreme authority, while Samuel, ruler of the southerners, was to be the religious leader. This alliance impinged upon the interests of the northern Levites and forced them to cede the limelight to the southern Aaronites. King David was more careful and farsighted than Saul. Taking into account the fact that during his conflict with Saul the northern priestly dynasty had demonstrated loyalty to him, he endeavored not to violate their interests and to maintain the fragile balance between the northern Levites, the southern Aaronites, and the Jebusite priesthood of Jerusalem. David remembered the northern Levites' resistance to his decision to move the Ark of the Covenant to Jerusalem, and, in order to avoid further exacerbating relations with them, he even renounced the idea of building the Temple of Jerusalem. However, Solomon, David's son, did not feel in any way indebted to the northern Levites; moreover, the Levites' support for David's other son, Adonijah, Solomon's main rival, badly strained relations between them and the future king. Accordingly, as soon as Solomon managed to overcome his rival, he lost no time in sending Abiathar, the leader of the northern priestly dynasty, into exile, back to his home city of Anathoth; Abiathar's powers and authority were given to the southern Aaronites who had supported Solomon from the very beginning.

Subsequently, King Solomon, unlike his father, failed to take into consideration the interests of the northern Levites, infringing them on repeated occasions during his reign. The construction of the Temple in Jerusalem and the transfer of exclusive rights to control religious worship at the Temple to the southern Aaronites banished the Levites to the shadows once and for all. Unsurprisingly, the northern Levites lent their full support to Jeroboam, the leader of the tribe of Ephraim, in his attempt to terminate the alliance with the southern tribes and to break free from the control of the Davidic dynasty. Like all the northern tribes, the Levites felt deprived and disadvantaged in Solomon's United Monarchy, where supreme power belonged to the Davidides and religious authority to the Aaronites. The biblical account of prophet Ahijah of Shiloh promising Jeroboam control of the ten northern tribes is circumstantial evidence of the absolute support provided by the northern Levites.

However, the dissolution of the union with the southern tribes and the formation of the Northern Kingdom failed to live up to the Levites' hopes. The main religious centers in Bethel and Dan, which had been intended to rival the Temple in Jerusalem, were never transferred to them. The temple in Dan remained in the hands of the southern Levite priestly dynasty, which had joined forces with the tribe of Dan in the 12th century BCE, when the Danites had been compelled to leave the south of the country and move to its far north, to upper Galilee, under pressure from the Philistines. Another, more important, temple in Bethel was operated by local priests. It is probable that the god initially worshipped there was El, whose cult in time merged with the old pagan form of Yahwism that existed before Moses' monotheistic revolution. The golden calves from Bethel and Dan were possibly similar to the calf sculpted by Aaron in the desert during Moses' lengthy absence. But Bethel had a special significance: it was one of the first and oldest religious centers in Canaan and was highly regarded by the Hebrew tribes during the pre-Egyptian period. At Bethel Abraham had often prayed and offered sacrifices; and it was there that his grandson Jacob saw the famous dream of the ladder leading to the sky. It is not accidental that Jacob said of Bethel: "Surely the Lord is in this place" (Genesis 28:16). The Bible tells that Jacob prayed there both before departing to visit his relatives in Haran and after his return. After Joshua's conquests Bethel – then known by its old name of Luz – fell into the hands of the tribe of Ephraim, and the priests from this tribe were in charge of conducting religious services there. The southern part of Bethel belonged to the tribe of Benjamin, and Benjaminite priests also took part in holding the religious services. The Levites initially made no claim to own this religious center; at any rate, neither during Joshua's time, nor during the period of the judges did they make such demands; it was clearly not the cult of Yahweh that prevailed there.

The situation changed when the United Monarchy fell apart and an acute need arose for a worthy alternative to the Temple of Jerusalem. The best known and most respected religious center on the territory of the northern tribes was that in Bethel; Jeroboam decided to make it a Yahwist temple by proclaiming it the Temple of the God who had led the Israelites out of Egypt. At this point there occurred two problems to which a resolution could not be found right up until the fall of the Northern Kingdom. Having proclaimed Bethel a Yahwist center that offered an alternative to the Temple of Jerusalem, Jeroboam was supposed to hand it over to the Levites, who represented the cult of Yahweh in the lands of the northern tribes. The latter status had originally been given the

Levites in the agreement between Moses and Joshua and had been observed both during the period of the judges and during the United Monarchy. But Jeroboam could not, and did not want to, enter into conflict with his own tribe, which was the leader among the tribes which had broken away. The possession of a respected religious center such as Bethel gave the tribe of Ephraim substantial political and economic benefits; moreover, the Levites, who represented the 'house of Jacob', were regarded as foreigners by the 'house of Joseph' and were perceived as rivals by the local priests. The Levites saw Jeroboam's refusal to give them Bethel as an act of betrayal by someone they had supported at great risk to themselves when confronting the Davidides and Aaronites. Another problem was the golden calves in Bethel and Dan: these were too closely associated with the notorious calf of Aaron. According to the old pre-monotheistic views of Yahwism that Aaron presented, the young bull was an embodiment of the cult of Yahweh; however, an identical symbol was used in Canaan in the worship of El and Baal. Clearly, a new syncretic cult, a combination of features of the cults of Yahweh, El and Baal, had come into existence in Bethel. Their merging was facilitated by their use of the same symbols – the symbol of the calf, for instance – and of similar epithets for god. Thus Bethel had become an attractive location for supporters of both El and Yahweh on the one hand and Baal on the other.

By setting up the calf in Bethel and refusing to hand over this religious center to the Levites Jeroboam inflicted two blows on them: he committed a profanation of Yahwism and created serious competition to the Levites' own religious centers. Furthermore, Jeroboam broke the historical agreement between Moses and Joshua regarding the division of powers, in accordance with which the Levites were to receive all religious authority within the union of Israelite tribes. This was the origin of the notorious 'sins of Jeroboam'– sins for which all the Israelite kings were blamed (admittedly, without much success).

The book of Chronicles notes an interesting detail: during the reign of Judahite King Rehoboam many Levites from the Northern Kingdom "[...] abandoned their pasturelands and property and came to Judah and Jerusalem, because Jeroboam and his sons had rejected them as priests of the Lord, when he appointed his own priests for the high places and for the goat and calf idols he had made" (2 Chronicles 11:14-15). It is likely that the Levites who came to the Southern Kingdom had previously served at those very 'high places' and conducted services before the same 'goat' and 'calf' idols, and that the real problem was not in where and to whom the services had been carried out, but in the question of by whom. Jeroboam quite rightly regarded the Levites as potential allies of the Yahwists from the Southern Kingdom and preferred to rely on the priests from the northern tribes. The fact that some of the Levites departed for Judah only proves their conflict with the new king and is a sign that the influence of Yahwism in the kingdom of Israel had waned, especially taking into account the fact that the northern tribes, particularly the 'house of Joseph', were historically closer to the Canaanite gods than to Yahweh.

Stone altar from Megiddo. Such horned altars were commonly used in Israelite and Judahite kingdoms.

Unlike in later times, the priestly castes of the Levites and Aaronites were not groups of kinsmen that were closed to outsiders. On the contrary, right up until the time of the Second Temple the Levites and Aaronites were periodically refreshed by influxes of priests from clans belonging to other peoples of Canaan. Indirect evidence of this is to be found in the Bible. The book of Exodus, for instance, in giving the entire family tree of the Levites and Aaronites following the departure from Egypt, names only three families – those of Gershon, Kohath, and Merari. On the other hand, the much later book of Chronicles, talking about the times of King Hezekiah of Judah, adds another four Levite clans to those given above: Elizaphan, Asaph, Heman, and Jeduthun. The latter four had nowhere been mentioned prior to this; at least, we may say that during the period of the Exodus from Egypt nothing was known about them. Even if we try to trace one of them, the clan of Elizaphan, to Uziel, who came from the clan of Kohath, that still leaves three Levite clans that were previously unknown. However, if the new clans were derived from old ones, the Bible would probably have mentioned this.

What peoples could the new priestly clans who joined the Levites and Aaronites have come from, and at what historical stage did this happen? We may suppose that the new priests did not come from among hostile peoples who had been subdued by force, but only from those ethnoses who were historical allies of the Hebrews and whose religion could have been similar to early Yahwism. Above all, such were the Kenites and the Kenazzites - or 'shasu Yahweh' – who joined the southern tribes of Judah and Simeon of their own free will even before the conquest of Canaan. The other likely candidates were the Jebusites – the traditional allies of the southern tribes, who naturally merged with the Judahites following King David's conquest of Jerusalem. It cannot be ruled out that Zadok, one of David's two high priests, had previously been the Jebusites' principal priest – especially since the Jebusites' religion was very similar, if not identical, to the new faith of the patriarch Abraham.

Finally, it should not be ignored that the priests of the southern Hivites, stalwart allies of the tribe of Judah, also joined the Levites. However, it was not just that priests from other peoples joined the ranks of the Yahwist priests, but that the latter themselves gradually assimilated with the Canaanite population around them. Confirmation of this is provided by Ezra, the lawgiver and evidently the principal and last editor of the Bible. In his book Ezra tells us that noble people had complained to him that "The people of Israel, including the priests and the Levites, have not kept themselves separate from the neighboring peoples with their detestable practices, like those of the Canaanites, Hittites, Perizzites, Jebusites, Ammonites, Moabites, Egyptians and Amorites. They have taken some of their daughters as wives for themselves and their sons, and have mingled the holy race with the peoples around them. And the leaders and officials have led the way in this unfaithfulness" (Ezra 9:1-2). Ezra goes on to adduce a long list of priests who have taken wives from neighboring peoples for themselves and their sons. If such a thing happened in the 5th century BCE, when Yahwism became a truly monotheistic religion, then we may imagine how considerable the mixing of Levites and Aaronites had been several centuries previously.

Yahwism and Canaanite Cults

We cannot but be struck by the curious fact that Elijah and Elisha, the best-known prophets of the Northern Kingdom, said not a word about the calves of Bethel and Dan. And yet it was these calves for which the keepers of the tradition blamed Jeroboam and all the kings of Israel without exception. How could it have happened that this clear instance of idolatry went unnoticed by these uncompromising crusaders against pagan cults – especially given that both prophets, as the Bible witnesses, visited Bethel on repeated occasions?

Evidently, the solution to this mystery has to do both with the specific nature of the age in which Elijah and Elisha lived and with their origin. We know that during their lives the main problem was not the calves of Bethel or Dan, but the cult of Baal. In order to resist this cult and its priests, the Yahwists of the northern tribes needed allies – and they found them in the influential priests of Bethel, whose interests had also been badly affected by the spread of the cult of Baal, especially under the kings of the dynasty of Omri. At that time the most dangerous enemy of the cult of Yahweh had been not the pre-monotheistic Yahwist cult of Bethel, but Baal and the priests of Baal. To a certain extent this is confirmed by Hosea, a prophet from the Northern Kingdom, who in his criticism of idolatry likewise highlighted the cult of Baal and the latter's priests and prophets, and only secondarily condemned the sins of Bethel, calling it Beth-Aven ("the house of deceit"). The problem of Bethel was especially a matter of concern for the northern dynasty of high priests who had, since the dissolution of the United Monarchy, claimed the right to manage this religious center. This dynasty comprised the keepers of the tradition in the Northern Kingdom who composed the biblical texts; this explains why their point of view was so well expressed in these texts. The prophet Hosea likewise belonged to this, the most literate and best educated caste among the northern Levites. As for Elijah and Elisha, the accounts given of their lives give us reason to think that they were probably vulgar prophets who lacked any kind of connection with the Levite establishment. Possibly they were not Levites at all by blood; after all, not every Yahwist was a Levite by origin. It was not for nothing that Jeroboam appointed priests of non-Levite provenance to conduct worship of Yahweh. Moreover, neither Tishbe nor Abel-meholah, the native cities of Elijah and Elisha, were named as places ceded to the Levites following the conquest of Canaan. It is likely that both these prophets were little interested in the claims made by the northern Levite dynasty of priests to the temples in Bethel and Dan. In a situation where the cult of Baal was everywhere advancing it is unlikely that they took part in the debate conducted by the Levite establishment concerning the admissibility of calves in Yahwist religious centers. Pagan symbolism was so intrinsic to the consciousness of that time that even a monotheistic religion could not fail to share certain of its elements. People of that age could not make do without visible symbols of the presence of God; the calves of Bethel and Dan were a concession to the religious views of that time.

Confirmation of the above is to be found in the cult of Nehushtan, which is first mentioned following the Exodus from Egypt. According to the book of Numbers, the people of Moses, who were then in the desert to the south of Edom, experienced great suffering when they were bitten by poisonous snakes, and then "Moses made a bronze snake and put it up on a pole. Then when anyone was bitten by a snake and looked at the bronze snake, they lived" (Numbers 21:9). The cult of Nehushtan (the Hebrew word 'nahash' means 'snake') existed quite happily until the religious reforms of the Judahite king Hezekiah, who was forced to forbid it as unquestionable idolatry. Possibly, the cult of Nehushtan came into existence even earlier, before Moses, and the fact that Moses himself accepted it was evidence of the inevitability of concessions to people's pagan views. If Moses himself could permit the depiction of a bronze snake, then Jeroboam and the priests of Bethel considered themselves entitled to set up golden calves, which were symbols not just of the pre-monotheistic Yahweh, but also of El and Baal.

Interestingly, the dwelling-place of the God of Israel was not the Promised Land – not Canaan – but the lands which lay to the south and south-west of it. The Bible gives several areas where the dwelling-place of the God of Israel should be sought. The triumphal Song of Deborah, for instance, names the following two places where the Lord lives: Mount Seir in Edom and Mount Sinai in the south of the Sinai Peninsula: "When you, Lord, went out from Seir, when you marched from the land of Edom, the earth shook, the heavens poured, the clouds poured down water. The mountains quaked before the Lord, the One of Sinai, before the Lord, the God of Israel" (Judges 5:4-5).

This evidence is all the more valuable given that the Song of Deborah is one of the oldest parts of the Bible, dating to the 12th century BCE. Another, just as ancient, biblical text, the Song of Moses, which offers up praise to the Lord following the successful crossing of the sea over dry land, states quite clearly that, after leaving Egypt, Moses led his people into the native dwelling place of Yahweh, to his holy place in the mountains: "In your unfailing love you will lead the people you have redeemed. In your strength you will guide them to your holy dwelling [...] You will bring them in and plant them on the mountain of your inheritance—the place, O Lord, you made for your dwelling, the sanctuary, O Lord, your hands established" (Exodus 15:13, 17).

As is well known, Moses led his people to Mount Sinai on the southern tip of the Sinai Peninsula. At least, the Bible on repeated occasions names this mountain and associates it with the Lord. For instance: "Mount Sinai was covered with smoke, because the Lord descended on it in fire" (Exodus 19:18). Or, slightly differently: "The Lord descended to the top of Mount Sinai and called Moses to the top of the mountain. So Moses went up" (Exodus 19:20). The latter words leave no doubt that the dwelling place of the Lord was Mount Sinai. However, the passage in the Bible which talks of Moses' mission of saving his people gives an utterly different name for the Lord's mountain, calling it Mount Horeb: "Now Moses was tending the flock of Jethro his father-in-law, the priest of Midian, and he led the flock to the far side of the wilderness and came to Horeb, the mountain of God" (Exodus 3:1). In confirmation that this is a reference to the holy place of the Lord, the biblical text says: "Do not come any closer,' God said. 'Take off your sandals, for the place where you are standing is holy ground" (Exodus 3:5). Further evidence that Horeb rather than Sinai is the name of the Lord's mountain is provided by another episode, this time involving not Moses but the prophet Elijah. Reduced to despair by the persecution inflicted by the idolaters, Elijah goes to the Lord's dwelling place in search of help: " [...] he traveled forty days and forty nights until he reached Horeb, the mountain of God" (1 Kings 19:8). Was Horeb a second name for Sinai or did it refer to an altogether different mountain? We do not know. However, if God's dwelling place could have been Seir in Edom and simultaneously Sinai, why could it not also have included a third mountain – Horeb in Midian? It is extremely likely that all three of these mountains were part of God's dwelling place and were considered holy places.

The Judahite prophet Habakkuk, who lived at the end of the 7th and beginning of the 6th centuries BCE, left his own indication of where the One God appeared from: "God came from Teman, the Holy One from Mount Paran" (Habakkuk 3:3). Teman was the name given to the area of Edom which was home to the eponymous tribe of Edom, and the desert of Paran was situated between central Sinai and southern Judah. There is further evidence in the Bible, even if of a fairly general nature, regarding the dwelling place of the God of Israel. In the description of the wars between Ahab, King of Israel, and Ben-Hadad, King of Damascus, there is an interesting episode in which it is said that "Meanwhile, the officials of the king of Aram advised him, 'Their gods are gods of the hills. That is why they were too strong for us. But if we fight them on the plains, surely we will be stronger than they [...] the Lord is a god of the hills and not a god of the valleys" (1 Kings 20:23,28).

Thus the dwelling place of the Lord of Israel was initially situated in the mountains – or, to be more precise, in a mountainous, semi-desert region in the triangle between south-eastern Canaan (Edom), north-western Arabia (Midian), and southern Sinai. But why were Yahweh's principal sacred places – Seir, Sinai, and Horeb – not situated where his people lived? Does this mean that the 'house of Jacob' adopted the God of the peoples who lived in these places – the Edomites, Midianites, and Kenites? Or had the southern Hebrew tribes themselves spent a long time living nomadically in this region? On the other hand, if Mount Seir in Edom was part of Yahweh's dwelling place, why did the Edomites not remain adherents of this cult, but, on the contrary, began worshipping the pagan god Qaus? The resulting picture is strange and difficult to explain: the 'house of Jacob', which had almost never lived in the dwelling place of Yahweh, with the exception of when the two southern tribes wandered the desert for forty years, became a permanent follower of the Yahwist religion, while the Edomites and the Midianites, who were constant inhabitants of the Lord's dwelling place, either never worshipped the Lord or, with the passing of time, exchanged worship of Yahweh for another cult. In order to understand why this happened, we need to take into account two very important circumstances: the close blood relations between the entire group of tribes whom the patriarch Abraham brought to Canaan and the special role played by Moses in forming monotheistic Yahwism.

In spite of the fact that the Bible talks of Abraham as the patriarch of a family clan, in reality he was the head of a large association of tribes which later split up into different peoples with whom we are familiar – the southern Hebrew tribes, the Edomites, Moabites, Ammonites, Ishmaelites, Amalekites, Midianites, Kenazzites, and Kenites. These peoples began to split from one another following the death of Abraham, when they started mixing with the local inhabitants of southern Canaan, north-western Arabia, and Sinai. All these nomadic Amorite peoples shared the same provenance, spoke the same language, worshipped the same gods, and occupied the same mountainous triangle of Seir-Horeb-Sinai, which was regarded as the dwelling place of Yahweh. The cult of Yahweh was probably one of the religions which they had in common – and it is not surprising that the Egyptians called some of these nomads 'shasu Yahweh'. It would hardly be a mistake to say that in the pre-Egyptian period all these peoples constituted one large ethnos of nomadic Amorites, within which there were only divisions into different tribes. Not only under Abraham, but during the rule of Isaac too there was not yet any division into the 'house of Jacob' and the 'house of Esau' – into Hebrews and Edomites. All these peoples at that time were one ethnos and consequently Mount Seir in Edom was their shared holy place.

The main reason why the southern Hebrew tribes acquired an identity distinct from this large ethnos of nomads and semi-nomads was that they spent four centuries in Egypt. Their stay in the Nile Delta fundamentally changed their lifestyle, turning them into a settled people and splitting the 'house of Jacob' from their nomadic brothers in Sinai, Midian, and southern Canaan; but on the other hand, the southern Hebrew tribes' stay in Egypt brought them closer to the Hyksos 'house of Joseph', which derived from an altogether different association of tribes of nomadic Amorites. Why could the descendants of Ishmael or Midian not have the same gods as the descendants of Isaac if their founding fathers were considered to be sons of the same patriarch, Abraham? The same goes for the descendants of Jacob and Esau – especially since both the latter were born to the same mother (Rebecca) as well as father (Isaac). The division of the tribes brought into Canaan by Abraham and the formation of particular peoples led to a situation in which the territory of the 'house of Jacob' lay outside the dwelling place of this house's God. Nevertheless, these peoples remained for a long time very close to one another in all respects. It is not surprising that the tribes of Moses which had come out of Egypt were joined in the desert by the Kenites, Kenazzites, and Jerahmeelites, who subsequently merged with the tribe of Judah. This alliance was made possible not just by their common ethnic and linguistic roots, but also by their shared religion. There can be no doubt that the cult of Yahweh was known to them even before the 'house of Jacob's stay in Egypt. Possibly, it had been brought into southern Canaan and Midian from their distant original homeland, the north-west of Mesopotamia, where they had lived likewise on highland plateaus or in mountainous districts. If this was the case, then another question arises: why was it only the Hebrew tribes who remained faithful to this cult and eventually made Yahweh the only God in their pantheon?

The special role played by the cult of Yahweh in the fate of the Hebrew tribes was only made possible by Moses. The latter's idea of a single, all-mighty, and everlasting God was embodied in the cult of Yahweh, turning the latter into a monotheistic religion – a religion which was thus unique for its time and which fundamentally changed the destiny first of Moses' tribe, the Levites, and then of all the Hebrews. The old, pre-monotheistic form of this religion had differed little from other pagan faiths. Moses not only radically changed its religious aspects, but also imparted to it a distinctive social and legal character which was unprecedented in religions of that time. The related nomadic peoples, who knew and professed cult of Yahweh, had nothing of this kind. So it is not surprising that in time the pagan form of Yahwism gave way to other pagan faiths, while monotheistic Yahwism established itself more strongly only among the Hebrew tribes.

The Judaism of the First Temple period was very different not just from the Judaism of today, but also from the Judaism of the Second Temple. Initially, Judaism was not a monotheistic faith; it became one only through the intervention of Moses. However, in spite of the categorical prohibition against worshipping other gods, a prohibition which was central to the commandments handed down on Sinai, Judaism of that time coexisted peacefully with other pagan cults. In the light of this characteristic of early Judaism, it would be better to call it 'Yahwism' – since its adherents, in giving preference to the cult of Yahweh, did not renounce worship of other divinities. Right up until the destruction of the First Temple in 586 BCE, the Hebrew tribes, not to mention the Canaanite and Amorite population, remained polytheists who worshipped both Yahweh and other gods (such as Baal and Asherah). It was only during two short periods – the reigns of the Judahite kings Hezekiah and Josiah – that the southern tribes returned fully to the monotheism of Moses. Yet these periods were the exception rather than the rule.

The state of affairs in the territory occupied by the northern tribes was still more complicated. Here there was an incomparably larger percentage of Canaanites and Amorites who were historically in no way associated with the cult of Yahweh. But the main problem was that the 'house of Joseph' – the leader of the northern tribes – traditionally preferred worship of El, Baal, and Asherah, the principal Canaanite divinities of that time. This was hardly surprising given that the cult of Yahweh was not widespread among the Amorite tribal group to which the 'house of Joseph' belonged. That was the main difference between the 'house of Joseph' and the 'house of Jacob'. The cult of Yahweh was initially more common among the Midianites, Ishmaelites, and Kenites, who came from the group of tribes descended from Abraham, than among the 'house of Joseph'. In this circumstance lay the objective weakness of Yahwism in the areas occupied by the northern tribes. Moreover, the 'house of Joseph' returned to Canaan from Egypt two and a half centuries earlier than the 'house of Jacob' and had thus become much more assimilated with the Canaanites than the southern tribes. The 'house of Joseph' adopted Yahwism following its alliance with the tribes of Moses and as a consequence of the agreement with Moses himself. The Levites and the Aaronites were, together with their cult of Yahweh, alien to the 'house of Joseph' and were perceived as an inevitable tribute and concession to their allies, without whom Joshua's conquests would have been impossible.

The situation in those tribes who had joined Moses during the Exodus from Egypt was only slightly better. The tribes of Issachar, Zebulun, Gad, and Asher belonged to the same Amorite tribal group as the 'house of Joseph' or were at least closer to the latter than to the peoples descended from Abraham. Admittedly, during the time that they spent with Moses in the desert they became followers of Yahweh; moreover, the union with the Levites, the majority of whom joined them following the split, obliged them to give preference to the cult of Yahweh. The only exception was the southern tribe of Reuben, which joined the northerners due to its conflict with the tribe of Judah over power in the 'house of Jacob'. The Reubenites, like the Levites themselves, were Yahwists, but this did not prevent them worshipping other gods at the same time. Worst of all was the situation with the Indo-European (Achaean?) tribe of Dan, for whom the cult of Yahweh was absolutely alien. But the Danites desperately needed a military alliance with the Hebrew tribes, without whose support they would have been unable to settle in Canaan. Furthermore, their forced state of homelessness and memory of living together in Egypt bound them still closer to the Hebrews. Initially, the alliance with the southern and then with the northern tribes had a merely military significance for them, and the Levites, as the Bible bears witness, had no place of their own among this tribe. But subsequently, as it became more assimilated with the Israelites, the tribe of Dan acquired its own Levites and even a Yahwist temple, and from the point of view of religion became no less Yahwist than the other northern tribes. In this respect the tribe of Dan is a very typical example of how a tribe that was not just not Israelite, but not even Semitic could start worshipping Yahweh under the influence of the Levites.

Given that Yahweh initially had no place in the pantheon of the northern tribes, the Levites were the main factor in this cult's expansion among them. Perhaps the only advantage of the northerners was the fact that amid them were the majority of the Levites and the latter's principal religious centers, and, above all, Shiloh. The role of the Levites in the area occupied by the northern tribes was considerably more important during the time of the judges than in the years of the United Monarchy and the Northern Kingdom. The period of the judges was when the entire history of Yahwism as we know it from the Bible occurred in the territory inhabited by the northern tribes, through the medium of the northern Levites. But Yahwism in the north differed from Yahwism in the south, although the Levites and the Aaronites were adherents of one and the same cult. Among the northern tribes Yahwism existed in the form of so-called Elohism, whereby the cult of Yahweh assimilated the cult of the supreme Canaanite god El, and made use of this cult's terminology and images.

The first time that the Bible links the names of El and Yahweh comes when Moses is given his mission to save his people from slavery in Egypt. It is at this point that it is revealed that Yahweh, is simultaneously the God of the patriarchs Abraham, Isaac, and Jacob, who knew him as 'El'. Thus the keepers of the tradition laid the foundation for a religious union between the houses of Jacob and Joseph, between the southern and northern tribes; without this foundation it is unlikely that their union would have survived for long. The identification of El with Yahweh made one cult of two, just as the identification of the name of Israel with Jacob unified the family trees of the two groups of Amorite tribes known as the Habiru.

In Canaan, his new motherland, the patriarch Abraham broke with the old gods from Sumer and adopted one of the varieties of the cult of El, which at this age prevailed in Canaan. The cult of El was recognized not just by Abraham, but by all the semi-nomadic Amorites – the Habiru who had arrived with him in Palestine. At the same time each group of Amorite nomads had its own tribal religion which they had brought with them from their former homeland in north-west Mesopotamia. For instance, the God worshipped by the 'house of Jacob' was Yahweh. For historical reasons, the northern tribes found themselves under the incommensurably greater religious and cultural influence of their Canaanite surroundings than their southern kinsmen. The 'house of Joseph' lived longer in Canaan and spent less time in Egypt than the 'house of Jacob'. Whereas the former's stay in Egypt was approximately 250 years, the latter were there for considerably longer – for 430 years; thus by the time that the southern tribes departed from Egypt the influence of Canaanite El had dissipated to a large extent in favor of these tribes' own tribal cult of Yahweh. In the 'house of Jacob' the cult of El suffered the same fate as the Sumerian pagan gods brought by Abraham into Canaan. The 'house of Joseph', where this cult was much more common, found itself in an entirely different situation. The term 'El' as a name for God was so generally accepted in the Northern Kingdom that even the Levites from Shiloh were forced to use one of its variants, 'Elohim'. However, the best memorial to the cult of El remained people's names, including the name of the legendary forefather of the northern tribes, Israel. When the biblical texts were first recorded, the keepers of the tradition – the Levites and Aaronites – combined Yahwism, their tribal cult, with the Elohism of the northern tribes and interpreted the Elohism of Abraham, Isaac, and Jacob as identical with Yahwism.

There is convincing evidence that these cults merged with one another. Above all, in the Old Testament there is a complete lack not just of any kind of criticism, but also of any mention, of the supreme Canaanite god El – something which in itself is very strange. In the light of the severe condemnation of the cults of the Canaanite gods Baal, Asherah, Astarte, and Moloch, Kemosh of the Moabites, Milcom of the Ammonites, Qaus of the Edomites, and Hadad of the Arameans (an incarnation of Baal), this 'forgetting' of El, the supreme god of Canaan, Phoenicia, and Syria, and the father of the gods can hardly have been incidental; on the contrary, it is a fact which is eloquent in itself. There is a simple explanation: the biblical text absolutely unambiguously identifies El with Yahweh. As a rule, the name 'El' is used in those parts of the Old Testament which were created by the Levites in the Northern Kingdom, while that of Yahweh predominates in texts written by the Aaronites in the Southern Kingdom. It is not incidental that biblical scholars call the first source 'the Elohist' (E) and the second 'the Yahwist' (J). A number of authors – for instance, F.M. Cross and M. Smith – note that epithets used of the Canaanite god El have parallels in descriptions of Yahweh. Studying Canaanite epic from Ugarit, Cross has come to believe that there is no significant difference between the Canaanite and Amorite El, on the one hand, and the Israelite Yahweh, on the other, and that these are merely different names for one and the same God. According to Cross, the description of the Lord in the Pentateuch and the poetic images of his might and power are a synthesis of descriptions of the god-creator El and the god-warrior Baal (Haddu).

Chief Canaanite deity El, the father of the gods, 13th century BCE limestone statue excavated at Ugarit.

The merging of the cults of Yahweh and El had both a poetic aspect and a religious one. From the point of view of poetry, it can only be admitted that the descriptions of the Lord in the Bible have parallels with Canaanite El and are inspired by poetic images and epithets from Canaanite/Amorite mythology and epic. This is quite natural and logical, given that the Hebrews were an integral part of ancient Canaan and direct heirs of indigenous peoples of this country. In terms of religion, on the other hand, the situation was more complicated. In Moses' monotheistic faith Yahweh was the One God, while El, even if he was the supreme divinity, was merely only one of a number of Canaanite gods. But the name 'Yahweh' was alien to the northern tribes, while 'El' embodied for them the God the Father and creator of the world who stood at the head of the Canaanite pantheon. The need to unite the Hebrew tribes compelled the Levites to call Yahweh 'El' and to declare that this was merely a second name for the same God. There were good reasons for such an affirmation: the God to whom Abraham had prayed in Canaan was probably the same El – or, to be more precise, 'El a-Elyon', the All-mighty Lord, the principal God of Abraham's ally, Melchizedek, the king and high priest of Jerusalem. It was a common phenomenon for a god to have a second name. The Arameans, for instance, knew the god whom the Canaanites and Amorites called 'Baal' as 'Had' or 'Haddu' (that is also the origin of the names of the kings of Damascus, the Ben-Hadads). The most difficult part of this problem was the need to transform a pagan cult into a monotheistic one. However, a similar task confronted the Aaronites in the south. The latter spent centuries trying to make the cult of Yahweh completely monotheistic, in the spirit of Moses, and found themselves up against the same kind of polytheism among the general population as the Levites in the north. Thus the northern tribes' lack of readiness to accept the monotheistic essence of El/Yahweh could not have been an impediment to these cults merging completely.

Moses' uncompromising monotheism, which was many centuries in advance of the development of the rest of the ancient world, could not be completely understood or accepted by either the northern or the southern tribes. It was only as society became more spiritually developed that Moses' legacy acquired increasing influence both on the Yahwists in the south and on the Elohists in the north and their attitude to other religious cults changed. Previously, they had been happy to co-exist with the pagan divinities, but with the passing of time they became openly intolerant of them. In the Southern Kingdom this process went further than in the Northern Kingdom, and during the rules of Hezekiah and Josiah the Aaronites and Levites tried to put Moses' monotheistic idea into practice. In the Northern Kingdom the Levites did not possess such an influence on the kings, but there too during the time of Elijah and Elisha they tried to resist and even destroy the pagan cults. Of course, the main body of the population in both the south and the north was not yet ready to accept monotheism, so Yahwism in Judah and Elohism in Israel were monotheistic only as a trend of religious thought among the more advanced Levites and Aaronites. In general, Moses' monotheism, which had arisen at the beginning of the 12th century BCE based on the cult of Yahweh, proved unable to subordinate to itself the religious life of the Southern Kingdom, still less of the Northern Kingdom. But it continued to exist inside both groups of priests – the Levites and the Aaronites – and then, in approximately the 5th century BCE, led to the creation of the first society in the ancient world to be based on a genuine monotheistic faith.

There can be no doubt that right up until the 5th century BCE it was the accepted practice among the Hebrew population – not to mention among the Canaanites and Amorites – to worship several gods at once (Yahweh, Baal, and Asherah, for instance). The biblical text has left us memories of the campaign waged by the prophet Elijah against polytheism: "Elijah went before the people and said, 'How long will you waver between two opinions? If the Lord is God, follow him; but if Baal is God, follow him.' But the people said nothing" (1 Kings 18:21).

In spite of the competition between the different priesthoods, for the most part all these religious cults co-existed peacefully given that polytheism was the accepted custom in the ancient world. Nevertheless, when dramatic events occurred in the life of a people, its leaders were not only capable of declaring a particular cult the principal religion, but also of demanding the destruction of rival faiths. This is what happened during the Exodus from Egypt, when Moses made the cult of Yahweh the only possible faith for his fellow tribesmen. And this is what Gideon the judge tried to return to when, after destroying the altars to Baal, he fought for liberation from the Midianites. The exact opposite – a kind of 'counter-revolution' – was attempted by the dynasty of Omri, especially during the rule of Ahab, when the cult of Baal not only became the principal religion, but also, thanks to the efforts of Queen Jezebel, almost drove out the cult of Yahweh from the Northern Kingdom. For his part, the prophet Elijah fought not only for the restoration of the Yahwists, but also for the destruction of his opponents, the priests of Baal. Elijah's follower and pupil, the prophet Elisha, and Jehonadab, the head of the Yahwist sect of the Rechabites, enthusiastically supported Jehu's military coup and enlisted his help in destroying the priests of Baal in Samaria. However, during ordinary times of peace, all these cults co-existed fairly harmoniously, as is evidenced by the fact that both rulers and common people in these Hebrew kingdoms usually worshipped several gods at the same time, i.e. were polytheists.

There were objective difficulties not just in accepting the monotheistic nature of the cult of Yahweh, but also in understanding the invisible and intangible character of this One God. The priests – the Levites and Aaronites – often themselves found the legacy of Moses hard to comprehend. Traces of these troubles are clearly to be seen in the description of the One God. One and the same book in the Bible, the Exodus, preserves two approaches. In accordance with the first approach, which reflects previous views on the matter, God was visible, like the pagan gods: "Moses and Aaron, Nadab and Abihu, and the seventy elders of Israel went up and saw the God of Israel. Under his feet was something like a pavement made of sapphire, clear as the sky itself. But God did not raise his hand against these leaders of the Israelites; they saw God, and they ate and drank" (Exodus 24:9-11). On the contrary, the other point of view, which is closer in spirit to that of Moses, warns: "You cannot see my face, for no one may see me and live" (Exodus 33:20). The same message is to be seen in the episode with the prophet Elijah, who, prior to coming before God on Mount Horeb, is forced to cover his face with a cloak (1 Kings 19:13). There were also serious differences in the way that the Lord's external manifestations were understood. Initially, it was thought that the presence of the Lord necessarily expressed itself in unusual natural phenomena or events and that it was in these that God revealed himself to people. For instance, the scene of God's descending upon Mount Sinai is described as follows: "On the morning of the third day there was thunder and lightning, with a thick cloud over the mountain, and a very loud trumpet blast. Everyone in the camp trembled [...] Mount Sinai was covered with smoke, because the Lord descended on it in fire. The smoke billowed up from it like smoke from a furnace, the whole mountain trembled violently [...]" (Exodus 19:16,18). The description of the prophet Elijah's meeting with the Lord puts the emphasis in an entirely different place: "The Lord said, 'Go out and stand on the mountain in the presence of the Lord, for the Lord is about to pass by.' Then a great and powerful wind tore the mountains apart and shattered the rocks before the Lord, but the Lord was not in the wind. After the wind there was an earthquake, but the Lord was not in the earthquake. After the earthquake came a fire, but the Lord was not in the fire. And after the fire came a gentle whisper" (1 Kings 19:11,12).

Only the cult of Baal was considered a serious rival to that of Yahweh. El, god the father and creator of the world, the supreme god in the Canaanite pantheon, soon merged with the cult of Yahweh and became merely another name for the One God. This assimilation was facilitated by the fact that the word 'el' or 'il' meant 'god' in all the Semitic languages. The epithets for El – such as 'El-Elyon' ('The Most High God') or 'El-Shaddai' ('The Almighty God') – automatically came to be used of Yahweh as well. However, the descriptions of god in all West Semitic languages were very similar, so we have to exercise caution in considering the question of the cross-application of particular epithets. In short, the keepers of the tradition, who came from the southern tribes, from the very beginning legitimized the northern tribes' El as the same Yahweh, only with a different and more universal name – 'el', meaning 'god'.

From the clay tablets found in Ugarit we know that the Canaanite pantheon comprised numerous gods; the children of the supreme god El and his spouse Asherah on their own numbered at least 70 divinities. But the Old Testament mentions only a very few of them – namely, those who constituted real competition for the cult of Yahweh and were a source of irritation to the keepers of the

The Levites and Aaronites – Keepers of Tradition and Memory 301

tradition. Usually, Baal is the only pagan god who is mentioned; he is followed by the goddesses of fertility and love, Asherah and Astarte. However, the latter were less common, attracting mainly the female part of the population, and so did not constitute serious competition for the cult of Yahweh. Moreover, among ordinary people, especially in the Northern Kingdom, it was commonly thought that Asherah was the wife of Yahweh (El) and so worship of her was regarded as a natural continuation of the cult of Yahweh. In Kuntillet Adjrud, in the Negev, an interesting inscription has been found: "Yahweh from Samaria and his Asherah". The Israeli archaeologist Ze'ev Meshel, who has carried out excavations on this site, has dated the inscription to the end of the 9th or beginning of the 8th century BCE. Thus centuries after Moses' monotheistic revolution, the Canaanite mother divinity found a niche for herself beside the God of Israel. As for Astarte, Canaanite mythology viewed her as the daughter of Asherah and El. This Canaanite goddess also assumed her place under the cult of Yahweh and for a long time coexisted with the latter in perfect harmony.

Bronze statuette of Canaanite god Baal from Megiddo, around 1200 BCE.

The situation with Baal was completely different. Baal not only did not make any kind of fit with Yahweh, but constituted a direct challenge to him. According to the ancient Canaanite texts from Ugarit, Baal, the god of thunder, had no connection at all with El; his father was considered to be Dagan, the god of grain or a storm god, who was the principal divinity of the Philistines. However, the cult of Baal was widespread among the population of Canaan and became even more popular from the middle of the second millennium BCE onwards. In time Baal even became more revered than El; at any rate, none of the gods in the Canaanite pantheon could compare with him in popularity. He became the principal enemy of the Yahwists and Elohists and the Bible abounds with mentions of the lengthy and dogged fight against the worship of this pagan god. Baal was an integral part of Hebrew history right up to the beginning of the period of the Second Temple and perhaps for longer. The Bible is evidence of the persistent influence which Baal had on the lives of the Hebrew tribes from the moment that they returned to Canaan from Egypt. Even before the death of Moses, when the Hebrews were in the region of Moab, "Israel yoked themselves to the Baal of Peor. And the Lord's anger burned against them" (Numbers 25:3). The Israelite judge Gideon battled with Baal, but unsuccessfully, as it turned out: "No sooner had Gideon died than the Israelites again prostituted themselves to the Baals. They set up Baal-Berith as their god" (Judges 8:33). The cult of Baal was the principal cult under Gideon's son Abimelech, who was loaned money "from the house of Baal-Berith" (Judges 9:4, 46). Following the death of the Israelite judge Jair "[the Israelites] served the Baals and the Ashtoreths" (Judges 10:6). Samuel, the last of the great judges, likewise called upon the Israelites to banish their Baals and Astartes (1 Kings 7:3), but evidently with no great success given that the house of King Saul of Israel himself was so closely bound up with Baal that this divinity's name was incorporated in the names of his children and grandchildren. According to the book of Chronicles, the real name of Saul's youngest son was not Ishbosheth, but Ishbaal, and his grandson's real name was not Mephibosheth, but Mephibaal. The cult of Baal became even more firmly established following the division of the United Monarchy, when the northern tribes gained independence from the rule of the Davidic dynasty and the Temple in Jerusalem. Baal's position was strongest in the land of the 'house of Joseph', which had joined this cult long before the return of the other Hebrew tribes from Egypt. The 'house of Joseph' not surprisingly supported the dynasty of Omri, which made the cult of Baal the principal cult in the Northern Kingdom. The kings from the Yahwist dynasty of Jehu tried to limit the influence of Baal and his priests, but even a century after the dynasty's founder had killed the priests of Baal in Samaria, the prophet Hosea disappointedly noted that "[Ephraim] became guilty of Baal worship and died" (Hosea 13:1). It is logical to suppose that even following the fall of Samaria and the removal of part of its population to Assyria, worship of Baal in the lands of the former Northern

The Levites and Aaronites – Keepers of Tradition and Memory

Kingdom did not cease. The fact that at the end of the 7th century BCE the Judahite king Josiah destroyed the sacrificial altars for the pagan gods there only reinforces this supposition. Thus, regardless of the Levites' opposition, Baal was just as much a god of the northern tribes as Yahweh/El. Furthermore, Baal's popularity grew to such an extent that some of the population started to view Asherah as the spouse of Baal and not El, although, according to the Canaanite myths from Ugarit, Baal's spouse was considered to be Anath, the goddess of love and war, one of the daughters of the supreme god El. But it is possible that Canaanite mythology had its own regional particularities and that the religious views of central Palestine did not necessarily coincide with the versions known to us from northern Syria, where ancient Ugarit was situated.

A representation of the god Baal on a relief from Ugarit (Ras Shamra).

In mentioning altars used in sacrifices to Baal, the Bible very often talks of the idol trees which were to be found near these altars. But these trees were symbols of Asherah. For instance, the judge Gideon, after destroying the altar to Baal, at the same time chopped down the idol tree which was situated nearby (Judges 6:28, 30). It was under this kind of tree – which is often translated as 'terebinth' (Hebrew: 'elah') – that Joshua placed the stone as a sign of his covenant with the people. This terebinth tree stood "near the holy place for the Lord", which for some reason the Bible does not name. Joshua called upon his people to "throw away the foreign gods that are among you and yield your hearts to the Lord, the God of Israel" (Joshua 24:23-26). What God did the leader of the 'house of Joseph' and the head of the northern tribes have in mind? Probably El, who was later identified with Yahweh. But at the time many of his fellow tribesmen, especially from the 'house of Joseph', would have been perfectly entitled to assume that he was talking about Baal, whose name in translation from all the West Semitic languages meant 'lord' and who was regarded as an absolutely Israelite god. Subsequently, following the victory of Yahweh/El over Baal, many epithets of the defeated divinity, including the name 'lord', passed to the victor as 'war trophies'.

For the sake of fairness, it has to be admitted that even in times – for instance, during the reigns of Ahab and Jezebel – that were highly favorable for the cult of Baal, Baal was unable to squeeze out his rival, Yahweh/El. Followers of Baal, including King Ahab himself, were compelled to accept the fact that a substantial part of the population remained Yahwists and that the latter included the most organized and strongest group of priests, the northern Levites. This is confirmed by the biblical text which tells of Ahab's unexpected repentance following Elijah's terrible prophecy about him: "When Ahab heard these words, he tore his clothes, put on sackcloth and fasted. He lay in sackcloth and went around meekly. Then the word of the Lord came to Elijah the Tishbite: 'Have you noticed how Ahab has humbled himself before me? Because he has humbled himself, I will not bring this disaster in his day, but I will bring it on his house in the days of his son" (1 Kings 21:27-29).

The fall of the kingdom of Israel inflicted irremediable damage on the northern Levites. Many of them, including their most literate and cultured members, fled to Judah, where they were compelled to join the local Aaronites as their junior partners. Others remained in the lands of the northern tribes, but, having lost their own religious centers and organizational unity, in time merged with other Elohist groups. The abrupt weakening of the Levites in the territory of the former kingdom of Israel led to a deepening of the religious differences between the northerners and southerners, and especially between Judah and Samaria. To no small extent, this was facilitated by migrants brought by the Assyrians from Mesopotamia and Syria. Subsequently, the Judahites' refusal to acknowledge the Samaritans as heirs of the 'house of Joseph' led to a political and religious split between them and resulted in the Samaritans' becoming an independent sect.

Epilogue

The Emergence of Judean People

The fall of the Northern and then of the Southern kingdoms did not interrupt two important processes – the unswerving evolution of Yahwism towards a truly monotheistic religion and the gradual formation of a single ethnic community in Palestine based on the Hebrew tribes. Paradoxically, the destruction of the Temple of Jerusalem in 586 BCE and the Babylonian exile did not put a stop to, but accelerated the transformation of Yahwism into the Judaism that is familiar to us. The fact that the Judahite elite spent a period of time living in captivity severely weakened the influence of the old Canaanite cults in Judah and strengthened Yahwist monotheism. After the Babylonian exile, the latent fighting between Aaronites and Levites ceased and both these groups of keepers of the tradition became part of a single priestly caste, in which the former were responsible for supervising worship and the latter acted as their assistants.

Palestine's ethnic composition was subject to change to no less an extent. The plundering incursions made by the Assyrians and, a century later, by the Babylonians led to the displacement of large parts of the country's population, and this facilitated the subsequent formation of a single people. The autochthonous peoples and peoples with origins outside Canaan, whether Semitic or non-Semitic, who had lived in pre-Israelite Canaan, had not been destroyed or driven out, but had merged in their entirety with the Hebrew tribes. In time a new Palestinian super-ethnos, given the ethnonym 'Judeans,' emerged and inherited the history and traditions of the 'house of Jacob'. However, in terms of ethnicity and culture, this super-ethnos had more in common with the Canaanite and Amorite peoples of Palestine than with the Hebrews, given that initially the Hebrew tribes had been the clear minority in the population of Canaan. The Judeans were an amalgam of all the peoples of ancient Palestine who are familiar to us – the Canaanites, Amorites, Jebusites, Hivites, Perizzites, Hittites, Girgashites, Rephaim, Kenazzites, Kenites, Hurrians, Indo-Aryans (Maryannu) and, finally, the Hebrew tribes themselves, which consisted of three different groups. Later, following the fall of both Hebrew kingdoms, the Judeans merged with the Edomites and likewise with some of the Moabites and Ammonites. The process of assimilation and Judaization also involved the Philistines who lived in the border cities of western Shephelah. It was thus that a new ethnos grew and consolidated – the Judeans, in whose veins flowed the blood of all the ancient peoples of Palestine, but who considered themselves to be descendants of only one of these peoples, the 'house of Jacob'. The only people not included in this ethnos were the Samaritans, who constituted a substantial part of the 'house of Joseph'. Their repeated attempts to join the Judeans were rejected by the leaders of the Judean community out of fear that the Samaritans, who considered themselves heirs of the 'house of Joseph', would lay claim to equal rights in worship and leadership. The reason given for this rejection was that the inhabitants of Samaria had intermarried with people from Mesopotamia and Syria, although the Judeans themselves were the best example of the assimilation of Hebrew tribes with the Canaanite-Amorite population of Palestine.

The enmity between the Judeans and Samaritans was not accidental; it reflected the historical rivalry between the 'house of Jacob' and the 'house of Joseph' for leadership of the Hebrew tribes and for the right to unify Canaan under their authority. This endless conflict over hegemony was rooted in the different histories and genealogy of the two groups of tribes. It had begun back in the pre-Egyptian period and continued even after the fall of the kingdoms of Israel and Judah. The 'house of Jacob' dominated in the southern half of Palestine and the 'house of Joseph' in the northern. Each of these houses was intent upon unity, but only under its own leadership. These two centers of power could unite voluntarily only at moments when they faced a common danger, as happened during the period of Philistine expansion. During times of peace, however, they were unable to share power in a common state, as was confirmed when the United Monarchy fell apart. These were the real reasons for the conflict between the Judeans and the Samaritans. Historically, it turned out that hegemony in Palestine passed to the 'house of Jacob' and that most descendants of the northern tribes, known previously as the Israelites, together with the remnants of the Canaanite-Amorite population, became a constituent part of the Judean people. A catalyst of the growth of the new super-ethnos was Judaism, the only monotheistic religion in the ancient world, coupled with an energetic policy of proselytizing. After absorbing the peoples of ancient Canaan, the 'house of Jacob' became the legitimate successor to these peoples' historical and cultural past. However, the 'house of Joseph' was not swallowed up by the Judeans, and the direct descendants of the 'house of Joseph', the Samaritans, after spending many centuries outside the main route of Jewish history, were able to preserve their distinctive character.

Selected Bibliography

Aharoni, Y. Nothing Early and Nothing Late. Re-writing Israel's Conquest. *Biblical Archaeologist* 39: 55-76.

Albright W.F., *The Biblical Period from Abraham to Ezra*, 1963.

Barns G.W., *The Ashmolean Ostracon of "Sinuhe"*, London, 1952.

Bar-Yosef, O., 'Prehistoric Palestine' in: *The Oxford Encyclopedia of Archaeology in the Near East*, ed. E.M. Meyers, 4.207-12, New York: Oxford University Press, 1997.

Ben-Tor D., 'The Historical Implications of Middle Kingdom Scarabs found in Palestine bearing Private Names and Titles of Officials' in *BASOR* 294 (1994), 7-22.

Ben-Tor, A. (ed.), *The Archaeology of Ancient Israel*. New Haven, 1992.

Bietak M., *Avaris: The Capital of the Hyksos*, London, 1996.

Boling, R.G. *Judges*. New York, 1975

Bourriau J., "The Second Intermediate Period," in *The Oxford History of Ancient Egypt*, ed. Shaw I., New York: Oxford University Press, 2000, pp.185-217.

Bright J., *A History of Israel*, 4th edition, New York: Oxford University Press, 2001.

Brinkman J.A., *A Political History of Post-Kassite Babylonia, 1158-722 BC* (1968).

Campbell E.F. Jr. 'A Land Divided' in: The *Oxford History of the Biblical World*, ed. M.D. Coogan. Oxford University Press, New York, 2001, p.237.

Clayton P. A., *Chronicle of the Pharaohs. The Reign-By-Reign Record of the Rulers and Dynasties of Ancient Egypt*, New York: Thames & Hudson, 1994.

Coogan M.D. (ed.), *The Oxford History of the Biblical World*, New York, 2001.

Coogan, M. D., ed. and trans. *Stories from Ancient Canaan*, Philadelphia: Westminster, 1978.

Cross, F. M., *Cananite Myth and Hebrew Epic: Essays in the History of the Religion of Israel*, Cambridge, Mass: Harvard University Press, 1973.

Dever W. G. "Archaeology and the Israelite 'Conquest'." *In Anchor Bible Dictionary*, ed. Freedman D.N., 3.545-58. New York: Doubleday, 1992.

Dever W.G., *Who were the early Israelites and where did they come from?*, Wm. B. Eerdmans Publishing Co., Cambridge, 2003.

Diakonov, I.M, 'Starovavilonskiy period v Dvurechye' in: *Istoriya Drevnego Vostoka*, ed. I.M. Diakonov, Moscow: Glavnaya redaktsiya vostochnoy literatury, 1983.

Dothan T., *The Philistines and Their Material Culture*. New Haven: Yale University Press, 1982.

Dothan, T., and Dothan M., *Peoples of the Sea*. New York: Macmillan, 1992.

Eichler, B. L, 'Nuzi and the Bible: A Retrospective' in: *Dumu-e-dub-ba-a: Studies in Honor of Ake W. Sjoberg*, ed. H. Behrens, D. Loding, and M. T. Roth, pp. 107-19, Philadelphia: University Museum, 1989.

Finkelstein I, Mazar A. and Schmidt B.B., *The Quest for the Historical Israel. Debating Archaeology and the History of Early Israel.* Society of Biblical Literature: Atlanta, 2007.

Finkelstein I. and Silberman N.A., *The Bible Unearthed: Archaeology's New Vision of Ancient Israel and the Origin of its Sacred Texts*, New York: Free Press, 2001.

Finkelstein, I. and Naaman, N. (editors). *From Nomadism to Monarchy: Archaeological and Historical Aspects of Early Israel.* Jerusalem, 1994.

Finkelstein, I. *The Archaeology of the Israelite Settlement.* Jerusalem: Israel Exploration Society, 1988.

Freedman D.N. and Graf D.F., eds., *Palestine in Transition*, Sheffield, 1983.

Frerichs, E. S., and Lesko L.H., eds. *Exodus: The Egyptian Evidence.* Winona Lake, Ind.:Eisenbrauns, 1997.

Friedman R.E., *Who Wrote the Bible?*, New York: HarperCollins Publishers, 1997.

Gernot W., *The Hurrians*, 1989.

Gitin, S., Mazar, A. and Stern, E. *Mediterranean Peoples in Transition: Thirteenth To Early Tenth Centuries BCE.* Jerusalem, 1998.

Giveon R., *The Impact of Egypt on Canaan*, Gottingen, 1978.

Gottwald N.K., *The Tribes of Yahweh: A Sociology of the Religion of Liberated Israel 1250-1050 B.C.E.* Maryknoll, N.Y.: Orbis, 1979.

Grabbe L.L., *Ancient Israel.* New York: T & T Clark, 2007.

Greenberg M., *The Hab/piru*, New Haven, Conn., 1955.

Gurney O.R, *The Hittites*, revised edition, New York: Penguin, 1990.

Halpern, B. "Erasing History: The Minimalist Assault on Ancient Israel." *Bible Review* 11/6, 1995.

Hayes W.C., *A Papyrus of the Late Middle Kingdom in the Brooklyn Museum*, Brooklyn, 1955.

Hazel M.G., 'Israel in the Merneptah Stela', *BASOR* 296 (1994), pp. 45-61.

Helck W., *Die Beziehungen Agyptens zur Vorderasien*, Wiesbaden, 1972.

Hoffmeier, J.K. *Israel in Egypt: The Evidence for the Authenticity of the Exodus Tradition.* New York: Oxford University Press, 1997.

Isserlin B.S. J., *The Israelites.* Minneapolis: Fortress Press, 2001.

Josephus Flavius, *Against Apion*, Book 1, Section 73 (P., 1912).

Kenyon K. M., *Archaeology in the Holy Land*, 4th ed, 1985.

Killebrew, A.E., *Biblical Peoples and Ethnicity.* Atlanta: Society of Biblical Literature, 2005.

King, Philip J. *Amos, Hosea, Micah-An Archaeological Commentary.* Philadelphia: Westminster, 1988.

Klengel, H., *Syria: 3000 to 300 BC: A Handbook of Political History*, Berlin: Akademie, 1992.

Krauss R., *Das Ende der Amarna-Zeit* (Hildesheim, 1976).

Kuhne C., *Die Chronologie der internazionalen Correspondenz von El-Amarna* Neu-Kirchen-Vluyn, 1973.

Kuhrt A., *The Ancient Near East c. 3000-330 BC*, 2 vols, London: Rutledge, 1995.

Selected Bibliography

Lemche N.P., *Die Vorgeschichte Israels. Von den Anfangen bis zum Ausgang des 13. Jahrhunderts v. Chr.*, Stuttgart, 1996.

Leonard, A., Jr, 'Archaeological Sources for the History of Palestine: The Late Bronze Age', *Biblical Archaeologist* 52, 1989, 4-39.

Lipinski, E. *The Arameans: Their Ancient History, Culture, Religion*. Leuven, 2000.

Lloyd S., *The Archaeology of Mesopotamia: from the Old Stone to the Persian Conquest*, 1984.

Loretz O., *Habiru-Hebraer: Eine sozial-ling. Studie*, Berlin, 1984.

Machinist, P. "Outsiders or Insiders: The Biblical View of Emergent Israel and Its Contexts." In The Other in Jewish Thought and History: Consructions of Jewish Culture and identity, eds. L. J. Silberstein and R. L. Cohn, 35-60. New York: New York University Press, 1994.

Manassa C., *The Great Karnak Inscription of Merneptah: Grand Strategy in the 13th Century B.C.*, Yale Egyptological Studies 5, New Haven: Yale Egyptological Seminar, 2003.

Manetho, *Aegyptiaca*, frag. 42, 1.75-79.2.

Mazar A., *Archaeology of the Land of the Bible, 10,000-586 BCE*, New York: Doubleday, 1992, p. 38.

McGovern P., *The Foreign Relations of the 'Hyksos'. A neutron activation study of Middle Bronze Age pottery from the Eastern Mediterranean*, Oxford, 2000.

Metzger, B.M., and Coogan M.D., eds, *The Oxford Companion to the Bible*, New York: Oxford University Press, 1993.

Miller, J. Maxwell, and John H. Hayes. *A History of Ancient Israel and Judah*. Philadelphia: Westminster, 2006.

Moran W.L., *The Amarna Letters*, Baltimore: Johns Hopkins University Press, 1992.

Murnane W., *Texts from the Amarna Period in Egypt*, Atlanta, 1995.

Na'aman N., 'Habiru and Hebrews: The Transfer of a Social Term to the Literary Sphere', *JNES* 45, No. 4 (1986), pp. 271-88.

Na'aman, N. "The 'Conquest of Canaan' in the Book of Joshua and in History." In *From Nomadism to Monarchy: Archaeological and Historical Aspects of Early Israel*, Jerusalem, 1994. ed. I. Finkelstein and N. Na'aman, 218-81. Washington, D.C.: Biblical Archaeology Society, 1994.

Nelson, R.D. *Joshua: A Commentary*. Louisville, 1997.

Nicholson, E. W. *Exodus and Sinai in History and Tradition* (Oxford: Blackwell), 1973.

Oren E., ed., *The Sea Peoples and Their World: A Reassessment*. Philadelphia: University of Pennsylvania, 2000.

Oren E.D. (ed.), *The Hyksos: New Historical and Archaeological Perspectives*, Philadelphia, 1997.

Orni, E., and Ephrat E., *Geography of Israel*. 4th ed., Jerusalem: Israel Universities Press, 1980.

Parrot A., *Abraham and His Times*, 1968.

Pitard, Wayne T. *Ancient Damascus: A Historical Study of the Syrian City-State from Earliest Times until Its Fall to the Assyrians in 732 B.C.E.* Winona Lake, Ind.: Eisenbrauns, 1987.

Postgate N., *The First Empires*, 1977.

Potts, D.T, *Mesopotamian Civilization: The Material Foundations*, Ithaca, NY: Cornell University Press, 1997.
Pritchard J.B., ed., *Ancient Near Eastern Texts Relating to the Old Testament*, Princeton: Princeton University Press, 1969.
Provan I., Long V.P., and Longman T. III, *A Biblical History of Israel*, Louisville, Kentucky: Westminster John Knox Press, 2003.
Quirke S., *The Administration of Egypt in the Late Middle Kingdom*, New Malden, 1990.
Rainey A.F., "Israel in Merenptah's Inscription and Reliefs", *IEJ* 5, pp.57-75.
Rainey, A. F. (ed.) *Egypt, Israel, Sinai: Archaeological and Historical Relationships in the Biblical Period.* Tel Aviv: Tel-Aviv University, 1987.
Redford D.B., *Egypt, Canaan and Israel in Ancient Times*, Princeton: Princeton University Press, 1993.
Roaf M., *Cultural Atlas of Mesopotamia and the Ancient Near East*, 1990.
Rogerson John, *Chronicle of the Old Testament King*, Thames and Hudson, 1999.
Ryholt K., *The Political Situation in Egypt during the Second Intermediate Period*, Copenhagen, 1997.
Sandars, N.K., *The Sea Peoples: Warriors of the Ancient Mediterranean 1250-1150 BC*. Rev.ed. New York: Thames and Hudson, 1985.
Sarna, N.M., *Exploring Exodus*, New York: Schocken Books, 1996.
Shanks H., ed., *Ancient Israel: From Abraham to the Roman Destruction of the Temple*. 2nd rev. ed. Washington: Biblical Archaeology Society, 1999.
Shaw Ian (ed), *The Oxford History of Ancient Egypt* (New York/Oxford), 2000.
Singer, I., 'A Concise History of Amurru', appendix in Sh. Izre'el, *Amurru Akkadian: A Linguistic Study*, 2, pp. 135-94, Harvard Semitic Studies, 41, Atlanta: Scholars Press, 1991.
Smith H.S. and Smith A., 'A Reconsideration of the Kamose Texts', *ZAS* 103 (1976), 48-76.
Smith M.S., *The Early History of God. Yahweh and the Other Deities in Ancient Israel*. 2nd ed. Dearborn, Michigan: Dove Booksellers, 2002.
Snell, D.C., *Life in the Ancient Near East, 3100-332 BCE*, New Haven, Conn: Yale University Press, 1997.
Stager L.E., 'Forging an Identity: The Emergence of Ancient Israel' in *The Oxford History of the Biblical World*, ed. D. Coogan. Oxford University Press: New York, 2001, pp.100-102.
Stern Ephraim (ed.), *The New Encyclopedia of Archaeological Excavations in the Holy Land* 4 Vols. (New York: Simon and Shuster), 1993.
Stiebing, W. H., *Out of the Desert? Archaeology and the Exodus/Conquest Narratives*, Buffalo, New York: Prometheus, 1989.
The Book of Jubilees or the Little Genesis, trans. R.H. Charles and G.H. Box, Kessinger Publishing, LLC, 2006.
Vaux R. de, *Ancient Israel: Its Life and Institutions*, 2nd ed., 1973.

Selected Bibliography

Wiener M.C.and Allen J., 'Separate Lives: the Ahmose Tempest Stela and the Theban eruption', *JNES* 57/1 (1998), 1-28.

Yurco, F. J. "3,200-Year-Old Picture of Israelites Found in Egypt." *Biblical Archaeology Review* 16, no. 5 (September-October 1990): 20-38. idem, 'Merenptah's Canaanite Campaign and Israel's Origins', in *Exodus: The Egyptian Evidence*, pp. 27-55.

Index

A'amu, Egyptian name of Amorites, 21, 23
Aaron, brother of Moses, 36, 38, 44-47, 67, 72, 134, 203, 273, 278-81, 283, 285-86
Aaronites, clan of priests, 3, 11, 37, 42-43, 45-48, 62, 67, 72-73, 84, 87, 98-102, 107, 112-14, 121, 125, 129, 134-36, 140-41, 182-83, 190-91, 194-95, 198-213, 216, 226-36, 242-43, 247-48, 251, 259-61, 265, 273-88, 294-300, 304
Abdon, judge, 77
Abel-mehola, birthplace of prophet Elisha, 289
Abiathar, high priest, 102, 107, 109, 111-13, 135, 283-84
Abijah (Abijam), king of Judah, 186-87, 189-90, 193-94, 212
Abiram, one of the chieftains of tribe Reuben, 45
Abishai, brother of Joab, 103, 107
Abner, military chief of king Saul, 95-97
Abraham, patriarch, 2, 5-15, 17, 22-25, 30, 37, 39, 50-54, 61, 85, 93, 97, 121, 129, 137, 178, 192, 269-71, 285, 288, 292-96, 298
Absalom, son of David, 102, 106-10, 120, 125
Achaean(s), 54, 79, 104, 106, 138, 268, 294
Achish, king of Gath, 91, 94
Adad, ruler of Edomites, 115, 127
Adad-nirari III, king of Assyria, 160
Adonijah, son of David, 111-13, 284
Adoraim, city of, 186
Adullam, town of, 59, 186

Ahab, king of Israel, 117, 143-50, 152-57, 160-61, 174, 191, 194-97, 213, 227, 291, 299, 304
Ahab, false prophet, 248-49
Ahaz, king of Judah, 168, 209-13, 215, 217, 224, 272, 274
Ahaziah, king of Israel, 148, 150, 193
Ahaziah, king of Judah, 153-54, 196-98, 201, 204
Ahijah, prophet, 100, 136, 285
Ahimelech, high priest, 207
Ahinoam, wife of David, 135
Ahio, son of Abinadab, responsible for Arc of Covenant, 101
Ahmose, pharaoh, 28-29
Ahshav, city of, 59
Ai, city of, 59-61
Aijalon, city of, 186, 210
Akhenaten (Amenhotep IV), pharaoh, 79
Akkadian, 181
Alalakh, city of, 44
Amalek, 53, 77, 87, 125
Amalekites, nomadic people, 15, 30, 41, 43, 50, 53, 57, 82, 87, 92, 94-95, 119-20, 267, 292
Amasa, military chief of king David, 103
Amaziah, king of Judah, 161, 201-6, 208, 212, 234, 258, 274
Amenhotep III, pharaoh, 79
Amenmessu, pharaoh, 35
Ammon, kingdom of, 62-63, 82, 85, 87, 93, 98, 102-3, 108, 118, 126, 131-32, 141, 144, 159, 162, 164, 168, 192, 206, 209, 218, 232, 235, 238, 250, 252, 257, 261-65, 270-71

313

Ammonites, people, 7, 15, 22, 30, 50, 52-53, 62, 72-73, 76, 84, 93-94, 103, 107-9, 114, 119-20, 135, 160, 192-93, 206, 209, 261-62, 265, 267, 269-71, 288, 292, 296, 305
Amnon, firstborn son of David, 108
Amon, king of Judah, 233-35, 243, 274
Amorites, West Semitic peoples, 5-7, 18-30, 33-34, 42-43, 49-53, 60, 62, 66, 76, 82, 93, 119, 132, 143, 181, 195, 241, 268, 271, 273, 288, 292-95, 298-99, 305
Amos, prophet, 160, 162, 164-65
Amurru, 20-21, 31, 138
Anakites, See also Rephaim, 53, 84
Anath, Canaanite goddess, 303
Anathoth, town of, 248, 251, 284
Anatolia, 20, 53
Aner, ally of Abraham, 6, 53
Aphek, city of, 59, 64, 81, 146-47, 160
Apiru (Habiru), people, 5-8, 15, 21, 30-31, 50-51, 61-63, 75, 89, 94, 97, 103, 117-18, 126, 129, 137-38, 295
Apries (biblical Hophra), pharaoh, 252-54, 264
Arabah, 255
Arabia, 7, 43, 50, 116, 193, 206, 267, 291-92
Arad, city of, 59, 61, 66, 92, 254-55
Arad ostraca, 254
Aram-Damascus, kingdom, 115, 139, 142, 144, 146-51, 156-62, 167-68, 189, 192, 196-97, 201, 204, 209-10, 217, 259
Arameans, West Semitic peoples, 51, 60, 103, 106-8, 131, 139, 141, 146-62, 168, 171, 174, 179, 181, 187, 189-92, 196, 201, 238, 267, 296, 298
Arauna (Arawena), Jebusite, 56, 116
Argolis, 79
Argos, city of, 79

Ark of the Covenant, 77, 81, 87-88, 98-102, 107, 109, 113, 134, 281-84
Arnon River, 155
Aroer, city of, 155
Arpad, city of, 174, 221, 267
Asa, king of Judah, 142, 151, 187-90, 193, 208
Asaph, clan of Levites, 288
Ashdod, city of, 53-55, 59, 83, 205, 223, 225, 239
Asher, tribe of, 12, 43, 64, 74-77, 80, 138, 177, 217, 294
Asherah, Canaanite goddess, 135-36, 145-46, 159, 175, 180, 186-87, 190, 200, 216, 227-28, 234-35, 241, 271, 274, 294, 296, 304
Ashkelon, city of, 55, 59, 83, 218, 230, 253, 267
Ashtoreth (Astarte), goddess, 74, 114, 235
Ashurbanipal II, king of Assyria, 231, 238-39
Ashur-uballit II, king of Assyria, 239
Asia Minor, 54-56, 79, 104, 107, 254, 268
Asiatics in Egypt, 35, 39-40
Assyrian empire, 174-75, 178-79, 218, 233, 239
Assyrian(s), 19-20, 26, 56, 147, 158-62, 165-66, 168-82, 206, 211-13, 217-31, 238-42, 244, 251, 268, 304
Astarte, See Ashtoreth, 296, 301-2
Athaliah, queen of Judah, 144, 153, 194-99, 202, 208, 234, 274
Avaris, city of, 20, 24-25, 28-29, 33
Avva (Ivva), city of, 175, 180-81
Avvites (Avvim), See also Rephaim, 52, 55, 78
Azariah (Uzziah), king of Judah, 205-10, 212
Azariah, high priest, 207
Azekah, city of, 186, 254

Index

Baal, Canaanite god, 47, 71-74, 88, 134, 136, 143-48, 150, 152-56, 159, 164, 175, 180, 191, 195, 197-200, 203, 227, 235-36, 241, 272, 274, 284, 286, 289-90, 294-304
Baalis, king of Ammon, 262-63, 265
Baasha, king of Israel, 141-44, 151-52, 189
Babylonia, 172-75, 180-81, 231, 238, 244
Babylonian empire, 132, 183, 244-46, 251-56, 260, 265
Babilonian exile, 119, 247-48, 250-51, 256-60
Balak, ruler of Moabites, 63
Bashan, 52, 155
Bathsheba, David's favorite wife, 112-13, 187
Bay (Irsu), pharaoh, 35-38, 40
Beeroth, town of, 50, 63, 140
Beersheba, city of, 76, 236
Benaiah, commander of David's guards, 112-13
Ben-Hadad, king(s) of Aram-Damascus, 146-49, 156, 159-61, 189, 196, 291
Benjamin, tribe of, 11, 14, 29-30, 74, 78, 82, 89, 95-101, 104, 111, 125, 137-42, 176, 185-87, 190, 202, 215, 259, 267, 283-85
Bethel, 9, 14, 59, 73, 99, 134, 136, 155, 159, 162, 164, 171, 182, 187, 189-90, 235-36, 238, 260, 274, 285-86, 289-90
Bethlehem (Ephrat), city of, 13, 90, 186
Beth-shean, city of, 59
Beth-shemesh, city of, 161, 210
Beth Zur, city of, 186
Bilhah, concubine of Jacob, 74-75, 77
Black Obelisk of Shalmaneser III, 157-58
Bubastite branch of Nile River, 20
Byblos, city of, 55, 157

Calah, city of, 170, 230, 239
Caleb, son of Jephunneh, the Kenazite, 47, 50, 66, 90, 92, 106, 281
Canaanites, 43, 49-52, 55, 60-72, 76-78, 97, 118-19, 132, 140, 143, 154-56, 181-83, 268, 270-73, 288, 294, 298-99, 305
Carchemish, city of, 172, 174, 244, 248
Carmel, Mount, 146
Chaldeans (Chaldees), group of Aramean tribes, 168, 171, 181, 217-18, 244-45, 248, 253, 257, 263-67, 270
Cilicia, 173
Crete, 54
Cush, Cushites, 42, 188, 196, 221-22, 230, 279
Cuth (Cuthah), city of, 175, 180-82
Cyprus, 54
Cyrus the Great, king of Persia, 180, 267

Dagan, deity, 302
Dan (Laish), city of, 6, 73, 80, 134, 136, 155, 159, 162, 285-86, 289
Dan, tribe of, 12, 73, 75-81, 138, 285, 294-95
Dathan, one of the chieftains of tribe Reuben, 45, 67
David, king, 3, 11, 52, 62, 89-125, 135, 138, 140, 153, 156-57, 162, 176, 185-87, 193, 195, 199, 270, 284
Dead Sea, 6, 53, 92, 132, 162, 192, 205, 266-67
Debir (Kiriath-Sepher), city of, 59
Deborah, Song of, 67-68, 76-77, 79, 92, 108, 290
Danyen (Danuna), Sea People, 79
Doeg the Edomite, 93
Dor, city of, 55, 59-60, 64, 171
Dothan Valley, 8, 13
Dur-Sharrukin, palace of Assyrian kings, 175

Eben-Ezer, site of battle, 81
Edom, 7, 12, 57, 62-63, 87, 93, 102-3, 115, 118-20, 126, 131-32, 150-51, 192, 195-96, 202-5, 218, 250-52, 255, 257, 263, 265-66, 270, 290-92
Edomites, people, 6-8, 15, 22, 30, 47, 50, 53, 57, 62, 76, 115, 119-20, 161, 168, 191, 193, 195-96, 203-5, 210, 255, 266, 269-71, 274, 291-92, 296, 305
Eglon, ruler of Moab, 72, 93
Egypt
 The Middle Kingdom, 18-19
 The Second Intermediate Period, 19-27
 The New Kingdom, 28-31, 33-44, 48, 60-62, 66, 79, 131, 139, 165, 171, 173, 186, 188, 221-22, 230-31, 238-54, 263-64
Ehud the Benjaminite, 72, 76, 93
Ekron, city of, 55, 59, 83, 218, 223
El, 37, 88, 136, 159, 243, 285-90, 294-98, 300-4
Elah, king of Israel, 142
Elam, 172-74, 218, 231, 238, 248, 252
Eleazar, son of Aaron, 47-48, 85, 176, 280-81
El Elyon, 300
Elephantine, 264, 273
Eli, high priest, 73, 81, 83, 86-87, 98-99, 102, 281-83
Eliezer, prophet, 193
Elijah, prophet, 145-46, 148-49, 152, 161-62, 194, 196, 289, 291, 298-300, 304
Elisha, prophet, 148-52, 161-62, 196, 203, 289, 298-99
Elizaphan, clan of Levites, 288
Elkanah, father of judge Samuel, 90
Elohist source (E) of Pentateuch, 3-4, 121, 296
Elonei Mamre, 10
El Shaddai, 300

Elteke, site of battle, 218
Ephraim, tribe of, 11, 13-14, 26-27, 29-30, 64, 73-74, 77, 82, 84, 100, 108-9, 117, 125, 133, 137, 139, 141, 164-65, 171, 177-78, 181, 183, 202-3, 210, 216-17, 238, 268, 282, 285-86, 302
Ephrain, city of, 187
Esarhaddon, king of Assyria, 230-31
Esau, 7-9, 11, 57, 110, 114, 266, 292-93
Eshkol, ally of Abraham, 6, 53
Ethbaal, king of Sidon, 144
Euphrates River, 7, 14, 22, 103, 107, 118, 129, 133, 240, 242, 244, 246
Exodus, 28-48
Ezekiel, prophet, 255, 258, 260, 266, 269, 272, 275
Ezion Geber, town of, 115-16, 148
Ezra the scribe, 3, 270, 288

Gad, deity of Fortune, 271
Gad, tribe of, 12, 43, 74-75, 77, 80, 89, 107-8, 138, 151, 155, 166, 176, 265, 294
Galilee, 69, 92, 116, 127-28, 132-33, 159, 169, 176, 181, 238, 285
Gath, city of, 53, 55, 83, 91, 104, 107, 186, 205
Gaza, city of, 44, 52-55, 59, 83, 172, 174, 218, 223, 253, 267
Gedaliah, governor, 249, 257, 259-63
Geder, city of, 59
Gerar, city of, 12, 188
Gershon (Gershonites), clan of Levites, 288
Geshur, Aramean kingdom, 65, 108, 120, 135
Gezer, city of, 59, 64, 98, 116-17, 268
Gibbethon, city of, 141
Gibeah, Saul's capital, 100-1, 259, 283
Gibeon, city of, 50, 63, 96, 110, 118, 140, 248, 259, 263

Index

Gideon, judge, 72, 76, 84, 108, 155, 299, 302, 304
Gihon spring, 219-20
Gilboa, Mount, 95
Gilead, 51, 84, 89, 93, 107-8, 155, 160, 167, 169, 171, 176
Gileadite(s), 108, 165, 167
Gilgal, 72, 80, 85-86, 99, 207, 281
Girgashites, people, 49, 51, 119, 305
Goiim, city of, 59
Golden Calf, 72, 134, 278, 280
Goliath, 52-53, 89, 97
Goshen, 28, 33
Gozan, 175, 178-79

Habakkuk, prophet, 244, 291
Habor River, 175, 178-79
Haddu (Hadad), Aramean god, 296, 298
Hagar, 24
Halah, city of, 175, 179
Hanani, prophet, 188, 190-91
Hananiah, false prophet from Gibeon, 248, 250
Hanun, son of Ammonite king Nahash, 103
Hamath, city of, 147, 162, 174-75, 180-81, 221, 256, 267
Haran, city of, 7-9, 178-79, 239, 242, 285
Harris papyrus, 39
Hazael, king of Aram-Damascus, 149, 155-61, 196-97, 201, 217
Hazezon Tamar (En-gedi), 192
Hazor, city of, 25, 59, 63, 68, 76, 79, 92, 116-17, 132, 144, 169
Hebron, city of, 13-14, 50, 52, 95, 97, 106, 124, 186, 266, 268
hekau khasut (Hyksos pharaohs), 20, 26
Herodotus, historian, 222, 239
Hezekiah, king of Judah, 177, 215-19, 221-29, 232-33, 235-37, 251, 255, 259, 261, 271-74, 288, 290, 294, 298
Hilkiah, high priest, 234-36

Hiram, king of Tyre, 115-16, 127
Hittite empire, 44, 54, 96, 106
Hittites, people, 20, 49, 52-54, 56-57, 66, 107, 119, 268, 288, 305
Hivites, people, 49-51, 63, 66, 68, 76, 96-97, 110, 119, 132, 140-41, 185, 268, 288, 305
Horeb, Mount, 36, 291-92, 300
Horites, people, 53, 57
Horma, city of, 59
Hosea, prophet, 164-65, 289, 302
Hoshea, king of Israel, 170-73, 175, 218, 251
Huldah, oracle, 236
Hurrians, people, 20, 49, 56-57, 305
Hushai, adviser of king David, 107
Hyksos, Amorite rulers of Egypt, 13, 18-21, 24-29, 31, 33, 50, 56, 60, 62-63, 74, 120, 129, 137, 178, 292

Ibadidi, Arab tribe, 181
Ijon, city of, 169
Indo-Aryans, See also Maryannu, 305
Indo-European peoples, 53-55
Ipuver, the admonition of, 18
Isaac, patriarch, 2, 7-13, 15, 17, 23, 37, 121, 129, 137, 187, 266, 292-93, 295-96
Isaiah, prophet, 108, 210, 218, 220-22, 224, 230, 264
Ishbosheth (Ishbaal), son of king Saul, 95-97, 106, 111, 302
Ishmael, son of Abraham, 9, 24, 292
Ishmael, assassin of Gedaliah, 262-63
Ishmaelites, nomadic tribes, 7, 15, 30, 50, 68, 292, 294
Ishtar, Mesopotamian goddess, 271
Issahar, tribe of, 74-75, 77, 80
Ivri(m), 5, 21, 51, 63, 88-89, 91, 94-95

Jabbok River, 9
Jabesh-Gilead, 166

Jabin, king of Hazor, 79, 92, 108
Jabneh, city of, 205
Jacob, patriarch, 2, 7-15, 24
Janoah, city of, 169
Jebus, pre-israelite Jerusalem, 50, 97
Jebusites, people, 49-51, 56-57, 64, 66, 97-98, 102, 107, 112, 116, 118-20, 132, 140, 183, 268, 273, 284, 288, 305
Jeduthun, clan of Levites, 288
Jehoahaz, king of Israel, 159-62, 204
Jehoahaz (Shallum), king of Judah, 242-43, 247
Jehoash, king of Israel, 160-62, 203-4, 217
Jehoiachin (Conia), king of Judah, 243, 246-48, 250, 257, 264, 275
Jehoiada the priest, 197-201, 216, 234, 241, 251, 274
Jehoiakim (Elyakim), king of Judah, 243-50, 262, 272, 275
Jehoram, king of Judah, 153, 194-96, 198, 201, 208, 212, 274
Jehoshaphat, king of Judah, 144, 150, 190-97, 201, 208
Jehosheba, wife of Jehoiada the priest, 197
Jehu, king of Israel, 133, 152-67, 171, 197-99, 203-4, 299, 302
Jehu, Judahite prophet, 191
Jephthah, judge, 72-73, 76, 93, 108
Jerahmeelites, 92-93, 293
Jeremiah, prophet, 243-44, 246-51, 253-58, 260-61, 263-66, 269, 271-73, 275
Jericho, city of, 169, 255
Jeroboam I, king of Israel, 100, 117, 123-24, 131, 134-36, 139-41, 144, 187, 237, 285-86, 289-90
Jeroboam II, king of Israel, 162-65, 206
Jerusalem, 50, 59, 63-64, 97-102, 106, 114, 116-20, 126-27, 131, 142, 161, 168, 177, 186, 199-201, 204, 206, 210, 218-22, 246-47, 253-56
Jeshanah, city of, 187
Jesse, father of David, 90, 109, 123
Jezebel, queen of Israel, 144-45, 152, 154-56, 195, 197, 213, 299, 304
Jezreel, city of, 150, 154, 197
Jezreel Valley, 49, 63, 128, 132, 154, 156, 268
Joab, military chief of David, 103, 107, 109, 111-13, 115, 119
Joash, king of Judah, 197, 199-202, 204, 207-8, 212, 216, 234, 241, 274
Johanan son of Kereah, Judahite commander, 263
Jonah, prophet, 164
Jonathan, son of Saul, 86, 90, 95, 97, 110-11
Joram, king of Israel, 148-54, 156, 191, 197
Jordan River, 9, 49, 53, 63, 89, 261
Jordan Valley, 128, 132, 141
Joseph, patriarch, 5, 11-12, 14-15, 24, 27
Josephus, Flavius, 19, 28, 257
Joshua, son of Nun, 41, 50, 62-64, 66-67, 75, 81, 85, 87, 108, 110, 121, 129, 131, 133, 138, 140, 280, 286, 304
Josiah, king of Judah, 136, 183, 200, 232, 234-43, 246-47, 261, 271-74, 294, 298, 303
Jotham, king of Judah, 207-10, 212
Jubilees, book of, 8
Judea, 67-69, 132
Judeans, 305-6

Karnaim, city of, 171
Karnak temple inscriptions, 139, 270
Kohath, clan of Levites, 288
Kedesh, city of, 59, 169
Kemosh (Chemosh), Moabite god, 151, 296

Index

Kenites, Midianite tribes, 15, 30, 49, 50, 66-67, 92-93, 183, 267, 274, 279, 288, 291-94, 305
Kenazzites, Edomite tribe, 47, 49-50, 66-67, 90, 92-93, 106, 183, 267, 273-74, 288, 292-93, 305
Kephirah, city of, 50, 63
Kidron, Valley, 188, 235
Kiriath-Arba (Hebron), city of, 52
Kiriath-Jearim, town of, 63, 100, 140, 248-49, 283
Kittim (Greeks), 254
Korah, Levite, leader of rebellion against Moses and Aaron, 45-46, 67, 279-80
Kuntillet Adjrud, 301

Laban, son of nephew of Abraham, 8
Lachish, city of, 59, 186, 205, 218-19, 221-24, 227, 254-55
Lasharon, city of, 59
Leah, 13-14, 42-43, 68, 74, 77, 141
Levi, tribe of, 7, 11, 36-37, 41-42, 45-46, 68, 74, 91, 95, 190, 277
Levites, 3, 11, 37, 42, 46, 48, 67, 73-74, 78, 80, 87, 99-102, 111, 135-36, 138, 140, 145-46, 148, 152, 155, 159, 171, 195, 199-200, 203, 215-16, 229, 260-61, 273, 277-88, 298-99
Libnah, city of, 59, 195-96, 222
Libyans, See also Meshwesh, 44, 56, 188, 238
Lot, nephew of Abraham, 5-7, 9
Lukka, Sea People, 56
Luwians, 54, 107
Luz (Bethel), city of, 285

Maacah, Aramean kingdom, 65, 103, 135
Maachatites, people of Aramean origin, 49
Machir, one of the chieftains of tribe Manasseh, 125

Machpelah, cave of, 13-14
Madon, city of, 59
Mahanaim, city of, 97, 106
Makkedah, city of, 59
Mamre, ally of Abraham, 6, 53
Manasseh, king of Judah, 227-34, 272
Manasseh, tribe of, 11, 13-14, 26-27, 29-30, 64, 74, 84, 107-8, 125, 133, 171, 176-78, 183
Manetho, historian, 19-20, 25, 28
Maon, Maonites, 90, 92, 205, 267, 274
Marduk-apal-iddina (biblical Merodah-baladan), 217
Mareshah, city of, 186, 188, 193
Marsimanu, Arab tribe, 181
Maryannu, 56, 268, 305
Mattan, priest of Baal cult in Jerusalem, 199
Medes, people, 173, 175, 179, 239, 242, 252
Megiddo, city of, 64, 116-17, 139, 144, 171, 240, 287, 301
Melchizedek, king of Shalem (Jerusalem), 97, 298
Memphis, city of, 19
Menahem, king of Israel, 165-67, 176, 206
Meni, deity of Destiny, 271
Mephibosheth (Mephibaal), grandson of Saul, 108, 110-11, 302
Merari (Merarites), clan of Levites, 288
Meri-ka-Re, instructions for king, 18
Merneptah, pharaoh, 35-36, 44, 56, 60, 66, 76, 79
Merneptah Stele, 34, 138
Mesad Hashvayahu site, 238
Mesha, king of Moab, 150-51, 191-92
Mesha Stele, 143, 150-52
Meshwesh (Libyan tribes), 188
Micah (the Ephraimite), 73, 80
Micah, prophet, 272
Michal, daughter of Saul and wife of David, 97

Midian, 38, 180, 188, 191, 196, 205-6, 267, 291-93
Midianites, nomadic tribes, 7, 15, 22, 30, 36, 38, 43, 45, 47, 50, 72, 82, 92, 196, 291-92, 294
Milcom, deity of Ammon, 271, 296
Miriam, sister of Aaron, 207, 279
Mitanni, kingdom of, 56, 60, 106, 133
Mitinti, king of Ashdod, 223
Mizpah, city of, 85, 257, 259, 261-62, 282
Moab, Moabites, 7, 15, 22, 30, 50, 52-53, 62-63, 93, 119-20, 135, 150-51, 160, 191-93, 206, 266-67, 269-71, 288, 292, 296, 305
Moloch, Canaanite deity, 72, 241, 271, 274, 296
Moses, 35-48, 66-67, 72-75, 77, 81, 87, 121, 135, 216, 277-83, 290-94, 298-300
Mycenae, city of, 54-55, 79

Nabateans, people, 270
Nabopolassar, king of the Chaldeans, 244
Naboth, 154
Nadab, king of Israel, 141, 187
Nahash, king of Ammon, 93-94, 103, 107-8
Nahshon, chieftain of tribe Judah, 47
Nahum, prophet, 239
Naphtali, tribe of, 12, 29-30, 64, 68, 74-75, 137, 169, 176, 238
Nathan, prophet, 112-13
Nebuchadnezzar II, king of Neo-Babylonian empire, 244-50, 252-53, 255-58, 260, 266
Nebuzaradan, 256-57
Necho II, pharaoh, 242-48, 252-53
Neferty, Prophecy of, 18
Negev desert, 48, 50, 64, 66, 69, 87, 90-91, 119-20, 132-33, 191, 205-6, 210, 267
Nehemiah, 270-71

Nehushtan, bronze serpent as object of worship, 216, 290
Nergal, Mesopotamian deity, 182
Nineveh, city of, 175, 179, 219, 222-23, 231-32, 239, 242
Nob, city of, 100, 282-83
Northern Kingdom (Israel), 137-183
Nubia, 29, 42, 252-53

Obadiah, prophet, 266
Obed-Edom, the Gathite, 101, 107
Oded, prophet, 168
Og, ruler of Amorites in Bashan, 50, 52, 57
Oholiab, artisan from tribe Dan, 77
Omri, king of Israel, 133, 142-45, 147, 149-50, 152, 154, 156, 191
Ophir, 115, 148
Ophrah, home town of judge Gideon, 72
Osorkon I, pharaoh, 188-89

Padi, ruler of Ekron, 218, 223
Paran, desert, 291
Parosh, ruler of Moab, 270
Pashhur, priest, 248
Passover (pesah), 38-39, 126, 177, 216, 237-38
Pekah, king of Israel, 167, 169-72
Pekahiah, king of Israel, 167
Pelethites, people, 106
Pentateuch, 2-4, 13-14, 17, 37, 41, 43, 54, 78, 119-21, 237, 281, 296
Penuel, city of, 141
Perizzites, people, 49-50, 66, 119, 132, 183, 268, 305
Philistia, Philistines, 40, 49, 52, 54-55, 60, 76, 78-91, 93-104, 106-7, 118, 131, 138, 141-42, 162, 167-68, 173, 178, 188, 191, 196, 201, 205, 210, 218, 226, 230, 239, 245, 253, 266-67, 283, 302

Index

Phinehas, son of Eleazar, 47
Phoenicia, Phoenicians, 21, 49, 55, 79-80, 96, 107, 115-16, 118, 132, 144-45, 147, 156-57, 159-60, 167, 169, 173, 209, 230-31, 239, 252-53, 267, 296
Phrygians, 173
Pithom and Rameses, 34
Potipherah, Egyptian priest, 78
Prayer of Manasseh, book of, 232
Psammetichus (Psamtik) I, pharaoh, 238-39, 242
Psammetichus (Psamtik) II, pharaoh, 252

Qarqar, battle of 853 BCE, 147, 167
Qaus, Edomite god, 271, 292, 296
Queen of Heaven, goddess, 273

Rabbah, capital of the Ammonites, 120, 265
Rachel, 11, 13-14, 68, 74-75
Ramah, home town of judge Samuel, 83, 90, 258
Rameses I, pharaoh, 33
Rameses II, pharaoh, 33-35, 60-61, 79
Rameses III, pharaoh, 44, 46, 48, 55-56, 62, 66, 79
Ramoth-Gilead, 147, 149-50, 154, 191
Ramseside pharaohs, 39, 48
Rebekah, 10, 13, 293
Rechabites, 154, 299
Rehoboam, king of Judah, 102, 123-25, 131, 135, 185-87, 286
Rephaim, pre-Canaanite inhabitants of Palestine, 52-53, 57, 78, 84, 98, 268, 305
Rephaim Valley, 98
Retenu, Egyptian name of Palestine, 22
Reuben, son of Jacob, 14, 68
Reuben, tribe of, 7, 11, 13, 36, 41-42, 45-46, 48, 67-69, 78, 91, 126, 139, 277, 294

Rezin, king of Aram-Damascus, 167, 171, 209-11, 259
Riblah, city of, 243, 255-56
Ruth the Moabite, 93, 120, 270-71

Saite Dynasty, 238, 248, 252, 254
Salitis, Hyksos pharaoh, 19
Samaria, 67, 69, 143-49, 153-55, 159, 165-69, 171-82, 211
Samaritans, people, 182-83, 241, 265, 304, 306
Samson, judge, 76, 78-79, 81, 86
Samuel, prophet and judge, 73, 76, 83-91, 94, 275, 283, 302
Sarah, 7, 10, 13, 25
Sargon II, king of Assyria, 172, 174-76, 181, 217-19, 225-26
Saul, king of Israel, 83-94, 97, 100, 104, 107, 110, 123-24, 127, 138, 185, 207, 273, 283-84, 302
Scythians, people, 239
Sea Peoples, 44, 52, 54-56, 59-60, 79-80, 96
Seir, Mount, 50, 57, 192, 290-92
Sela (Joktheel), city of, 203
Sennacherib, king of Assyria, 218-20, 222, 225, 230, 259
Sepharvaim, city of, 175, 180-81, 221
Seti I, pharaoh, 33, 60-61, 270
Seti II, pharaoh, 35
Setnakht, pharaoh, 35-36, 38-41, 44, 79
Shallum, king of Israel, 165
Shalmaneser III, king of Assyria, 147, 156-58
Shalmaneser IV, king of Assyria, 162
Shalmaneser V, king of Assyria, 171, 173-74
Shamgar, judge, 81, 86
Shaphan, scribe, 236, 249, 256-57
Sharuhen, city of, 28
Shasu, see Sutu, 7, 31, 50, 76, 93, 132, 270, 288, 292

Sheba, son of Bichri, Benjaminite chieftain, 109-10
Shechem, city of, 8, 13-14, 29, 50, 59, 68, 76, 97, 99, 118, 123-24, 131, 140-41, 143, 261, 277, 281
Shekelesh, Sea People, 56
Shemaiah (of Nehelam), priest among Babylonian exiles, 248, 251
Shemaiah, prophet, 123, 125, 185, 190
Shephelah, 49, 132, 195, 223, 226-27, 254, 259, 268, 305
Sherden, Sea People, 55-56, 60
Sheshonq I (biblical Shishak) pharaoh, 131, 139, 186, 188, 217
Shiloh, religious center of northern Levites, 73, 83, 86-88, 99-100, 111, 135-36, 139-40, 261, 281-83, 285, 295-96
Shimron-Meron, city of, 59
Shobi, Ammonite ruler, 103, 107
Sidon, city of, 49, 64, 73, 144, 157, 218, 230-31, 250, 252-53, 267
Sidonians, See also Canaanites, 49, 114, 235
Sihon, ruler of Amorites in Transjordan, 50, 132
Sillibel, ruler of Gaza, 223
Siloam inscription, 219-20
Simeon, tribe of, 7, 11, 14, 36, 41-42, 46-48, 57, 66-68, 74, 76, 78, 82-83, 85, 91, 99, 126, 138, 190, 238, 267, 277, 280, 282
Sinai, Mount, 42, 73, 75, 121, 290-93, 300
Sinuhe, tale of, 22
Siptah, pharaoh, 35-36
Sisera, military chief of the king of Hazor, 79, 92, 108
Soco, city of, 186
Sodom, city of, 7, 272
Solomon, king, 3, 11, 29, 102, 111-27, 131, 135, 186, 235, 272, 284

Southern Kingdom (Judah), 185-276
Sumer, 129, 133, 137, 295
Sutu, nomadic West Semitic peoples, 7, 15, 30-31, 41, 118

Taanach, city of, 59
Taharqa (Tirhakah), pharaoh, 230
Tammuz, Mesopotamian god, 271-72
Tamud, Arab tribe, 181
Teman, 266, 291
Tekoa, city of, 186
Tell Halaf, city of, 179
Tell el-Amarna letters, 31, 56, 60, 137
Temple of Jerusalem, 29, 72, 114, 127, 134-35, 161, 190, 197-201, 207, 211-12, 215-16, 226, 228-32, 235-36, 248, 250, 256, 271-72, 281, 284
Tausret, queen, 35-36, 38
Thebes, city of, 24, 55-56, 60, 62
Thutmose I, pharaoh, 29
Thutmose II, pharaoh, 29
Thutmose III, pharaoh, 29, 44, 60, 242
Tibni, military chief of Israel, 142
Tiglath-pileser III (Pul), king of Assyria, 143, 166, 168-70, 174, 176, 210, 213
Tigris River, 22, 129, 133
Timnah, city of, 210
Timnah, copper mining site, 48
Tirzah, city of, 140-43, 165
Tishbe, birthplace of prophet Elijah, 289
Tjeker, Sea People, 55, 60, 80
Tobiah (the Ammonite), 271

Ugarit (Ras Shamra), city of, 44, 296-97, 300, 302-3
Ur, city of, 8
Urartu, kingdom of, 159-60, 166, 173, 230
Uriah, high priest, 211
Uriah the Hittite, 107

Index

Uriah, prophet from Kiriath-Jearim, 248-49
Uzzah, son of Abinadab, responsible for Ark of Covenant, 101

Wen-Amon, tale of, 55

Yahwism, 180, 182, 200, 255, 278, 280-81, 285-86, 288-305
Yahwist source (J) of Pentateuch, 121
Yarmuth, city of, 59
YHWH, tetragrammaton, 37, 73
Yokneam, city of, 59

Zadok, high priest, 98, 102, 107, 112, 288
Zebulun, tribe of, 42, 64, 68, 74-75, 77, 80, 138, 176-77, 217, 294
Zechariah, king of Israel, 165
Zechariah, priest, 200
Zedekiah, false prophet, 249
Zedekiah (Mattaniah), king of Judah, 247-57, 264, 272, 275
Zephaniah, priest, 248, 251, 256
Zeruiah, family related to king David and Ammonite king Nahash, 95, 103, 112
Ziklag, town of, 91
Zilpah, concubine of Jacob, 43, 74, 77
Zimri, king of Israel, 142, 152
Ziph, 90, 92, 186
Zipporah, wife of Moses, 289
Zorah, city of, 186